MOUSEHOLE
a documented history

'BUTTS'

Mousehole – a documented history

© Mike 'Butts' Buttery

Cover Photograph: Mousehole Harbour Construction 1871 (author's collection)
Cover Design: Tobi Carver

First Edition published 2012

Published by:
Palores Publications,
11a Penryn Street, Redruth, Kernow TR15 2SP, UK.

Designed & Printed by:
The St Ives Printing & Publishing Company,
High Street, St Ives, Cornwall TR26 1RS, UK.

ISBN 978-1-906845-31-5

MOUSEHOLE
a documented history

'BUTTS'

PALORES

CONTENTS

Introduction & Acknowledgments

RESEARCH IS A strange thing, it is very much like gardening. You start of with a small seed of an idea which gradually grows out of all proportion as branches shoot off in all directions. Then you have to prune it back to keep it in some sort of shape. That is what I had to do with my research on Mousehole. I started off with the idea of just researching the fishing side of our village, but as you will see it does branch off in other directions. Some I have included others I had to leave out, the main reason being space.

I have tried to keep everything as short as possible without losing to much of the actual history but it was difficult. It is the harbour that makes Mousehole what it is, a fishing village, and it was this industry that basically shaped nearly everything in our village for several hundred years. Mousehole was once two separate little villages that over the years, as houses where built, gradually became one village, the same thing happened in Newlyn and probably countless other villages and towns in Cornwall. Details on Porth Ennis are very sketchy so in all probability it was only a very small hamlet but Mousehole, in all its various spellings, can be traced back for over a thousand years.

I started my research in about 1962 basically to solve arguments who owned what lugger back in the 1800's. All the boat information was taken from the Customs and Excise registers held at County Records Office in Truro and I would like to thank the staff of this office for all their help during the months I spent there. I ended up giving them some old barking ledgers etc on permanent loan. There are also several old personal diaries from the 1800's that will be sent to them.

The other place where I spent a lot of time doing research was the Cornish Studies Centre in Redruth. Once again the staff where very helpful during the months I was researching and a very big thank you to all those people who helped me. The same goes to the staff of the Royal Geological Society of Cornwall that used to be based at St Johns Hall, Penzance. I spent a lot of time there and the staff regularly sent me information through the post regarding the monks of St Michaels Mount, the flooding of Mounts Bay and what it was like geologically in this area during the last Ice Age. Thank you all for the help given me during those months.

A special thanks must also go to the Mousehole Harbour Commissioners who let me look at their Minutes Book from 1869 when the construction and enlargement of the present day harbour was started. Without their help I could not have written a comprehensive account of our harbour.

Thanks must also go to Trevelyn Richards and Tommy Rowe who lent me note books from the 1800's when their grandfathers where Harbour Masters, this is where all the PE registered fishing boats came from. Clifton Pender leant me an old book on Cornwall that contained some of the old Cornish words still used in some villages which I have included.

I would like to thank all the people in Mousehole who have given me so much help over the years with newspaper cutting and old notebooks regarding the history of our village. The unknown person who sent me photocopies from the *Sherborne Mercury* regarding several very interesting articles about Mounts Bay in the 1700 and 1800's, a lot of which have been used.

Then there are the newspapers of the day, *The Cornishman, Cornish Telegraph, Western Morning News, Falmouth Packet* and numerous others that have all yielded information during the last 300 years or more.

If I have forgotten to thank anyone please accept my apologies but after 50 years it is a job to remember where all the information came from.

Everything in this book comes from documented information, nothing is hear say, and the vast majority can be seen at the places I have mentioned.

yours sincerely
'Butts'

Section I

Mousehole – Its Name

THE EARLIEST KNOWN traders in Mounts Bay were the Phoenecians and Syrians who sailed up the tidal inlet past Mousehole, then on to Gwavas Lake and at high tide sailed through the marshes to St Michaels Mount to trade for tin. There were and still are several streams that empty into the sea between Mousehole, Newlyn and Marazion. Those to the east of Mousehole were highly polluted at this period in history from the 'tin streaming' industry. They would be running red in colour from cleaning and winning tin and contain a high proportion of arsenic in the water. This coloration of the streams around the western tip of Cornwall in all probability gave the name 'Red River' to so many of them – if there was tin to be won then it invariably involved a stream in the separation process.

Mousehole's two streams were never used for this purpose, there was no quantity of tin in the immediate vicinity, if there had been then they would probably have ended up like the others. There was a copper mine that is now situated in the middle of the New Estate. Mousehole is built on a fault line, to the west of the stream it's granite, to the east it's blue elvin and tin is only mined in granite. These two streams were the only safe drinking water in Mounts Bay. Lamorna's river was highly polluted and if you walk up through the nature reserve you can still see the large piles of earth from this industry, which have never been levelled. It is also possible to see the last remains of the dams (they take some finding) where they diverted water to use in the separation process.

It is known that these early traders 'called at an inlet with two streams to fill up their water barrels.' There was only one inlet open to the sea at that time which had two streams and that was Mousehole. We also know that all the tin trade was carried out from either Marazion or St Michaels Mount. Satellite pictures taken in the 1970's clearly show all the old 'tinners tracks' converging at Marazion from as far away as Newquay. These old tracks cut straight through what are now towns, villages, farms, buildings etc and the A30 from Hayle to the Marazion roundabout is built on top of an old tinners track. These old tracks must have been used for hundreds, if not thousands of years, to have packed down hard enough to alter the water content in the ground and so be visible to satellite photography after all this time. These photographs can be seen in Penzance reference library. An interesting thing about these tinners tracks is that metal detector enthusiasts using the satellite photographs have found numerous gold coins along these tracks and in one case a hoard of gold jewellery that was being taken to St Just by a commercial traveller trying to sell his wares to the rich miners. He was attacked by robbers and hid his gold in a wall behind a stone. He never returned to collect it and was presumed murdered. These reports come from the *Cornishman* newspaper.

When trying to trace the origin of a place name the researcher is looking back into the past, the older the village the further back into time you have to look, and in the case of Mousehole that is a long time.

There are more ways of spelling Mousehole than there are letters in its name, but one thing I have noticed is that all the variations contain only three vowels, e, o and u, except for one spelling in 1302, 'Mowssal.' The normal spelling was 'Mowssel' so the 'a' might have been a mistake. The earlier spellings included 'Mozul,' 'Muzel,' 'Mosel,' 'Mossel,' 'Musel,' with 'Mozul' probably being the commonest. Then in 1242 it was 'Mosehole,' this was the first time that the word 'hole' was used in the name. Then in 1267 there is this quotation, 'Near the Cornish village of Mosehole there is a place called *Portheness.*' In 1310 another states 'Porthenys beside Mosehole.' From these and other accounts it would appear that there were two places close together, Mosehole and Porthenys. The records clearly indicate that they were separate, but close together. For just over 100 years until the late 1600's the village was known as 'Porthennis' – some of the charts from this period show the name as 'Porthennis.' Then in the early 1700's the name was again changed to its present day spelling of Mousehole, but even during the 1600's it was still known, called and written as 'Mossel, near Porthennis, in Mounts Bay.' The actual name, regardless of spelling, was still used even though Porthennis was added.

There have been several explanations regarding the name Mousehole. One says that it applied to the cave near the village, 'the mouses hole' – another Cornish word 'Maews-holh' which means 'hollow or valley of the gulls.' The last one is very plausible but I have not come across this spelling on any chart or other records regarding the village name. The oldest name I came across from the 900's was spelt 'Mozul' and during the next 600 years it was always spelt differently but they all sounded the same. So that was where I began my research.

Now remembering the tin trades from the Mediterranean 'that filled their water barrels at an inlet with two streams,' I made enquiries regarding the name Mozul etc in the languages around the Middle East. It turned out that this name is very common in and around the Mediterranean countries in all its various spellings. Further enquiries showed that the name means 'fresh water,' 'place of fresh water,' 'drinking water,' etc.

Remembering our Syrian and Phoenecian traders who filled up their water barrels then they would call that inlet by a name in their own language which indicated or meant fresh water, and that name would be 'Mozul,' or a similar spelling.

They would also have bartered for fresh vegetables and meats for their journey home. What better way to encourage this trade than to build a small breakwater to protect the small rowing boats from the mother ship while they collected water. Perhaps these early traders were the instigators of the village all those years ago.

There is no documented proof that this is how our village got its name but it is the only explanation that actually fits all the known facts together. From the early tin traders some 2,000 or so years ago, the fact that the two streams were not polluted by tin streaming or drying out, that it was a sheltered safe inlet with a good anchorage, that there would be ample fresh vegetables and meats from the farms that then existed in what is now Mounts Bay, that the oldest spellings of Mousehole are common place names in the Middle East and that they indicate or mean fresh drinking water. A study of present day maps of the Middle East clearly shows there are still numerous places called Mossel or Mozul, probably the best known is Mossal in Iraq where a lot of fighting took place during the Iraq war. I wrote to a couple of embassies regarding the name Mossel, Mozul etc and they all replied with the same answer, fresh water, drinking water, oasis.

Unbeknown to me another very well known Mousehole gentleman was also researching the name Mousehole, this was Jack Pender the artist. He was still teaching art at school and had access to computers. He took a very similar line of enquiry by starting with the oldest spellings and working through various languages that were known to have been used by early traders in Cornwall. It only took him six months to arrive at the same conclusion, that Mousehole in its old spelling is an Arabic word meaning fresh water.

There are also several Mossels, Mouzels, Mousels etc on the continent and at least two beers and a wine bearing this name, as before all to do with drinking.

Mounts Bay – 12,000 Years Ago

I THOUGHT IT might be interesting to find out the lost history of ancient Cornwall and with the help of the Royal Geological Society of Cornwall and various other institutes have managed to form a picture of what it was like during the last ice age. All the facts below can be authenticated by anyone who cares to look. Most of the people I talked to say that Cornwall and Devon would be very like present day tundra near the Arctic Circle. All the animals mentioned below did live in this area and their remains have been found in the famous Kents Cavern in Devon along with early human bones.

12,000 years ago the ice age had reached its peak and was starting to retreat. It has been estimated that some 90% of all the world's fresh water was locked up as ice.

Surface water evaporates from the sea and rises to form clouds which eventually falls as rain. This rain finally completes its journey back to the sea as streams and rivers. During an ice age a lot of this rain falls as snow and gets compacted into and onto the ice sheets. When this happens and the ice sheets are on land the sea levels fall dramatically. This is what happened during the last ice age which covered some 11 million square miles (35 million square kilometres) of land and lowered the sea level by 250 to 350 metres (different researchers give different figures for this).

During the height of the ice age it has been calculated that the ice cap on the continent over Norway was at least 2½ miles thick. The vast weight of such an ice cap slowly forced the magma (subsurface molten rock) sideways lowering the actual ground underneath it. As the ground sank the magma was forced sideways to the east and west causing the land to tilt and rise in the direction of the magma flow. England was still connected to the continent at this point in time and the raised and tilted ground started near Holland and extended to the eastern and southern parts of present day England. The western side of England was tilted downwards.

The ice caps never reached Cornwall but it would still have been a very inhospitable place with a tundra like appearance. Lashed by severe snowstorms with most surface water frozen during the winter months. The sea was estimated to be 200 miles away at this period in time, borne out by core samples from the continental shelf.

During the brief summer months Mounts Bay would be like a vast luxuriant bog supporting herds of mammoth, woolly rhino, reindeer, elk, wolves and arctic foxes. Bones of these animals have been found in some bogs and caves. As with present day tundra it would also support a seething mass of mosquitoes. The vegetation would consist of tundra grasses, flowers and bog plants that would eventually turn into peat. There would be no tall trees, just the ground hugging arctic willows, birches and junipers.

Pollen counts from core samples taken for the Royal Cornwall Geological Society in the late 1800's show that pine, hazel, birch, oak, elm and lime trees grew near the Continental Shelf nearly 200 miles away.

During the next 5,000 years as the climate grew warmer, the melting ice retreated with the resultant rise in sea level, and the trees around the Continental Shelf migrated slowly northwards to enter present day Devon and Cornwall and to finally cover the whole country in a vast forest of trees as the sea inundated the lower ground. The sea was still over 100 miles away from the present day Mounts Bay.

6,000 Years Ago

THE ICE WAS rapidly retreating and sea levels rising quite quickly at this period of time. Melt water from the retreating ice caps would start as a trickle and end up as raging rivers that gouged out valleys and shifted countless millions of tons of silt, gravel and rock fragments to form the large flat fertile plains that now create Englands 'green and pleasant land.' This did not happen in Cornwall because there were no thick ice caps, but erosion on a smaller scale did take place. The granite tors of Cornwall would have been a lot higher than present day and during the cold winter months would be topped in quite thick snow. This would melt during the summer months and turn the small streams and rivers into powerful water courses with the resultant erosion around them. Lamorna Cove was formed in this way and is a good local example of how the power of water can change the appearance of the coast to cut out and erode a large deep inlet. The two small streams in Mousehole also helped to form an inlet which was utilised by man to make a harbour.

Between the Lizard and Lands End there are numerous small streams and rivers that emptied into the bay, some of them were very powerful during the summer months. They carried vast amounts of mud and silt out into what is now the bay. This erosion had been going on for several thousand years and made the bay a low boggy fertile plain. The underlying strata on the western side of the bay from around Lamorna to Newlyn and underneath Long Rock and Marazion to St Erth is a soft slate rock. This is overlayed with peat which was formed when the bay was a large bog. Parts of this peat bog can be seen at Perran and Praa Sands where it lies on the surface of the beaches. During the 1700's peat was regularly cut at Marazion to be used as fuel.

The underlying slate is very soft and out in the bay the piddock shellfish bore deep holes into it where they live. This weakens the slate even more and after severe storms you can often pick up this slate from Marazion beach. When fishing with ground nets in the bay they will often snag up on the rough edges and when the nets are brought to the surface you will sometimes see large pieces of slate complete with piddocks in their holes.

The streams between Marazion and Newlyn emptied into a large lake known as Gwavas Lake. The water from this lake flowed along the shore past Mousehole and Lamorna and was further increased by the waters from the streams from these places. This river flowed roughly parallel to the present day shoreline and somewhere off Lands End was joined by the very large river that flowed from what is now Wales. The remnants of this once very powerful river is today known as the River Severn. This river was responsible for the present day Bristol Channel and helped create the steep sea cliffs along the north Cornish coast and helped shape the Lands End peninsula.

A similar effect to this created the Lizard peninsular with its two rivers. One, the Fal River, is still in existence, all that remains of the other is the large lake behind Loe Bar near Porthleven which occasionally breaches its shingle bank to empty into the sea. At one stage of their life the two peninsula waterways from the Lizard and Lands End must have joined together and formed a very large and powerful river because it gouged out an extremely deep trench as it poured off the Continental Shelf. Core samples taken near the Continental Shelf show serpentine fragments that came from the Lizard. These rivers were probably at their strongest towards the end of the ice age some 12,000 years ago.

5,000 years ago the increasing sea levels were making great inroads into low-lying areas in the northern hemisphere helped in no small way by the land tilting back towards an even keel. This was when the present day North Sea was formed as a shallow salt water lagoon and turned England into an island. From that date the North Sea has been steadily getting wider and deeper and this process is still continuing at the present time.

The Scillies were still connected to the mainland and Mounts Bay was a fertile boggy land covered in trees. Carbon dating old tree stumps indicates that 3,000 years ago the sea had reached the Scillies and drowned a forest but it does not indicate that this was when they actually became islands. There is evidence to suggest that when they became separated from the mainland it happened very suddenly and encompassed a very large area of land, possibly to within a few miles of Lands End. The Royal Geological Society of Cornwall states that there had been a flood to the height of 18 foot and that such a flood must have drowned a whole territory and not simply Mounts Bay. They also say that this drowned landscape would have been inhabited because of the useful timber, fruits, nuts and berries, and that its one time population with its houses, villages and parish churches would have been instantly overwhelmed. This basically agrees with what the monks on St Michaels Mount told William Worcestre in 1478. But without those old records that the monks kept there is no evidence to prove when this catastrophe occurred, it could have been 3,000, 2,000 or 1,000 years ago. That these monks kept old records is well known because when they left the Mount for Brittany they 'took great quantities of writings with them.'

Mousehole Harbour

THE HISTORY OF Mounts Bay is inextricably tied to the fishing industry. It was the fishing that gave the bay all its little coves and harbours that characterise it at the present time. It was also the fishing and protection of vessels during storms and the ever changing face of this industry that caused some harbours to expand rapidly. As in all other types of industry centralisation would inevitably take place. There are several reasons why this happened in the fishing industry but the main ones were the availability of ground space to locate fish stores on a large scale, this then encouraged fish buyers to congregate in that area, the ease in transportation of bulk fish and somewhere that the larger boats could stay afloat at all stages of the tide. The above is why the construction of Newlyn harbour was carried out in the 1890's.

The lack of suitable 'safe' harbours in the Mounts Bay area restricted the growth of the fishing industry for some 1,000 years or more. They were restricted to vessels that could be pulled up out of the water above high water mark during severe storms by horses. There were of course small harbours around the bay during that period, some no more than wide breakwaters, Newlyn old harbour being a good example. Mousehole's old harbour was quite a large construction for those days and at one stage of its history was the largest in the bay. Penzance also had a small harbour but with the expanding population and the increased commercial trade this harbour grew in leaps and bounds to keep up with the amount of ever larger cargo vessels that now called on a regular basis. Up until the late 1890's this was classed as the only 'safe' harbour of refuge in the bay during severe southerly storms. But as will be seen later the word safe was hardly appropriate.

Up until the 1880's Mousehole had the largest fleet of fishing boats in the bay, mostly luggers, ranging in size from 16 foot to 60 foot in length. Newlyn vessels main port was Penzance during poor weather. On the other hand Mousehole boats did have quite a lot of protection because during storms baulks of timber would be lowered into slots in the gaps to stop the surges during such storms.

By the 1860's Mousehole's fleet had grown to such an extent that the old harbour was no longer large enough to hold them all. The commissioners at that time decided that a larger harbour had to be constructed. They applied to the Government Loans Commission for a grant to do just this.

But before any grant would be given the commissioners had to have a civil engineer down to draw up plans for the proposed new harbour, they also had to purchase the old harbour and surrounding ground so that 'no other person or persons could have prior claim once the harbour was constructed.'

The plans for the new harbour where drawn up by a Mr James Douglas, later Sir James Douglas, better known for designing the present day Eddystone Lighthouse in 1862. Tenders were invited for the construction of the new harbour in early 1868. All tenders had to be in before the end of 1868.

In January 1869 the commissioners met at the offices of solicitor, Mr Thomas Cornish, in Penzance. The new registered name would now be 'The Harbour of Mousehole Improvement Commissioners'.

At the first meeting of the Harbour of Mousehole Improvement Commissioners held after due notice at the office of Mr Thomas Cornish in Penzance in Cornwall on Friday 5th February 1869. Present were: Messrs William Angwin, Henry Wright, Martin Wright, John Bodinnar, Richard Angwin, William Humphreys, Richard Pentreath, Charles Mann, John James Pentreath, Richard Jacka, John Thomas Wallis, Joseph Trewavas, Michael Wright Pender, and Joseph Hockin. It was resolved that Mr Henry Wright be the first Chairman of the Board. That Mr Martin Wright be the first Secretary of the Commissioners and that Mr William Angwin be the first Treasurer of the Commissioners. It was resolved that the seal now produced be adopted as the seal of the Commissioners and be entrusted to the care of the Chairman.

The following minute was adopted as the basis on which the Commissioners receive the money for the purchase of the pier and give receipts for the same.

The memorandum dated 1st February 1869. The commissioners have contracted with the trustees of Edwin Ley Esquire, deceased, for the purchase of their interest in the existing piers and harbour at Mousehole for the sum of £1,000. The money for said purchase to be obtained by subscriptions from the boats and fishermen. The harbour and piers are to be the absolute property of the Commissioners for the purpose of their incorporation and order and none of the subscribers are to have any right or title to the same or any part thereof by reason of their subscribing.

The necessary money was raised and the old piers and harbour now belonged to the new commissioners. Their next job was to raise money for repayment and other expenses that would be involved with the new harbour construction, and once again that money would come from the fishermen. 'All the boat owners in and using Mousehole have signed an agreement to pay £1 per year for every vessel in the mackerel fishery, 13s 6d per year for boats on pilchards and herrings and 10s per year for pilchard fishery only until the £1,000 at £5 per year interest is paid. The Commissioners are to levy the dues under the Agreement and to pay the same to the subscribers until the £1000 subscribed with interest at 5% per annum is repaid to them but no subscriber shall have any claim on the Commissioners or on their property in respect of this Agreement other than a right to see that the Commissioners collect the dues aforesaid and distribute the same as aforesaid so far as the law will allow and to the best of their ability. The Agreement for the purchase of the present piers and harbour was read and approved and the Chairman was authorised to affix the seal of the Board to it'. 'The Treasurer reported that he had received on the Memorandum above set out £630 and he was authorised to pay the same as a deposit on the contract.'

Share List as follows:

One thousand pounds to be raised in one thousand shares at one pound per share.

Henry Wright	65	Henry Harvey	50
Martin Wright	50	William Angwin	15
Richard Angwin	30	James Trenoweth	50
Joseph Hockin	55	William Maddern	10
Francis Richards	5	Robert Richards	50
Charles Mann	10	John Pentreath Snr	10
William Humphreys Snr	10	Henry Harvey Snr	10
Charles Pezzack	5	Capt John Maddern	20
Henry Williams	50	John James (Dunbarton)	10
John Bodinner	10	Abraham Wright	25
Josiah Trembath	5	William Barnes	20
John Maddern Snr	5	Richard Trembath	20
John Jasper Richards	50	Martin Wright Jnr	10
Richard Jacka	20	John Thomas Wallis	10
Thomas Edmunds	20	William Hall	10
Richard Berryman	10	William Harris	50
John Thomas Wright	30		

This is the exact copy of the first minutes of the Mousehole Harbour Improvement Commissioners, another meeting held on the 9th February 1869 added the following before the seal was stamped.

'Resolved that subscription list, memorial of Pilots and statement of facts be adopted.' They also agreed to accept the tender of Mr John Freeman and sons from Penryn of £5,200 to construct the new north pier and extend the south pier by 75 yards as per specifications laid down by Mr James

21

Douglas. The commissioners borrowed £5,500 from the Government Loans Commission to pay for this work, plus Mr Cornish and James Douglas' bills.

During the early meetings when the Commissioners were setting new byelaws they always included their solicitor Mr Thomas Cornish from Penzance. This was because any new byelaws had to go before the Board of Trade and be passed by Parliament. The letter below sets out the way Commissioners were elected.

> At a meeting of the Commissioners held at the house of Mr William Angwin in Mousehole on Saturday 11th June 1870 at 6pm on a ballot to determine the rotation of retirement in pursuance of the Provisions of the Commissioners Clauses Act 1867 the list was settled as under.
>
> To retire in 1870:- Charles Mann, Richard Pentreath, Abraham Maddern, William Angwin, Michael Pender.
>
> To retire in 1871:- Joseph Hockin, Richard Angwin, John Bodinner, John Thomas Wallis, Richard Jacka.
>
> To retire in 1872:- John James Pentreath, Joseph Trewavas Jnr, Henry Wright, William Humphries, Martin Wright.
>
> It was resolved that the day for the Annual Meeting for the election of Commissioners shall be the second Saturday in June. It was resolved that the year for payment of all yearly dues shall expire on 31st December and that all yearly dues shall be payable in advance. The solicitors were instructed to endeavour to embody the above Resolutions of the meeting in the order now before the Board of Trade. On reading a letter from the Board of Trade to the effect that all boats must be excepted equally whether owned in Mousehole or elsewhere – it was resolved that the proposed amendment be accepted.

Prior to 1869 the harbour was only half its present size. The old quay was 75 foot shorter and there was no north quay. There used to be a breakwater come pier extending from where the Lobster Pot Hotel used to be out toward the steps on the old quay. During the extension of the old quay and the construction of the new quay this breakwater pier was demolished and the stone used in the building of both quays until it was used up. The final facing stones on both quays was faced granite which can be plainly seen to this day.

A list was also drawn up after 'a ballot being taken to determine the rotation of retirement in pursuance of the provision of the Commissioners Clauses Act of 1867.' This list was made out for the next three years. As it turned out this list was illegal because their solicitor Mr Cornish produced 'the new order of the Board of Trade confirmed by Act of Parliament that the retiring commissioners were all elected at the same time and so will all have to retire at the same time, that time being 1873.' Three years was the maximum time that any one person could hold the position of being a Harbour Commissioner, this act applied to all harbours. It was agreed that Mr Cornish draw up papers inviting nominations for new commissioners to take the place of those retiring. It was also agreed that the first public annual general meeting be on the first Saturday of June when most of the boats will be home 'changing over their nets.'

Messrs Freeman started work on the harbour during 1869 but from the reports it appears that the first six to eight weeks was spent getting all the equipment ready and down to the harbour. Some of this equipment was constructed on the site while others such as the cranes, used to dismantle the small breakwater, and the steam crane, which ran on railway type tracks, had to be erected in situ. As did all the scaffolding and ramps – the ramps and temporary roadways were for the benefit of the horse and carts. Some of the granite used in construction was brought in by sailing vessels, but in March of 1870 Freemans opened up a quarry near the harbour 'which is said to be excellent in quality and apparently inexhaustible, a short distance from the harbour and connected the two by tram rail.' On 29th June 1870 'the freehold of what promises to be a very valuable quarry near the base of the southern pier, has been purchased by Messrs Freeman who are erecting sheds, stables etc.' Exactly where this quarry might have been is very unclear as there is no sign of any quarry near the old quay today. Granite from Lamorna and Sheffield was also being used. By 1871 Messrs Freeman had completed the bulk of the actual construction of the new pier, the extension was already finished. A cheque for £5,000 was paid to John Freeman on 11th November 1871, the balance to be paid when all work was finished. By that it was meant clearing and removing all rubbish plus finishing off the slip road leading to the new quay.

There was a problem between Messrs Freeman and the Commissioners regarding the completed work. The specifications stated that the paving stones on the quay should be laid in a foot of cement, this had not been done. There were also problems with the infill which should have been of stone but was just dirt and rubble. This had caused some of the paving stones to sink. The engineer, Mr James Douglas, refused to sign the document from Messrs Freeman saying that the work was not carried out to specifications. The Commissioners refused to pay the outstanding amount until the work was done to specification. Mr Freeman said they wanted a cheap job done and did not pay enough money for those jobs not completed. There was stalemate as none of the parties would budge.

I suppose that living in todays mechanical world one tends to forget or probably do not realise the difficulties that must have been an every day commonplace occurrence for large heavy deep-drafted wooden fishing luggers entering or leaving harbours in certain weather or wind conditions. They were built to stand the rigours of everyday commercial fishing and to carry large heavy canvas sails, large quantities of heavy cotton nets and even larger amounts of fish. They would not have the speed or manoeuvrability of modern motorised fishing vessels built of steel or fibre glass.

On 22nd February 1872 a buoy was moored between the island and harbour so that boats could warp out of the harbour during easterly winds when they could not sail out. The buoy would have been made from cork and then a thick canvas covering would have been sown over this, then there would have been two or three coats of tar applied to the canvas. Running from the buoy would have been a thick rope or a chain to an anchor, the anchor was supplied by Mr Joseph Trewavas. They also hung chains over both pier heads so that 'vessels coming in during any surf have something to make fast to and prevent them from being carried onto the rocks at the back of the pier.' These chains would have been essential when coming in under sail with a surf running. Even today with motor powered boats this is always the most difficult time to leave or enter the harbour. If you time it wrong the surf can spin your boat around making her hit the quay and there is nothing you can do about it, in a fifty foot boat with only sail power it must have been very difficult. Later in the year a large esparto grass warp was laid from the pier head to this buoy. In 1886 this warp was extended to the island where a large ring bolt was fastened, chain ran from this to deep water clear of the island so that the rope warp would not chaff out on the rocks. This rope was made of 'Esparto Grass' which was imported into Mousehole by schooner for Mr George Laity who paid sixpence per ton landing dues on esparto. As well as making ropes for the boats he also used the esparto to make bags, handbags, mats and carpets, even outer clothing and a type of shoe or sandal. All 1st class vessels were charged one shilling per year for the use of the warp, all other vessels sixpence per year, cargo boats paid four shillings for each time of using.

In 1905 this warp was renewed with a '3 inch 130 fathom cohair rope, right handed hawser laid by Mr Stephens in Falmouth.' On Monday 4th September 1905 the new warp was placed out between the island and harbour 'so that it might be stretched and in readiness when required.' The distance between the island and harbour is approximately a quarter mile (220 fathoms) so this new hawser would not reach the island, this report did not mention how far out the buoy was or how much chain there was from the island.

1872 was the year that a large wooden crane was erected on the old quay head to lower the baulks of timber into slots in the gaps (harbour entrance) during storms. It was quite usual for these baulks to be lifted and lowered twice a day during times of severe weather to let vessels either in or out. This was no easy job either, believe me, I did it for 40 years, if you could take them up in 3 hours that was considered fast, lowering was always easier and quicker. Ideally there would be three men on each winding handle, most times there were only two, then there was the brake man who locked the gears once the baulk was in the air, then there were the hookers, one on each quay. Their job was to get the hooks on the crane chain into the eyes of the baulks ready for lifting, I did that on the New Quay for 40 years. So it was not only hard work but required some nine men each time. This old wooden crane was dismantled in 1975 because of insurance problems, there was nothing wrong with it but because it was wood no company would insure people to use it. When it was finally taken down and cut up the wood was in perfect condition with no rot anywhere. A mobile crane is now used to lower and lift the baulks, they are lowered in November and remain down until March when they are taken up for the summer. Without these baulks across the harbour entrance the surges running into the harbour during extremely stormy weather would under-mine the quays and wharfs. Once they collapse all the harbour front properties would also be at risk especially those on the old wharf which are extremely low and only just above high water mark. They used to have great difficulty in insuring these against flood damage – maybe they still do?

Also in 1872 the slipway near the monument was constructed. This was used by horse and cart to load and unload nets and fish. At this time the area now occupied by the harbour office, cottages and shops was still open ground used by fishermen as a storage area. Fishing boats were also built on this land.

During November 1872 it was decided that all fish buyers keep an account of all the fish they buy and to deliver an account of the same to the harbour master each week. The only reason I can think of why this should be done is that fish buyers must have been paying some sort of dues for this privilege, probably on the amount of fish bought. The actual number of fish buyers in Mousehole is unknown but there are numerous mentions concerning them from the earliest records. One such mention states 'that fish buyers be requested to keep the quays clean of offal and all other dirt after the cleaning of fish thereon and that the mooring posts be not used for opening fish on.' There is also a much quoted bylaw that appears in every harbour bylaws which 'forbade any person from throwing offal, dung or dirt into the harbour.' This bylaw still applies to all harbours at the present time, although in a more modern terminology. During research there was one recurring complaint concerning Penzance, Newlyn and Mousehole harbours and that was the 'nauseating smells coming from the harbour at low tide during hot weather.'

By the end of 1873 the matter concerning fish buyers and cleaning up came to a head as an extract from a report clearly shows. 'That the Harbour Master do mark off the north quay into sections that each fish buyer have his own place for packing fish and they be obligated to keep their own place clean after using the same.' Not all the fish would be packed on the quay, there were probably more fish cellars, net lofts and storage buildings, plus the pilchard presses, sailmakers lofts and bark houses than actual dwelling accommodation in those days. Even if some of the fish were taken ashore it is more than probable that they would be cleaned on the quay.

There was no electricity in Penzance, Newlyn or Mousehole in those days and refrigerators had not been invented so the only way of preserving fish was to split and clean each fish and then pack it in salt or ice. Any salt or ice that fell into the harbour would not make any difference but fish guts, fish heads or broken and damaged fish most certainly would, gulls can only eat a certain amount and the rest would just rot away on the harbour bottom. During the height of the fishing season at low tide in hot weather the smell must have been very ripe to say the least. In Mousehole's case this would have been aggravated even more because a lot of the sewers emptied straight into the harbour. It was not until 1962 that the Water Board put in large pipes to take the sewerage from the harbour and pipe it through the old quay out to sea. In 1997 during operation 'Clean Sweep' a new sewerage system was installed in Mousehole harbour with everything being pumped to St Erth Sewage Works. The new pumping station is situated in the harbour next to the slip road running down towards the new quay and has created a very nice viewing and seating area.

In the early 1800's, and of course a long time prior to that, very few houses would have any way of disposing of sewerage or other rubbish, especially in the smaller communities. An extract from a letter illustrates this quite well. 'Mrs Beddon is requested to remove all her dung and refuse from a spot occupied by her as a dung pit which belongs to the harbour or pay an acknowledgement of sixpence per year for the same.'

It must be remembered that Mousehole had no running water, electricity or gas in the 1800's and early 1900's. We still do not have a gas supply. Most houses in the 1800's did not even have any waste pipes and those that did were invariably close to the harbour or sea so without running water to flush things away they either had to have a cess pit or dung pit. It was the dung and refuse pits which was the cause of such aggravation.

But, as in all such cases, there is always someone who can see a way of making money and that is what happened in this case. 'Dung boats' came into existence. They charged three pence (1½p) per week per house to dispose of dung and refuse. Once a week they would go around the houses with a horse and cart filling up barrels from the dung and refuse pits. The barrels were then loaded aboard the boat, taken out to sea and dumped overboard. Originally these dung boats were not charged harbour dues as it was considered they were doing the village a service. By the 1870's there were several vessels employed in this service and harbour dues of seven shillings and sixpence per year was required. By the mid 1880's this was increased to twelve shillings and sixpence per year, from the increase in harbour dues it would appear that these dung boats had a very good if somewhat smelly trade. Dung boats also operated from both Newlyn and Penzance.

A census taken in the 1880's showed that the population of Mousehole was 1,602, while Newlyn's population was 3,323.

It was after one very long hot summer in September of 1909 that the Commissioners decided that the harbour had got to the stage where something should be done about cleaning it up. They decided to have 24 posters printed and posted around the harbour 'prohibiting fish being thrown into the harbour.' They had already stopped, or tried to stop, 'the dumping of dung and household rubbish into the harbour' but it appears that this was still going on. It was decided that a 'boy be paid one shilling to go around with a bell on Monday morning warning the fishermen and also ask them to put their boats between island and shore so that the harbour might have a thorough clean.' The Harbour Master was to employ men and carts to remove all the refuse and fish offal from the harbour. It did not say where all the refuse etc was to be dumped but that in itself would have caused quite a smell, not unless it was taken further along the shore to be dumped.

In 1876 the first iron railings were erected on the new quay head. In 1882 railings were fixed from where the slip is to the start of the new quay near the toilets. Mr James Harvey's bill for the job came to £21 6s 1d. This was done by the commissioners after a few children fell from the road into the harbour. During 1889 a Mousehole fisherman, William H. Worth, fell from the top of the quay onto the granite steps and was killed. At the inquest the County Coroner, G.P. Grenfell, suggested that railings should be put around this area and also on the steps.

A letter was sent to the Commissioners on 21st November 1889.

Gentlemen,

The jury at the inquest on William H. Worth, fisherman of Mousehole, request me to notify you that they consider a hand rail should be at once placed at the steps of Mousehole pier where the fatal accident occurred to this man.

I accordingly now give you notice.

Mr G.P. Grenfell, County Coroner.

In 1890 the whole of the new quay was fitted with hand rails, life rings were also fixed to both pier heads at the same time. The whole bill came to £9.4.2.

It was not until 1905 that railings were fitted along the whole length of the old quay by a Mr William Henry Harvey. This same gentleman had just finished putting iron railings along the whole of the harbour frontage for the Council. All the railings the Commissioners put up only had one parallel iron bar, those being erected by the Council had two.

It must have been extremely dangerous walking along the harbour front at night during a gale with only a paraffin lamp for light before any railings were erected. There was no electricity in those days and no street lighting, it is possible that the odd house might have had a paraffin lamp outside their front door but this would only give the odd pool of light in an otherwise dark street. From the records it appears there was only one death from falling off the quays and that was Mr William H. Worth in 1889. There are other reports of people falling but suffering 'only broken bones.'

In February 1878 it was decided to 'deepen the harbour so that boats could lie better in the inner part of the harbour.' Mr George Eddy was asked to do this work and also level such areas as was found necessary, his bill came to £8.15.6. It was also in 1878 that the first board giving the depth of water at the entrance was erected. In latter years this was also done at both sets of steps on each quay.

Due to a series of long running disputes concerning the use of and who owned the Banks the commissioners solicitor put an insert in the local paper in 1879 to the effect that anyone using the Banks at Mousehole harbour will have to pay sixpence per year rent. This small acknowledgement ensured that there would be no more disputes about who owned that area but it did create other problems. Some of the masons and carpenters who only used the Banks occasionally, like George Eddy who stored his cart there and William Grenfell, carpenter, who used the Bank for mending carts etc, complained that the boat builders who had a permanent space on the Bank should pay more. It was finally agreed that the boat builders pay £1 per boat during construction.

In 1880 the first harbour entrance lights were erected on the New Quay pier head. This was done in accordance with the Board of Trade regulations, two white lights in a vertical position six foot apart on an iron mast of twenty foot in height. The lights were paraffin lanterns made to the Board of Trade specifications. The making and fixing of mast and lights was carried out by a Mr Roberts at a cost of £11 6s 5d. The first 'Keeper of the Lights' was a Mr Robert McClary who received 20 shillings per year.

It was not until February 1903 that the Commissioners decided that something should be done to let vessels at sea know when the harbour was closed with the baulks down. It was decided that 'a red light be placed at the corner of Mr Hockin's house (if agreeable) when the booms are down or if it was considered dangerous in taking the harbour.' It must be remembered that very few boats had engines in 1903, most relied entirely on wind power. There are numerous reports of vessels getting damaged leaving or entering the harbour, and at least five boats being wrecked or very seriously damaged due to missing the warp between the island and harbour entrance. The addition of this red light would of course have to be done via solicitors, then the Board of Trade and then passed as an act in Parliament. The reason why any alteration to harbour lights had such a lengthy procedure was simply because it had to become law and then could be incorporated into any new maps or Mariners Orders.

The severe storm of 1880 during February not only completely wrecked several boats in the harbour when their moorings pulled out but also did considerable damage to the harbour. Baulks were smashed, the paving between the gaps was torn up and both quays were damaged. A notice was printed inviting tenders to replace the harbour entrance paving and repairing the quays. Also included in the tender was for putting down granite mooring posts in the harbour, namely under 'Mr Henry Mann's wharf.' This was the first time that granite posts were sunk into the harbour to use for mooring. Some of these large granite posts can still be seen today. The top harbour mooring chain now runs behind them. At the same time iron rungs were let into the granite under the steps on both quays so that fishermen could climb down into the harbour. On the new quay there used to be a drop of some four to five feet from the bottom plat to the harbour. Even in the 1960's there was still a two foot drop and we occasionally used this to our advantage by putting the bow on the step with an ebb tide to either mend or replace keel irons.

29

Most of 1881 was taken up with repairing the harbour, Mr John Tregenza, Mr James and Mr White appeared to be the three main contractors. Mr Corin made a new lamp mast and lamps for £6 5s 0d. A new rail was erected on the parapet as a guard rail for the Light Keeper and Robert McClary's wages were increased to £2 per year as Light Keeper. The oil for the 'lighter of the lamps' was put out for tender and was awarded to Janie Wallis whose bill was £2 0s 2d per year. Towards the end of the year all the new cement work on the old quay was coated in coal tar 'for added protection.' the ground under the Ship Inn was levelled so that boats 'could lay fair on the ground.'

In 1882 the new quay was once again badly breached and Mr John Tregenza was asked to fill in the cavity with 'concrete of cement' and that he order three tons of cement. When an engineer was consulted about the continual damage to the new quay his reply was 'because the pier has not been filled in or laid fair.' By that he meant the infill should have been rocks 'not stuff that do wash out,' 'laid fair' meant the paving should have been laid in cement. Exactly as Mr James Douglas stipulated 12 years ago, no wonder he would not sign the completion form from Messrs Freeman.

Extracts from a letter written on 27th February 1884. 'Knowing the inconvenient and unsatisfactory postal arrangements at Mousehole there is a new house where one or two rooms could be used as a Post Office that is more accessible, central and convenient for the inhabitants of Mousehole at large.' Extracts from the Postmasters reply. 'It is admitted that the present Post Office is in a somewhat inconvenient position at Mousehole and a more central position would be more favourable. But there is one obstacle which I do not see any way clear to get over. Miss Trembath is a very old servant of the Post Office and has scarcely any thing to live on except her salary as Post Mistress. I feel sure that you would not care to displace her after so many years service unless a very strong case indeed could be made out. To remove the office would in fact entail her dismissal.'

As can be seen from the above two extracts postal arrangements were not good but it also shows that some large companies at least were prepared to look after their employees. The two rooms talked about were in fact the two rooms at the bottom of the newly built harbour office.

Prior to 1882 all the steps leading down into the harbour were constructed in wood. In front of the present day Ship Inn there was a large wooden landing area level with the road that was used by fishermen and fish merchants, and would also double as a passing place for horse and carts.

Leading from this was a flight of wooden steps leading down to the harbour. In December 1882 it was decided to replace these wooden steps with granite steps, this work was carried out by Mr John Tregenza at a cost of £13 14s 4d. In 1891 the other granite steps leading down into the harbour by the present day pumping station were constructed by Mr Charles Tregenza at a cost of £30.

There had been a long running debate between the Commissioners and the Highway Board regarding boundary stones, exactly where these boundary stones were is very unclear. It could well be the area where they were proposing to build the new harbour office. 'On the plot of ground in front of William Rowe's house.' This was obviously sorted out because that is where the harbour office stands today. Tenders had been asked for the masonry and carpentry work. It was decided that Mr John Tregenza's tender for £49 10s 0d be accepted for the masonry work and Mr William Grenfell's tender of £36 for the carpentry, 'and that the work be attended to as early as possible.' At this period in time the harbour office would have looked somewhat different than it does today. There was no clock or clock tower and it appears that the idea of having a village clock had not been thought of. That all started with a cancelled regatta and harbour sports day due to bad weather. The money collected that day was given to the harbour commissioners to put towards a village clock and the ladies of the village held tea parties to help raise money. On 2nd July 1898 the commissioners decided 'to go the whole expense of erecting the clock in the harbour office and that Mr Charles Tregenza be employed to do the work.' His bill for alterations and erecting the clock was £14. He had to build the clock tower and alter the insides of two rooms to accommodate the pendulum and bobs, so the bill was not that excessive. A few months after the clock was installed it was decided that a cast iron pillar be fixed under the clock in the shop below to prevent any accidents and that Mr Grenfell get and fix this. His bill for all the woodwork during the clock tower construction came to £15 6s 9d. There was also a bill from Messrs Berringer and Schwerer for six guineas (£6 6s 0d) for the clock. There was also a bill for 14s railway charge and carriage from Penzance to Mousehole. Exactly what this charge was for, clock or building materials, I do not know. The whole amount spent on the building and clock came to £36 6s 9d, and the same clock is still working and keeping perfect time, although it did have a new face in 1999. A paraffin lamp was 'got to go behind the face so that it could be read in the dark.' It was the Harbour Masters job to light the lamp and look after the clock for which he was paid £2 per year. On October 20th 1898 the clock was illuminated for the first time.

An interesting letter appeared in the *Cornishman* newspaper on 1st July of that year.

> We (Newlyn folk) jubilate at Street-an-Nowan on Wednesday but Newlyn Towners, so far, are doing nothing. Pity it is that a united demonstration could not take place. Mousehole folk do things much better. There they will have a Jubilee Memorial clock in the harbour office. To this we hear Mr Bolitho MP has subscribed £10. If the people of Newlyn had been united something permanent might have been provided to the benefit of the two villages of Street-an-Nowan and Newlyn Town.

The Jubilee they are talking about was the celebrations of Queen Victoria's 60 year reign.

The bottom of the new Mousehole harbour must have been very rough indeed because from around 1870 there was always complaints from boat owners about the damage to keels caused by 'carns of blue elvin sticking up.' Mr George Eddy was always being asked to level or break up stones in the harbour. In 1886 he was also asked to clear a deeper channel leading into the harbour entrance and to blast out the larger blue elvin to the eastward side of the channel, 'to make a safer approach.' It was also decided to hire two horse and carts, two drivers and two labourers to 'excavate a portion of ground in the pier so as to allow the inner tier of boats to lay on fairer ground.'

There were now so many boats landing fish in Mousehole that the Harbour Master was instructed to tell all vessels to land end on instead of side on. This would allow more boats to land at the same time and also make it easier for the fish buyers.

It was not only fishing and cargo vessels that used the harbour, there were also a few pleasure boats and occasionally high class racing yachts that some of the young men took berth on. Once or twice a year the Salvation Army yacht would call in for a day or two, usually during the spring and summer. They were always greeted enthusiastically by the people of Mousehole. From the reports it appears this vessel would sail all around the coast calling in at every harbour for a few days. Harbour dues were waived at every port they called in. How far up the Bristol Channel they actually went is not recorded but they did get as far as Padstow.

The first advert for a 'Pleasure trip around the bay aboard Steam Ship *Nora* leaving Mousehole daily according to the tides' appeared in 1911. The *Nora*, PZ29, was built in 1909, she was 43 foot long, 8½ foot beam and weighed 9½ tons. She was owned by Philip Nicholls of Penzance and was finally broken up in 1930. Due to the vast number of fishing boats in the harbour during the 1890's there had to be a reshuffle in the way they were moored up to accommodate them all. This was accomplished by laying down new heavy chains and forming three semicircular tiers of boats that stretched from pier to pier. The larger 1st class vessels were given the moorings closest to the entrance, the next tier was for boats of 30 foot and the inner most tier was for boats under that size. The vessels next to the quays in the outer most two tiers were moored up one boats length astern of each tier to enable other craft to get in and out without too much difficulty. I am not to certain about that phrase 'without too much difficulty' though. Especially when you consider that only a very few of the 1st class vessels had an engine in those days, they were mostly sail powered. The smaller ones from the inside tier could probably scull out, and with all those masts it would be rather difficult to be pulled out with ropes. Anyway it must have worked because that is what they did. Once the three tier system was up and running another problem reared its head. The chain ladders were now all in the wrong place. An advert was put in the local papers asking for tenders 'to make and fix three chain ladders in Mousehole harbour.' These were for the new quay, it did not mention the old quay at all. Anyway the tender was given to a Mr Harvey, blacksmith, his bill for the first two ladders came to £12 19s 10d, his bill for the pier head ladder and fixings came to £9 4s 6d. They were installed during January 1895. Later another chain ladder was installed for the inner most tier as well, the rungs are made to move up and down slightly and only protrude out far enough to give a booted foot a fair grip.

Tenders were invited for 'boarding with half inch planking the Barbers Shop and for the door and windows to be painted outside.' The barbers shop they are talking about is the room on the left hand side of the harbour office and by a strange coincidence it was once again turned into a barbers shop in the 1980's and is known as the Barbers Arms.

Tenders were invited for 'Mr Joseph Hockin's drain which do empty itself onto the pier to be excavated to a proper depth and lay pipes from Mr Hockin's drain and cover in the same and carry the run right through the pier to the satisfaction of the Commissioners.' Mr George Eddy's tender of 10 shillings was accepted. It did not state what the drain was used for but it could have been waste water from the house, or cleaning fish or even a sewer. It was most probably all three.

During 1905 there was another dispute between the Commissioners and Paul Urban District Council concerning a roadway. From the report it appears that the Commissioners wrote to Paul Council 'thanking them for laying the road from Mrs Lugg's to the pier and asking them to have nothing more to do with it seeing it was harbour property.' This roadway was the slip road leading to the new quay. The report does not mention it but this was probably the first time that the main roadways in the village were 'tarmacadamed.' Prior to this covering all the streets were cobbled and they just tarred over the top of them. It was in April 1911 that Paul Urban District Council agreed 'to hand the slip over provided the Commissioners widen the road.' The slip was lengthened by 30 foot 'so as to make an easier gradient.' The work was carried out by Mr Charles Tregenza for £30. At the same time the blacksmith, Mr Harvey, put a one inch iron hand rail down the side. On the 2nd November 1907 the District Commander thanked the Commissioners for 'allowing the Board of Trade to fix a pillar on the south quay for the purpose of calling the Rocket Crew.' The 'Rocket Crew' were all volunteers and part of the Coastguard Service. They were responsible for firing a rocket across onto a shipwreck, and once the main rope was across using the breeches buoy to haul seamen to safety. They were summoned to the Coastguard hut, which is now an estate agents near the Coastguards Hotel, by firing one maroon, two maroons was for the lifeboat and three maroons was for both companies.

It appears that the Board of Trade were often writing to the Commissioners on various aspects of the harbour and its workings. A letter from the Board of Trade to Mousehole Harbour Commissioners on 30th September 1905 stated that 'attention of the Board had been called to the 25th section of the Mousehole Harbour Improvement Order 1868 by which the Commissioners are constituted a Pilotage Authority with the powers conferred on such authorities by the Merchant Shipping Act.' They then go on to ask whether this 'section in question remains unrepealed and if so whether the commissioners have exercised or do exercise the powers conferred upon them with respect to Pilotage.'

The Commissioners replied saying 'they have never exercised their powers with regard to Pilotage and that NO part of the Improvement Order has been repealed.' They then ask what powers were conferred upon them by the Merchant Shipping Act.

The Board of Trade reply states that 'the powers in question are contained in Part 10 of the Merchant Shipping Act 1894.'

When the Commissioners decided to fix harbour entrance lights they had to apply to the Board of Trade 'to fix a light to conduct boats into the harbour entrance on dark nights.' Before this was granted the Commissioners had to send a scale drawing of the harbour, piers and position in Mounts Bay to the Board of Trade. On 31st January 1880 they received a reply from the Board of Trade. 'Sir with reference to recent correspondence on the subject of the lighting of Mousehole pier – I am directed by the Board of Trade to state that they are of the opinion that two white lights placed vertically will be most suitable for this position and I am to signify the statutory requirements of the Board of Trade accordingly. Board of Trade, Whitehall Gardens, London SW, C. Cecil Trevor.' Nothing could be done to alter the harbour without the Board of Trade approval in those days and those two white lights would be paraffin lamps.

In 1887 Mr James Runnalls from Penzance asked the Commissioners if he could use the harbour for shipping stone. They agreed and said 'he be allowed to rest about 100 tons of stone on the upper end of the quay so as not to interrupt the passage or in any way interfere with the business of the harbour – until the vessel come to take it away but for not longer than ten days – and that Mr Runnalls be allowed to break up and take away the blue rocks in the north part of the harbour free of charge.' A crafty way of getting a large carn of blue elvin rock cleared from the harbour. Some of the blue elvin can still be seen jutting out of the harbour wall by the slip road, the rest was concreted over when sewers were laid in the 1960's, where the pumping station now sits.

It was also passed at a meeting in 1879 that 'Mr William Grenfell, carpenter, that he have to pay sixpence a year acknowledgement for occupying the bank, property of the Harbour Commissioners, for repairing carts and other implements thereon.' These small rents for the use of the banks were made by the Commissioners so that they were retained by them and not taken over by someone else. There are several instances in the old ledgers where they had not charged rental and ended up having to prove that in fact they owned the land.

From the records of February 1883 it appears that boats employed in crabbing did not pay any dues and it was proposed that they pay 10 shillings a year for the crabbing season and then pay as other boats of their class for the pilchard season.

It becomes clear from the records that at one stage the harbour bottom alongside the old quay was paved with granite blocks and there are several references to these in the ledgers over the years. It is possible that some boats owners complained about the state of them because George Eddy was asked to remove them to within 8 foot of the pier. At the next meeting it was decided to take the whole lot away and 'keep the stones for the villages use.' These paving stones would have been faced on at least one side and squared up so would be very useful for building purposes.

The Liberal Committee asked the Commissioners if they could use the harbour office and reading room to hold a meeting. This was agreed to providing the Conservatives were extended the same privilege and by giving 48 hours notice.

During September 1887 the Harbour Master reported that the last cargo vessel to leave had struck rocks outside the pier head and it was decided to consult George Eddy about removing all the high rocks on both sides of the channel. George Eddy's first tender was for £150 which was turned down, his next tender was for £75, he was offered £70 and 4 pence per ton shipping dues for the removal of rocks, which he accepted.

In 1892 six meetings had to be cancelled because all the Commissioners were at sea and a Special Meeting was held towards the end of October to discuss this. After a lot of discussion they decided 'all owners or part owners of a boat of 30 foot or upwards on the keel to be eligible to stand as a Commissioner.' Mr Joseph Trewavas and Richard Angwin were asked to see Mr T.B. Bolitho MP whether they could have an amendment to the Provisional Order relating to the choosing or standing of Commissioners. During October to December there were numerous letters from a Mr R. Giffen, Secretary to the Board of Trade, Harbour Department, London SW which stated that any intended application for a Provisional Order must be advertised for a month before the next ensuing session of Parliament. The Board of Trade would also require the fee of £35 in connection with the Provisional Order, also other expenses regarding printing, advertising and legal fees as a letter from J. Bolton & Co, 3 Temple Gardens, Temple, London EC, explains. 'Impossible to estimate accurately but over fifty pounds plus £35 for the Board of Trade.' The Commissioners were looking at a bill of over £100 to have a new Provisional Order made out and they decided to 'stop any further proceedings in the matter.'

Over the years there were numerous requests from Newlyn fishermen to winter their boats at Mousehole. They were nearly all turned down because there was just no room, even for wintering on the banks and they were usually told 'the space we have on the banks is so small that we cannot allow strange boats to be brought here to winter.' At the present time this rule still applies and only residents of Mousehole are allowed to have moorings in Mousehole.

If you stand by the newsagents and look across the harbour it is hard to imagine that there were once three tiers of fishing boats that stretched from quay to quay in vast semicircles. Each vessel would be touching each other and lashed together with short ends fore and aft so that the whole tier would move together as one. This was to prevent boats from rubbing against each other and causing damage (this practice is still carried on today and can easily be seen in Newlyn with boats against the quays). Each boat would have heavy chains running fore and aft across the harbour bottom and fastened to even heavier harbour chains. One chain ran around the harbour walls, another chain from steps on the new quay to the old quay and the third chain around the harbour gaps. At the present time there are only two chains, one by the gaps and the other around the top of the harbour.

Mousehole fishing industry declined rapidly in the early 1900's due mainly to the use of Newlyn harbour where the boats could stay afloat at all stages of the tide. The easiest way of calculating the decline of the fishing industry is by looking at the income obtained from fishing boats. In the 1870's to 1900 it was between £450 dropping to £300 per year. This was made up as follows, 90% coming from fishing boats, the other 10% from cargo dues, coal, salt, seaweed, lumber, esparto grass etc. By 1912 the income from all sources had dropped to £114 8s 1½d, down by about two thirds, and £70 of this came from fishing boats. Fish landing dues were increased in the 1900's by the Commissioners but that was still down, using the old 1870's tariff the decrease was again about two thirds. From the foregoing and the records it becomes clear that by 1912 Mousehole fishing fleet had decreased by about two thirds, but this still left a considerable number using the harbour. By 1960 there were only 10 full time fishing boats using the harbour and about the same number of part timers.

Another loss of income for the harbour was cargo vessels dues, in the 1800's this varied between £120 to £60 each year, by 1900 it was around £20, by 1912 it was £12 4s. This was mainly due to the railway which terminated at Penzance, better road transport and improved roads.

In 1894 the Commissioners decided to 'post a notice for tenders for the letting of the piers by the year for fishing, from Monday morning 1 o'clock until Saturday evening 8 o'clock, all Sunday fishing to be excluded.' This was for mullet that were around the harbour in huge shoals, gill nets or poles with hooks were used. Three tenders were received, first Mr J.M. Johns, £2 2s, second Mr James Trenoweth £1 1s, third Messrs Richard Pezzack Thomas, Joseph Johns, John M. Johns, A. Johns and Richard J. Harry for £3 per year. The last tender was accepted. At the present time fishing from the quays is free. £3 might not sound very much money but when you consider that the average rent in the 1890's was one shilling a week, £2 12s per year for a small cottage then that £3 was equivalent to a years rent.

After some severe storms in 1899 the Commissioners decided to advertise in the *Cornishman* newspaper for builders to meet them on the pier to consider

37

strengthening the old quay. 'It was decided to build a buttress 32 foot long, 10 foot high and 10 foot wide at the back of the old pier.' The buttress they are talking about was built on the seaward side on top of the new old quay, this joined up with the existing buttress, Mr George Eddy was awarded the contract for £70. Today this buttress runs the whole length of the quay.

In 1901 a pipe was laid down through Keigwin Street which came out half way down the harbour, it was finally finished in 1902. This pipe was for carrying sewage and household refuse. Not the ideal way of getting rid of sewerage but that was the way it was in those days. It was not until the 1960's that it was connected to a pipe that ran under the old quay and discharged 100 yards or so out at sea.

Another interesting fact that I discovered was this. A letter was received from Mr Roach of Penlee Stone Quarry asking whether they would be allowed 'to ship siftings from the pier at two pence per ton which was the price charged at Newlyn.' This was agreed to and the Harbour Master was asked to see the quarry manager and 'ask them whether they could not ship a few more cargoes of stone from Mouse-hole.' The vast majority of stone from Penlee Quarry was transhipped from Newlyn where the vessels were permanently afloat, during any busy periods the smaller cargo vessels were loaded with stone in Mousehole. The Commissioners were always trying to increase this side of the harbours activities but being tidal owners preferred Newlyn or Penzance for their transhipping agreements.

During the winter of 1908 Mrs M.G. Thornton offered the amount of '£15 towards a siren to be used on the pier during fogs.' Charles Tregenza and Bruce Wright were asked to get a list of prices. A letter from Messrs Barlow and Haddon offered 'a slightly worn siren, worked by hand, which could be heard a distance of half a mile for £15.' This foghorn was duly presented to the Harbour Master by Mrs Thornton. This same foghorn is still in the Harbour Office but not used these days.

By 1909 the harbour income had dropped considerably and was causing concern with the Commissioners regarding paying the Public Works Loans back for the £5500 borrowed to enlarge the harbour. They had paid back £5553 13s in interest and £1339 1s of the capital making a total of £6892 14s all together. They asked Sir Clifford Cory MP for St Ives to try and get the debt cancelled. Sir Clifford Cory wrote to the Loan Board giving all the figures and explaining the harbour income was now not enough to pay the interest let alone anything off the principle and that the money received was just enough to keep the harbour in good repair. The letter goes on to say, 'I most earnestly request that your Board will agree to wipe out and cancel the entire debt on Mousehole Harbour so that men will only have to pay a due for the upkeep of the harbour, which I fear from past experience will even then necessitate their having to pay a much larger due than in the Irish ports above mentioned.' The Loan Board reply stated that 'the Board have no power to cancel the outstanding debt on Mousehole Harbour which can only be done by an act of Parliament.' During June and July of 1909 some twelve letters were sent between the Public Works Loan Board, Sir Clifford Cory MP and Sir George Murray GCB, Treasury Chambers, London, concerning 'the remission of the amount now outstanding in respect of the loan granted by the Public Works Loan Commission to Mousehole Harbour Commissioners.' 'This debt could only be repelled by an act of Parliament.' 'My Lords are not satisfied that the case is one in which they would be justified in proposing such legislation.' So the Commissioners were stuck with the debt but it appears that the interest payable each year was dropped slightly.

On 2nd March 1912 the Commissioners wrote to 'the Sub Commissioners for Pilotage for the Port of Customs for Penzance' whether they could get two pilots appointed for Mousehole. 'For many years there were several pilots out of this port and the Commissioners thought that now they have all died out it would be an advantage to the seafaring community if two were appointed.' Reply 'Dear Sir, in reply to your request that two pilots be appointed for Mousehole I am directed to inform you that the Elder Brethren of Trinity House see no sufficient reason to accede to that request but that when a vacancy occurs in the Penzance district the matter will receive further consideration. Yours faithfully W.J. Hiscox, sub commissioners.'

2nd Jan 1892, three elm baulks were bought for £21 3s 9d. In 1896 two American elm baulks were bought, this appeared to be a regular occurrence. Broken baulks were always sold by auction but not until the fishing fleet was home when a boy would go around ringing a bell before the auction, he was paid 1s. In August 1892 the Harbour Master was asked to measure some boats keels that were doubtful on size, smaller boats paid less dues. In 1893 they stopped 'all persons taking sand from the beach for any purpose.'

7th July 1894, the Harbour Master was instructed to 'paint the crane with coal tar and pay a man not exceeding 10s to do it.' Land Tax was then 2s 9d per year. June 1896, 'Pier head lights to be kept on for 12

39

months instead of 9 months during periods of darkness.' This had to be passed by the Board of Trade and the Government.

On 3rd January 1914 a firing point was erected on the North Pier for the purpose of calling the lifeboat at 1s per year. Up until the 1990's maroons were fired for calling the lifeboat or LSA, now they use bleepers.

Mousehole Quay – Its Age

A QUESTION THAT is regularly asked is when was the old quay built. In all my research I have not come across any mention of when the old quay was started. It must be remembered that Mousehole was not an important place like Marazion or the Mount, and according to the Royal Geological Society the only thing that connected them over a thousand years ago was a brackish water inlet that led to Gwavas Lake and a shallow river leading through the marshes to Marazion. The bay was then a forest and farm land.

It is known that some 3,000 years ago tin trading was carried on at Marazion from the Mediterranean countries, some people say tin wasn't known about that long ago, it was because they made bronze axes, spear heads etc, and you can't make bronze without tin, that is what makes bronze so hard. The earliest tin was probably won from streams and silt deposits where water was used to separate the tin, in a similar way that gold was first won. You have probably all heard of the Golden Fleece, well all that was was a sheep's pelt (fleece) anchored in a stream by heavy stones, any gold dust washing downstream was caught in the pelts fine hairs and worked its way down to the skin. That was your Golden Fleece that Jason was after. After a few weeks this would be taken out and after drying the gold dust would be shaken out onto another flat skin. This method of winning gold dust is still used in the fast streams in remoter regions of the world and has been documented and shown on TV. I can't see the Cornish tin streamers using that method but maybe it has never been tried.

When tin trading was carried on 3,000 years ago one must presume there was some record kept of their trading. Most of the Mediterranean countries had mastered the art of writing by then but it was usually done by the High Priests or such like. We do know the Mount was occupied by Monks but whether Monks were about 3,000 years ago I don't know, but considering how easy it would be to defend the Mount then it is reasonable to assume if it wasn't Monks it would be some other religious sect or important person who would be able to write. This would be invaluable to these traders.

Before these traders left for the Mediterranean they would have to replenish their water barrels for the long journey and as stated before tin streamers were using the streams to win tin, this would poison the water with arsenic and turn the water red. Mousehole on the other hand had no tin to talk about with blue elvin rock to the north of it. So their two streams would be clear of any colouring or arsenic, that would be the obvious place to fill up their water barrels *(see Mousehole – Its Name)*. They could only do this with the aid of small boats (punts), it would be too shallow for the mother ship to get in close enough. To protect these small punts from any damage by waves or wind blowing up the creek a small breakwater would have been built by these men. That would ensure the safety of these small boats when drawn up the beach while collecting water. Maybe the farmers cultivating the ground in the bay would also take advantage of these traders to provide them with fresh vegetables or meat or the few fishermen to trade their catch. It will never be known how the original breakwater started but it is known that these traders stopped for water at a place with two streams and Mousehole is the only place with two streams.

The old quay was gradually built up over several hundred years and this can be seen in the way the old quay is constructed. It is difficult to see the inside of the start of this quay because it has been buried under the car park. The outside has been repaired numerous times over the years and does not give a clear picture, also the parapet or coping was not added until the 1800's *(see Mousehole Harbour)*. The last 75 foot from the steps being added in 1869.

It is possible to pick out the various stages of construction in the older part, differing ways that stones are laid or stone size and rough joins where one lot of the building meets the other, but actual documented evidence of when any building took place is virtually non-existent until the 1800's.

There must be some sort of report regarding Mousehole harbour because in the 1700's and 1800's it was the largest and most important fishing port in the bay, as yet I have not found anything.

Fishing

RECORDS FOR THE earlier fisheries are scarce to say the least but how far back they can be traced depends a lot on were the sea levels where at that time. It is known that Mounts Bay was once all forested land so there would be no fishing in those times. 4,000 years ago it is known that the tin traders from the Mediterranean sailed through the marsh to St Michaels Mount to collect tin, they then called at an inlet to fill up their water barrels, that inlet proved to be present day Mousehole. *(see Mousehole, Its Name)*. At this period of time Mounts Bay was still covered by forest. It was not until 1099 that the bay flooded and assumed its present day shape. Fishing must have been pursued before this date as there was a wide inlet running right up to Gwavas Lake, which was outside present day Newlyn. What type of fishery was carried out in those days is unknown but in all probability it would be for pilchards, mackerel and herring. They formed very large shoals up until the early 1900's.

By the 1200's there was a thriving fishing industry in Mounts Bay but only on a very limited scale, the limiting factor was the lack of large quantities of salt for curing the fish. Salt was obtained by evaporating sea water but this could never produce the quantities required for fishing purposes. There were salt mines in England but they were far away from the west country and in all probability the salt they produced was required for the growing population of the country. It was not until the early 1200's when King John granted licences to merchants in Bayonne to fish 'for whales, conger and hake from St Michaels Mount to Dartmouth,' that this lack of salt was overcome. These merchants imported vast quantities of salt from France and from this time onwards the fishing industry began to prosper.

There were basically two ways of preserving fish in those days, wet salting and dry salting. Dry salting was the most commonly used method, this entailed splitting the fish open and usually removing the backbone in the large types of fish, they would then be laid on a bed of salt belly up, then more salt would be sprinkled or rubbed onto the exposed flesh. These would then be left until the salt had drained all the moisture out of the flesh, quite often this would be done outside in the sun to help with the drying. This dry salting would be carried on until, as one merchant put it, 'they be hard enough to knock in nails.' I do not think that would have been possible but it does give you some idea how dry and hard fish ended up. In this condition, provided they were kept dry, they would last for years and could be transported anywhere. Dry salting is still carried on in the remoter parts of the world where there is no electricity and is a valuable source of income for the isolated fishing villages, especially in desert regions where it not only provides food but also much needed salt. It does need several hours of soaking in fresh water before cooking.

Wet salting, or pickling, came into use a long time after dry salting and was used mainly for pilchards. It did the same job but was a lot less time-consuming. Wet salting was done in wooden containers and later in cement pits. A layer of salt was first spread across the bottom then pilchards would be tipped in along with more salt until about eighteen inches deep, then a large oak board was placed across the pit or container on ledges inside, this was to stop the bottom fish being crushed by the weight above. This stepping process would go on until the pit or container was full. They would then be left for about six months to cure, pickle, in the thick brine that was formed as the salt removed the moisture from the fish. This process for curing pilchards was carried on in Newlyn at the Pilchard Works until it was closed down and turned into housing during the late 1990's early 2000.

Before wet salting came into being pilchards were cured by 'bulking' which was a type of dry salting. This was done in cellars and rather labour intensive and invariably carried out by women and boys. A thick layer of salt was first spread across the bulking area, then pilchards would be laid out on their sides, another layer of salt and then fish, this would continue until it reached a height that made it awkward to work, then another bulk would be started.

Regardless of which way they were cured pilchards had to be pressed after curing. This was done to remove oil from the fishes flesh. The original way of pressing was done with a 'beam press.' When you walk into some of the older cottages around the harbours of Cornwall you can always tell if at some stage it was a pilchard press. These were built purely for pressing purposes, the back wall would be built up some four foot then it would be widened by about three inches or so to form a ledge. This was where the end of the beam went. The beams were up to 20 foot long and a third of the way along a forked pole went under the beam, this pole went down to a pressing plate that fitted the top of a barrel full of pilchards, on the very end of the beam would be hung a large granite stone that weighed about one hundredweight (112 lb). This was then left to press, each day more pilchards would be added until the barrel was full of pressed fish. The pilchards were placed in the barrel in a circle so that during pressing not one single fish was damaged or marked in any way. The oil that was pressed out would be collected and used in cooking and lighting. I would imagine the smell of cooking and burning this oil in lamps would be quite overpowering but if that is what you grew up with then it would not have been noticed. A barrel of pilchards was known as a Hogshead and weighed about 50 stone (700 lb). They were exported to the Mediterranean countries.

Wet salting was also used by the fish smokers, this hardened the flesh enough for them to be hung and smoked without damaging the fish and also helped in curing. This process still applies to smoked fish to this day, the yellow colouring comes from the hardwood chippings used in smoking although some do now use artificial colouring.

With the plentiful and abundant supplies of salt that was now available to the fishermen this industry grew very quickly, so much in fact that by the late 1400's it had assumed a position of national importance and the government of the day passed rules and regulations regarding it. These were mainly to do with distribution and 'conserving this profitable fish for all the people of the realm.' During this period of time there were a considerable number of fast days, it has been calculated that there were at least 153 fast days when 'it was officially forbidden to eat meat,' but eating fish was permitted. It is quite possible that more fish was eaten per head of population in those days than at present time, it is a great pity these fast days are gone as it would certainly do the countries fishing industry a power of good.

By the early 1500's another fishery was underway which would prove to be the most valuable and of great national importance, this was the Newfoundland cod fishery. This was carried out by boats from Devon and Cornwall. They would sail to Newfoundland at the start of the season and land their catches in this country. Towards the end of the season they would keep their catch aboard, salted down, and return home laden with Newfoundland cod. Some fifty vessels took part but by the 1580's there were over 100 boats fishing for cod. This did not go unnoticed by the pirates and Spanish men-of-war who had taken to capturing these boats and their valuable cargo.

On 20th July 1594 Sir Walter Raleigh wrote to Sir Robert Cecil pointing out that:

. . . certain great Spanish men-of-war had recently given chase to several British vessels as far as Dartmouth. It is likely that all our Newfoundland men will be taken up by them if they are not speedily driven from the coast, for in the beginning of August our 'Newland' fleet are expected, which are above one hundred sail. If those should be lost it would be the greatest blow ever given to England.

British men-of-war escorted these fishing boats to Dartmouth and successfully kept the Spanish at bay. Dartmouth was the main landing port for these Newfoundland vessels. It was decided that for better protection the boats engaged in this fishery should sail in convoy and be escorted by British warships, especially when returning laden with fish. By the 1630's there were over 200 vessels leaving Devon and Cornwall for Newfoundland. The main ports in Devon were Dartmouth, Teignmouth and Exmouth while in Cornwall boats from Saltash, Looe, Mevagissey, Fowey, Falmouth, St Mawes, St Keverne, Mounts Bay (presumably Mousehole, Newlyn and Porthleven), St Ives and Padstow were engaged in the Newfoundland cod fishing. It must have been a fantastic sight to see 200 plus sail stretching out across the sea.

Besides the extremes of weather the fishermen had to contend with pirates from Spain, Turkey and Algeria and their activities became so bold and devastating that fishing and cargo vessels around the Lizard and Mounts Bay area virtually came to a standstill. By 1608 it was estimated that 'there were five hundred sail of pirates in English waters,' around the Lizard and Mounts Bay 'the pirates have taken divers ships and barks taking out their principle men and suffering the rest to depart.' In 1625 Penzance was petitioning MPs to have a fort because of the activities of the Turks 'whose men-of-war were sighted daily off the shore so that no fishermen dare go forth.'

In 1636 Sir Francis Godolphin and his lady, along with his servants, his brother, Captain Godolphin, and his wife left Penzance for the Scillies. They had no sooner cleared Lands End when they were taken by Turks. One of the Turks attempted to abuse the Captain's wife and he ran him through with his sword. 'Whereupon they cut him in a hundred pieces and carried Sir Francis and the rest away captives, God of His mercy send us some relief.' There are numerous reports from around this time telling of such activities, or the capture of fishing boats and men but eventually all the pirates were destroyed and driven from the western approaches.

Once the pirates were driven off fishing local waters for the pilchard, herring and mackerel made great strides. By the mid 1700's the pilchard fishery was the largest fishing activity in the country, nothing could compare with it for the amount taken, and the largest proportion of fish was taken in seines. In 1868 the largest number of fish taken in one seine was 5,600 hogshead, 1,750 ton, 16 million eight hundred thousand fish, although a few years later a seine at Newquay was estimated to contain 8,500 hogshead, 2,656 ton, 25½ million fish. These very large catches could take up to ten days to empty the seine, the time taken depended on the availability of the workforce, women and boys, and how fast they could be 'balked' or 'pickled.' Once a shoal was enclosed, and the ends 'tucked,' then the seine would gradually be towed into shallower water. At dead low tide there still had to be enough depth of water for fish left in the seine to swim around without damaging themselves as they might have to be there for several days. 'Tucking' was done by a small net carried in another boat which was used to seal the two ends of the seine after it was shot. This was always a delicate operation and required both skill and speed if the shoal was not to be lost. The 'tuck' net had to be sown onto the two seine ends to close the gap if they did not meet, and to keep the fish away from this area the men would beat the water. Beating the water will frighten fish but if you can make it sound like gannets diving into the shoal this works even better. I used to use a 7 lb mackerel lead on the end of a rope to produce the right sound when trying to get mullet to mesh up.

In 1827 it was estimated that there were some 316 seines in Cornwall and 350 drift boats employed in the pilchard fishery, by 1877 this number was estimated to be 390 seines and some 540 drifters engaged in this industry. The largest concentration of drifters in Cornwall in the 1800's was loosely called the Mounts Bay fleet, but this fleet was comprised of vessels from St Ives, Mousehole, Newlyn and Porthleven, but even so it still amounted to over half the total number of drifters in Cornwall. In 1790 the fishery produced 52,000 hogshead of pilchards, 16,250 tons, 156 million fish. This was exceeded in 1796 with a catch in excess of 65,000 hogshead, 20,313 ton, 190 million fish. The 1796 catch was so great that merchants and curers ran out of salt and several thousand tons had to be imported from France. These two years were exceptional and have never been surpassed in quantity taken, nor ever will be because the huge shoals of pilchards that frequented the Cornish coastline are no longer there. Their decline was blamed on a new type of fishing that sprang up in the late 1880's, trawling. It was claimed that the trawlers destroyed the spawn and spawning areas. Whatever the reason their decline was very rapid and the fishery had finished by the 1950's early 60's.

During the 1700's, leaving out 1790 and 1796, the number of exported hogshead varied between 25,000 and 40,000 per year, prices also varied considerably, in some instances they could not be sold and were then used as fertiliser on the ground by farmers, but normally they fetched between £1 10s and £2 10s per hogshead, the average price was around the £2 mark. In 1800 it was calculated that it cost £1 3s to cure a hogshead of pilchards, the salt alone came to 6s which was nearly a quarter, the rest was taken up in the cost of the barrel, pressing and wages for the women and boys. So the actual profit per hogshead was not that great, especially when fishermen sold their catch to curers rather than putting them down themselves. On top of this the government paid a subsidy of 8s 6d per hogshead, it is not clear who actually received this subsidy, the exporters and merchants or the fishermen who caught them. The export trade of hogshead was mainly to Italy with the main ports being Genoa, Leghorn, Civita Vecchia, Naples, Venice and the Adriatic. So important was this export trade to the life of Cornwall that songs and poems were often sung or chanted in the local hostelries.

One such goes like this.

'Here's a health to the Pope, may he live to repent and add just six months to the term of his Lent and tell all his vassals from Rome to the poles there's nothing like pilchards for saving their souls.'

This was a popular chant in the early 1960's with the older fishermen of Mousehole and always said with a full glass raised high on a Saturday night in the Ship Inn.

On 9th December 1886 the largest single cargo of pilchards ever to leave England was aboard the steamer *Palmyra* which left Penzance for the Mediterranean with 3,252 hogshead of pilchard, 1,016½ tons, nine million seven hundred and fifty-six thousand fish. The records show that there could be up to ten vessels waiting or loading hogsheads of pilchards at the same time in Penzance harbour. Both Mousehole and St Ives exported cargoes of pilchards but not on the same scale as Penzance. All the coves from St Ives to the Lizard had pilchard seines and most of these places also had curing and pressing facilities, but due to their location the hogsheads had to be transported to a main loading area, and that was invariably Penzance. During the 1400's the herring fishery around the coast of England was largely untouched and the records show that the only vessels engaged in this fishery were from the south-west. The North Sea herring was being exploited by the Dutch but there is no record of East Coast vessels engaged in this fishery, which I feel sure there must have been. In the west country there are reports of herring being taken from Plymouth to St Ives, mostly by drifters, and also of large quantities being occasionally taken in pilchard seines. Seining for herring appears to have been sporadic and it must be assumed that they did not come as close inshore as the pilchard. By the 1580's the south-west vessels were following the herring as far as Ireland, it appears that the majority of these boats came from Mousehole, Newlyn, Porthleven and St Ives, with the largest fleets coming from Mousehole and St Ives. By the mid 1600's some of these boats were even working up around Scotland. It was in the 1700's that the east coast herring fishery really got into its stride and once again the boats from Mounts Bay were amongst those drifting for herring. They would follow the herring to Ireland, up to Scotland and then down the east coast, fishing the shoals as they moved. Most, but not all, would arrive back in December or January for the start of the mackerel season. There are records of some Mousehole vessels being away from their home port for nearly three years, the crews would obviously come home several times a year as the seasons slackened. From all the reports, records and documents relating to the herring fishery during the 1600's and 1700's it was the boats from Mousehole that followed the herring all the way round the coast, from Ireland to Scotland and down the east coast. This is quite understandable as during this period Mousehole did have the largest fleet of drifters in Mounts Bay and St Ives. One report mentions 'some 80 to 100 sail have left Mousehole for the herring fishery.' I find this number hard to believe, simply because the old harbour of Mousehole was only half the size of the present day, and if you then include the smaller pilchard drivers I cannot see where they could all possibly have fitted in. Although it is known that the larger boats from both Newlyn and Mousehole did use Penzance in times of bad weather. If the report had stated 'some 80 to 100 sail have left Mounts Bay for the herring fishery' then this would have been more acceptable as the combined fleets of Mousehole, Newlyn and Porthleven's larger drifters would probably be around this number.

The mackerel fishery was another large industry carried out by drifters and again confined to the extreme south-west of Cornwall during its early years. The market for mackerel was very limited up until the early 1700's and then consumption and demand for this very meaty fish increased dramatically. The sudden increase in demand for mackerel is rather unclear but in all probability it had something to do with the influx of east coast drifters who arrived at Penzance in January to exploit the vast shoals that frequented the area. From the mid 1700's the mackerel fishery had become very large and was only beaten by the pilchard fishery for importance, by the mid 1800's it had become the most important fishery in Cornwall and employed more boats than any other. Nearly half of these vessels came from other ports around the country, especially from the east coast.

During May of 1891 the fishing was so heavy that 'a powerful steam tug named *Gamecock* takes all the luggers mackerel from the Scillies, Newlyn and Mousehole to Plymouth to load onto special trains for London.' Why they should want to transport these fish all the way to Plymouth is unclear because in June 1870 it is recorded that,

> . . . when boats were working out of Scillies or further a steamer called *Earl of Arran* would load other boat's fish aboard and deliver them to Penzance to be put aboard the fish train for London, and during times of slack fishing a smaller vessel named *Little Western* was used for smaller loads, both of these vessels were owned by Messrs Hicks of Scilly.

It is more than probable that these fish trains had insulated compartments for carrying fish as ice was now becoming available as the following extract shows. 'Mr Ashwells new ice factory at Gulval can make 100 tons of ice per week, the steam machinery for making this ice cost between £4,000 and £5,000.' This was a considerable amount of money in those days but it most certainly appeared to pay for itself because on 12th August 1886 'new ice works are being constructed for Mr Ashwell near the Tolcarne river.' Even with two plants producing ice this was still nothing like enough needed for the fishing industry and as late as 1897 ice was being imported from Norway and Bergen as the following shows, 'four schooner have arrived from Norway each carrying between 300 and 450 tons of ice for the fishing industry.'

These large quantities of both salt and ice that were regularly imported can be understood from the following extract which gives some idea of the number of vessels employed.

> 19th April 1894, a large contingent of fishing boats, sail and steam, from all along the south and east coasts now work out of Newlyn, this year a record number of fish buyers are attending sales, 54 of them, which accounts for the steady and good prices.

This number of buyers was noted by the fishermen of Mousehole who on the 13th July 1893 'hold a large meeting with the Commissioners to discuss the selling of fish at Mousehole quays by open auction, previously they sold direct to curers in the village.' They did sell fish by auction from the quays for a number of years but it was far too late as Newlyn now basically had the monopoly.

It was not all that easy for the fishermen and they could easily lose a considerable amount of money. Not only did they have to contend with the vagaries of the weather, which often caused damage to boats etc, but the fish themselves could also be a problem and there are numerous reports of vessels 'losing all their nets from weight of fish, which caused the nets to be torn and all that was retrieved were headlines and footlines, the fish taking the rest.' This happened quite regularly in all the drift fishery.

Another problem that regularly affected them, especially the mackerel drifters which worked further from the shore, was the damage caused by dogfish and sharks. From the accounts it appears that 'Spur dogfish' (Squalus Acanthias) was the biggest problem. A large pack of dogs can number thousands and if they pitched into a net full of fish and start feeding then it is soon reduced to ribbons. One of the worst years on record for this was 1905. By the middle of April the packs of dogfish were so large and numerous that it brought the mackerel fishery to a close. A large majority of the east coast drifters returned to their home port with 'what little nets they have left.'

A few steam drifters went off 200 miles from Lands End but even out here they were 'belittled by dogfish and shark,' they also left for their home port. There was hardly any sale for dogfish in those days and merchants did not bother with them because, as one merchant put it, 'they do have to be skinned.' Due to the lack of mackerel and the apparently inexhaustible supply of dogfish a group of merchants held a meeting in a Newlyn pub on April 20th of 1905 to 'see what could be done about marketing dogfish.' They did agree that 'they were considered inedible due to their name dogfish shark,' the merchants thought that if the name was changed they 'could get the general public to eat them.' Someone suggested that 'salmon was known by all' and various names were put forward such as 'Deep Sea Salmon,' 'Princes Salmon' etc, then one of the merchants came up with the name 'Rock Salmon,' this was the name they all agreed on. This name became known all over England and was the nations favourite fish with chips and even outsold the cod for several years. This was the start of a big national fishery as dogfish were common and very abundant all around the coastline. Sadly these huge packs of dogfish were gradually over-fished and the last big landings made at Newlyn were in the 1970's. Very few are landed these days and the amounts are usually only a few stones in weight. Dogfish can grow to 1½ metres in length and live for 20 years, the gestation period is between 18 and 22 months depending on water temperature, the live independent free swimming young are between 20 cm to 30 cm long (8 to 12 inches). The Trades Description Board decreed that the name 'Rock Salmon' was misleading as it had nothing to do with a salmon and was in fact a shark, so they are now marketed under the name 'Dogfish,' 'Huss' or 'Dogfish Shark,' the same name that put the general public off and the Newlyn fish merchants changed so successfully in 1905, and they call that progress?

Seining for pilchards, herring and mackerel has long since finished but there is still one branch of this industry that survives to the present day, mullet seining. One of the first mentions I have come across of this fishery was in the 1200's when 'a vast shoal of mullet has been enclosed in a seine at Sennen.' Mullet do not form huge shoals all the year round, throughout the summer months they tend to be in small heads of fish which only group up to form the very large shoals during the early part of the year when they are spawning. Once they have spawned the shoals break up again. During the early part of the year there is always someone high up on the cliff tops around Sennen looking for the 'colour' of a shoal. They might watch this 'colour' for weeks and still not be able to shoot their seine, the mullet have to come onto the sand and be in the right place before any seining can take place. It might be several years before this happens but when it does the rewards are high, they only get one chance and if it goes wrong then that is it for another year. Mullet are one, if not the, hardest fish to catch, and even when you have them enclosed you still might lose all or part of them, they are the Houdini's of the fish world. Seining is still carried out at Sennen, the only difference is in the nets which are of man-made fibre, not the huge heavy net of cotton.

An interesting article I came across regarding the sharing of mullet after the catch is worth repeating.

> On being brought ashore the fish is thrown on to the ground in piles, pile being as equal as they can make it, generally two piles to each man. When all the fish has been divided another man goes around with a basket and each person puts in some personal belonging, pipe, tobacco tin, knife etc. These are then thrown at random on each pile of fish, by which means each man will be able to identify his pile and feels that he has received his share by a fair and impartial allotment.

I wonder how such a system would go down with today's share fishermen?

The oldest form of fishing is handlining and bone hooks from thousands of years ago have been found all over the world. This fishery employed a lot of boats during the 1200's but they would undoubtedly be the smaller vessels. During the 16, 17 and 1800's the number of vessels gradually increased, these were the pilchard drivers that worked 'hooking,' handlining, during the early part of the year until the pilchard season started. The records show that from the late 1700's the number of boats that continued this fishery for the whole year was increasing. One reason for this was undoubtedly financial regarding the cost of fitting out a tier of nets compared with the cost of a handline. Handliners tended to catch the more expensive prime fish such as hake, turbot, halibut and bass. Hake was the main quarry sought and probably the most abundant, with most of it being sold fresh locally, although by the early 1800's there was a large dry salting industry for hake around Mounts Bay. At this period of time hake were fetching '9/-s per burn of 21 fish,' by the 1880's it was '16 to 21 shillings per burn of 21 fish,' it was probably the availability of ice that brought about this sudden increase in price.

On 18th January 1883 one handliner landed 'three turbot weighing 40 lb, 22 lb and 16 lb, and these were sold to a Mr Richard Roberts from St Ives for the princely sum of £3 5s.' This was by no means an isolated case and turbot were landed on a regular basis by handliners. Halibut were another flatfish that was very common and they were even caught off the rocks with handlines during certain times of the year. Although the very large fish caught were not favoured by merchants as 'on a handlining trip in June 1898 Mr William Humphreys from Mousehole caught a large halibut on a handline that weighed 112 lb, but the buyers were shy of such a large fish and it sold for only 5s 6d.'

Sports fishermen also took large amounts of fish such as:

. . . on 4th August 1898 amateur fishermen are having fine sport off Mousehole pierheads catching quantities of mackerel, pollock, bream, black jacks, plaice and bass, one amateur caught two bass weighing 19 lb.

The report does not say whether these fish were sold or salted down for winter food.

An interesting report from 22nd September 1881 illustrates the selling of fresh fish by local 'fishwives.'

When business is to be done Newlyn and Mousehole fisherwomen get over the ground smartly, not withstanding a cowl full of fish. (A cowl was a large wicker basket carried on the back). On Tuesday morning two of them, with red faces and freely perspiring, might be seen racing down Bread Street in Penzance to a house of a customer who had ordered some hake. The leading one made a mistake at the turning which gave the other an advantage, whereupon loud talking ensued as to who would supply the fish. Judging by their appearance they had raced all the way from Newlyn.

I think this paints a lively picture of life in those times.

Handlining boats increased rapidly until the 1960's when in Mounts Bay alone, from the harbours and coves, there were some 100 or more, by 1970 and up until 1980 the number of vessels employed in this industry in Cornwall was over 2,000 boats ranging in size from 14 foot to 60 foot. During those ten years this was the biggest fishery in Cornwall and vessels from around the country took part in this bonanza. It was estimated that 5,000 fishermen were employed and twice this amount ashore, sorting, packing, weighing, icing, smoking and all the people involved in the distribution side of this business. These vast shoals of mackerel showed up around September or October and dispersed in February or March after they had finished spawning. The main area for this fishery was from Lands End up to Mevagissey with the largest concentrations being in Falmouth Bay and Mounts Bay. If the fish set in Falmouth first then we would leave Mousehole, usually by the end of September, and work from that port until they moved to Mounts Bay, quite often we would be in Falmouth for the whole season. If this fishery had been left purely to the handliners it would still be going today, but permission was granted to the 'industrial' fishing vessels that would catch more in one night than the handliners would catch in the whole season. It was estimated that there were some 50 to 80 'industrial' vessels from Scotland, Ireland and other ports from around the coast most of whom landed to 'factory ships' from Russia and other Communist countries to very large 'factory ships' from Japan which apparently had a crew of 500. They were so large that when the *Scillonian* passed them she looked about the size of a rowing boat. In the winter of 1980 we all left and steamed around to Falmouth, no fish, we ventured up as far as Plymouth and finally got back to Newlyn on December 22nd, during those three months we never landed one fish, that is how fast this winter mackerel fishery collapsed.

A natural follow-on from handlining was 'longlining' which appears to have made its appearance at the beginning of the 1800's. They caught conger eels, ling, ray, turbot etc.

The first longlines reported were of 100 hooks and by the 1900's the hooks numbered in the thousands. A longline is made from two coils of rope, 240 fathoms, 480 yards, and every 9 or 12 foot a three foot strop of hake line would be tied onto the rope, on the end of the strop was tied a large swivel hook. This line would be coiled into a large wicker basket and the hook points stuck into a cork rim tied onto the basket top. The larger vessels would carry up to 30 baskets or more which would be shot in one long line. This fishery has now virtually died out.

Another fishery which started about the same time was trawling. This is now the largest fishery in the world but it had humble beginnings. The first trawlers were sail powered and from the records there were only some six vessels working from Mousehole and Newlyn. By the 1880's this way of fishing was becoming more popular and visiting trawlers from other ports were working Mounts Bay. Some with not much success as 'Plymouth trawler *Maria* PH34, ran ashore on Gear Rock and sank on 24th April 1879,' and even earlier 'Plymouth trawler *Baron*, while becalmed, was swept by the tide onto a reef between Mousehole Island and the harbour on 23rd April 1873,' it does not say whether she was lost.

Mounts Bay's fishing grounds were becoming nationally known for trawling, this caused a rift between the drifters and trawlers when trawlers were cutting through tiers of drift nets. It was on 15th March 1888 that 'two Grimsby trawlers work from Newlyn for the first time and they land one and three quarter tons of sole.' This did not go unnoticed by the local boats and a report from 14th March 1889 states 'large numbers of drift boats are turning over to trawling at this time due mainly to several bad drift seasons, plus they are not away from home for months on end.'

On 12th April 1894 'Because of the uncertainty of the mackerel fishing quite a few more Mousehole boats have changed over to trawling and long lining during the first half of the year, some permanently.' One reason why there was such a changeover probably has a lot to do with a report from 18th October 1894. 'Steam capstans were fitted to more Mousehole boats at a cost of between £80 and £100 per steam capstan, the boats just fitted out are *Bonnie Lad, Vesta, Gleaner, Humility* and *Onward*.'

Surprisingly enough very few fishing vessels had engines fitted for propulsion at this period, although they were of course getting more common. The vast and abundant shoals of fish that used to inhabit Mounts Bay have all long since been caught and decimated by overfishing, or the destruction of spawn and breeding areas, but occasionally other unexplained factors happened as reported on 9th March 1870. 'Boats engaged in the mackerel fishery found the sea covered in large quantities of floating dead pilchards 10 to 15 miles offshore, the cause of all the dead pilchards was never discovered.' Another report from 8th March 1888 states 'that the coast around Mounts Bay is full of dead congers, presumed killed by a heavy frost.'

On 1st July 1911 it was reported that:

> . . . a huge shoal of whales, 60 in all, beached themselves at Eastern Beach near Ponsondane, Penzance. At the time the tide was ebbing and they all ended up high and dry. It was a very hot day so they soon died.
>
> The problem was what to do with them. At first it was suggested to slice them up and have them taken up country to a place where the oil could be extracted, but the excessive heat made this impossible. So in order to prevent a menace to public health, a large number of men were engaged to dig deep pits in the sand. After working night and day for some time several deep pits were dug and the whole shoal of these denizens of the deep were rolled in and buried.

I suppose the skeletons of these poor creatures must still be under the sand.

Crabbing and lobster fishing was mentioned way back in the 1200's but for some reason this branch of the industry warranted little attention from the recorders and reporters down through the ages. One reason could be that this fishery was invariably carried out from small coves around the bay where reporters would have little reason to go unless for something more important. Nowadays crabbing is big business and carried out by much larger vessels than the small cove boats, the home-made willow pots have long since been replaced by modern man-made materials which last for several years. Cove boats tend to concentrate more on lobsters and have their pots in tiers of five or more, depending on the boats size. The larger crabbers will have as many as fifty pots in a tier, again depending on their size, and they fish basically for quantity which means crabs, lobsters and crawfish (spiny lobster) are a bonus.

Another large fishery that has taken off during the last few years is gill netting, I was the first to exploit this fishery in the 1960's using nylon nets that I got from Bridport Gundry. To stop the knots slipping I used to have them tarred, it also stopped broken ends frizzing up. I still have one ball of 2z tarred mending twine, what it will get used for I have no idea now. When monofilament netting became available I changed over to that and it proved to be much better, easier to use and it caught more fish. This type of gill netting differs from drift fishing in that today's gill netting is done with static nets that are anchored to the bottom. I was lucky because in those days the type of ground and fish had not been fished this way before and I did not need a large boat or have to go very far. At the present time gill netters need miles of netting and consequently large boats and they now have to go a considerable distance from the shore. A virgin wreck is like finding a gold mine in this fishery as these man-made reefs contain huge quantities of top quality fish.

The main fisheries carried out by the Mounts Bay vessels today are trawling, gill netting, crabbing and handlining in about that order of importance.

A survey carried out in 1883 regarding the fishing industry in Mounts Bay as a whole is worth relating.

Mackerel drift boats	Newlyn	116
	Mousehole	60
	Porthleven	43

Newlyn harbour was not built until the mid 1890's so it is strange that they had so many fishing boats. Their main harbours were Penzance and Mousehole but listed as Newlyn where all the fish buyers were now to be found.

Pilchard drifters	Newlyn	24
	Mousehole	30
	Porthleven	68

Total number of boats, seiners, crabbers, hookers etc 430, but this does not include the herring vessels that were away all winter in other parts of the UK.

Total number of fishermen	2,624
Seiners hands	540
Women and children in curing etc	1,000 approximately
Total number involved in industry	4,164
Cost of mackerel boats and seines	£89,660
12,000 boxes at 1s 4d per box	800
12,000 pads at 18s per dozen	900
12,000 tons of ice	2,000
total	£96,360
Pilchard drifter	£42,560
Pilchard seines	15,000
Cellars and other premises	35,000
Cooperage	550
Salt, 600 tons at 25s a ton	750
Materials, pressing etc	500
Total investment	£94,360
Total mackerel and pilchard boats	£187,000
62 other boats, crabbers etc	1,250
Total invested in boats	£188,970

This figure would have been a lot higher if the herring boats had been included, but these worked away from Mounts Bay and that is probably why they are not listed.

Barking

THE OLDEST TRADE in the world that survives to present day is not, as is so often quoted, prostitution, but fishing. Over 1 million years ago, before humans had started wearing clothes, man was already harvesting fish from rivers, lakes and estuaries and quite possibly the sea. It is also known how they caught fish all those years ago. Fossilised remains have been found of spears with serrated bone ends and also the pointed bone sting from the tails of certain rays, which are naturally serrated, that had been lashed onto the end of wooden spears. From some of the fossilised remains it appears they split the wooden ends then slid the bone harpoon into this before lashing the whole thing together. Bone fishing hooks have also been found from around this period and that indicates the making of a thin twine suitable for fishing. When the first net was constructed will probably never be known but it would be a natural follow-on from the wooden stake traps that used to be driven into the river beds to trap fish moving up stream. On the east coast of Africa this type of trap was still being used in the 1960's, maybe they still are. These wooden stake traps stretched out nearly a quarter of a mile from the shore into the sea inside the coral reef, there were two circular stake ends on each side and fish following the line of stakes got trapped inside the circles. It has been documented that some 2,000 years ago nets were being used for fishing, the Bible mentions this several times, but all the old records do not show what type of net, how big, how long they lasted and if they were cured or what type of fish they were used for. The earliest records I have come across that mention curing nets was in the 1600's, but that is all it says. In 1963 I found an old 'barking' ledger that was being thrown out to the dustmen that dated from the 1860's which gives details regarding this process of curing, including the poundage required and the type of bark used as well as the cost. This old ledger I gave to the County Records Office in Truro on permanent loan and it is there for anyone to look at.

For hundreds of years the most important building in any fishing harbour would have been the 'Barkhouse.' Every single port and fishing community, large or small, depended on these Barkhouses. It was not only the fishing industry that needed these resources they would also be required by leather and canvas manufacturers and cloth mills. Barking was the only known way of preventing things from rotting in those days. There was one major drawback to this though and that was it tended to wash out if continually submersed in water. That is why fishing nets were barked every two weeks or so during the season, most vessels had at least two tiers, one they were currently using and the other drying ready for barking. The old ledger clearly shows the boat's name every two weeks during the mackerel season as they barked their fleet of nets. The same applied during the pilchard season. Because the herring fishery was carried out away from Mounts Bay the only references to herring net barkings was at the beginning of the season before they sailed to Ireland.

By the early 1900's creosote was taking the place of bark. This lasted longer and was a lot easier than barking. From the records it appears that one or two soakings in creosote would last the season, but just like bark it does wash out in water. The nets would be put into a large cement pit filled with creosote, left for a few minutes to soak up and then taken out and left to drain, the excess creosote running down channels back into the pit. The nets had to be dry for this process to be successful and they were always done at the end of the season before storing. Up until the 1950's all the nets used in fishing were made from cotton and there are still mackerel, herring and pilchard nets at the present time that were made in the 1800's and still being used. If nothing else it does prove that the old ways of preserving them did work.

Man-made fibre did not really become generally available until the 1950's. The fishing industry made good use of these man-made substitutes because they did not rot and were also a lot stronger and more resistant to wear than cotton, hemp or sisal. They were also a lot lighter to work and handle for the simple reason modern twines do not hold water like natural fibres do.

There were and still are a lot of drawbacks with man-made twines. The first nets were made from nylon and they were, to put it mildly, a pain in the backside. The major problem with them was the knots would not stay tight and consequently the meshes would slip giving you odd shaped meshes that threw the whole net out of shape, then they would not fish. We tried soaking the nets in cuprinol to stop this happening but found the only way to overcome the problem was to soak the net in tar. Bridport Gundry, the net manufacturer, finally sold nylon nets tarred. They eventually overcame this problem by making the nylon hairy which stopped the knots from slipping. In the 1970's nylon gill nets were superceded by monofilament, both these man-made fibres have one enormous disadvantage compared with natural fibres. Any nets lost on wrecks or reefs will continue to catch fish indefinitely because they do not rot, these 'ghost nets' can and do kill off wrecks and reefs because any fish around will eventually get caught, they just die and rot away, the same happens to crabs and lobsters.

Over a period of time, which could be years, the action of tidal movement will gradually chafe out the rope and netting and cut its killing potential. They are now made biodegradable but this only applies if they are left in direct sunlight, not underwater.

Polypropylene twine is used in the trawling industry and without this man-made twine trawling would not be the biggest fishery in the world. No other twine could stand the wear and tear imposed on it from being dragged along all sorts of ground, sand, shingle, shell and rocks, and still retain its strength even when nearly chafed through. Its biggest fault is that it floats and this fact has probably cost insurance companies millions of pounds, it has probably cost human lives as well. Because it floats any netting lost overboard is a potential hazard to all other propeller driven vessels. Back in the 1960's it was a common occurrence to get your propeller bunged up with this netting. In some cases it stopped the engine dead resulting in damage to propeller, shaft or gearbox. If that happened then you were towed into port where insurance claims for damage and towing resulted. If you did manage to keep the engine and propeller turning and limp back to harbour there could also be another nasty shock in store. If the netting was tight around the shaft it had a nasty habit of melting and running up the shaft into the stern tube. It always surprised me how it could melt underwater, but it certainly did. If it did go up the stern tube this was always a major operation and quite often very expensive. It nearly always involved splitting the engine and shaft coupling and removing it, drawing the shaft out of the stern tube if possible. In some instances the stern tube and shaft had to be taken out in one piece, if that happened then it required a lot of heat to melt the polypropylene before the shaft could be removed. Any damaged parts then had to be replaced before rebuilding, a time-consuming and expensive job. Very few boats during the 1960's and 70's got through that period of time without getting their propeller bunged up, and VHF radios did not become available until the early 70's so you could not call for help, that is why most of us had two engines installed in our boats, it gave you a second chance of getting home. Luckily these days fishermen do not discard net offcuts which caused so much trouble during that period. With the natural fibre nets the propellers just chopped them up into bits and spat them out.

So how were natural fibres preserved and what was the Barkhouse? There used to be two Barkhouses in Mousehole owned by the same person, Mr Charles Tregenza. The largest of which has now been turned into six holiday flats, the other was a lot smaller. Before the main Barkhouse was built in the 1860's most of the fishermen used to bark their own nets in small boilers in their garden. As you walk around the village you may notice the small square gardens in some of the cottages, these were where their small boilers used to be, housed in granite sheds, some of these are now used as garden sheds.

The largest Barkhouse had three large round bottomed cast iron boilers that were built into a huge granite housing under which a fire was lit. The boilers would be filled with water and brought to the boil, depending on what type of net was being cured, and what the fishermen considered the best for fishing, decided what type and poundage of bark was used.

It is a well known fact that bark from certain trees contain preserving properties, this was not so much to preserve the trees or bark but acted as an insecticide against attack from insects, but over time certain insects have adapted and become immune. It obviously also preserved the bark as all trees rot from the inside out and the actual bark is always the last to succumb to rotting.

The most commonly known use, in England at any rate, for tree bark was that used in the leather industry and continues to the present day. Oak bark solution is used for tanning leather although I suspect that other chemicals are now taking over. During all my research I can find no reference to oak bark being used for nets, ropes or canvas. Perhaps oak made the nets and ropes too stiff for this type of work.

The fishing industry bark arrived in one hundredweight (112 lb) bales, these were chopped up into smaller pieces with an axe and boiled in the furnace to release their preservative properties. The used bark was then taken out and burnt to keep the furnace going. Once the solution had cooled down nets, ropes, sails and fishermens' duck frocks were soaked in this solution until they were thoroughly impregnated. After this soaking they were taken out and left to drain, the excess solution ran down channels back into the collecting pit, this could then be used again.

Each type of tree produced a different type of barking solution, usually called 'cutch,' and the colours ranged from black, brown to yellow depending on which tree the bark came from. The darker the colour the stiffer the nets ended up. The 'Barking Ledger' I transcribed covered six years from 1875 to 1881 and from this it becomes clear that each fisherman had his own idea about what strength and colour fished better.

Black was the hardest and also the most expensive and came from the 'Shumac' bark. In the ledger it is called by both names when used, 'black,' 'shumac' or sometimes both. The softest and cheapest was yellow which appears not to have lasted very long in the water as these had to be treated more often, 'Gambier' and 'Memosa' bark produced this colour. 'Myrabolanes' and 'Valonia' appear to have been brown although there are several instances when fishermen had a mixture of 'shumac' and one of the others. From the ledger it appears the brown was collectively known as 'cutch,' although some old business cards from 1840 give the impression that 'cutch' was a separate type of bark.

George Lewis, Chemical Manufacturer and Drysalter, Suffolk Street, Cambridge Road and Ocean Street, Stepney, London E.
Shumac, Cutch, Gambier, Myrabolanes, Valonia, Memosa Bark. 1840.

The mackerel season between January and June was the fishery which used the most nets and consequently the most bark. All the Ist class vessels carried between 40 and 50 nets each depending on their size with the 2nd class boats working between 30 and 40 nets apiece. This fishery tended to use the 'brown cutch' or a mixture with 'shumac' and the poundage of bark per net was normally 2 lb, some fishermen preferred 2½ lb and a few 3 lb. There must have been a reason why some preferred the heavier barking but there are no records to indicate why, it could be any number of reasons, twine thickness, net size or an awkward boat that required a stiffer net, but without proof this is pure speculation.

Each net barked using 2 lb of 'brown cutch' per net cost the fisherman 11d (just under 5p), so 50 nets required 100 lb of bark which amounted to £2 5s 8d, the ledger shows that each boat barked every two or three weeks during the mackerel season which lasted approximately 24 weeks. If the vessels only barked six times during that period then the total cost of preserving their nets came to £13 14s 0d. This might not seem a lot of money but when you consider that a years rent for a cottage was £5, or you could buy one for around £50 or even have one built for less than £100 it puts the preserving costs into an expensive essential. Although having a boat built was even more expensive than a house, Charles Pezzack paid £200 to have the 40 foot 14½ ton *Nautilus* built and fitted out ready for sea, which included two sets of sails. Craftsmen's wages varied between £1 2s 6d up to £2 12s 6d per week for the top craftsmen, unskilled labourers between 7s and 11s per week and boys were paid one shilling a week.

At this period of time J. Avery's Co-operative Ironmongers, 3 to 8 Victoria Place, Truro were selling 'single breech loaders, £1 3s 6d each, double barrel breech loaders, £2 15s 0d each, 5% off for cash, cartridges filled with best powder 7s 6d per 100, empty brown cases 2s 4d per 100.' So a double-barrelled shotgun was equivalent to a craftsman's wages for a week. A bottle of rum was 2s 0d, about a quarter of a labourer's weekly wage and beer was one penny a pint. So for £1 you could get 240 pints of beer, if it was that price today there would probably be a lot of rather tipsy people about. A price list from 1866 shows the price of the most popular alcoholic drinks of the time.

Port 1s 3d per bottle, 10 year old port 5s 3d per bottle, gin 1s 11d per bottle, rum 2s 0d per bottle, Irish and Scotch whisky 2s 0d per bottle, brandy 2s 2d per bottle, cognac brandy 3s 4d per bottle.

To save any confusion a table of pre-decimal coinage seems appropriate. It might appear rather confusing compared with today's but this was the currency of the day.

Copper coins were, farthing = quarter of a penny, halfpenny and a penny.
Silver coins, 3d, 6d, 1/-, 2/- (florin), 2/6 (half-crown), 5/- (crown).
Gold coins, half sovereign = 10/-, sovereign = £1, guinea = £1 1s.
Paper money, 10/- note, £1 note, £5 note, £10 note.
12 pennies = one shilling (1/-), and 20 shillings = £1
240 pennies = £1, 10 florins = £1, 8 half-crowns = £1 and 4 crowns = £1

Once the mackerel season was over the first class vessels would change over for the Irish herring fishery. This was usually done in June or July and the Barkhouse would then be a hive of activity as all the boats nets were barked before they set sail for Ireland. Some forty odd vessels from Mousehole were engaged in this fishery and the number of nets employed by each vessel was between 18 and 30, about half the size of a mackerel fleet. Herring tend to be in much denser shoals than mackerel and would require less nets to catch the equivalent amount of fish.

Herring nets were barked a lot harder and would be a lot stiffer than mackerel nets. Each net took 4 lb of black 'shumac' to bark which cost the fisherman 1s 9d per net. So the total cost of 30 nets would be £2 12s 6d and use up 120 lb of bark. As these vessels were away from Mousehole fishing it is impossible to say exactly how often they barked, the only entries in the ledger are for the first barking before they sailed to Ireland. If we assume they barked 6 times up until December then the cost would be £15 15s 0d, which would be £2 1s 0d more than the mackerel season.

There is no record of why this fishery used twice as much bark per net as the mackerel nets but talking to some of the very old fishermen back in the 1960's they said the extra stiffness made it easier to shake out the herring. Whatever the reason this was the amount used.

The pilchard fishery ran from July until December and was carried out by the smaller 2nd class vessels. The size of these boats ranged from 16 foot to 40 foot and the number of nets carried was between 5 and 26. These were stiff barked in black 'shumac' at 3 lb of bark per net at a cost of 1s 5d per net, on 22nd November 1880 this was increased by 1d per net to 1s 6d. So 26 nets would require 78 lb of bark and cost the fisherman £1 19s 0d, 6 barkings per season would come to £11 14s 0d. Pilchards are one of the softest fish swimming and easily damaged which could explain why they were barked at 3 lb as against 4 lb for herring, the softer more supple brown 'cutch' would enable the pilchard to mesh up harder but would also cause more damage when being shaken out.

Ropes were always cured in black 'shumac' while sails used the brown 'cutch,' fishermen's outer clothing tended to be a mixture of yellow and brown 'cutch' which would be reasonably pliable.

Pilchard seines in Mousehole did not conform to any specific type of bark as there are mentions of black 'shumac,' 'cutch,' 'gambier,' 'memosa' as well as various mixtures of barks all being used. There does not appear to be any reason for this not unless that was the only type of bark available at that time. The Mousehole seines were classed as 10 pilchard nets and charged 15s per seine.

The actual size of each net for all the fisheries varied slightly from port to port but they were usually around 100 yards to 120 yards long and about 10 yards deep and all made of cotton twine. I was told by some of the old fishermen that were still alive in the 1960's, that Mousehole pilchard nets were only 80 yards long, and the reason given was they made smaller bundles which could be carried up the narrow steps of the net lofts without catching on the sides. From talking to them it appears that the smaller one man boat owners in the pilchard fishery used to store their cured and dried nets above the living accommodation in the driest part of the cottage.

The mesh size was different for each of the main fisheries with mackerel being the widest followed by herring, and pilchard nets had the smallest mesh. The mesh sizes were made so that the fish's head would only go in as far as its gills and no further and as each species of fish is slightly larger or a different shape the mesh was made specifically to catch that type.

These nets would be shot in a long line and suspended from the surface by cork or skin or leather buffs. The depth the actual net fished was governed by long rope strops hanging from the surface buoys with the end of the strop being made fast to the net headline. The weight of the cotton kept the net hanging straight down in the water. When shooting drift nets this was always done downwind and once the tier was shot the boat made fast to a rope leading from her bow to the last net shot, once the mizzen sail was set the wind kept the boat and nets in a straight line. They were always shot just before dark and as the sun went down the fish would rise towards the surface and get meshed in the net, hopefully. Nearly all catches were made in the first two hours of dark before the phosphorescent plankton rose to the surface, once this happens the net is like a shimmering green wall in the water and can be seen from the boat for over 100 yards. Sometimes the phosphorescence gets very dense and bright, and as Jack Worth used to be fond of saying, 'you could read a newspaper by it,' a very colourful description but also sadly very untrue. Jack used to be coxswain of the Penlee lifeboat and if we had a late call out on a fine night, usually a medico when a doctor was required, we would often stand up the bow chatting, one of us would stamp down hard on the deck and you would see the phosphorescent shapes of fish darting away. The boat rushing through the water never seemed to frighten them that much but a hard thump on the deck did.

Seine netting was a smaller mesh again as the last thing the seiners wanted was fish meshing up in the net. It might take several days to empty a seine full of fish and during that time the fish had to be able to swim and stay alive undamaged.

Seining was an art, it required a lot of skill and cooperation, one mistake and the shoal could be lost. The most important man in any seining operation was undoubtedly the 'Huer,' he was usually a retired fisherman.

By daybreak the Huer would be ensconced in his little stone hut on the highest point overlooking a sandy beach or cove from August until December. From this high vantage point he would watch the huge shoals of pilchards that appear as large dark shadows underwater. Suddenly the dark shadow would be blood red as the shoal turned head out showing their gills briefly before circling back to head along the shore. (This blood red colour is caused by the sunlight shining on their red gills as they circle and is only visible for a few seconds as the fish turn, this can be seen in most dense shoals if the sunlight is at the right angle, especially mullet.)

The Huer might watch these shoals for days before one of them comes in close enough and in the right position to shoot the seine. The boats and nets would have been ready for days just waiting for the Huer to give the signal. He would then direct the men and boats where to go, when to start shooting, when to turn and when to tuck. The Huers method of communicating this advice is often quoted as being 'with two furze bushes, one in each hand.' This method was undoubtedly used but the commonest reported signalling devices were 'two rounds of wood some two or three feet across painted black and nailed onto short sticks.' Back in about 1962 there used to be three such 'black rounds of wood' tucked away in a corner of the old Barkhouse by Abbey Place, they were riddled with woodworm and split across in several places from drying out.

From his high vantage point the Huer would be able to see exactly what the fish were doing and signal directions accordingly to the men out in the boats. Once the seine was tucked and secure the whole community would turn out with wicker baskets to brail out the pilchards. Horse and carts would transport the fish to wherever they were to be cured, they would only take out from the seine the amount of fish they could salt down that day, the rest would be left swimming around in the seine until next day.

The largest fishery carried out from Mousehole was from January until June during the mackerel season and consequently they used the most bark.

The actual amount of bark used in the whole village over the period of one year for the three fisheries is very hard to calculate. The only figures I have are for one Barkhouse which used three furnaces, but taking into account that there was another such Barkhouse plus numerous privately owned boilers then the final figure for the whole village would probably be at least twice the quantities listed below.

These amounts were taken from an old Barking ledger and are the actual quantities used each year for the three fishing seasons.

	mackerel	herring	pilchard	total
	Jan-Jun	Jun-Dec	Jul-Dec	
1876	5,803 lbs	2,664 lbs	2,485 lbs	10,952 lbs
1877	5,792 lbs	2,350 lbs	2,233 lbs	10,375 lbs
1878	7,182 lbs	2,271 lbs	2,301 lbs	11,754 lbs
1879	7,077 lbs	2,662 lbs	2,234 lbs	11,973 lbs
1880	7,348 lbs	2,555 lbs	2,874 lbs	12,777 lbs
Total for 5 years	33,202 lbs	12,502 lbs	12,127 lbs	57,831 lbs = 25.81 tons

It must be remembered that the herring boats only did one barking in Mousehole before they left for Ireland so the actual poundage used in this fishery would be at least six times of that shown, making the quantity used a minimum of 75,012 lbs. The herring industry was by far the largest user of bark due to the fact of using 4 lb of black shumac per net.

The total poundage of bark used in Mousehole by the other large Barkhouse and all the smaller privately owned furnaces would nearly double the figures above.

Taking into account all the other fishing ports around the coastline of England, Ireland, Scotland and Wales, who all had to use the same process for preserving their nets, then the total poundage of bark used each year must have been astronomical. It must have taken tens of thousands of trees just to keep the fishing industry supplied for one year. If you multiply this by all the other countries that had a fishing fleet then the amount of trees that had to be felled each year just for the fishing industry becomes awesome.

It would be interesting to know which industry used the most timber. At first glance it would appear that building construction would be the biggest user but let us consider the facts. In the 1700's and 1800's there were vast numbers of merchant vessels sailing the oceans with cargoes and passengers. At Falmouth alone there were sailing vessels docking along the wharfs all the way up to Truro every day of the year. The Shipping Registers at County Records Office in Truro list tens of thousands of cargo vessels, and the larger ports around the country would undoubtedly have dealt with more, a lot more. Then of course there were all the fishing boats around the British Isles, and we must not forget the British Royal Navy who had the largest fleet in the world. All these vessels were constructed in timber so perhaps the ship building industry was the largest user of wood. It takes a lot more timber to build a ship than a house and there were very few, if any, buildings constructed purely of wood, stone and plaster was always cheaper.

The last bale of bark I actually saw was in 1961 pushed to the back of the Barkhouse behind some furniture, the wire bindings had rusted through, the bark had dried out completely and it was rapidly being turned into dust by woodworm, as was the furniture.

A typical barking day would probably have been something like this. The furnace would have been booked a week ago, there were only three boilers in the Barkhouse to which the ledger refers. The furnace had been lit, the bark chopped up and boiled, the cutch drained off into the dipping pit and cooling. The boiler refilled and more bark chopped up and boiling. The time would be around 0800, a boy was paid one shilling a day to light the furnaces and fill them with water at 0500 and keep the fires going and boilers full of water until all the barkings for that day were done. Quite often it would be late evening before all the boats nets were barked. 15 hours a day for a boy of 14 years was quite common in the 1800's, especially up until July, after that there were only the few small pilchard drifters nets to bark, and for 15 hours work he was paid one shilling.

Our boat has been mackerel drifting all night and we arrive back in Mousehole just coming daylight. Our fish are counted or weighed by two men and loaded aboard a horse and cart. The other five men pull up the 50 nets from the vessels hold and spread them over the railings on the quay to dry in the wind. Once they are all spread out one man walks the whole length of the netting picking up any bights of net that are touching the stone quay and adjusts the net accordingly. This is done to stop the twine chafing out on the granite stones in the breeze. The time is about 0500 so the men go home for breakfast. 0700 they are back down the quay inspecting the nets. Its a good breeze and the nets have dried enough to be barked. Wet nets do not soak up enough cutch to cure them properly and were always entered in the ledger as 'Wet Nets.' Our nets are dry so we load them onto a horse and cart which takes them up to the Barkhouse. Once there we off load and soak each net in the cutch for a few minutes until they are completely saturated. The boy topping up the cutch pit after every few nets. Each bundle of netting is left to drain for several minutes before being loaded back onto the horse and cart, it could take three trips with wet nets as they are twice the weight of dry ones. These are taken down the quay and spread over the railings to finish draining. Just before we sail for our nights fishing we pull all the nets aboard, join them together, tie on the cork floats and skin buffs ready for shooting. Cast off, hand warp ourselves out between the Island and Harbour, haul up the sails and away for a nights mackerel drifting.

And they were the good old days???

Of course this was not always how it worked. There are references to the horse and cart being used to take their second fleet of dry nets from the loft. The ledger does not say but presumably this was done because the used nets had not dried out enough for barking. There are also references to the Barkhouse crew collecting the nets from the quay, barking them and then spreading them out on the railings again, or in a few instances putting them in the owners loft.

By the turn of the century creosote, called 'crease oil' by the fishermen, was starting to take the place of bark. It was cheaper and also lasted longer in the twine than bark. One drawback was that it tended to impregnate everything it came into contact with which was dry, namely wood in the lofts and boats and of course all your clothes. It did not affect the caught fish in any way because they were wet, creosote just runs off wet things. The few boats that still use cotton nets for pilchards now preserve them in creosote.

Modern man-made fibre does not work as well as cotton in the pilchard fishery. Pilchards are a very soft fleshed fish and nylon is a much too harsh a material for this fishery, nylon catches just as much fish but they cannot be shaken out of the net without a lot of damage, usually cutting the fish's head off which makes them unsaleable. Cotton does not do this and the fish can be shaken out in perfect condition. The White Fish Authority has been trying for several years now to manufacture a material that can be used for gilling pilchards in drift fishing, they have as yet not come up with anything to compare with cotton. The nearest their scientists have found that works reasonably well is a mixture of nylon and cotton, but as we have seen from the forgoing, cotton rots without being cured. All the nylon does is give the twine extra strength. With all their modern technology man has not yet been able to produce a rot proof twine which has the same properties as natural cotton with regard to the pilchard fishery.

Luckily for the modern day pilchard men their catches are sold by weight, in the 1800's they were sold by the 1,000. Just imagine having to count your catch out into piles of 1,000 fish, its hard enough catching them, let alone counting them afterwards. Imagine counting up into the 900's, then someone comes and talks to you. Now lets see, what number did I get up to!!! From talking to some of the old men in the 1960's the fish were counted in 100's and then one fish put aside for each 100 until they had ten single fish, that would give them the 1,000 and also indicate how many hundred were left at the end. One thing this system did do though, it certainly improved the counting abilities of all those involved in the fishing industry.

All that is left from the old barking days in Mousehole is one cast iron boiler with its granite surround and large fire box or furnace underneath, and the large cutch pit where the nets used to be dipped. The other two boilers were knocked down and broken up in the 1970's. I rescued the old hand beaten axe, still with its original handle and accumulated layers of cutch, in the late 1960's. The steel has not rusted away like present day steel would but just has a very thin rust coloured coating, you can also see every hammer mark from when the blacksmith made it some 200 years ago. The hole where the handle fits was forged and bent around and has a large iron rivet fastening to hold it together and stop it springing apart.

Up until 1998 you could still see and read the white chalk reminders written in the 1800's on some of the bare wooden walls regarding bark imports expected, or boats to bark, or reminders about the weight of bark borrowed or owed. The earliest date was 1865, the last was some time in the 1940's with two drawings and underneath was written 'Hitler,' 'Musso.' All these were in white chalk.

On the cleaner newer wood there were also quite a lot of pencil drawings but these I'm afraid were done by me in the late 1960's. Two of them concerned the sizes of a mizzen mast, gaff and boom I was making for my boat, others were for the pulleys, ropes and fixings etc for the mizzens. There were also lists of net rigging staple lengths and number of meshes to pick up to give the correct amount of slack for certain size gill nets etc. The only thing I marked in white chalk was the lengths of ropes in each stack, 10 fathoms, 20 fathoms or 30 fathoms, these were dahn ropes and it made life easier to just come in and pick up the length required without having to measure everything each time.

Unfortunately these little written gems from yesteryear were lost forever when the building was gutted and turned into six holiday flats.

The outside of the building has not actually changed although all the wooden rollers that used to be fixed under the windows have obviously gone. These rollers were used to pull nets over after barking when they were going to be stored in the net lofts above the Barkhouse. At the back of this Barkhouse there used to be three large openings, again fitted with rollers, which were used to either put nets down into the barking area or pull them out after treatment. These openings had large heavy wooden hinged shutters which were pulled open by means of a rope which went through a pulley high up the buildings back wall. These have now all been blocked up but the outlines can still be seen.

Where there was a lot of horse and cart traffic around Barkhouses, salt and coal stores and large net lofts, the corners of all buildings were built rounded on the outside. These buildings were designed like that for a very practical reason, to allow the cart following the horse to get around without jamming up. On very tight corners a large angled rock was built into the base – a flat blue elvin rock. When the iron rimmed cart wheel hit the angled rock this forced the outer wheel to slide on the flat blue elvin enabling the cart to negotiate these tight bends. It obviously worked as there are still numerous examples of the angled corner rocks around Mousehole, and even more rounded building corners. So as you walk around the village and notice these rounded areas you can, with some imagination, picture the straining sweating horses and their drivers hauling some heavy load around that corner.

When the telegraph poles were taken down around the harbour front and the electricity cables put underground in the early 1970's, the contractors digging the trench alongside the Barkhouse corner came across these large flat blue elvin stones. They were arranged in a fan shape around the corner, unfortunately they had to be removed so the electricity cables could be laid.

During construction work on the Barkhouse in 1998 the builders had to dig up the yard in several places to lay sewer pipes and put in foundations for new steps etc. Between six and eight inches down they came across a layer of large cobble stones, twelve inches below these was another layer of cobble stones. In the earth between the two layers of cobbles was found old rusty nails, a horse shoe, and a lot of brass pins, hinges, screw eyes and other bits from boats and masts. It would be very interesting to know when the first lot of cobbles were laid as they are some two foot below present day soil level. The top layer of cobbles was laid around 1860 to 1870, and they vary from two to twelve inches below present day ground level.

It is a great pity that from the three tea chests of ledgers and notebooks that were being thrown out in the early 1960's I only managed to salvage one, the others were all completely ruined by rain and mildew and were falling apart. Some of the bottom ledgers had turned into soggy paper lumps and been squashed into some very strange shapes, nothing resembling a book. There was probably some hundred years plus history contained in these ledgers which are now sadly gone forever.

Yawling in Mousehole

AN INTERESTING ARTICLE written by Herbert Richards of Mousehole in 1940 about an 1860/70's custom in the fishing village.

Although each mackerel drifter had its own punt it was never taken to the mackerel grounds. The reason being that the little craft took up too much room and interfered with working the sails and nets. The risk was, however, very great and when accidents happened there was no second chance of saving life. When drifters of a large type were built a law was passed that every boat should carry its punt to the fishing grounds, but before the law became operative a large number of boys who had just left school were taken on by crews during the period of the mackerel season to take charge of the punts and attend on the drifters. They received 2s per week (10p). I was yawler to the ill-fated Mousehole boat *Jane* which was struck by a heavy sea when about to enter Penzance harbour on her return from the North Sea herring fishery with the loss of all the crew.

At an early hour large numbers of yawlers could be seen off Mousehole harbour sculling about, anxiously awaiting the arrival of their boats. Sometimes many hours were spent in this way. When the lugger came near the yawler a rope was thrown and made fast. The punt was then towed to Newlyn which at that time was the fish market. The catch was put into the punt, sold by auction, and placed in maunds (Mounds?). The North Pier was not then built so the fish were taken out on the beach. This presented a very busy scene. Scores of punts laden with mackerel, fishermen in oilskins and seaboots, counting up the fish and loading wagons for Penzance, in order to catch the early trains for up-country markets, while just outside at anchor could be seen a large number of Mounts Bay drifters as well as large numbers of East Coast craft.

People on shore were always anxious to know the catches of mackerel and the following method was adopted. When just off Mousehole on the way to Newlyn, some person on shore took off his hat and held it high. This sign meant 'How many mackerel have you?' One of the crew observing the held up hat replied in this way. If the catch was say 800 the man on the lugger lifted his hat high and brought it down 8 times, each stroke indicating a hundred. If, however, the catch was 1,000 the hat would be swung around his head once, if 2,000 twice, and so on. By this means it was known what each boat had. Yawlers were expected to keep the boats spick and span and vied with each other in this respect. There were quarrels among the boys, and often during the night a boy took out the plug of his rival's punt, and

71

when the boy came to scull off to await the arrival of his boat burst into tears on seeing his little craft sunk to the water's edge. Yawling trained the boys to become good fishermen, but those days are long past and will never return. The mackerel industry too has completely gone in western waters and if one were to ask today what a 'Yawler' was it would be very difficult to get the correct answer.

Section II

Newfoundland Cod & the Spanish Invasion

WHEN DOING RESEARCH it does tend to branch out in all directions, a date or something you've read sticks in your mind and you wonder why. That happened to me when I was researching the Newfoundland Cod Fishery. It was over a month before I made the connection and to start with I couldn't believe it. Further research on the Newfoundland Cod Fishery finally gave me the answer. I had often wondered how a small fleet of Spanish Men of War had managed to sail into Mounts Bay and do so much damage – it was all to do with the Newfoundland Cod Fishery.

In the early 1500's a new fishery was under way which was to prove the most valuable to Britain – the Newfoundland Cod Fishery. This fishery was carried out by about 50 vessels from Devon and Cornwall. The returning fishing fleet with their cargoes of salt cod were easy targets for the pirates that roamed the Western Approaches and numerous boats were taken by them. The Navy had two Men of War patrolling this area and other vessels patrolling west of the Lizard, but the pirates had been joined by Spanish Men of War also intent on capturing the valuable cargo of salt cod on returning fishing boats. By the 1580's over 100 boats were taking part in this fishery and one report states that for every one of these fishing boats there is a pirate or Spanish Man of War ready to take them. From the reports it seems that Dartmouth was the main port for landing the huge quantities of salt cod.

On 20th July 1594 Sir Walter Raleigh wrote to Sir Robert Cecil pointing out that Spanish Men of War were now chasing returning fishing boats right to Dartmouth. Returning boats that had British Men of War guarding them successfully kept the Spanish at Bay. It was decided that the fishing fleet should sail in convoy and be protected by British Men of War, especially when returning.

This concentrated the warships into a small area off Devon during July, August and September as they sailed out to escort the returning Newfoundland fishing fleet. This left the Western Approaches unprotected. This did not go unnoticed by the Spanish who were suddenly robbed of easy pickings. Taking advantage of the lack of patrolling British warships Spanish Men of War attacked several isolated villages in Devon and Cornwall. Three Spanish boats anchored off Mousehole and after a sustained cannon ball bombardment they came ashore, it was July 1595. Finding little resistance they murdered, robbed, raped and burnt Mousehole to the ground before marching up to Paul, after that Newlyn and Penzance. They were eventually beaten and driven back at Marazion by soldiers before they could reach that village and the Mount, but for the village of Mousehole it was much too late. One report states that there were over two hundred Spaniards in these attacks and that over half of them were killed before they fled back to their ships. If that report is true then those three warships would have been seriously short-handed.

Cannon balls are very occasionally found during some excavations. The last one I know about was in 1995 when South West Water were digging out the harbour for the new sewer system, these are invariably credited to the Spanish Invasion. If the records are correct when stating that Mousehole was raised to the ground except for the large granite built Keigwin then that would indicate the oldest cottages in the village date from around 1595.

By 1630 there were over 200 vessels leaving Devon and Cornwall for the Newfoundland Cod Fishery. The records state that the main fishing ports in Devon were Dartmouth, Teignmouth and Exmouth, in Cornwall, Saltash, Looe, Mevagissey, Fowey, Falmouth, St Mawes, St Kevern, Mounts Bay (presumably Mousehole, Newlyn, Penzance and Porthleven), St Ives and Padstow. The report did not specify the number of vessels from each port which is a great pity. It must have been a fantastic sight to see 200 plus boat's sails stretching out across the sea escorted by British Men of War. The Navy did not make the same mistake again and kept a strong fleet guarding the water of the Western Approaches. One interesting fact that came out of this research is the mention of the first Naval Fishery Patrol that was carried out by British Men of War in 1580. That is the first mention of Naval Fishery Patrol I have come across in all my research and must make it one of the Navy's oldest non-stop patrol tasks because it is still carried out today. Protecting our fishing fleet.

A legend I came across purely by accident is worth repeating. Just outside Mousehole cave there is a large flatish rock that is surrounded by sea, this is named Merlin Rock. Legend has it that the wizard Merlin, of King Arthur fame, lived in the cave for a while and sat on this rock casting spells, or whatever wizards do. He prophesied that, 'There shall land on the rock of Merlin, those who shall burn Mousehole, Paul and Newlyn.' That was all he apparently said regarding those villages?

Privateers in South-West Cornwall

I HAVE INCLUDED this because Mousehole men were involved in this trade. I would also like to thank the people of Mousehole and everyone else who sent me newspaper cuttings regarding the history of Mounts Bay in general. The following comes from the *Sherborne Mercury* newspaper sent to me by an anonymous person. I do have other snippets from this newspaper but not specifically about Mousehole.

It should be emphasised that all privateering ships were privately owned and were armed and manned completely independent of government. Officialdom was only necessary to licence ships to act against an enemy. The need for such ships was rooted in previous times when there was simply no navy, it was only through King Henry VIII who provided initiative and finance that a navy came into being. Although well established by the reign of Queen Elizabeth I there were only 146 naval vessels of all sizes in the year 1573. When the Spanish Armada sailed into the English Channel in 1588 many units of the fleet sent to oppose it were private ships.

In time it was realised there could be a very fine line drawn between privateering and piracy, the former being thought patriotic while the latter was criminal and carried a death penalty on conviction. Hence official authorisations known as letter-of-marque were issued by the Admiralty to the bona fide privateers and a register kept to record them.

The registers of the letters-of-marque issued in the latter half of the eighteenth century are today held at the Public Records Office. The information includes the name and tonnage of the ship, its home port, armament and number of men in the crew, one third of which were supposed to be 'landsmen.' The names of the owners, captain and other ship's officers, (mate, gunner, carpenter, bosun, cook and surgeon), are all recorded although there is good reason to doubt the accuracy of some details, especially in naming the ship's officers. A few obvious examples, it cannot seriously be accepted that the surgeon of the *Active* of Penzance was John Dresswound, the surgeon of the *Truro* from Falmouth was Benjamin Cutts, the surgeons of *Desire, Dolphin* and a second *Dolphin*, all from St Ives were respectively John Probe, Samuel Dockshort and Samuel Trim. Surely too no surgeon would be named Andrew Hurt, *Penryn*, Thomas Addonleg, *Hind's*

Tender, Abraham Morearm, *Lucy* or John Carbuncle, *Fox*, and no crew would include John Lee, James Dee, William Lee, Simon Ree, George Bee and Alexander See all from the *Eagle*.

It seems that when information for the records was lacking the scribe resorted to improvisation, but disregarding his wit the registers contain a wealth of information on the British privateers from that era and a schedule of those with Cornish connections has been completed though there may well may be omissions. The issue of a letter-of-marque cost the boat owners thirty shillings and a commission (an abbreviated document which gave only the name of the ship and captain but carried the same authority) cost one pound with the cash being banked at the Tower of London.

While ships of the Royal Navy were empowered to make captures from any nation at war with Great Britain the letters-of-marque issued to privateers were only valid against one country and most owners would choose either France or Holland because the returns would be a lot higher than the Americans, all of whom were at war with Britain during this period.

Most of the Cornish privateers engaged in this war came from Falmouth, Penzance, St Ives and Scilly Isles, most of these were not commissioned until 1780. The first Cornish vessel to be commissioned in this war against America was the large sloop *Swallow* owned by John Carter of Prùssia Cove. The letter-of-marque dated 10th December 1777 records Henry Carter as her captain. The *Swallow* put into St Malo with a sprung bowsprit and was commandeered by the French. Although not at war with France at this time relations were very strained between the two countries, not long after this France sided with America against Britain. The loss of the *Swallow* was a heavy financial loss to the Carter family but they pooled resources with Richard Champion of Marazion and bought the 60 ton *Phoenix* and obtained a letter-of-marque in June 1778. She was armed with eight cannon and ten swivel guns and carried a crew of fifty men under the command of Roger Carter.

The *Phoenix* cruised in company with the Guernseyman *Hunter*. The alliance was well rewarded and in a very short time six French ships were sent back to Mounts Bay, they were *St Etienne, St Francoise, Rustique, Ville de Rouen, Arlequin* and *Courrier de la Rochelle*. The French vessels were sold with their cargoes of salt in the spring of 1779. The sharing of the prize money was not completed until October 1780 when final payments were made at Edward Hambleton's King's Arms Tavern at Marazion.

Late in 1780 the Carter family decided to sell the *Phoenix* and *Friendship* as they were too small for the business in hand. *Friendship* was sold to Thomas Roberts and Francis James of Penzance. *Phoenix* was sold by candle. This was a form of auction in which a short piece of candle was lit and the last bid before the flame went out was accepted.

The Carter family purchased a large 16 gun cutter named *Shaftesbury*. Her early successes included a French merchantman named *Fantaise*, her cargo of coffee, ebony wood and pepper was valued at £30,000. About this time they bought a large three-masted lugger named *Phoenix* which was three times the size of the previous sloop having twenty 6 pounder carriage guns and sixteen swivel guns. The *Phoenix* was lost off Portreath in a battle with a French privateer, fourteen of her crew were lost including Francis Carter.

Nine Dutch vessels were captured by the sloops *Dolphin* of Penzance and *Grace* from Scillies and sent back to Scilly Isles. They were *Jonge Gillis* carrying raisins and figs, *Resolutie* with raisins and rice, *Jonge Jacobus* with butter and beef, *Vrow Delania Maria* with wool and wine, *Vrow Hendrika* with wine, *Zelden Rust* with wine, *Jonge Petronella* with hides and wine, *Jonge Jan* with claret, and *Kristina Magdelina* with figs and raisins.

An interesting observation from merchantmen captured during the 1700's is what their cargoes consisted of and from these records it becomes clear that expensive wood like ebony, spices, figs, raisins, rice and wines were the main cargoes. This was presumably what the general public in various countries were asking for.

One of the celebrities of St Ives during the 1700's was a 'Gentleman' called John Knill who had a mausoleum/monument on Worvas Hill, he was also Collector of Customs for St Ives and used this post for smuggling purposes. He also had several privateer ships and from the records it appears these vessels were very successful in their privateer careers. He also appeared to be a kind and reasonable man towards the crews of his privateers as an advert in the *Sherborne Mercury* for prize money owed to some crew members shows.

Benjamin Banfield, ordinary seaman,	£8 1s 7½d
Thomas Bryant, ordinary seaman,	18s 6d
William Corner, land boy,	£5 5s 0d
Edward Davies, ordinary seaman,	18s 6d
Thomas Gilbert, landman and cook's mate,	18s 6d

William Giddy, able seaman,	15s 0d
Thomas Tepper, land boy,	8s 3d
John Pollard, carpenters mate,	9s 8¼d
John Trethecoat, able seaman,	£1 4s 9d
John Millet, 1st mate,	£2 2s 9d

By the late 1780's the Cornish privateers were all but finished due to the larger ships of developing navies. The smaller lighter Cornish craft were unable to cope leaving just the larger Cornish vessels to go privateering, a lot of these privateers then turned to smuggling for a living.

Vessels owned by the Carter family from Prussia Cove. *Swallow, Phoenix* (1), *Friendship, Shaftesbury, Active, Phoenix* (2).

Vessels owned by John Knill of St Ives. *Brilliant* (1), *Greyhound, Brilliant* (2), *Desire*.

Vessels owned by Richard Oxnan of Penzance. *Elizabeth, Two Brothers, Dolphin, Swift, Tartar*.

These three were the biggest privateer owners in each port although other families also had up to three vessels. The most influential family was without doubt the Carters who had privateer vessels stationed up as far as the Isle of Wight. Considering that some cargoes were valued up to £50,000 it was a profitable venture. It must be pointed out that privateers and Admiralty shared the profits between them, what the percentages were I do not know but it must have been very profitable for owners to buy and fit out vessels with cannons etc for a life of privateering. It would be interesting to find out if the old laws regarding privateering and registering are still on the statute books.

As can be seen from the above not all privateers were large vessels and it appears that the swivel guns were more affective than the larger fixed cannons in subduing merchantmen. From the records merchant ships invariably gave up without a fight and surrendered their ship and cargo without a shot being fired, all the privateers were also armed with pistols and cutlasses. It must be remembered that the cannons, swivel guns and pistols could only fire one shot and then had to be loaded by hand before another shot could be fired. Privateers that encountered other countries privateers would occasionally engage in battle but most times they kept clear of each other. There was little or no money to be made by engaging in combat and ships could get damaged which could put an end to a profitable career as a privateer. From the records it becomes clear that as

PENZANCE, ST IVES & SCILLY ISLES PRIVATEERS
1777 to 1782

Earliest letter of marque	Ship	Home Port	Tonnage & Rig	Crew	Cannons	Swivels
Jun. 1778	*Phoenix* (1)	Penzance	60 sloop	50	8x 3 pounders	10
Aug. 1778	*Brilliant* (1)	St Ives	50 lugger	14	8x 3 pounders	8
Aug. 1778	*Greyhound*	St Ives	150 cutter	47	14x 3 pounders	8
Aug. 1778	*Dolphin*	Penzance	30 sloop	20	none	8
Oct. 1778	*Swift*	Penzance	40 sloop	30	2x 2 pounders	8
Oct. 1778	*Tartar*	St Ives	65 sloop	40	8x 3 pounders	5
Nov. 1778	*Tartar*	Penzance	70 schooner		12x 3 pounders	12
Apr. 1780	*Grace*	Scilly	50 sloop	50	4x 2 pounders	8
Apr. 1780	*Speedwell*	Penzance	30 sloop	25	6x 2 pounders	8
May 1780	*Friendship*	Penzance	30 lugger	30	none	10
May 1780	*Brilliant* (2)	St Ives	86 shallop	19	10x 2 pounders	–
Dec. 1780	*Shaftesbury*	Penzance	200 sloop	60	20x 6 pounders	12
Dec. 1780	*Elizabeth*	Penzance	20 lugger	20	none	10
Jan. 1781	*Active*	Penzance	60 sloop	40	10x 4 pounders	6
Jan. 1781	*Admiral Rodney*	St Ives	35 sloop	30	4x 3 pounders	6
Jan. 1781	*Alexander*	Scilly	6	10		4
Jan. 1781	*Caesar*	St Ives	30 lugger	20	none	6
Jan. 1781	*Carmarthen*	Penzance	30 lugger		none	6
Jan. 1781	*Desire*	St Ives	50 lugger	30	6x 2 pounders	4
Jan. 1781	*Firm*	Penzance	30 lugger	20	none	4
Jan. 1781	*Fisherman*	Penzance	30 lugger	20	none	4
Jan. 1781	*Lands End*	Sennen	30 lugger	30	none	6
Jan. 1781	*Neptune*	St Ives	16 lugger	24	none	4
Jan. 1781	*Phillis & Betsey*	Penzance	30 lugger	24	none	4
Jan. 1781	*Polly*	Penzance	160 cutter	30	8x 3 pounders	3
Jan. 1781	*Pork and Greens*	Scilly	16 lugger	20	none	4
Jan. 1781	*Prince of Wales*	Penzance	120 cutter	30	8x 3 pounders	8
Jan. 1781	*Resolution*	St Ives	20 sloop	15	none	2
Jan. 1781	*St Peter*	St Ives	25 lugger	15	none	4
Jan. 1781	*Sluice*	Penzance	20 lugger	20	none	4
Jan. 1781	*Success* (1)	Penzance	50 sloop		none	4
Jan. 1781	*Success* (2)	Penzance	30 sloop	24	none	4
Jan. 1781	*Two Brothers*	Penzance	30 lugger	20	none	4
Jun. 1781	*Phoenix* (2)	Marazion	150 lugger	50	20x 6 pounders	16
Jun. 1781	*Ranger*	Scilly	25 lugger	25	1x 2 pounder	6
Oct. 1781	*Dolphin*	St Ives	150 cutter			–
Mar. 1782	*Resolution*	Penzance	140		12x 3 pounders	6

the privateers began to find less merchantmen unaccompanied by naval boats they turned their attention to smuggling. It might appear strange with England being at war with France that such a profitable enterprise for both countries should prosper and continue unabated, but as they say money is money.

Smugglers & Excisemen

SMUGGLING HAD BEEN carried on in Cornwall from the 1500's and probably long before that but it is not until about 1850 that it reached its height and it is from that period all the stories relating to this trade originate. They were known as 'Free Traders' and this trade was considered to be legal by those who carried it out and those who prospered from it and that is probably why it is still remembered to this day as being considered daring, dangerous and romantic. Daring yes, romantic no, not in those times, and it was more dangerous to the Excisemen, called 'Searchers,' tasked with catching them than the actual smugglers. When you consider that for every Exciseman employed there were 50 men involved in smuggling both on the sea and those who hid and distributed the goods. There are numerous reports of Excisemen being attacked, stoned or murdered while carrying out their job and it appears from the records that more Excise, Revenue, Preventative men or Searchers were killed than the actual seafaring smugglers. It must also have been a very disheartening job because even if they did manage to catch any smugglers they were invariably released by the courts to continue their illegal trade. It does make you wonder how many high ranking officials were involved in smuggling during that period as a few extracts from the records clearly show.

In 1770 the Mayor of Penzance was bound over for a considerable sum of money 'not to be again guilty of smuggling,' no jail sentence just a fine. This happened to several other notables and judges that should have been upholding the law, even clergymen were involved with the smugglers but not one of them was ever charged.

In 1768 William Odgers an Excise Officer stationed at Porthleven was murdered by smugglers in a most barbaric manner. £100 reward was offered to anyone who could give information. The principle witness against these men was a Mr Hampton, he was offered £500 by the smugglers to get out of the country and stay away for at least two years. He refused and the commissioners granted him seven shillings a week as he was afraid to go about his ordinary work. In 1780 Mr Hampton was receiving ten shillings a week. At the inquest Melchisideck Kinsman from Gwennap and four others unknown were convicted of wilful murder, but these men had disappeared, not abroad but skulking underground in the tin mines. Eventually three of the supposed murderers gave themselves up and promised to effect the capture of Kinsman which they succeeded in doing after an affray in which one of them was seriously injured. All four were tried at the Assizes but contrary to the opinion of the judge and the amazement of the whole court were found not guilty. The collector stated in his report that there was no doubt that the jury had been bribed by Kinsman's relatives and that three of the jury had disappeared after the case.

There are numerous reports similar to the above where Excisemen were murdered and the smugglers being found not guilty. Those that were found guilty invariably escaped from jail within two or three days.

The piece below is not exactly attributed to smugglers but it did concern them. Whether the cottages mentioned are still there I do not know because I can't now get there as my left leg has been amputated just below my waist but the story goes as follows.

> On the western side of Trencom Hill near Lelant there are two old granite built cottages that were known locally as 'Newcastle.' *(Newcastle is a derogatory Cornish name for a Folly)*. One of these cottages was used as a 'Kiddleywink' in the 1700's and 1800's, a noted haunt of smugglers who had excavated a cave where supplies of contraband were hidden. Apparently the cave is in a hedge and can still be seen. *(Kiddleywink is another name for beershop, public house etc)*. It was owned by two brothers one of whom joined the army. Finding that smuggling was more profitable than army life he deserted and joined his brother. A press-gang was in the district and hearing about the deserter descended on the cottages and after a fight the brother was killed, the deserter escaped through a hole in the roof. The press-gang left empty handed, the deserter lived there for the rest of his life and was never bothered again. The reason given was that having killed one brother 'they were debarred from laying hands on the other since the law did not allow the taking of two men (brothers) for one.'

In October 1751:

> . . . a good haul of smugglers was made including a notorious smuggler named Green. Penzance Magistrates committed them to Launceston Jail. The smugglers escaped in November of the same year through the wall.

Once again it becomes clear that those men must have had help. It would be impossible to dig a large hole in a wall without being heard by the jailers.

It becomes clear when one reads all the reports that smugglers did have certain privileges from persons in authority, especially in those early years. The local Squires, who were also Magistrates, were undoubtedly involved with the smugglers and it has been suggested that these Gentlemen financed the larger vessels of 250 plus tonnage and also armed them with up to 50 cannons. Not one of these Gentlemen were ever brought to justice. They became a law unto themselves and in 1753 ordered the soldiers based at Penzance, who were helping the Customs men, to leave without being replaced.

In 1778 Mr Edward Giddy, a judge, wrote a very lengthy letter to the Chief Customs Officer regarding the subject and its consequences, a few relevant extracts from this letter follow.

> . . . smuggling, since the soldiers have been drawn off has carried on almost without control . . . Their crews armed with pistols and swords escort the smugglers a considerable distance from the sea . . . In this way goods are

carried from one part of the country to another almost every night . . . The Excise men obtained from me a search warrant but were forcibly hindered from executing it by 4 armed men. They were told if they persisted they would have their brains blown out. As the law now stands I fear a criminal prosecution would have been useless for the reason, which it shocks me to mention, that a Cornish jury would certainly acquit the smugglers.

As can be seen from the above smugglers had friends in high places who could protect them, even to the extent of getting away with murder. This state of affairs continued until the 1850's when the tide slowly turned in favour of the Customs men, but before that date smugglers appeared to be able to do as they wished as the following few reports indicate.

In 1757 William Allen Carter of Penzance broke into the Customs warehouse and stole 15 large bags of tea, each bag weighing 56 pounds, he was caught and sentenced to 7 years transportation. The officer who was sent to retrieve the goods from Carter's house was promptly seized by two Mousehole men, William Keigwin and John Yeoman known as 'Lean Jack.' They locked the Customs man in a room while they removed all the tea. Once all the goods were loaded they released the Customs man who then had to walk back to Penzance.

A Government report in 1783 found that some vessels of three hundred tons were manned by as many as a hundred men. These large vessels were able to make seven or eight voyages a year and bring back large quantities of goods. Three thousand half ankers of spirits and twelve tons of tea in defiance of Revenue Cutters that most large smugglers vessels out-gunned. It also stated that these large armed vessels escorted back smaller lighter armed smugglers. Reserve price for brandy was 5s 6d a gallon, smugglers were selling it for 3s 3d a gallon.

A certain James Rogers from Breage injured two Excisemen trying to remove a keg of smuggled brandy from his house, they were attacked with a poleaxe used to kill cattle. The two officers were charged at Helston by James Rogers of having entered his property without a warrant. This was a common occurrence with smugglers charging Excisemen over such, like 'entering premises without a warrant.' On another occasion a marine on board the Revenue Cutter *Wolf* shot dead a smuggler and was charged with murder at Launceston, the trial was adjourned because of gaol fever.

On another occasion the controller obtained evidence against another smuggler, John Maddern from Mousehole. He struck an Excise Officer with a silver tankard and 'cut his head in a vile manner, so that he was presently in a gore of blood.' The informant, John Bodilley, afterwards stated when he signed the affidavit he was 'excessively overcome with liquor and had not been sober for several days.'

Smuggling in Mousehole had reached such a pitch that goods were openly transported through the village at midday for hiding in the countryside. The Excisemen, were at various periods during the 1700's and 1800's, in league with the smugglers and some paid the price for their involvement with jail sentences. There were of course some very good excuses put forward by these men when later questioned.

. . . I was in fear of my life as the smugglers tried to stave my head in with boat hook and poles . . .
. . . I was confined to bed from being stoned by village people a few days ago . . .
. . . the people of this village are all thieves and smugglers who stole my horse and tied it to a tree some half mile away . . .

These are just a few of the excuses put forward by the Customs men but it appears they wanted for nothing in the way of spirits, wines, silks, baccy, tea and coffee. They didn't catch the smugglers of Mousehole but instead arrested all the Customs men in Mousehole during 1780 for assisting the smugglers and taking bribes.

Mounts Bay smuggling was remarkably free of bloodshed compared to other areas. Whether this was due to the smugglers restraint or Excisemen's tact in keeping out of the way is unclear. It was said at the time that when not being terrorised by smugglers the Excisemen 'wore fog glasses with banknote shades.'

The Revenue Cutters would likewise put up a token fight by firing a few cannon balls and in most cases departed the scene, with good reason as the majority of these smugglers cutters, luggers, schooners and wherries invariably carried more cannons and swivel guns than the Government vessels. There are numerous references to smugglers boats with 20, 30 and up to 50 cannons and swivel guns. It was only when two Revenue Cutters were together that they dared take on the more heavily armed smugglers.

In 1778 a smuggler landed 2,000 ankers of spirits (an anker is just over 9 gallons, so 2,000 ankers would be over 18,000 gallons), 20 tons of tea, bales of silk and other goods on a sandy beach between Penzance and Marazion. The public road was sealed off with armed men until all the goods were landed and hidden in the countryside, this would have taken a considerable time to accomplish. The vast amount of goods landed would indicate a very large vessel that was probably well armed with cannon and swivel guns. Next time you are travelling along the Penzance to Marazion road try and imagine what activity was going on during that dark night in 1778.

In 1872 a Penzance Customs boat was plundered and sunk by smugglers, again in 1772 on 29th November another smuggler sailed into Penzance harbour, boarded and sailed away the Revenue Cutter *Brilliant* which had a captured cargo in her holds. She was one of the more successful Customs boats and responsible for intercepting a large number of smaller smugglers in Mount Bay.

It appears from the records that the majority of smugglers were also staunch methodists and supported the chapels both financially and in other ways. In

1771 the Chief Collector of Customs in Penzance described Richard Pentreath, also known as Doga from Mousehole, as 'an honest man in all his dealings although a notorious smuggler.' Thomas Mann of Mousehole was also spoken of in the official records as a 'reputed smuggler but an honest man.' Such references were also made about other smugglers in the Mounts Bay area. Even the Carter family of Prussia Cove and their famous leader John Carter, known as the 'King of Prussia,' was seen as being honest as the following shows. He broke into the Custom warehouse in Penzance to recover goods taken by the Excisemen during his absence from home. He explained to his comrades that he had agreed to deliver these goods to his customer on a certain day and not to do so 'would forfeit his reputation as an honest trader.' When the Customs men arrived next morning and found their store had been broken into and certain goods taken away they said:

> John Carter has been here and we know it because he is an upright man and has taken nothing which was not his own.

It seems strange in the modern world that smugglers who were defrauding the Government and breaking laws should be classed as honest upright men.

The tin miners and tin streamers were all in league with the smugglers and often hid their goods in disused mines or caves used by tin streamers. Their pay was an anker or two of brandy, or a bag of tea, or maybe tobacco, whatever it was the miners and streamers were well rewarded for their efforts. In Porthgwarra, a favourite landing place for smugglers, miners cut a tunnel from the beach to the centre of that little village. It was easier than trying to get goods up their steep slipway. This tunnel is still there and used by both visitors and local people alike, it gives easy access to their sandy beach. If you get down to Porthgwarra and go through the tunnel just pause for a few moments and look at the entrance and try to imagine what happened there during those far off smuggling days.

On 13th February 1802 the *Cornish Gazette* reported:

> A squadron of frigates being ordered to cruise on the Cornish coast against smugglers has raised a formidable idea in the public mind of the extent of the illicit trade carried on here. We shall be very much surprised, however, if the frigates shall, at the end of twelve months, have seized as much spirits as will be equal to the regular consumption of their crews. The fact is that while the war establishment is kept up, some employment must be found for it, when children are doing nothing they are doing mischief.

By 1803 however the forces of the Crown were once again diverted to help Nelson in the battle of Trafalgar and so once again the smugglers of Cornwall had a free hand.

After the peace treaty was signed the Government set up a much more efficient preventative force of Excisemen, soldiers and Naval vessels to counteract smuggling along the Cornish Coast in 1816/17. That marked the end of the large heavily armed smuggling craft, instead the smugglers turned to the smaller faster vessels to run across to Roscoff with the emphasis being on fast. This enabled the smugglers to outrun most of the vessels sent out to catch them, but that didn't last long with faster boats being deployed by the Navy and Excisemen.

The heyday of the smugglers was over by the 1840's but there was always someone who would risk all for a quick profit but the consequences were now very harsh for those who were caught. The protection afforded by the Squires and gentry was very much reduced as to be almost non-existent. Anyone caught smuggling was made to watch as his boat was reduced to matchwood before being sentenced usually with very heavy fines. There were long jail sentences for those who used 'threatening behaviour' when Excisemen relieved them of their illegal cargoes. By the 1850's and 60's smuggling was all but finished. The massive fines, loss of boats and jail sentences imposed by the 'New Courts,' and the large number of Revenue Men, soldiers and Naval craft had finally put the 'Free Traders' out of business.

Is has been estimated that some of the larger smuggling vessels made up to £18,000 in the 1770's early 1800's which was a lot of money back in those days, especially when you consider you could have a good cottage built and furnished for less than £40. Even in the 1860's you could have a cottage built for between £50 and £100 as mentioned earlier in this book.

In the early 1960's a man called Dennis Allen lived at number 2 Gurnick Street. He was a tall man being 6 foot 3 inches high, wore very thick pebble lens glasses and drank nothing but mild ale in the Ship Inn at Mousehole. He was also addicted to snuff which he continually took and promptly sneezed into a very brown stained handkerchief. He was a philosopher and writing a book about that subject which was about a thousand pages long. I used to see him regularly and went to his house a few times where he showed me something very interesting in his cellar one day. It was an old smuggler's tunnel that was running in water. I put on oilskins one day and armed with a torch went into the tunnel. It was very cramped and extremely wet with running water underfoot. The tunnel went in a little way then climbed steeply upwards. I never actually reached the end because it looked very unsafe, there appeared to be loose rocks in the roof that were running in water. It was eventually breeze blocked up in about 1969 after drains were put in to take the water away. I doubt very much if the present owners of this cottage know about the tunnel. I might call in there one day and tell them. I doubt if there is anyone else left alive who knows exactly where the entrance is now.

King of Prussia

PRUSSIA COVE IS three miles across the bay next to Praa Sands with the large headland of Cudden Point guarding the northern side. If you look to the right of St Michaels Mount from Mousehole you can easily pick out the large grey headland of Cudden. If you get the Mount just peeping clear of Cudden and slowly steam across Praa Sands there is a large reef that is just underwater. There used to be day marks in Praa Sands that marked the top of this reef with the Mount just showing, whether both day marks are still there I do not know. This reef would be right in the way of any Revenue Cutter that was sailing in towards Prussia Cove and if the Captain was unaware of it it could seriously damage any vessel. Whether this actually happened is not known but it was another benefit for those smugglers at Prussia Cove. Mousehole was well known for its smugglers and without any doubt there must have been Mousehole men aboard some of the Carter families boats engaged in this activity. The Carter's themselves skippered the smuggling boats and were well known to the authorities but most of the crews names were not known and going by the records kept fairly secret from the Customs men for obvious reasons.

The most famous and probably most successful smuggler in south-west Cornwall was undoubtedly Captain John Carter, known as 'The King of Prussia.' He was the leader of the Carter family of smugglers based at Prussia Cove. His exploits and deeds will probably live on forever. He was known as 'an upright and honest man but a notorious smuggler' by the authorities of that time and it appears they respected him in a strange sort of way. The very name of Prussia Cove was by John Carter's own making. It is said that as a boy playing soldiers with other children he always called himself the 'King of Prussia' and that name stuck and followed him into manhood. The original name was Porthleah but as his fame and notoriety grew it became known as 'The King of Prussia Cove,' today it is simply called Prussia Cove. That is how this well protected hidden little cove arrived at its present day name.

The cove hasn't really changed since the 1700's except there are now fishermen instead of smugglers using it. The fishermen's main catch is lobster, once clear of Praa Sands the ground is rough, rocky and shallow right out past Mount Moppas Buoy. I bought a new 12 foot punt and 2½hp Seagull outboard from Prussia Cove in 1962 and motored it back to Mousehole. By a strange coincidence my punt ended back at Prussia Cove when it was used in the filming of the Poldark series for television. There have been numerous films, like *Jamaica Inn,* about smugglers that have been filmed at Prussia Cove.

For 37 years from 1770 until 1807 John Carter landed smuggled goods all along the Cornish coast including Prussia Cove, in all probability it was a lot longer than that. It was John Carter who made the cove as it basically exists today, cutting it back into solid rock and making the steep track that leads to a steep slipway. In all probability it was miners who carried out all the work under John Carter's guidance. The vast majority of the numerous caves were cut into the solid rock at his request for the purpose of storing smuggled goods. Some of these caves that led up to the house on the cliff top now have their entrances sealed. The other caves are used by the cove's fishermen for storing their fishing gear. When you walk down the steep track towards the slip it is difficult to imagine what went on in the 1700's during dark stormy nights with just oil lamps or candles to give a flickering dim light as burly bearded leather clad smugglers smelling of snuff struggled to manhandle heavy casks and sacks up the steep slip towards the caves. All you have to go on are the ancient records, the way men dressed, type of vessels and punts employed, the rest you have to imagine.

To guard the cove from Revenue Cutters he built a large granite house with battlements on the north-east point of Prussia Cove and then installed cannons, which can still be seen today, and these cannons were not just for show as the following indicates. A Revenue Cutter had sailed into the cove with the intention of putting men ashore at Prussia to search for smuggled goods. Led by John Carter the smugglers manned their battery cannons and opened fire on the Government boat. They in turn opened fire at the shore battery, how long the actual battle lasted is not made clear but eventually the Revenue Cutter left the area and the smugglers counted that as a victory. In actual fact the Revenue boat easily outgunned the smugglers few small cannons with more guns and heavier firepower but it was a wise decision of the ship's captain to withdraw as there is very little searoom to manoeuvre a large vessel due to the shallow water, reefs and sandbars leading in towards Prussia Cove. Several Revenue vessels did enter the cove area but this was the only time that I came across a battle taking place, and not once was the large house with its cannons raided although some goods were seized that had been hidden nearby.

John Carter's brother Harry was also a very successful and notorious smuggler who commanded his own vessel of 20 cannons by the time he was 18 years old. Although a ruthless man in pursuit of his smuggling trade he forbade all swearing and unseemly conversation aboard his boat. In later years when he was living in Roscoff with a price on his head he conducted religious services every Sunday afternoon for the 30 or 40 other Cornish smugglers that were forced to live in Roscoff to avoid being arrested for their deeds. They were all reprieved in 1805 and from the records it appears they all came back to Cornwall, some to continue smuggling or privateering.

The Carter family were also heavily involved with the privateering business that was carried on at the same time as their smuggling activities. The first privateer to be licensed was John Carter's vessel in 1777. Henry, Roger and Francis Carter were all involved with privateering, Francis was killed in a battle with a French privateer in 1800. *(see Privateers in South-West Cornwall)*

Imports & Exports in Mousehole

UP UNTIL THE 1930's the main method of transporting reasonably large quantities of materials was by small cargo vessels that could negotiate the narrow harbours and shallow waters of the countries smaller harbours. Road haulage was still in the future although during the 1800's trains were beginning to transport perishable goods in larger quantities.

The first known import/export trade was carried out by the Phoenecians and Syrians about 4,000 years ago when they traded for tin at Marazion. The second oldest harbour in Mounts Bay after Marazion is Mousehole, exactly when Mousehole started trading will probably never be known but it is a fact that all these early traders called in here to fill their water barrels as all the other streams were polluted by tin streaming.

Way back in the late 1400's the records show that French salt was imported to Mozul, (Mousehole) for the pilchard fishery. One report states that three French boats were unloading at the same time. Taking into account how small the harbour must have been during this period one must assume that these cargo vessels were also not very large, in all probability they would be French drifters.

There are several references to French vessels unloading salt but it is not until the late 1500's that there is any mention of pilchard exports, hogsheads. The first mention claims that 'some 200 hogshead of pilchard are loaded aboard a boat at Mouzul for Leghorn and Civita Veschia.'

There obviously had to be other imports such as wood for building or making barrels, or even the completed hogsheads as well as coal but it is not until the 1700's that any mention is made of these imports. The first I have come across was in the 1780's when it just says 80 tons of coal landed at Mousehole. It is not until the 1800's that any regular mention is made of imports and these again are very few and far between with very little detail.

The Government on the other hand were forever making new laws and Parliamentary Acts which were sent to all harbour authorities in the country,

for regulating the shipping and unshipping – lading – warehousing – stowing – depositing and removal of all goods of a dangerous explosive and inflammable nature.

91

Further on it describes these as:

. . . benzoline and certain descriptions of petroleum etc which give off inflammable vapour at low temperature.

It then states that:

. . . the harbour authority appear to have sufficient powers for this purpose under the 83rd section of the Harbours, Docks and Piers Clauses Act 1847 which is incorporated with this special act.

Why Mousehole should have been sent one of these I have no idea, but I suppose they just sent them to every harbour in the country.

From the records it appears that the Government was sending out letters and forms to all harbour authorities on a very regular basis regarding all sorts of subjects relating to the importing of goods. An extract from one such letter from the Local Government Board, Whitehall on the 18th September 1884 is as follows:

Ordered that an account be laid before this House an account of all dues, duties and taxes, local and imperial, levied on the importation and exportation of coals and cokes in any part of England and Wales and Ireland in the year 1884.

On the reply form it stated that:

. . . an account of the number of tons of coals imported into Mousehole pier for the year 1883, 1,050 tons of coal at 3d per ton landing dues making £13 2 6. There is no coke imported here.

Why the Government should want these figures it does not say, the same applies to stone imports and exports, although I can find no record of the actual tonnage of stone exported it must have been considerable.

On 9th February 1883 Mr George Eddy was paid £10 to remove some 200 tons of stone from around Mousehole piers to make 'a safe passage for vessels entering or leaving,' he was allowed to export these without paying any dues. Presumably the waiving of these dues was part of his contract but the report does not say so. Over the next 20 years George Eddy was regularly employed removing stone from around the quays and exporting the same.

In the 1870's Mr Runnels, owner of Penlee quarry, was charge 1d per ton to export stone from Mousehole and he was allowed to lodge 200

92

tons on the pier. How many tons he actually exported is unknown but he must have had quite a large export business because after Newlyn harbour was built he used both ports for shipping stone. By the early 1890's it was 6d per ton for exporting.

During the 1880's the harvesting of seaweed for the Hayle factory had become quite a large industry employing 21 boats. They used to be charged 6d per cart load when landing/importing. During October 1885 Mousehole Commissioners changed this to 6d per ton to fall in line with the import tariff. This caused a lot of arguments and the owners refused to pay the new tariff. A court order was issued against the said boat owners but as no actual court proceedings were ever reported it is assumed that some agreement was reached, probably by paying the 6d per ton.

The seaweed that was harvested each year was oarweed and this was taken by horse and cart to a factory in Hayle that extracted iodine from the weed, oarweed was and still is the only plant that produces this. The weed was harvested towards the end of the year after it had stopped growing and before the winter storms ripped it off the rocks. Exactly how they harvested the weed is not recorded but it must have been with some sort of scythe, probably similar to that used by farmers. From the records it appears that most harbours and ports had seaweed gathering boats. California and Florida are now the world's largest producers of iodine taken from the 60 to 100 foot oarweed forests. The Hayle factory closed in the early 1900's.

The largest import into Mousehole after coal was undoubtedly salt which was used in the fishing industry. Again it is impossible to tell exactly how much tonnage was landed each year but from those imports that did get reported it appears to be in the region of 500 tons. In 1893 a Mr Matthias Dunn landed 113 tons and a Mr S. Truscott from Charlestown, St Austell landed 328 tons, they were charged 5d per ton landing dues. There must have been a different tariff for salt as all other imports were charged 6d.

On Sunday 28th January 1894 a large three-masted vessel *Hanseign* entered Mousehole harbour from Spain with 320 tons of salt for the curers. This is the largest craft ever to enter Mousehole harbour.

Unfortunately for researchers the *Cornishman* reporters of this period did not go into very much detail regarding the type or size of the *Hanseign*.

In July 1879 both of Mousehole's quays were fitted with large ring bolts for 'the benefit of vessels discharging cargo and that new wider quay planks are being made for the discharge of goods on the quays.' The report also stated that 'some goods landed by Messrs Roose and Trewavas were not numerated on the harbour tariff.' It must be presumed that they had to pay some sort of landing dues and I expect that these goods were soon incorporated into the tariff.

Esparto grass was regularly imported by George Laity and he was charged 6d per ton landing dues. Esparto was used for making ropes, mats, fabrics etc., but where this was carried out in Mousehole is unknown. I can find no record relating to this but he did export esparto 'goods' for which he was again charged 6d per ton. Mr William Harris, sailmaker, was also charged 6d per ton when he imported sailcloth. There is no mention of any exports regarding sails but it is known that he fitted out vessels from other ports as well as Mousehole boats.

From the records it is apparent that the Commissioners were regularly updating the tariff regarding imports and exports. This was always mentioned in the local press but no actual tariff of goods was published, the report just stated that 'the present tariff for Mousehole piers to be abridged, printed, varnished and posted as early as possible.' Posted meant that they were on display for all boat owners to see. One would obviously be in the harbour office and there are mentions of them being on the quays but exactly where is not said.

This import and export trade had one rather bad disadvantage for the harbour as a whole as reported in August 1885.

The Rates Assessment Committee held a meeting regarding Mousehole piers and new harbour office. At this meeting it was decided that these rates be increased from £10 10s per year to £180 per year. A deputation from Mousehole harbour commissioners headed by chairman William Barnes attended a meeting of the Assessment Committee to try and get these rates reduced. They were told that the Commission could not be relieved from these rates but after much talk it was reduced to £175 per year.

This was a massive increase by any standards and the money had to be found from somewhere. From this period all vessels landing anything in Mousehole had to pay, this included the dung boats, seaweed boats, crabbers, seiners and all persons storing things on Mousehole harbour property. Dues were increased for boatbuilders, cartwrights and carpenters using either of the banks. It was a time of unrest in the harbour and several court orders were issued during the next twelve months when some men refused to pay the new dues. There is no record of anyone actually being taken to court so it must be assumed that they all eventually paid the new dues. The tariff of 6d per ton on all imports and exports was not altered but now the dung and seaweed boats also fell into this category, however it did not stop either from trading.

At the yearly AGM of Mousehole Harbour Commissioners on Saturday 6th February 1886 the question of the new rates was raised and recorded as such.

> Respecting the excessive rating of the pier it was put to the views of the public meeting when it was proposed that the Treasurer not pay the pier rates before it was fairly tried in court.

This proposal was carried unanimously at the AGM.

> On Wednesday 5th May 1886 the Secretary of Mousehole Harbour Commissioners appeared before the Magistrates in Penzance to try and have the rates struck off altogether or greatly lessened. He was defended by Mr Wellington Dale. It was decided that Messrs Joseph Trewavas, Francis Blewett, William Drew and Richard Angwin should meet the Overseers on Saturday 15th May at 5pm to try and get the pier to its former rate. If they cannot succeed in doing so to call a Parish Vestry meeting for the last Saturday in the month.

No agreement was reached and so a letter and notice was posted.

> To the Overseers of the Parish of Paul. We the undersigned ratepayers of the Parish of Paul request you to call a special Vestry meeting for the purpose of considering the question of rating for the property belonging to the Mousehole Harbour Commissioners and for making such arrangements as may be thought best as to the rates now due or hereafter to become due.
> The meeting to be called on the last Saturday in May 29th of the month at 7pm.

This was signed by 30 fishermen from Mousehole.

> On the 3rd of June 1886 the Magistrates in compliance with a Vestry meeting called on 29th May and having a majority of 27, the Magistrates reduced the new assessment to its former rate.

This was £10 10s per year but for some reason this was not accepted by the Overseers of Paul Parish. There followed several meetings throughout the following months until on Saturday 16th October 1886 they both agreed on a payable rate of £24 per year. At least it was a large reduction from the original assessment of £180, and it also showed what could be achieved at an AGM when the whole village backed the Commissioners.

What I do find odd is not being able to discover a completed list of the tariff on imports or exports for Mousehole harbour. There must surely be a complete list surviving somewhere.

Harbour Masters

ONE OF THE first jobs of the newly formed Mousehole Harbour Improvement Board of Commissioners was to advertise for a Harbour Master. The report did not mention how many applied but Mr Charles Mann was appointed Harbour Master with a salary of £4 per year. In 1871 his salary was increased to £8 per year due to his extra duties which included collecting all landing dues from fish and cargo. He resigned in January 1885.

In January of that year tenders were invited for the Harbour Master's job, eight were received and their salaries ranged from £12 to £25.

Mr Benjamin C. Harvey was duly elected Harbour Master at a salary of £15 per year plus 5% of all fish landing dues that he collected. He held this post until August 1893 when he resigned due to ill health.

It was in 1885 that the rates on the harbour were increased with the consequent increase in landing dues that made his job harder. It was during this period that the first rules and duties of the Harbour Master were laid out, printed, varnished and posted on the piers alongside the new tariff.

They were as follows:

The Duties of the Harbour Master

1st. To regulate all boats and vessels – to attend to all moorings and to the putting down of the booms and to secure them when taken up.

2nd. To attend to the lighting of the lights from sunset and putting them out at sunrise from 1st August to 1st May – when booms are down to take the lanterns up in a secure place.

3rd. To collect all dues from boats and vessels – also all landing dues from fish or other commodity imported in the harbour according to the tariff on the pier – and all other unmentioned duties of a Harbour Master.

4th. That the Harbour Master is to pay into the Treasurer every week the amount of money in his hand or at any time agreed to by the Commissioners.

5th. To court no mans favour nor fear no man's frowns – to be impartial in every case – for each party to take or give one months notice on either side – to attend all meetings.

These were the basic rules laid down for the Harbour Master but over the years his duties did increase and were covered by rule 3 'all other unmentioned duties.'

These unmentioned duties included collecting warping dues, fish buyers dues, calculating the tonnage of stone being shipped out and collecting those dues before the vessel left the harbour. Keeping the quays clear so that horse and carts could pass, moving and mooring up boats, checking all moorings to ensure that these were strong and safe enough for the vessels moored on them and also oversee any work being carried out in and around the harbour. He was also responsible for ensuring the crane and harbour walls were all in good repair. The phrase 'fear no man's frown' in the 5th rule most certainly applied as the Harbour Master came in for a lot of abuse and aggravation when trying to collect some dues, especially the increases during 1885 and 1886, as the number of court summons's served proved.

After Mr Benjamin Harvey resigned tenders were invited for the position of Harbour Master along with the rules applying to the job. Six were received.

Joseph Trewavas VC	£25 plus 5% on fish dues
Thomas Lugg	£20
William Harris jnr	£20
William Harris snr	£18
Richard P. Thomas	£15 plus 5% on fish dues
Francis Praed	£16

This was the second time that William Harris snr, sailmaker had applied but seamen or fishermen were preferred for obvious reasons. The three seagoing men who had applied were asked whether they intended to give up fishing altogether. Mr Trewavas said he would give up seagoing after the present season for the sum named. Mr Praed said the same but would require £20. Mr Thomas said he would give up seagoing immediately for £30. The three men were told that whoever was accepted would have two months grace given him for the present season. When the ballot papers were opened it was found that Francis Praed had 7 votes and Joseph Trewavas 2 votes. Mr Praed was called in and the duties were read to him and he agreed to abide by these. He started on 1st August 1893 and resigned in June 1895 when the job was once again put out to tender. Five were received.

Henry Potter	£20
John Humphreys	£20
Michael Pender	£20
Charles Brookman	£20
Joseph Trewavas VC	£25 all plus 5% on all landing dues

When the ballot papers were read it was found that Mr Pender had 1 vote, Mr Trewavas 3 votes and Mr Potter 8 votes. Mr Henry Potter kept the job of Harbour Master until his sudden death in October 1905.

This time the position of Harbour Master was advertised at a salary of £23 per year plus 5% on all landing dues. Fifteen applications were received and they came from Penzance, Newlyn, Paul and Mousehole. It took 6 ballots before a winner for the job was finally arrived at and Mr Francis Blewett was duly elected as Harbour Master with his duties to start the next day, Sunday 5th November 1905. This was now a full-time job and one of the stipulations was that he give up seagoing. How much the 5% on all landing dues came to is unknown but it must be assumed it was a goodly sum to make up his wages to a liveable standard. As a major fishing port Mousehole was losing out to Newlyn which was by now the main port for all fishing boats and where the majority of fish buyers were situated, so over the next few years the amount of revenue coming into the harbour from fish landings would drop quite drastically. Mr Blewett was the last Harbour Master who had to give up seagoing to keep his job. Due to the influence of Newlyn harbour and the number of Mousehole vessels now using this as their main port for berthing and landing the income for Mousehole harbour was drastically reduced. In fact the income from fish landings was virtually nil with only pilchard boats now landing some of their catch. In October 1913 Mr Francis Blewett was asked to take a cut in his wages, he made no reply to this and in December 1913 he was given three months notice to quit his position as Harbour Master. In March 1914 Obediah Reseigh was elected Harbour Master at £16 per year plus 5% on all landing dues. It was becoming a part-time job and later Harbour Masters were allowed to go fishing to top up their wages. Although there was still a thriving import trade with salt, coal, building materials etc.

Watch Keeping

MANKIND HAS BEEN afloat in various types of sailing craft for several thousand years. One of the earliest documented accounts comes from the ancient Egyptians who used large papyrus rush vessels to explore the Mediterranean Sea and River Nile, they were also used to transport large stone blocks to build the pyramids. Even back in those days, some 4,000 years ago, they would have employed some of the crew as lookouts, watchers, to ensure the safety of both boat and crew. As the voyages got longer, some lasting months into uncharted waters, the need for lookouts or watchers during 24 hours would become of paramount importance. This shift system during each 24 hours became known as 'Watches' with a Port Watch and Starboard Watch divided up as follows. Port is red and on the left hand side, Starboard is green and on the right hand side.

The Watches were of four hours duration except for the two 2 hour Dogwatches. The Dogwatches were brought in to prevent the sailors doing the same Watch and number of hours each day. Probably the first instance of flexible working hours.

First Watch 2000 hours until 2400 hours, midnight.
Middle Watch 2400 hours until 0400 hours.
Morning Watch 0400 hours until 0800 hours.
Forenoon Watch 0800 hours until 1200 hours.
Afternoon Watch 1200 hours until 1600 hours.
First Dogwatch 1600 until 1800 hours.
Last Dogwatch 1800 hours until 2000 hours.

Way before there were clocks or chronometers shipboard time was measured with the use of 'Sand-glasses' – bigger versions of the three minute sand-glass used for timing boiled eggs. Shipboard sand-glasses recorded half-hour, one hour and a normal Watch of four hours. Each glass had to be turned either half-hourly, hourly or every four hours to reset them, failure to do this incurred severe punishment because the safety of both boat and crew relied on the Watchkeepers during the hours of darkness.

Watchkeepers would also have to call out the number of bells rung each half-hour and which side and Watch it was. For example, "First Port/Starboard Watch 6 bells and all's well" would indicate it was 2300 hours, 11.00 in the evening and our local pub in Mousehole had just stopped serving beer. Likewise "Forenoon Port/Starboard Watch 6 bells and all's well" would indicate that it was 1100 hours in the morning and opening time at our local pub.

The cry "All's Well" indicated to the Watch Officer that all the rigging and sails were correct on both Port and Starboard sides and there was no need to call the crew out to change or alter any rope or sail. It must have been a rather wet, cold and dangerous job walking the side decks in a gale for four hours. The system of Watches and bells was originated in the British Navy, later the Royal Navy, and was adopted by both Merchant and Naval vessels across the known world.

Even in today's modern sophisticated highly technical electronic world a system of Watchkeeping is still carried on by both Naval and Merchant vessels, although this is now done in the comfort and warmth of a large wheelhouse and nobody has to walk the side decks calling out "All's Well".

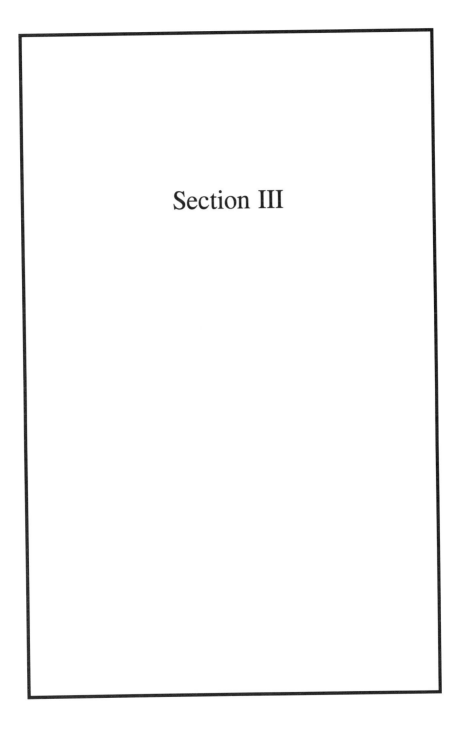

Section III

Tom Bocock

THE LEGEND OF Tom Bocock has now become inextricably linked with the children's book *The Mousehole Cat*. In actual fact the legend of Tom Bocock has nothing whatsoever to do with a cat. The basic legend is as follows.

A storm had been blowing for several weeks and the small community of Mousehole were starving and wondering where the next meal was coming from. One man, driven by the cries of hungry children, put to sea in his little boat. His name was Tom Bocock. Amid the storm driven waves he fished for the life of the village and won. He caught enough fish to last for over a week, and when he came ashore they found seven varieties of fish, one for each day of the week, and the week in question was Christmas week. The seven varieties of fish were dogfish, sand eel, ling, hake, scad, pilchard and herring.

Tom Bocock's Eve is celebrated each year on the 23rd December with the traditional Starry Gazey Pie and the locals singing the song commemorating this event.
The chorus for this song is sung between each verse and goes as follows:

A merry place you may believe
was Mousehole on Tom Bocock's Eve
to be there then who wouldn't wish
and sup on seven sorts of fish.

1: When Mergy broth had cleared a path
come Launces for a fry
and then us had a bit of scad
and starrie gazzie pie

2: Then came Fairmaids and thrusty Jades
that made our ousles dry
with ling and hake enough to make
a running shark to sigh

3: When each we clunk and health was drunk
with brumbers brimming high
and when up come Tom Bocock's name
we praised him to the sky.

So what are the facts regarding the above legend? Basically none – I have as yet not found any documented evidence relating to Tom Bocock and the legend about saving the village, but all legends are based on fact which over the years and countless retellings invariably gets very distorted.

The basis of this legend is the fact that Mousehole was starving. Take that away and there is nothing to build a story around, and for the village to be that short of food you are looking for a major disaster that encompassed a large part of the extreme south-west of Cornwall. A disaster on such a scale that livestock, crops and fishing all failed at the same time over a large area. There is one such occurrence that did just that in 1099.

In actual fact there are two documented floods that occurred in Mounts Bay, the first in 1014 which stated that, 'Mounts Bay inundated by 'mickle sea flood,' many towns, villages, hamlets and people drowned.' The second great flood would appear to be even worse as the records say that in '1099 all the hamlets and villages were inundated by the sea with great loss of life, all the cattle, horses, swine and fowl were drowned and crops washed away. A great famine swept the land.'

The *Anglo Saxon Chronicles* start at year 1 and finish in 1154 and throughout these records there are innumerable references of floods inundating low-lying ground. In these modern times it is taken for granted that we can all read and write, but 1,000 years ago this would not be the case. Even so there are a considerable number of documents that still exist from this period, but equally so there is an even greater amount missing which tends to leave gaps in certain areas of research. Considering how important Marazion and St Michaels Mount were 3,000 years ago during the very early tin trade then it is reasonable to expect that there must have been some sort of written record by the monks relating to this trade. If such records were kept then what happened to them is unknown. It is possible that these old records, including the floods of 1014 and 1099, were hidden behind walls by the monks who then lived on St Michaels Mount. As with all old priories and monasteries the monks were very fond of making hiding places and walling up records etc. Another possibility is that when the monks left St Michaels Mount and sailed across the channel to Mont Saint Michel, another priory in Brittany, they took these old records with them. It is known that when they left for Brittany they took vast amounts of written text with them, but I still like to think that somewhere in the older part of St Michaels Mount these records are resting in a secret enclave that has been walled up, although it is known that one vessel was lost to the sea.

When researching the old records of the Royal Geological Society of Cornwall there are plenty of accounts and references to floods and also the proof that such a disaster did happen. In 1478 when William Worcestre visited the priory on St Michaels Mount he was told the name was 'le Horerok in the Wodd,' 'The Hoar Rock in the Wood.' When he enquired about the wood the monks told him that:

. . . there were both woods and meadows and ploughland between the said Mount and the Scilly Islands and 140 parish churches were drowned between that Mount and Scilly.

For the past 3,000 years and longer it was the monks in their priories and monasteries that were the scribes of their era and recorded major events that happened in their area. In fact the vast majority of the very early history of England comes from these monks writings, they were all well versed in the art of writing and recording. They had one bad habit and that was they tended to guard and hide these old writings.

For the monks on St Michaels Mount to know how many parish churches were lost and also about the ploughed ground indicates that they must also have had access to old records in 1478. It is also highly probable that they had names for the villages and hamlets around those old churches. It is also highly conceivable that some of the high rough ground that fishermen now work pots and nets over was once the site of a village or hamlet. All these fishing marks have names and it would be interesting to know if some of these matched the drowned villages. Without the old writings this will never be known.

During the latter part of the 1400's and early 1500's a John Leland found that:

In the bay betwyxt the Mont and Pensans be fownd neere the lowe water marke rootes of trees yn dyvers places, as a token of the grounde wasted.

Below is a passage taken from Michael Drayton's 1612 *Poly-Olbion* which mentions the flooding of the bay, the original basis of which in all probability came from the monks on St Michaels Mount.

Strange things, that in his daies times course had brought to pass,
That fortie miles now Sea, some times firme fore-land was,
And that a Forrest then, which now with him is Flood
Whereof he first was call'd the Hoare-Rock in the Wood.

In 1690 Nicholas Boson of Newlyn wrote:

Tradition calls it 'Carrack Looes en Cooes,' a hoary or venerable rock in the wood or forest, but we have not record extant when this furious inundation made wonderfull changes upon this part . . . That bodyes and roots of trees lye along the sand betwixt this and Newlyn is very evident . . . I have likewise seen the form of various leaves in the washed earth as of oak, nutt, elm, ash, willow and holm.

An extract from the Royal Geological Society of Cornwall Annual Report in the 1960's.

Once again, more markedly than in the case of the Wolf and Seven Stones, and for different causes, the implication was clear throughout past centuries. The Mount once stood in a wood, the wood was occasionally still seen, and, since its remains lay below all but the lowest scouring tides, there had been a flood, and one in the order of the Mounts Bay tidal range (the height of three grown men, about 18 foot). Such a flood must have affected a much larger area, and therefore a whole territory, not simply Mounts Bay, had in the past been drowned. But landscapes with deciduous trees, useful timber, and with nuts and berries, are normally inhabited. Therefore this one had been, and in the event its one time population, with the houses and villages and parish churches, had all been instantly overwhelmed – unless, that is, anyone with foresight or with some means of travel swift enough to out-run the waves had managed to escape in time.

This is an exact copy as printed by the Royal Geological Society of Cornwall. William Worcester recorded in 1478 that 'even a man on a horseback could not outrun this flood,' this was told him by the monks.

It is a proven fact that at sometime the Scillies were joined to the mainland and that this area was also populated, and if the monks were correct we know that there were 140 parish churches and villages on this land. Even today in clear seas on the Scillies you can see stone walls that run underwater between some of the islands with stone walls to match up with those underwater on the islands. But when and how did this vast area flood.

The how is reasonably easy to explain. During the last ice age the 2½ mile thick ice cap in central Europe was large and heavy enough to force the underlying magma to flow sideways. This had the effect of tilting England, it raised the east and south coast and lowered the west and north coast. The land at this period in time extended out nearly 200 miles towards the Continental Shelf. Pollen counts from seabed core samples give an accurate picture of the trees growing. At the end of the last ice age, approximately 12,000 years ago, when the ice began to melt there would be a gradual increase in the mean depth of the seas around the northern hemisphere. This was a very slow process to start with but as the climate warmed the meltdown would also increase and so would the amount of flooding. 5,000 years ago the North Sea was formed and England became an island, but the Scillies were still joined to the mainland, although by this time the sea was only some 50 to 60 miles away.

In 1958 Sir Gavin de Beer arranged a radiocarbon dating on a petrified piece of oak, this gave its age between 2,700 to 3,500 years old but as he points out 'in the absence of a closer location and a vertical fix in tidal range, further extrapolation of the kind given here is not possible.' What this means is that our piece of oak could have come from anywhere and been carried by tides to where it was finally found. If it was from between the Scillies and the mainland that would indicate a severe flooding. The *Anglo Saxon Chronicles* were started over 1,000 years ago and finished in 1154 and their pages are full of flooding reports.

There are two main reasons for all the flooding activity that occurred during the last 2,000 years. One was the acceleration in the melting of the ice cap and the other more significant reason was that the land that had been tilted by the magma was now starting to flatten out. The magma that had been displaced by the 2½ mile thick weight of the ice cap, which had now virtually melted, was starting to slowly flow back under central Europe. The land underneath the ice cone was, and still is today, rising. The displaced magma that tilted England was, and still is, slowly flowing eastwards. Consequently England is levelling out to its normal flat stable position. This levelling has two major significant factors that affected, and are still affecting, England as a whole. The east and south-east coastlines are sinking into the North Sea, there has been widespread coverage of this erosion on the television during the last few years. Remember how they moved the lighthouse away from Dover's white cliff edge in early 1999.

As this coastline sinks then the west and north-west coastline rises. This gives the west coast its famous raised beaches, the average height above sea level at the present time is between 50 and 60 foot. The coast road between Mousehole and Newlyn is built on top of a raised beach. With this tilting effect levelling out and the rise in sea level it is easy to understand the increase in these sudden and disastrous floods that claimed so much land along with its inhabitants.

It is hard to imagine that what is now called Cornwall was once over two hundred miles from the sea some 12,000 years ago. In the Royal Geological Society of Cornwall older pamphlets there is ample evidence that cold climate trees grew as far out to what is now called the Continental Shelf. Core samples taken from the sea bed out there indicate that trees grew and flourished because they have recovered petrified leaves and nuts of various trees and as stated before there must have been ancient humans living in that area as well. If there is a plentiful supply of fruit, nuts and game then there would be humans. Core samples also show from the pollen counts that it was a very diverse forest that covered this area out to the continental shelf. Unfortunately the Royal Society has now been moved from Penzance to the Camborne School of Mines but it is worth the effort to go and browse through the very informative and eye opening reports regarding the formation of this area of Cornwall.

From the above pages it is possible to form an opinion regarding Mr Tom Bocock and his legend. The village and whole area of West Cornwall would have been starving after such a catastrophe and for the legend to hold water it had to be a wide area otherwise food could have been brought in from other villages. Considering the large amount of ground churned up by the inrush of water the sea would be just a very thick mud pool and no fish can live in that because it would block up their gills and deprived them of life-giving oxygen. It also appears from the records that what is now Mounts Bay was once a fertile low-lying area where all the crops were grown. It is easier to till flat fertile ground than steep hills that were extensively used by tin streamers way back in those days. The inlet that ran past Mousehole to Gwavas Lake and then through the marshes to Marazion is known about and the two streams in Mousehole and the Lamorna stream emptied into this inlet. The devastating flood of 1099 must have been lethal for all sea life that was caught up in the flood. Thick muddy water would have killed those off that didn't swim fast enough and find clear water. After several days the mud would have settled to the sea bed and formed mud stone after a thousand years or so. (Three or four miles back of Mousehole Island mud stone often comes up in the bottom nets and these soft rocks are riddled with Piddock Shells that have bored into the rock.) After a week when the outer seas had cleared the flood tide would have brought clear water into the bay and that is where the fish would be, on the out skirts of the muddy water where there would have been plenty of plankton. So Tom Bocock would have had to fish a flood tide in that clear water. That would be the only place where fish lived during that stage. Once the tide started ebbing then muddy water would return. Some people might find this hard to understand but the tide only moves six hours one way then six hours back so muddy water would take a long time to disperse. The inner Longship tides are slightly different. They have eight hour ebb and four hour flood tides, this is due mainly to the River Severn that flows into the Bristol Channel.

England is getting smaller as an island and the civil engineers and scientists all agree that there is very little that can be done in the long term to prevent the east coast disappearing into the North Sea. The city of London will also be lost, drowned, inundated, call it what you like but it will be lost and there is little that can be done to prevent it happening. Embankments have already be raised in areas of serious risk but even modern man with all his technology cannot go on building embankments even higher, at some stage the government of the day will have to say, 'enough is enough, let the sea have its way.' They have already agreed with engineers and scientists to let the sea 'have its way' along most of the east coast. Farmland, houses and villages have already been lost and there will be a lot more before England gets back on an even keel.

So when exactly did the Scillies get cut off from the mainland? At the moment the exact date for this is unknown but probably within the last 2,500 years, this would tie in with the carbon dating of the oak log. The increase in sea level and the ground returning to a more even keel would make this flooding inevitable. The pollen counts from core samples taken between St Michaels Mount and the Scillies show that it was a very fertile area covered in a forest of oak, willow, alder, birch, hazel etc and that it was inhabited. There is no evidence to show that when it did flood the waters reached Mounts Bay, in fact this flooding would be more likely to have happened in sudden rushes that reached several miles inland taking huge bites or swathes of land with each successive encroachment. The action of waves on a beach naturally builds up a bank of sand or shingle which will hold the sea back for a considerable time but when it eventually does break through then the ensuing flood is usually very severe. The steepest angle a natural shingle or sandbank can be built up by the sea is 45 degrees. A simple experiment will bear this out, a bucket of dry sand tipped out on the ground will form a pyramid of 45 degrees.

At the present time there are two such places in Mounts Bay that will eventually flood and one of these will turn Penwith into an island. The ground between Marazion, St Erth and Hayle is only just above sea level and in numerous places below sea level. It is a very wet marshy extensive area of land which the railway line follows and is continuously flooded during the winter and periods of heavy rain. All that keeps the water back is the large sandbank that the sea has built up over the years, but there is an optimum height to which the sea can build any bank depending on how steep the shoreline is shelving. Once that height is reached the base will be continually eroded and the barrier will move slowly inland, once it is breached then the force and amount of water rushing into the low-lying ground behind would wash away more sand and each successive tide would enlarge and deepen the breach. Once it reaches Hayle then the massive, strong tides that swirl around Lands End would utilize this short cut and soon gouge out a permanent and very deep channel, Penwith would then become an island, 'Isle of Penwith.' It will happen – when depends on how quick the remaining landlocked ice melts and how much further the tilt in the land has to go. The large pond or lake at Marazion is man-made and is the result of an extensive peat cutting industry some 200 years ago.

The other area at risk is Loe Bar near Porthleven. This shingle bank holds back a very large amount of water and every few years it breaks through and rushes into the sea. If this shingle ridge disappeared then the sea would reach the outskirts of Helston.

This building up and breaking through the natural barriers made by the sea between Scillies and the bay might have only taken 1,000 years, it could be even less as the monks appeared to have thought, but for the sea to claim all the land between Scillies and Mounts Bay at one flooding would truly be a major catastrophe and undoubtedly be recorded several times by writings and legends.

Then we come to the two major floodings of 1014 and 1099, which happened 'with great loss of life and livestock' and the even worse disaster of 1099 which says that:

> . . . all the hamlets and villages were swept away with great loss of life, all the cows, horses, swine and fowls were drowned and a great famine swept the land.

Could this be the flood the monks were talking about, and what area was flooded?

There is an old shoreline that runs from Low Lee Buoy to the back of Mousehole Island in a southerly direction before heading towards the Lizard for about 3 miles, then it runs parallel to the shore as far as Lamorna. It then heads once more towards the Lizard for several miles before curving in towards Mullion. This old shoreline varies in height from a few feet to 10 fathom (60 foot) and is well known to all the local fishermen who regularly work nets and pots along its outer edges. The highest and roughest parts all have names, 'The Drop Off,' 'Shannock,' 'The Hump,' etc., and this outer edge is very easy to follow with todays modern echo sounders and nearly always yields a good catch of fish because the seaward side consists of mud or sand.

The outer edge of the old shoreline to the north-eastern edge of the land varies between 3 and 8 miles and it is about 15 miles long. This large area of low-lying fertile ground was where the hamlets and villages were situated and where they grew crops and kept their livestock, it was basically the bread basket of West Cornwall. Very little cultivation took place on the hills surrounding the bay, it is easier to farm a low-lying fertile flat area than cultivate a stony hillside. Mousehole was not connected to this land because a small tidal river flowed from Gwavas Lake past Mousehole and into the open sea, the village never had a great farming tradition, they were all seamen or fishermen.

As the water depth increased the natural barriers holding it back would have more strain put on it and when this reached a critical point in 1099 it would only have taken a heavy storm or perhaps a tidal surge or wave to breach the sand or shingle bank. The surge of inrushing sea water would be so fast and great that 'no man could outrun it' as the Royal Geological Society of Cornwall explained earlier. A piece of land up to 8 miles wide by 15 miles long was inundated within a few hours and as the records show 'all the hamlets and villages were swept away with great loss of life, cows, horses, swine and fowls were drowned and a great famine swept the land.'

112

Another report states 'that no man could outrun the flood and even men on horseback were engulfed.' We have to thank William Worcester who visited St Michaels Mount and whose scribes wrote down what the monks related to them in 1478. It must also be remembered that during the last ice age sea levels were estimated to be some 200 metres lower than present day levels, which would place the shoreline approximately 100 to 200 miles further out, Cornwall Geographical Society core samples indicate trees once grew that far from present day shorelines.

Taking into account the large area of land that had been engulfed in 1099 by the sudden inrush of sea water then this would also have another equally devastating effect. All the earth inside this area would be churned up and held in suspension by the movement of tide and waves turning the waters tens of miles offshore into a virtual mudbath. This mudbath would have two effects on the fish life. Those bottom living creatures would all die from suffocation caused by suspended mud, those fast enough to swim away would stay away, otherwise the same fate awaited those that returned. Each successive tide would gouge out new earth and so renew the suspension problem for a considerable time, probably for several weeks.

For those that survived this disastrous flood there would then be the added burden of suddenly losing 99% of their food supply, in other words a famine, 'and a great famine swept the land.'

Perhaps this was the disaster the monks were talking about in 1478 when they said 'there were both woods and meadows and ploughland between the said Mount and Scilly Islands and 140 parish churches were drowned.'

Crops and livestock take time to grow or obtain but the sea would yield food if clear clean water could be found. It would probably be several weeks before this happened and fishermen could help alleviate some of the hunger and suffering. For those left alive food in large enough quantities to stop them dying would have to come from the sea, there was no other place it could come from, and if the date in the legend is correct this flood must have happened in the fall of the year, probably late October early November, just after harvest time.

Maybe in 1099 there was a fisherman in Mousehole who found clear water and caught enough fish just before Christmas to save the village from starving. Perhaps this is where the legend originated and after 1,000 years of retelling has been handed down to the present generation. But during all that time what has been added, and more importantly, was has been omitted? Whatever, the legend of Tom Bocock is now a permanent fixture in Mousehole's history.

1099 is the only date I have come across that brings all the necessary ingredients together to form a major famine, and for any community to starve it would have to be a very large disaster otherwise food could be brought in by horse and cart from the surrounding countryside.

I have found no documented proof which indicates that Tom Bocock's Eve was a festive occasion or in fact even celebrated although this is quite understandable because even in the 1950's early 60's it was a very low-key affair celebrated mainly by fishermen. An old fisherman named Jack Wallis used to wear a bowler hat, throw a bit of pilchard net over his shoulders, kiss all the ladies and get very drunk. That was Tom Bocock's Eve, true we all used to sing the song but there was no Starry Gazey Pie. The first modern Starry Gazey Pie was made by Rose Tregenza in the early 1960's, the pilchard heads sticking out of the pie are to let the steam out. Then in the late 1960's the landlord of the Ship Inn invited the local radio station and the following year the television. That was the start of the end for our local celebration. Within five years very few Mousehole people bothered to go out in the evening because of the massive crowds. Those that did tended to steer clear of the 'Ship.' The rest, as they say, is history.

Bocock is not a very common name and never was going by my research. In the 1998 telephone directory there are only three Bococks listed for the whole of Cornwall and Devon and only one Bowcock. Bacock and Bawcocks are not even listed. Badcock on the other hand is a very common name in Cornwall and this name was well represented in Mousehole until the early 1900's. Badcock's have been living in the village as far back as it is possible to trace people's names so it is just possible that our fisherman was named Tom Badcock and that over countless retellings has gradually been altered by mispronunciation to Bocock. The very old Cornish language did have the habit of dropping letters on some words, probably to do with how it was pronounced, and inserting an apostrophe. So Badcock could be written as Ba'cock, then the apostrophe would gradually be dropped and so Bacock and depending on how you say this name to Bocock. There is no proof that this happened but it is a fact that I have come across countless times that when a letter was dropped an apostrophe was inserted, and over a period of time the apostrophe was done away with and not used. Some of the reports in books relating to local customs spell the name in three different ways, Bawcock, Bacock, Bowcock and Bocock but the generally accepted version is Bocock. As can be seen from the above, even Tom's surname is not entirely clear let alone the complete legend, but the reader must remember that all legends are based on truth, regardless of how much they get embellished.

Mousehole Foundry

THERE ARE NUMEROUS references to a foundry in Mousehole during the early 1800's but the actual location is unknown. From the reports it would appear to have been somewhere in the bottom south-western end of the village but actual records for its location have not been found. Builders and fishermen also mention using the foundry. In all probability it was a small foundry although by pure chance I have located a very large blacksmith's anvil that was made in Mousehole along with all the old blacksmith's tools.

A Mr Michael Selby who lives at 'The Forge' in Fenny Drayton, Nuneaton, called in to see me regarding the location of the foundry in Mousehole, I was unable to help him. He then explained that he had a large anvil that belonged to his grandfather and possibly his great-grandfather that was made in Mousehole. He can remember his father using the anvil and old tools but neither of them knew how old it was, his father told him that his grandfather used it as he was also a blacksmith and that it came from Cornwall. The gentleman who came to see me was unsure who brought it up from Cornwall, but it was made in Mousehole. The only inscription left on the old anvil is a hole with a mouse's head sticking out, the actual lettering had long since been beaten flat. When he spoke to me I suggested that he get in touch with Flambards at Helston who would be delighted to have the anvil and tools that were made in Mousehole. He is seriously considering this as he is not a blacksmith, his talents are working with clay in pottery and sculptures, his father was the last blacksmith in the family. This is the second anvil I know of from England and one from America, all of them have a hole with a mouse's head sticking out, none have any lettering left.

Another report I came across regarding foundry work is rather vague and does not say or indicate that it was made in Mousehole, although why such a heavy piece of casting should be hauled through the narrow streets of Mousehole is rather odd. I doubt very much if there was a foundry in Mousehole capable of casting something of this size so in all probability this large heavy casting was made at St Just. If it was it seems rather strange that they should come through Mousehole instead of using the St Just to Penzance road which has less corners and steep hills.

23rd June 1897. On Thursday a heavy piece of casting was drawn by ten fine horses through Mousehole for the Penlee Stone Quarry. Three additional horses were attached to pull it up the steep hill at the entrance of the quarry. The casting weighed several tons and is to replace the crusher bed which some weeks ago broke while at work.

On 28th July 1887 Mr W.P. Harvey, boot and shoemaker of North Cliff (where the large gift shop on the corner is) was appointed the first agent in Mousehole to sell the *Cornishman* newspaper. They cost 1d each.

An interesting report from 1790 that I came across is once again lacking in detail so all I can do is copy the small paragraph that was printed.

In 1790 a company was formed for the extensive manufacture of salt. Ponderous machinery and pans of every description were provided, but those who fixed the plant were greatly disappointed to find that the salt water was not strong enough without rock salt, which made it unprofitable. The venture and works were closed down in 1796.

The name 'Salt Ponds' still exists in Mousehole to this day and is an area in the south-western part of the village.

Salt extraction from sea water is possible but the only areas of the world where it is profitable are in the tropics where they have access to large areas of flat ground that can be flooded from the sea and then closed off. These evaporation tanks are as large as a football pitch and only flooded to a depth of 3 to 4 inches(10 centimetres), the sun does the rest. In the Middle East these tanks were quite often flooded twice and sometimes three times a day. The dried salt would then be hand brushed into large heaps and shovelled onto the bank to finish drying, where it was left until needed.

During all my research on Mousehole there was very little on the agriculture side of the village. There must obviously have been agriculture and farms but for some reason it appears to have been overlooked regarding the actual reporting of the day. There are a few scattered reports regarding farming around Mousehole but invariably it was included with general farming news. Such as 'Mousehole is reporting a fair crop of broccoli, or spring greens etc' and that was all. Although on 19th April 1900 there is one report that states 'some 300,000 to 400,000 daffodil blooms were sent away by train today for the market in London, prices fair to good.'

One report that appeared with terrible regularity and must have been devastating for the farmers was the yearly caterpillar plague. They do not mention which type of butterfly was responsible but in all probability it was the Cabbage White. There is mention of boys being employed to 'pick off the caterpillars' but they do not mention what the boys did with these pests. Obviously they would be killed but whether it was by squashing between their fingers or under their feet the reports failed to tell us. The devastation must have been on a large scale as a few of the following extracts indicate.

> August 1873. Mousehole is again plagued with caterpillars and all the ground is bare with hardly any green to show.

> The only green to show is that of plants the caterpillars do not like.

> September 15th 1898. The caterpillar plague in Mousehole has at last started to lessen. These pests have devoured everything that came in their way. The hearts of the green crops have all been eaten out and gardens are bare and woe begone.

We have all seen what these caterpillars can do on a small scale and the mess they leave behind but these reports indicate that it was very widespread and on a massive scale. Even with boys picking them off it was probably a losing battle.

I came across this report, which has nothing to do with Mousehole, but thought it worth including because it could very well be the first recorded incident of anyone rowing across the Atlantic, assuming the report is correct.

> 6th August 1896. On Saturday August 1st the inhabitants of St Mary's, on the Scillies, were greatly surprised by the arrival at 10.00 of a small boat rowed by two men and flying the Stars and Stripes. The surprise was intensified when it was found this boat was the *Fox*, a 16 foot clinker built boat containing no mast, sail or rudder, and that she had been rowed from New York to Scilly.

I have not bothered to do any research on this as it has nothing to do with the history of Mousehole, just interesting.

Dolly Pentreath

IN THE YEAR 1768, the Honourable Daines Barrington, the brother of Admiral Samuel Barrington, travelled around Cornwall to ascertain whether the Cornish language had become extinct.

After his extended tour of Cornwall he wrote to John Lloyd Esquire, Fellow of the Society of Antiquaries on 31st March 1773 giving the results of his journey, which referred to Dolly Pentreath.

I (Daines Barrington) set out from Penzance with the landlord of the principle inn as a guide, towards Sennen, or the most westerly point, and when I approached the village, I said that there must probably be some remains of the language in those parts, if anywhere, as the village was in the road to no place whatever, and the only alehouse announced itself to be the last in England. My guide however told me that I should be disappointed, but that if I would ride about ten miles about in my return to Penzance, he would conduct me to a village called Mousehole, on the western side of Mounts Bay, where there was an old woman called Dolly Pentreath who could speak Cornish fluently. While we were travelling towards Mousehole, I inquired how he knew that this woman spoke Cornish. When he informed me that he frequently went from Penzance to Mousehole to buy fish, which were sold by her, and that when he did not offer her a price that was satisfactory, she grumbled to some other woman in an unknown tongue, which he concluded therefore to be Cornish.

When we reached Mousehole, I desired to be introduced as a person who had laid a wager that there was not one who could converse in Cornish, upon which Dolly Pentreath spoke in an angry tone for two or three minutes, and in a language which sounded very like Welsh. The hut in which she lived was in a very narrow lane, opposite to two rather better houses, at the doors of which two other women stood, who were advanced in years, and who I observed were laughing at what Dolly said to me. Upon this I asked them whether she had not been abusing me, to which they answered, 'Very heartily, and because I had supposed she could not speak Cornish.' I then said that they must be able to talk the language, to which they answered, that they could not speak it readily, but that they understood it, being only ten or twelve years younger than Dolly Pentreath. I continued nine or ten days in Cornwall after this, but found that my friends whom I had left to the eastward, continued as incredulous almost as they were before, about the last remains of the Cornish language, because, among other reasons, Dr Borlase had supposed in his natural history of the county, that it had entirely ceased to be spoken. It was also urged, that as he lived within four or five miles of the old woman at Mousehole, he consequently must have heard of so singular a thing as her continuing to use the vernacular tongue.

I had scarcely said or thought anything more about this matter, till last summer, having mentioned it to some Cornish people, I found that they could not credit that any person had existed within these few years, who could speak their native language, and therefore, though I imagined there was but a small chance of Dolly Pentreath continuing to live, yet I wrote to the president then in Devonshire, to desire that he would make some inquiry with regard to her, and he was so obliging as to procure me information from a gentleman whose house was within three miles of Mousehole, a considerable part of whose letter I shall subjoin.

'1772. Dolly Pentreath is short of stature, and bends very much with old age, being in her eighty-seventh year, so lusty however as to walk hither, to Castle Horneck, about three miles, in bad weather, in the morning and back again. She is somewhat deaf, but her intellects seemingly not impaired, has a memory so good, that she remembers perfectly well, that about four or five years ago, at Mousehole, where she lives, she was sent for by a gentleman, who being a stranger, had a curiosity to hear the Cornish language, which she was famed for retaining and speaking fluently, and that the innkeeper where the gentleman came from, attended him. *(This gentleman was myself, however I did not presume to send for her, but waited upon her.)* She does indeed talk Cornish as readily as others do English, being bred up from a child to know no other language, nor could she *(if we may believe her)* talk a word of English before she was past twenty years of age, as, her father being a fisherman, she was sent with fish to Penzance at twelve years old, and sold them in the Cornish language, which the inhabitants in general, even the gentry, did then well understand. She is positive however, that there is neither in Mousehole, nor in any other part of the country, any other person who knows anything of it, or at least can converse in it. She is poor, and maintained partly by the parish, and partly by fortune-telling and gabbling Cornish.'

(It is a great pity that Daines Barrington omitted to give the writer's name and address)

I have thus thought it right to lay before the Society this account of the last sparks of the Cornish tongue, and cannot but think that a liguist, who understands Welsh, might still pick up a more complete vocabulary of the Cornish than any we are yet possessed of, especially as the two neighbours of this old woman, whom I have had occasion to mention, and not now above seventy-seven or seventy-eight years of age, and were healthy when I saw them, so that the whole does not depend upon the life of this Cornish sybil, as she is willing to insinuate. If it is said that I have stated that these neighbours could not speak the language, this should be understood that they cannot so readily converse in it as she does, because I have mentioned that they comprehend her abuse upon me, which implies a certain knowledge of the Cornish tongue.

Daines Barrington.

The rest of Daines Barrington's letter concerns other parts and languages in England and does not mention Dolly Pentreath again.

Dolly Pentreath lived for another 15 years after the Daines Barrington letter and died in December 1778 at the age of 102. She was buried in the churchyard at Paul and her epitaph is written in both Cornish and English.

Coth Doll Pentreath cans ha Deau
Marow ha kledyz ed Paul plea
Na ed an Egloz, gan pobel bras
Bes ed Egloz-ha coth Dolly es.

Old Doll Pentreath, one hundred ag'd and two
Deceas'd and buried in Paul Parish too
Not in the church, with people great and high
But in the churchyard doth old Dolly lie.

The above epitaphs were written by a Mr Tomson who lived in Truro and was an engineer by trade.

In July 1776 Mr Daines Barrington presented to the Society of Antiquaries a letter written in both English and Cornish by a William Bodener, (Bodinner), a fisherman of Mousehole. He asserted there were still four or five people in Mousehole who could speak Cornish. In 1777 Mr Barrington found another man named John Nancarrow, 45, from Marazion who could converse in Cornish.

From the foregoing it is clear that the Cornish language did not die with Dolly Pentreath but lingered on, gradually becoming more and more forgotten.

The last stronghold for the spoken Cornish language was Mousehole and a Dr Bryce indicated that it was still known and spoken in this village until the 1800's.

The survival of the Cornish language owes a great debt to the Society of Antiquaries, Mr Daines Barrington who spent so many years pursuing, tracking and recording the last speakers and off course to Mousehole where the mother tongue was spoken until the last.

121

In *Lake's Parochial History of the County of Cornwall* it states that the Parish records of Paul contain the following entry. 'Dorothy Jeffery was buried December 27th 1777.'

On the monument in the church wall placed there in 1860 by Prince Louis Lucian Bonaparte and the Reverend John Garrett, vicar of Paul, it says. 'Here lieth interred Dolly Pentreath who died in 1778.' Clearly these two dates do not match.

Lakes history also says:

Jeffery, Dorothy (generally known by her maiden name of Dolly Pentreath, daughter of Nicholas Pentreath) baptised at Paul 17th May 1714, died Mousehole December 1777, buried Paul 27th December.

All the accounts state she was 102 years old when she died, if that is correct then Dolly Pentreath was baptised when she was 39 years old.

To add more confusion Polwheles *The History of Cornwall* clearly states that 'her maiden name was Jeffery.' If this is correct then she married a man named Pentreath and so was naturally called this during the rest of her life. It also states that Dolly never had any children.

Regardless of whether her maiden name or married name was Jeffery she will always be known and remembered as Dolly Pentreath.

Another Cornish historian named Mr Hitchens who died in Marazion on 1st April 1814 must surely have known Dolly Pentreath before she died and being such a fine historian would hardly have the dates wrong. He says that Dolly Pentreath died on 26th December 1777 and was buried in January 1778.

This appears to be born out by a letter from a Mr Bernard Victor of Wellington Place, Mousehole. He not only gives the date of her death but also details on the exact position of her grave. An extract from his letter is below.

The house in which the ancient dame lived, at the time she followed the occupation of a fish seller, is still to be seen at Mousehole, and at present is occupied by two fishermen as a net loft.

She died on the 26th December 1777 at the age of 102. The undertaker was George Badcock, my grandfather, that is the reason I am so well informed, and there were 8 chosen fishermen bearers to take her to her last resting place.

There was not anything erected on the old lady's grave as a tablet to her memory. I know quite well the grave where her remains are deposited.

This letter was sent to a Dr Jago, 21 Lockyer St, Plymouth.

In May 1882 Dr W.T.A. Pattison and Bernard Victor visited Dolly Pentreath's grave so that the exact position could be recorded.

Extract from a letter written by Bernard Victor to Dr Jago on the 16th May 1882.

Dear Sir,

I beg to inform you that I have visited the graveyard of Dolly Pentreath this day at noon, and I will give you the correct distance and compass bearing of the grave to the monument that was erected by Prince L.L. Bonaparte. Also the distance from the chancel door of the church and compass bearing. I took a mariners compass and a rule to measure with so that it should be correct.

1st. The head of the grave from the monument erected by L.L. Bonaparte is south-east, a point easterly, distance 47 feet.

2nd. The head of the grave from the chancel door is south, a point westerly, distance 52 feet.

I have sent you a plan of the church, also the grave and the present monument, so there can be no mistake.

The grave is quite close to the front wall of the churchyard, as you will see I have placed it in the plan of the graveyard.

Dr Jago wrote back asking how such a mistake could have been made and that 'the public require proof and how was such a mistake made about the exact place of Dolly's grave.'

Bernard Victor wrote a very long letter to Dr Jago on 22nd May 1882, some of which is below.

I will give you an opinion of where Prince L.L. Bonaparte got the information from to erect the monument. I never saw L.L. Bonaparte, if I had the monument would have been erected in its right place.

There was a William Bodiner, a fisherman of this place, who wrote a letter in the Cornish language on 3rd July 1776. So when L.L. Bonaparte came to Mousehole he came to the descendants of the before mentioned William Bodiner. I am not prepared to inform you whether they gave him any information as to the present erection of the monument, but the information I gave you is from my grandfather, who was the undertaker at her funeral.

If you were in Mousehole at this present time you could see an old fisherman named Stephen Blewett who could give you the same information about the grave which I gave you. What he and the others know about Dolly is handed down from sire to son.

I remember my grandfather quite well, he died with us, and I was 15 years old when he died.

I gave you the plan of the churchyard wall, and you see there are two gates in the long south churchyard wall. The monument is placed in the position below the upper gate, but it should have been placed below the lower gate, so there was the mistake by the person who gave the information to the Prince.

123

This I can further say, that there was no person who could satisfy visitors who came to make enquiries about the grave before they came to me. There was always a doubt by the folks that the monument of 1860 was not in its right place.

Who knew better about Dolly Pentreath's grave than my grandfather who made the coffin and superintended the funeral.

It is not to be said that the monument is in its right place because it was put there by the order of Prince L.L. Bonaparte, or by the Rev John Garrett, the one a Frenchman and the other an Irishman.

I remain yours faithfully
Bernard Victor

On 17th August 1887 the memorial was removed and placed where it stands today. Bernard Victor was present and it was placed where he said. They did unearth the bones of a single body and the coffin was consistant with what Bernard Victor had said his grandfather had made. When the monument was moved the date of her death, 1777, was corrected.

There seems no doubt that an epitaph in ancient Cornish and a translation into English was written around 1778, as referred to by Drew, Hitchens, Polwhele and others, but there is no evidence to prove that such an epitaph was ever inscribed on stone or placed upon her grave at or after the time of her death.

Yet there are tantalising memories that suggest there was a tombstone, as reported by Mr Trewavas of Mousehole in 1881 when he was 88 years old.

He does not remember anything on her tombstone himself but he has heard that the first or old inscription on the tombstone was.

Here lieth old Dolly Pentreath
who lived one hundred year and two
was born and buried in Paul Parish too
not in the church amongst people great and high
but in the churchyard doth old Dolly lie.

Poets & Artists

THERE ARE MENTIONS of artists and sightseers going back to the 1600's in Mousehole but unfortunately the records fail to mention any artists by name. One of the earliest references regarding this was from the late 1400's 'when the yearly fair came around with lots of painters and promenaders.' It is not until the 1800's that reporters decided that such trivia as artists were worthy of naming, and even then the reports are rather brief to say the least.

Songs, poems and sayings relating to fishing and mining were nearly always recorded by the old scribes, that was easy enough but in relation to the old songs they failed dismally to record the music. It must be assumed that these very early reporters did not have the knowledge or ability to write down music. Most of these very old songs etc that remain today owe their existence to the amateur historians, those learned gentlemen with plenty of money whose hobby was researching ancient Cornwall, they usually made their enquiries about one specific subject. A few actually had some of their work published but the biggest majority was just written down in longhand in large ledgers. Some of these very early writings are now lodged in the County Records Office in Truro but in all probability the majority are either lost or residing in some attic.

One such researcher was a Mr John Boson of Newlyn who died in the 1700's. Several years after his death the following song, written in longhand, was found amongst his papers in the attic. There was no date and I have copied it down exactly as it was written. It mentions 'Grey rock in the wood,' St Michaels Mount surrounded by trees, also boats going out to Gwavas Lake, presumably when this was written trees still surrounded St Michaels Mount.

> I will sing of the Pilchard, by boat and net
> Taken in ye bay of the Grey Rock in the Wood
> The boats are come home
> From the sea, the Man of the Port, Tyth, Tyth cries
> And every woman comes near her Husband
> With her Kawal and 300 pilchards on her back
> To make Bulks in every House
> With their mouths, 'Much Pilchards, Pilchards, more Salt'

When they are well salted for about a Month
Ready to break them up the Porter
Afterwards He makes them clean in salt water
And will give them a good name to all the Maids
That put them shining in the Barrel, the Head Man
And He reward every good thing, come the Handsome Merchants
Look you for a Tree 13 foot long
Put upon it Stones 5 Hundredweight
3 times in a Day look you to it
For in the middle of ye Month from it Oil will fall
This is the True way Pilchards to prepare
In the best Markets they will sell
Year after Year let the Ships come
And with Pilchards full go out to Gwavas Lake
From the Shore let the North East wind blow them far
For the People of hot Countries to eat em all
As is the plenty of Pilchards on all ye Coast
The more the People are impoverished, or enriched.

'Grey rock in the wood' – St Michael's Mount.
'Kawal' – basket for carrying fish, usually strapped to the back.
'Bulks' – laying of pilchards in cellars for salting.
'Markets' – Mediterranean countries.
'Gwavas Lake' – between Newlyn harbour and St Michael's Mount.

There are of course a lot more sayings, poems and songs relating to the fishing industry but the one above appears to be the oldest.

Anyway back to the artists. Remembering the earlier chapters when it was mentioned you could buy a cottage for £30 and how much various items cost the following few extracts relating to the price of paintings is rather special and worth recounting.

> 19th March 1885. A fine painting by Walter Langley 'News of the Missing,' a Newlyn subject which took well at the Royal Academy last year, was purchased by a lady lover of fine arts for £250.

In July 1897 Walter Langley married Miss Pengelly from Tolver Road in Penzance.

The following report does not mention any price but the purchasers name is very familiar with art lovers, namely the Tate Gallery.

9th May 1889. Mr Henry Tate is the fortunate purchaser of Stanhope Forbes' splendid 'Cornish Wedding'.

Perhaps this extract will give some idea how much Mr Henry Tate paid.

14th April 1892. Stanhope Forbes' painting 'The Village Forge' was sold to a Mr Tullock, an Australian merchant, for £1,000.

A truly amazing amount of money for this period of time, Mousehole's rateable value was only £900, but even this amount was surpassed with his next painting.

21st May 1896. Mr Stanhope Forbes's painting 'The New Calf,' one of the most attractive exhibits at this year's Royal Academy, was sold to Mr Daniel Delins of Yorkshire for 1,000 guineas, it was painted in Newlyn.

During the 1800's there was a large contingent of artists living in Mousehole, there are plenty of references to this, but trying to find out their names is virtually impossible. There were probably a lot of unknown artists at that time who became famous later in their life, it was in the 1800's that the Newlyn School of Artists started and Mousehole was always a favourite place and subject as this report shows.

August 17th 1893. Mousehole is becoming very popular with visitors, and artists are taking up abode in this clean if old fashioned village, and those fortunate to have apartments to let have no difficulty in finding occupants.

Mousehole is still a very popular haunt of artists and it also has a very strong contingent of resident artists, some of whom are renowned worldwide.

There used to be a short cut between Duck Street and Commercial Road that was regularly used by the local people. It ran between two cottages, over the top of the alley was one of the cottages bedrooms, this made a covered area. After that it went past the back of my cottage, over some steps, through another garden and into Commercial Road. About 1965 or so Arnold and Rodney Gartrell had the job of blocking off this covered alley and incorporating it into the cottage. Rodney called me around to look at the paintings covering the walls. They were all of Mousehole fishing boats and painted by such well known artists as Harold Harvey, Stanhope Forbes and his wife, plus other artists. I always regret not taking photographs before they were plastered over or knocked down.

Joseph Trewavas VC

ON 1st JULY 1897 a letter to the *Cornishman* newspaper was published, some of which is below.

Right glad am I to find, at last, steps are being taken to duly recognise the services rendered to his country by Joseph Trewavas, Victoria Cross, hero of Mousehole. Mr Trewavas is known amongst his townsfolk and fishermen as 'Joe' and a more upright, high principled and fearless character it would be hard to find. Unobstencious, intelligent, good natured and good looking, Joe might well come in for a popular ovation.

As a boy I have heard him tell, in the foredeck of his fishing boat, the story of the deed which at length seems destined to bring him some consideration. He told it modestly, regarding it as a simple act brought about merely in the execution of his duty.

A week later on the 8th July the following report was printed.

THE PRINCE AND THE GALLANT CORNISHMAN TREWAVAS

A garden fete in aid of the Soldiers and Sailors families association was held on Monday afternoon at Chelsea Barracks and attracted a large and fashionable assemblage.

At 4.30 the Prince of Wales arrived accompanied by the Princess of Wales, Princess Victoria, the Duke and Duchess of York, Prince and Princess Charles of Denmark, Princess Lonise, and the Marquis of Lorne, the Duke of Cambridge, the Duke and Duchess of Saxe-Coburg, the Grand Duke of Hesse, Prince Edward of Saxe-Weimar, the Duke and Duchess of Teck, and the ladies and gentlemen in attendance on various royal personages. Their Royal Highnesses inspected 400 representative veterans from various parts of the country who had participated in naval or military engagements during the Queen's reign. Many wore quite a collection of medals and clasps, some the Victoria Cross, and a few the Ribbon of the French Legion of Honour. The Prince addressed every individual, shook hands with many, and had a long chat with some. Particular interest attached to Joseph Trewavas, the gallant Cornishman wearing the Victoria Cross and numerous medals, to whom the Prince announced that £130 had been collected to purchase him a small annuity.

The Prince also spoke approvingly of the medals, whereupon the veteran remarked that he would not surrender them for any amount of money. The royal party subsequently saw the veterans at tea, and Jubilee pipes and tobacco were distributed.

In July 1897 Joseph Trewavas was interviewed by the *Western Daily Mercury* newspaper and the story he told them is as follows.

When scarcely eighteen years old I joined the navy and served on board the *Agememnon* (he later called his fishing boat by the same name, she was a 1st class lugger, PZ17, of 42 ft and 16½ tons) during the Crimean War, being in her on October 17th at the bombardment of Sebastopol. A week later I landed on the Crimea with the naval brigade and did duty on shore until February 1st 1855.

I was in the battery during the Battle of Inkerman and we were under arms prepared to defend our camp if the necessity arose at the time of the charge of the Light Brigade. We experienced terrible weather. Snow lay feet deep on the ground and we wanted food and clothing. We were obliged to take boots from the Russian dead, our clothes were so patched that you could not tell what part remained of the old garments and raids had to be organised to secure food. On one occasion I went to assist at the removal of a number of wounded to Balaclava and we had fifty funerals on the journey, burying the men in the deep snow by the roadsides.

Well, we came aboard again on February 1st and remained there until May 24th when I was lent to the *Beagle* gunboat under the command of Lieutenant Hewett. We went to the Sea of Azoff under the command of Captain Lyons of the *Meranda*, son of the Admiral (Sir E. Lyons) who had orders to burn, sink and destroy everything hands could be put on, with the object of weakening the enemy. In the first forty-eight hours we destroyed 247 sail (ships), so there were plenty of bonfires I can tell you.

There was a military pontoon bridge across the Genitchi Strait connecting Genitchi with the Arabat Spit, and across this the enemy marched troops and conveyed stores as it shortened the distance by 21 miles, a great consideration at that time. Inside this (in the Sivash or Putrid Sea) there were a lot of merchant ships that had gone out of our way, and as the water was very shallow they were perfectly secure. Lieutenant Hewett had orders to destroy that bridge at all costs, and this he tried to do without loss of life. He landed forces to reach it by night marches but the enemy prevented that. Next he endeavoured to send men in boats by night to take the enemy by surprise and cut the bridge adrift. But the Russians were too wide awake to our movements. We went in one night but they began to fire and we were forced to retire. Next day however, the thing had to be done, no matter at what cost. To reach the bridge we had to go around a stretch of low lying land, and thus got out of cover of our vessel. So we were provided with a paddle box boat with one gun to cover us to the bridge. When we had the paddle box boat moored in a position we could see Russian soldiers marching about on shore and our gunner fired to where they were. In the very first round the gun drew her bolts and was thus rendered useless. That left we six men with a four oared boat, one rifle, ten rounds of ammunition, and a cutlass apiece to face the two hundred or more soldiers who were on shore behind the heaps of coal. The gunner who was in charge said 'the gun is dismounted but my orders from the Captain are to destroy the bridge, let the consequences be what they will. Now lads, we may as well go in there and be shot as go back to the ship and have a four brace block for an awning.' So we went in. As we paddled we got out of sight of the ship. On a little mound we could see a Russian motioning the soldiers on shore to keep down, and our man in the bow with a loaded rifle wanted to have a go at him, but the gunner gave him orders not to do so. I was pulling the bow oar, and when we were near the floating bridge the gunner told me to get on the bridge, cut the hawser, jump back in the boat again and shove off. I was not as long doing that as it takes to tell. In less than ten seconds I had cut the hawser and was back in the boat again. During this time the Russians, who were only eighty yards off had not fired a shot. But when they saw the boat two hundred rifles were pointed at us, and the men shook their fists as much as to say 'if you don't come back we will fire.' Our man in the bow could not stand that so he let drive, and to this day he will tell you that he shot his man. Then the Russians let fly. For some time we could not get much away from them as the water was shallow and we had to keep on their side as we went towards our ship. The shot came amongst us like hailstones. We gradually increased the distance between us, and at last, when we came within cover of the ship and those on board had no cause to fear killing us, they put shots amongst the Russians and silenced them. Three of those in the boat were wounded, and the boat was riddled and full of water when we reached the vessel.

On getting aboard the gunner told the Captain we had destroyed the bridge and that I had cut the hawsers. That was reported to the Admiral, and I never expected to hear more about it, but a short time after I received this medal for 'conspicuous gallantry' and £5, and when the Victoria Cross was instituted I was recommended and received that from Her Majesty, which carries with it £10 a year.

I always thought the others in the boat ought to receive something, but they never did. The gunner was promoted. As we were then the allies of the French I received the star of the Legion of Honour, which is thought as much of in France as the Victoria Cross is in England. I also have a Crimean medal with three clasps (Azoff, Sebastopol and Inkerman) and a Turkish Crimean medal. That finished the Crimean experience. For a long time we wondered why the Russians did not shoot us when we were near the pontoon bridge at Genitchi, as they could easily have done, but later it was explained to one of our officers by a Russian officer that they had no idea we were going to destroy the bridge, and, believing we were coming to destroy the shipping, they were ready to take prisoners.

On 27th July 1905 a report was published in the *Cornishman* newspaper on the inquest into the death of Joseph Trewavas, which was held at

Mousehole Wesleyan schoolroom on Friday afternoon by Mr Edward Boase, County Coroner. Mr Bruce Wright was the foreman of the jury.

The Coroner in his opening address said they had met there to inquire into the circumstances attending the death of Mr Joseph Trewavas. It appeared that Mr Trewavas was taken with a seizure about three months ago and since that time been more or less under medical care. On Tuesday Mr Trewavas was found under circumstances which would be detailed in evidence, with a wound to his throat which was apparently self inflicted. The question the jury would have to consider was what state of mind was the deceased in when he committed the act. He knew Mr Trewavas and the jury knew as well as he that he was always a bright, cheerful and sanguine man, and the last man one would have expected to have committed an act of this kind if he were in his normal state of mind, as they knew Mr Trewavas was a man who had served his country in days past, he had served it with great distinction and had earned the most coveted honour in the land, the Victoria Cross. He was sure they would all join with him in expressing their sympathy to the bereaved friends in such a sad termination to a career which had been certainly very gallant and conspicuous.

Miss Sarah Trewavas, daughter of deceased, said she lived with her father at Dumbarton House. He was 69 years of age and many years ago he was in the Navy when he won the VC. He retired from the Navy some years ago and for some time had followed the occupation of a fisherman. He retired from fishing about ten years ago. Witness had lived alone with her father latterly, in fact for eight years. Deceased was usually of a bright happy disposition. About three months ago he was taken with a seizure and since that time has been attended by Dr Fox. He had never 'been himself' since he had the seizure, though he seemed to be physically strong. On 18th instance witness saw her father in his room and he said he would come down stairs for breakfast. He seemed to be fairly well. That was about 8 o'clock. There was a girl named Ethel Wright who helped witness in the domestic duties. At the breakfast table he appeared to be rather quiet, and he said to witness, you can talk as much as you like. He talked in a most unusual manner. He made a good breakfast and after the meal went upstairs. Shortly after she followed him and said, come down stairs father into the sitting room. The reason why she wanted to bring him downstairs was because she liked to look at him. About ten o'clock he came to her and said, where are my keys. Witness replied, I do not know, you have never lost them have you. Deceased replied, you do. She went with her father to try and find the keys upstairs but was not successful. Shortly after he put his hands on his head and said, what shall I do. She said that she would go and look for them. When she went upstairs she left a small cheese knife on a round table in the kitchen, but when she came down she did not notice it was missing. Deceased walked out of the kitchen, but she did not see him take the knife. He went into the sitting room and locked the door. A little time after she went and looked through the keyhole and found he was not sitting in his usual chair. She shouted, father what are you doing, but she received no reply. She asked him if he would open the door several times and there was no response. She sent the girl away for her uncle, and while she was away witness heard peculiar sounds. Her uncle came back and burst open the door and gave an awful cry when he saw what had occurred. She noticed that her father was rather childish since he had been ill. He had often said, I wish I was dead, I am no good in this world. But he never mentioned that he would put an end to himself. He died on Thursday morning. There were four attendants watching to him after he was found in the sitting room. In reply to questions from the coroner witness said her father underwent an operation for a growth on his lip but it did not seem to affect him in the least.

Henry Trewavas, brother of deceased, said he was on intimate terms with his brother. Witness had noticed a mental difference in his brother since the seizure. He talked incoherently. He was sent for on the morning of the 18th about 11.30 or 11.40. He burst open the door of the sitting room and saw his brother crouching in a pool of blood. Witness cried, my God what have you done. He was in a crouching position, his right hand, which held the knife, being near his throat. Witness came out and ran for assistance. He afterwards met his wife who went into the room and took away the knife. A young man named J.S. Tregenza sent for medical assistance.

Mrs Trewavas, wife of previous witness, said she had never heard deceased say he would take his own life. She took away the knife from him and threw it into the passage. After her husband had fetched assistance he went off in a faint. The knife used was a small cheese knife with a white bone handle.

Dr Fox said he had known deceased for many years and until he was laid aside with seizure he appeared to be a bright and cheerful man. It was on the 23rd April that the deceased was first taken ill and witness had attended him since that date. At times Mr Trewavas was depressed but he never heard him threaten to do anything out of the way. Witness arrived at Mousehole at one o'clock on Tuesday afternoon and saw deceased lying on the floor of the sitting room partially attired with his throat cut. He examined the wound and found it was a jagged cut extending across the throat almost from the left ear to the right. The knife had cut the windpipe and it had evidently been sharpened with a stone just before being used. None of the big blood vessels were injured. With the aid of Dr Jago witness sewed the wound, but it was a hopeless case from the first as nothing could be done to save him. The cause of death was haemorrhage and shock, the result of the severance of the windpipe.

By a juror. He had not noticed anything in the condition of Mr Trewavas to cause any alarm. It was only at times that they did not understand what was said.

A juror. Were you notified of the attempt he made to jump out of the window.

Witness. No, that was shortly after he got out of bed. I do not give much credence to the story. I believe the man simply tried to push the window down.

A juror raised the question as to whether Mr Trewavas might have been depressed after the operation on his lip.

Dr Fox replied that the operation for the growth on the lip did not affect the deceased's state of mind in any way. The wound was a very jagged one and it was a determined effort to end his life.

P.C. Wells, stationed at Mousehole, said he was called to the deceased's house about 12 o'clock on Tuesday. He distinctly heard the deceased say, I was mad when I done it. Mr Trewavas asked for some milk just before he died.

The jury, without retiring, returned a verdict of 'Suicide whilst of unsound mind.'

There is a large slate plaque on the outside of the house were he lived and died halfway down Parade Hill on the right-hand side as you enter Mousehole on the Penzance road.

After he left the Navy Joseph Trewavas took over his father's boat called *Monarch* PZ106, a 2nd class lugger of 42ft which he worked until she was wrecked in 1871. In 1872 he bought a 1st class lugger of 42ft and 16½ tons and named her *Agememnon*, PZ17, after the Navy vessel he served aboard during the Crimean War. He worked her, along with his crew, following the shoals of fish around the British Isles until he sold her to Lowestoft in 1898. His other boat was a 2nd class lugger of 22.5ft and 5 tons used for pilchard drifting and crabbing, named *Annie*, PZ200, which was built in Penzance in 1872. He bought her in 1884 and sold her to William Pender in Mousehole during 1900. This was his last boat when he retired from full-time fishing.

Temperance Society & Court Cases

THERE WAS A very strong movement in the country as a whole regarding the evils of alcoholic drink and there were regular meetings in every city, town and village relating to this. It has become clear during my research that certain gentlemen travelled the width and breadth of the country giving lectures on the benefits of 'total abstinence.' They were paid a small sum of money for this but after each lecture a collection was made and these proceeds were also handed to the speaker.

They might not have imbibed in alcohol but one temperance speaker in Somerset during the 1850's was imprisoned for 'fornicating with the wives of some parishioners.' It's a good job that the courts have a more lenient approach to this subject than they apparently did in the 1800's.

Mousehole, like other villages, had a strong temperance society and there are plenty of reports and references to meetings held at various places over the years. One such on February 23rd 1870 says:

> A Mr Lloyd Jones gave a lecture in the United Methodist Free Church on the 'History and experience in relation to total abstinence.' It was a capital lecture and gave great satisfaction. Several people signed the pledge after the lecture.

It must be remembered that most couples had large families. There were no contraceptives in those days, and money was always in short supply for the majority of the population, so temperance societies would and did have a large following.

They also had a considerable amount of power in certain areas of village life as the following report from 4th July 1895 shows.

> A large public meeting was held in the Wesleyan Chapel to discuss the closing of the 'Keigwin Arms.' They all voted to keep the 'Keigwin Arms' closed and not renew the licence. After the meeting several people signed the pledge.

Not everything was done according to the law and on 9th February 1899 'a wilful attempt to burn down the Ship Inn was followed by all the windows being smashed.' Nobody was ever charged with this offence and about three years later the Ship Inn was again attacked and burnt but the fire damage was slight. As before nobody was ever caught or charged.

Both the Keigwin Arms and Ship Inn were used by the coroner when any inquest was held in Mousehole as the following shows.

2nd July 1885.
The body of Fredrick Davey 13, son of a Mousehole stonemason, was discovered lifeless in the water where he had gone to bathe. The inquest was held at the Keigwin Arms before Mr G.P. Grenfell, coroner. The verdict was accidental death due to fits.

Both of these hostelries were used extensively for at least 150 years, and probably a lot longer, until the early 1900's as courthouses for inquests like that above and also to sentence persons who break the law, although in most cases a serious crime was referred to Penzance after the preliminary hearing in Mousehole.

As well as the above both establishments were also used as auction houses several times each year by various auctioneers from Penzance when selling property, fishing boats, nets, cattle etc by public auction. The following account is interesting because it gives the landlords name and also indicates the approximate price of property.

27th March 1884. 3 leasehold dwellings at Dumbarton Terrace for auction at Ben Pearce's Ship Inn. The bad fishing season attributed to only two turning up, Captain William Pentreath and Thomas Kneebone. Only £120 and £140 was offered, the sale was withdrawn.

As can be seen from the foregoing both the Ship Inn and the Keigwin Arms played an important role in village life although the temperance society appeared to have other ideas. Their cause and beliefs would be further strengthened though when reading such reports as the following.

30th October 1884. At Penzance, a Mousehole fisherman, Sampson Roberts, was charged with being drunk and incapable at Street-an-Nowan, Newlyn, on Saturday evening. PC Rowe proved the finding of Roberts perfectly helpless and he could not get anyone to assist him to Mousehole, so he had to bring him to Penzance Police Station. He was perfectly quiet however. Mr Bolitho remarked on fining Roberts 5s plus 2s 6d costs, that it is seldom a Mousehole fisherman is charged with being drunk and hoped it would not occur again.

The following account does not mention anything about being drunk and I could find no other report relating to where, when or if he did appear in court or if he was arrested. In certain sections of the community they would probably assume he was drunk anyway.

1st December 1898. To be arrested if necessary. Edward Maddern, fish hawker, Mousehole. Who was charged at Camborne on Tuesday with furiously driving a horse and cart at Phillack. He did not appear in court. The case has been adjourned from the last court and now a warrant has been issued for his arrest to be used if necessary.

Some very strange things happened in courtrooms up to the early 1900's, one could fill a book on nothing else but old courtroom dramas. Some of them sound quite alien to our modern society but they were once quite a common practice in some courtrooms. One such incident that is well documented and actually happened goes like this.

9th October 1884. A woman named Tamar Humphries was charged before Sherborne magistrates with assaulting an old lady of 83. The defendant, Tamar Humphries, ran a stocking needle through the old lady's hands and arms with a view to drawing blood so that the complainant, the old lady, might not bewitch her daughter.

It would be interesting to know if this old law or act had been repealed. Imagine what the judge would say in a present day modern courtroom if you demanded to draw blood from your accuser to stop being bewitched.

It must be admitted though that even in the 1850's property held more value than human life and during my research I came across plenty of evidence for this. The following has nothing to do with Mousehole or even the west of Cornwall but the bare bones are worth relating to indicate the above statement.

'Man gaoled for three years for killing his wife,' The report said that this man killed his wife when he found she was having an affair with another man. The actual report of the court case took up nearly a quarter page but he only received three years for this offence.

Directly below this report was another court case which only took up part of a paragraph. This gentleman was accused, found guilty and prosecuted for stealing twelve chickens from his neighbour. His sentence was twelve years, one year for each chicken stolen.

The following is a copy of a report from the *Cornishman* newspaper from 18th June 1891. It will undoubtedly upset some people but whether you like it or not it is part and parcel of Mousehole's recent history, and like everything in this book, readily available for those who care to look.

AN UNENVIABLE REPUTATION

Certain Mousehole boats have the unenviable reputation of having passed floating bodies encased in lifebuoys and lifejackets without taking them on board or reporting the fact. It is also alleged that bodies were robbed by Mousehole and Scillonian fishermen and thrown back into the water.

A condensed eyewitness account by a young Stephen Jeffery who was aboard the fishing boat *Gratitude*. Master was William Humphreys, crew were John Benjamin Trewavas, Stephen Downing, John James and John George.

About five weeks ago we anchored off a little island outside Annet in the Scillies. We had run out of firewood so the Captain, Trewavas, Downing and myself put out the punt and landed. Stephen Downing called out he had found a man's body. It was between two rocks, brown barragan trousers, sea boots and a flannel rolled up around his neck. Trewavas slit down one of the pockets but found nothing. At the other end of the island they found a canvas bag full of men's changes. The bag was taken by Trewavas and Downing. They told the Captain they had found a body, he said if we had the materials here we ought to bury it. Once on board Trewavas and Downing began to divide the contents of the bag between them. Mr James found fault with the two men for keeping the clothes. He, the Captain and Mr George went below very much put out by what the other men were doing. The two men offered me a pair of drawers, I told them as they were keeping the other things they could keep that as well.

No one told me to keep quiet so I told my mother.

Mrs Downing said, when interviewed, that the letters J.W. were on the things her husband brought home but she would have nothing to do with them as it was wrong to keep them and she would not have them in the house. He never wore them.

Mrs James said she heard about it at the shute and has shed hundreds of tears since because I have relatives drowned at sea and know what it is to have them buried properly. When she asked her husband he explained he did not see the body, just the clothes being divided up. He was very vexed and said, 'what sort of devils am I with now' or something of that kind, and went below. My husband don't make a great profession of religion, but he's certainly got more than those who rob the dead and go to class meetings.

The body was finally identified as that of a young Padstow fisherman from the *Eliza* which was lost during the terrible blizzard of March 10th. The little island was called Melledgan one sea mile from Annet, the body was interred at Scilly.

Legal proceedings might be taken by Mr Mitchell, Superintendant of HM Customs, Penzance.

The following week the *Cornishman* was full of letters regarding the above, all of condemnation and all from Mousehole.

I can find no further reports or records concerning the above so it must be assumed that no legal proceedings were ever brought against anyone.

Fishermen are not basically cruel but because the nature of their job entails killing fish and constantly fighting the vagaries of the weather they do tend to get hardened towards life in general compared to those who work ashore. Fishermen are the last true hunters left on the planet and they all know that each time they leave the harbour could very well be their last, the sea is very unforgiving. Fishing is the most dangerous occupation in the world and no other industry loses such a high percentage of its work force. It was not until the 1960's that fishermen could get a life insurance in case they were lost at sea. The premiums for fishermen against accident or death at sea are very high compared with other occupations. This does not in any way excuse what happened above but it might help the reader to understand why.

THE SECOND OLDEST PROFESSION

Perhaps the above paragraph might also go some way to explaining the following account that occurred on 17th November 1892.

> Much disgust was felt at Newlyn on Saturday when a well known young woman from Penzance had, after spending a portion of the night aboard a steamer with some sailors was thrust on shore with only a chemise, and wrapped around with a seaman's blanket. In this condition the young lady promenaded the streets imploring to be let into some house. In most instances the strange attire and peculiar circumstances ensured a point blank refusal.

As can be seen from the above, even the second oldest profession has its ups and downs and ins and outs.

Mousehole Population 1851 – 1891

MOUSEHOLE IS IN the parish of Paul and the census forms only give the population of that parish not of individual villages such as Mousehole. Not only that the old Paul parish boundaries were very much different than today as stated on the 1851 census form.

> The parish of Paul is situated in Deanery and Hundred of Penwith. It was bounded on the north by Madron, on the east by Mounts Bay, on the south by St Buryan and on the west by St Buryan and Sancreed. It is located south of the fishing port of Newlyn and contains the small village of Paul with its fishing port of Mousehole.

Part of the above might have been altered otherwise it would say 'is bounded on the north' not 'was bounded'. The boundaries of Paul parish were changed in 1974 to make it smaller.

The 1851 census also contains a list of fishing vessels and crews that were in the harbour during the census and comes under the Merchant Shipping Act, this was discontinued for the 1861 census. Those fishermen away in other ports around the coast of the British Isles fishing would not be included in the Mousehole census but on the census for whatever port they were fishing out of. This is illustrated by entries for Mousehole which clearly states 'visitor' followed by their name and home address further up country.

There are numerous confusing entries in the 1851 census and some street names or place names that do not exist anymore, or maybe it was just written down wrong or spelt wrong, and some of the addresses in the same street are classed as Mousehole while next door it says Paul. Two good examples are Ragginis Hill and Duck Street with both Mousehole and Paul mentioned in their addresses. Likewise Regent Terrace in Mousehole is written down as Recent Terrace in some instances, again with both Mousehole or Paul given as their address. Gurnick is also written down as Garnic or Gernick.

In the 1851 census there are 21 boats listed along with their crews. These were:

> PE13 *Albion*, Abraham Jacka, master 48 years. 6 crew.
> PE231 *Amity*, William Humphreys, owner/master 34 years. 6 crew.
> PE47 *Betsey*, Benjamin Harvey, Captain part owner, 38 years. 6 crew.
> PE48 *Brothers*, Nicholas T. Mann, Captain owner, 48 years. 6 crew.

PE42 *Britannia*, Richard Tonkin, Captain owner, 48 years. 7 crew.
PE67 *Barbados*, Edwin Quick, Captain owner, 59 years. 7 crew.
PE89 *Three Brothers*, William Ladner, Captain owner, 24 years. 7 crew.
PE26 *Daring*, Richard Bodinner, Captain owner, 28 years. 7 crew.
PE34 *Storm*, Richard Humphreys, Captain owner, 38 years. 6 crew.
PE82 *Charles Nisley? (Wesley?)* Charles Wright, Captain owner, 44 years. 5 crew.
PE40 *Gregor*, John P. Blewett, Captain part owner, 50 years. 5 crew.
PE232 *John Wesley*, Thomas Pentreath, Captain owner, 42 years. 6 crew.
PE46 *Liberty*, William Beadon, Captain owner, 46 years. 7 crew.
PE95 *Mariner*, Nicholas Praed, Captain, 35 years. 6 crew.
PE24 *Nile*, John Pentreath, Captain owner, 41 years. 7 crew.
PE29 *Peterel*, Henry Richards, Captain owner, 37 years. 6 crew.
PE207 *Vivid*, Thomas Matthews, Captain, 34 years. 7 crew.
PE31 *What You Will*, John Harvey, Captain owner, 59 years. 7 crew.
PE189 *Wanderer*, Richard Pentreath, Captain owner, 32 years. 6 crew.
PE27 *Muon? (Jason ?)* Charles Mann, Captain, 29 years. 7 crew .
PE226 *Zephyr*, John Ash, Captain owner, 40 years. 7 crew.

The above is a copy of the boats listed although there are discrepancies with some boat's names, I know this because of a Harbour Master's notebook loaned to me from this period of time. This also applies to some of the men's names being written down wrongly.

Each vessel named above had a young boy aged between 15 and 17 years old as part of their crew. Some of the older fishermen from the 1960's told me that most fishermen aboard a boat also had their own nets which increased their share of any payout for the catch. This is the first documented proof I have of this happening because each crew member had 'and nets' after his name, except for the boys employed.

The census forms for 1851, 61, 71, 81 and 1891 list every single person living or staying in Mousehole during those years, as mentioned earlier some of those listed were visitors. Rather than count each individual I counted the number from six random pages and took the average then multiplied that by the number of pages listing the inhabitants of Mousehole. The actual number does not include those fishermen that were working from other ports around the British Isles so the actual number of people would be a lot higher than those on the census forms. So if for example the village had 20 vessels each carrying 7 crew working away from Mousehole that would increase the population by 140. It is also known that some fishing boats working around Scotland on the herring could be away for up to two years. It would be easier and quicker to come home by train than sail a boat from Scotland to Mousehole and then have to go all the way back again.

1851 census population 1,503 persons registered
1861 census population 1,472 persons registered
1871 census population 1,636 persons registered
1881 census population 1,702 persons registered
1891 census population 1,656 persons registered

If you take the average of these 5 census forms then you arrive at 1,594 people living in the village for that 50 year period of time.

There were a lot less houses in the village in 1891 than there are now because the most important thing was storing and keeping your nets dry. For every inhabited building there would be an equal area in size for curing or storing nets and boat's gear, plus sailmakers and all the other trades connected with the fishing industry. Fish curing tanks and cellars, pilchard pressing buildings and storage for barrels and boxes of pressed and cured pilchards. If you live in a property where the wall juts out six to nine inches then that used to be a pilchard press years ago. To my knowledge all the pilchard curing tanks that were usually let into the ground have now been filled in and all the barking boilers have gone except one opposite my cottage that has now got a preservation order on it thanks to me. Mr Vaughan Tregenza, who was Chairman of the Old Cornwall Society at the time, knocked down and took out two boilers and was attacking the third and last one when I stopped him and got hold of the Old Cornwall Society. The large long three storey high building opposite me was and still is known as The Bark House where most nets, ropes and sails were cured, there is still one old cast iron boiler and firebox left. The last lot of cutch was drained out of the holding tank in 1971. I also managed to rescue, and still have, the old hand beaten axe with its original wooden handle used for chopping up the cutch (tree bark). *(See Barking)* This building, The Bark House, has now been turned into 6 holiday flats, as have all the other old buildings connected with the fishing industry. There is one left up Duck Street still used by fishermen and the Christmas Lights Brigade to store electrics and displays. It is hoped to turn it into a community hall one day, it is called the Solomon Browne Hall in memory of our lifeboat.

A lot of the cottages in the 1800's had as many as seven people living in them, parents plus five children but the majority was five or six. That is still a lot when you consider how small some of these cottages were. Quite a few small cottages have now been knocked into one to make a larger living area for present day occupants. In the 1960's and 70's two new large estates were built where we used to go hunting for rabbits, plus numerous other houses built around the village. We now have three times the amount of living accommodation in Mousehole compared with 1891 with probably

143

half the number of permanent residents living here, most properties are now holiday lets or second homes. I very much doubt if this year's census, 2011, will be near the one thousand mark for residents. A few years ago those entitled to vote on the Polling Register was either just over or just under 500. We are now down to one newsagents general store to serve the whole village. In 1960 there was a large greengrocer, bakery, 2 butchers, 2 dairies, 2 fish and chip shops, 5 general stores, newsagents/barbers and a taxi.

Besides the usual jobs such as stone mason, carpenter, boatbuilder, etc there are a few that give you some idea how village life was back in the 1850's. I haven't read the whole census of 1500 or so people but one or two did come to my notice. Servant, housekeeper, dressmaker, tailoress, coastguard, net maker, net mender, shoemaker, sailmaker, matron, head-master, headmistress, maker of straw hats, lamplighter, cordwainer, rope maker, bread maker, baker and cake maker This is just a small selection of various jobs that people put down on their census forms back in 1851. By far and away the majority of men were classed as fishermen, captains or pilots and these made up the most as regards working jobs, very few farm workers or farm labourers are mentioned for Mousehole, understandable as this village was basically run for fishing.

Lifting the Baulks, 1962.
From left to right: Frank Wallis; Billy Worth; Cecil Thorbyn; Norman Wallis; Clarry Williams, Harbour Master and in the foreground Jack Worth. I stood back from helping to take the photograph.

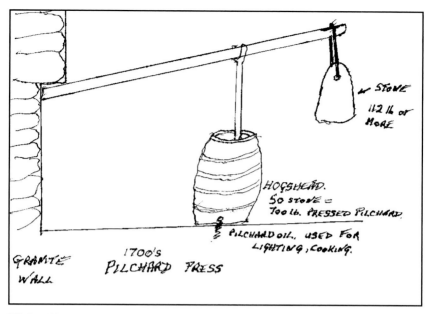

Pilchard Press

27th February, 1963.
Part of the South Quay, damaged in the Ash Wednesday southerly storm force 12, Mousehole. There were four such breaches in the South Quay.

Rescue practise off Penzance prom, circa 1970, using a relief lifeboat while the *Solomon Browne* was undergoing a refit. From left to right: Trevelyan Richards*; Barry Torrie*; Mike 'Butts' Buttery; Lewis Brown; Nim Bowden; Coxswain Jack Worth; Lifeboat Inspector; Stephen Madron* and two unknown youngsters. In the water is Elaine Bowden, later WPC Bowden. (* lost with the *Solomon Browne*)

On the 19th December, 1981 the *Solomon Browne* was lost with all hands. Wreckage washed ashore at Lamorna Cove on December 20th 1981.

28th December, 1977.
Grimsby midwater trawler *Conqueror*, ashore 200 yards past Mousehole Cave.
She was a total loss.

18th December, 1983.
Southerly storm force 10. Mousehole quays battered by huge waves.

15th January, 1987.
Snow shovelled up against the harbour railings. A blizzard hit the village on the evening of 12th January – by the 19th the roads were cleared of snow.

South West Water's 'Clean Sweep' sewerage scheme, 1994 – 1995.

1998 – Reinforcing the North Bank car park.

2002 – Southerly storm damage along the concrete walk.

22nd December 1977.
Part of the 1,000 plus Mounts Bay mackerel handlining fleet return from Falmouth and Plymouth without catching a fish. This was the last winter mackerel season – killed off by midwater and purse seine fishing boats.

Section IV

Buildings

IN A LARGE number of houses constructed before 1900 the rafters and main beams were timbers reclaimed from shipwrecks or fishing vessels being broken up. Masts were also used extensively, some as props to hold up loft floors that overhung courtyards while a few were actually incorporated into the main building.

All ship's main deck beams were cambered so that after planking any water falling onto them could run away through the scuppers. In some buildings these deck beams were put camber side down so that the flat side could be built onto and it is still possible to see these in some of the oldest buildings. Nothing was wasted, if you know what to look for you can see numerous parts of boats incorporated into most of the older buildings. Some are easy to pick out because of the decorations carved into them and one such large beam has the word *Tobago* carved into it. This vessel was wrecked at the Runnel Stone in the 1860's. Tobago is an island near Trinidad, the main towns are Plymouth and Scarborough, she was carrying a cargo of timber when she sank. This beam and several other ship's timbers can be seen over the 'Barkhouse' gateway, which is up the alley between 'Cliff House' and 'Cliff Cottage' on the harbour front. Well worth a visit.

One large ship's timber with 1781 carved into it was condemned and replaced with an iron girder. This very large timber was eaten out with woodworm and dry rot, but it still had the old wooden belaying pins running through it and you could plainly see where ropes had worn into the main beam. There must still be timbers like this in some of the oldest buildings but they are invariably out of sight. The one mentioned above was resting on top of a granite and earth wall and carried the loft beams of the Barkhouse. It was only when the place was being renovated that this old timber came to light.

Granite was the building stone for all of old Mousehole, not all of it was good stone though. Some came from the fields and was known as brown or field granite, this type of stone has started to decay and is very soft and porous, just rubbing your hand across it makes grains and flakes fall off onto the floor. Other stone came from the shoreline and was known as beach granite, these form large crystals of salt on the outside which again makes the granite soft, porous and always damp. The best granite was always quarried but it did cost money, you couldn't pick it up from the beach or fields.

Clay subsoil (rab) was used to bind the granite together in the earlier buildings, the wall thickness in these very early constructions could be up to four foot thick, very good insulators. Beach sand and lime was also used but being full of salt the walls always felt damp and huge salt crystals would form on the outside within a very short period of time. Even after the walls have been repointed, treated with all the modern salt inhibitors or completely cemented over, the salt still keeps rising to the surface forming large crystals, keeping the wall damp. It's amazing where the salt keeps coming from after 150 years or so. The builders tell me that the only certain way of curing a bad wall is to build another leaving a gap of several inches.

A lot of the properties were built with rough stone and then faced in cut quarried granite. In conservation areas of old Mousehole new buildings are built with breeze blocks and then faced in thin cut granite to be in keeping with the older cottages.

Because Mousehole is surrounded by hills (we call them mountains), a lot of the cottages in old Mousehole are built into the actual hillside, and these retaining back walls can be up to six foot thick. These substantial walls are needed to hold back the earth. Where I live the floor level is nine foot below the soil level at the back and in some properties up in the mountains they are cut into the hillside nearly level with the roof. This stepping into the hillside can be seen in nearly every street, especially when you get towards the back of Mousehole and onto the steeper part of the hill. It does cause problems with damp and occasional flooding when there is a heavy continuous downpour of rain though. During an average winter my place lets water in through the base of the back wall about six times, luckily for me only occasionally does it cause a major problem. I have cut the carpet back from the wall by three inches which lets the water trickle alongside the wall where it collects in a pool by the fire.

Years ago there used to be a saying in the west of Cornwall that went like this – 'If it stands up straight, doesn't move, limewash it.' Going by the thickness of lime on both the inside and outsides of some of the buildings I have seen being renovated this limewashing must have been practised for hundreds of years. Still, it did the job. Made things look clean and light, filled in all the cracks, and over a period of time levelled out all the lumps and bumps, plus helping to waterproof the outside. Nearly all the buildings have now been 'needle gunned' back to bare granite and those that have been repainted are coated in modern stone paint.

From the 1860's until the early 1900's the main dealers in Mousehole for nearly everything was the Tregenza family. They owned the largest 'barkhouses' and were the main builders in Mousehole. They were undoubtedly the largest importers of a wide variety of goods into the village, the majority of which came in by cargo vessels. They were the general merchants of Mousehole selling everything from fishing nets, rope, cutch for curing the first two, all types of building materials, salt for curing pilchards, barrels for the same, and a wide variety of foods.

John Samuel Tregenza was foremost a builder but he must also have carried a considerable stock of building materials because throughout the Barking Ledger there are numerous inserts relating to supplying building materials. One such is listed below.

Supplied by John S. Tregenza, 5th April 1880
William Pollards Account

	s	d
400 bricks	4	0
3020 slate	6	0
1 ton 5 cwt cutch	5	0
1 range, 1 sack of flour	1	6
Plaster of Paris		6
½ ton blue lias	2	0
½ barrel coal tar		6
Two blocks Gambier, 1 ton black	5	0 (cutch)
Timber	2	6
200 nails	1	0

Interspaced throughout the Barking Ledger there are pages and pages of other materials supplied by John Samuel Tregenza and more pages regarding building work that he carried out for various residents in Mousehole and Newlyn. I have picked out just one such from 1880 which gives an idea of the cost of each part of the construction.

Work carried out for Mr Abraham Wright, 1880	£	s	d
236 perches walling at 2s 8d per perch	31	9	4
37 yards stone nogging at 7d per yard	1	1	7
541 yards plastering at 1s 3d per yard	33	16	3
16 square 4 feet roofing at £1 11s 0d per square	24	16	0
228 yards flat pointing at 6d per yard	5	14	0
51 yards round pointing at 8d per yard	1	14	0
Paving cellars as per agreement	2	0	0
Cutting, setting front steps as per agreement		14	0
Total	£91	5	2

To help the reader understand some of the measurements and get an idea of how much work was actually carried out the following tables should help.

1 Rod, Pole or Perch =	5½ yards	4.96 metres
1 Chain = 4 Rods =	22 yards	19.84 metres
1 Furlong = 10 Chains = 40 Rods =	220 yards	198.5 metres
1 Mile = 8 Furlongs = 80 Chains = 320 Rods =	1760 yards	1588 metres

As well as all the bills for building properties there were also several agreements drawn up between John Samuel Tregenza and clients. As below.

A memorandum of an agreement entered into this day June thirteen in the year of our Lord one thousand eight hundred seventy eight between John Tregenza, Mason, of the one part and John Ash, Fisherman, of the other part. Whereas the said John Tregenza do hereby agree to leave a space or roadway betwixt the new houses sold to John Ash and the new houses now in the course of erection twelve feet from wall to wall all the length of the buildings.

John Tregenza, John Ash
Witness Thomas Ash

A memorandum of an agreement entered into this day August 23rd in the year of our Lord 1884 between Josiah Trembath of the one part and John S. Tregenza, builder, of the other part. Whereas the said Josiah Trembath doth agree to let and the said John S. Tregenza doth agree to build and complete the whole of the work of a new dwelling house situated in Mousehole in the Parish of Paul for the said sum of £100.

John S. Tregenza

It is a pity that these agreements failed to mention the locality of these buildings. Specifications were drawn up for all building work being undertaken but very few are entered into the ledger, the one below was but it was not dated.

Specification of Masons, Plasterers and Slaters work to be done at the Wesleyan School Mousehole, to take off the roof and carefully remove the slate to a proper place.

Walls. To raise the present walls twelve feet higher than present walls to form an upper room, the walls to be two feet thick and form all openings for windows, chimneys, stacks etc.

Roof. The roof to be laid to the 4½ pin, the whole of the slate on the present roof to be used up and the deficiency to be made up with new slate to be laid in blue lias lime and blacks from the smelting house, to be lathed with baltic heart lathes and cut lathe nails, the whole to be plastered against the pin with common lime and sand with hair in due proportions.

Plastering. The whole of the walls to be plastered inside with three good strong coats of lime, sand and hair, the first coat pricked and scratched, the second coat floated true and the third coat to be plastered with fine stuff and trowelled smooth on the surface, the exterior of the walls to be pointed with aberthno lime and sand and the mortar well raked out, the lower rooms to be ceiled.

The materials for the entire work listed above came to £9 16s 11d. The labour costs for this job were unfortunately not listed.

A lot of the older buildings in Mousehole were built with rounded corners rather than the usual right angled walls. The reason for this was to allow horse-drawn carts to get round without damaging their wheels. This was usually where businesses had regular deliveries of various commodities that were either too heavy or bulky for a handcart. Most of these rounded corners were where there was a lot of activity involving the fishing industry which was the biggest employer in ancient times. The Barkhouse on the harbour front where nets had to be barked (cured) to stop them rotting is a prime example of rounded corners and can still be seen to this day. This building was in constant daily use preserving nets all of which had to be brought in by horse and cart. Once barked the nets would be twice their dry weight and a heavy load for horses to pull. These rounded corners made it easier for both the horse and cart to get round in a tight circle and saved the wheel hub from being damaged by making heavy contact with the granite walls. When walking around the streets of Mousehole you will notice dark blue elvin stones protruding at an angle at road level. These again were placed on building corners for the sole purpose of helping a horse-drawn cart to get round. The iron clad wheel rim would ride up on the stone and keep the wheel hub clear of the buildings wall. Blue elvin stone was used because it is a very dark close grained rock and extremely hard. This stone was often incorporated into some of the oldest buildings in Mousehole but it does not work very well, it always feels cold and sweats badly which inclines to make other things damp.

Mousehole has had numerous Abbeys, Churches and Chapels over the years and when they fell down or were pulled down the stones were used in the construction of cottages. The carved stone was used as it had been faced and you can still see granite stones in some buildings that have parts of carvings showing, probably the best place to see these is up Duck Street but you will have to look hard, oh yes, Duck Street has nothing to do with the quack quacks but was to do with pilchards. Exactly what I have not been able to find out. One explanation was that it was where pilchards were washed before being salted down and pilchards were always salted whole. Another explanation says it is a bastardisation of the word Duke. It always causes a lot of laughter with the local people when visitors see the sign because our Street is no more than five foot across, you can touch both sides with outstretched arms. My electric wheelchair can just about get down with a foot to spare each side.

Water Supply

MOUSEHOLE HAS TWO streams that have never been known to dry up but now that the Water Board have given permission to sink a bore hole and extract water from Paul moor the stream that empties into the harbour by the monument occasionally all but stops running during the height of the summer. The water from this bore hole is piped to Newlyn and used by the Ice Works. The other stream runs down from the 'mountains' and out under the Lobster Pot. It used to empty into the harbour but this stream has now been covered over and it runs into the old sewer system which empties at the back of the old quay.

Water from both of these streams was piped around the village, originally they were stone culverts but later cast iron pipes were used. The biggest pipes fed the numerous mills in the village, the smaller pipes led to 'shutes' where people would come to collect their water. There were three main shutes and also smaller outlets around the village situated where it was most convenient for people generally. From the records it appears that some of the more popular shutes did get rather muddy and work was constantly being carried out to alleviate this problem as the following shows.

> 16th August 1888, Annie John's Shute at Mousehole is much used for its excellent water, unavoidably there is much slopping of water near it, about 12 yards of paving is to be laid down and waste water turned into a drain.

There had been numerous public meetings over the years regarding Mousehole's water supply and the building of large water tanks near the three main shutes. The records are very unclear as to whether water from these tanks was to be piped directly to houses or just make a reliable steady outflow of water at the shutes. At one meeting in early 1894 it was proposed that Mr Edward Maddern look into the available springs and ascertain the amount of water discharged and the viability and cost of building water tanks.

On 22nd March 1894 he reported back to the meeting that:

> Several springs had been found which were good ones but thought many would be expensive to pipe down. A spring in Fox's Lane would give a good supply and if piped might make a good reservoir. The quantity of water per day at Fox's Shute is about 13,000 gallons.

On 5th April 1894:

Mr Maddern reported that he had made an estimate as requested at the last meeting. He calculated the complete cost of a tank at Annie John's Shute would be £350, Fox's Shute £245 and Peddan-Caunce Shute £105. This was the full cost unless they had to pay for the land they went through which is Mr Bedford Bolitho's. Much laughter at this remark.

Mr Trewavas thought that if they built a tank at Fox's Shute and another at Peddan-Caunce there would be no necessity for one in the middle of the town.

Mr Carne replied I don't see why we need tanks at all as there is water enough around Mousehole to supply London. Much laughter at this remark. After further discussion it was proposed by Mr Trewavas and seconded by Mr Carne that the scheme of three tanks be accepted with liberty to make any improvement if possible. This was carried.

Now that all the plans and cost had been worked out it was down to the Government Inspector to decide whether this scheme was given the go ahead.

On the 3rd of May 1894 at a public meeting Mr Maddern explained that:

The last census showed that the population of Mousehole was 1,602, Newlyn 3,323. Assessable value for Newlyn £4,870 10s, Mousehole £943 5s. The Government Inspector then closely examined Mr Maddern's plans. These provided for 70,000 gallons per day for Newlyn, or 23 gallons per head of population. 31,000 gallons per day for Mousehole or 10½ gallons per head of population.

Source of supply for Newlyn, Green Shute where a reservoir will be built to hold 25,000 gallons, Jacob's Well to take 30,000 gallons and Belle Vue where a tank is to be made in the adit to contain 30,000 gallons, total storage 85,000 gallons.

Mousehole tanks to be erected at Peddan-Caunce 5,740 gallons, Fox's Shute tank 5,300 gallons and Annie John's Shute 5,300 gallon tank, all to be built.

These tanks were completed and working by 17th November 1898.

When looking at the above figures it must be remembered that Newlyn was already a large fishing port with a considerable amount of industry associated with the fishing trade and it was at this port that all boats took on water, that is why they needed more water per head of population than did Mousehole.

Sewer System

MOUSEHOLE'S FIRST SEWERAGE system was in the late 1960's, prior to that sewage discharged into the harbour or small pipes at the back of both quays. When you went swimming in the harbour everybody used the breaststroke to push away floating sewage, strangely enough nobody seemed to pick up any illness of any sort, I suppose we were all immune to any bugs by then. The worst part was pulling in running moorings to boats. It was amazing what got caught or was balancing on the ropes, but a good flick of the rope usually dislodged the thing you didn't want to put your hand on.

It was the time of the 'Flower Power' people who all wore T-shirts that said 'Make Love Not War,' and some of the young girls were very good at it as well, making love that is. Where all these people actually came from I have no idea but the ones I met all came from the London area.

There was a large stack of sewer pipes laid out on the beach waiting to be laid after the diggers had made a trench long enough and deep enough to take them. Every morning just after 0800 one of the workmen, a Mousehole man called John Gruzalier, would take a sledge hammer and hit each pipe. The metal pipes would make a ringing sound and all these Flower Power people would crawl out of the pipes where they had spent the night. Most would crawl out and stay on all fours shaking their heads in a dazed state to get rid of the ringing sound, but they would all be back in the pipes the next night, this went on until all the pipes were laid. Then the Flower people just disappeared. The pipe banging was one thing I do remember clearly and always had a laugh about.

Anyway back to the sewer system. They connected up most of the pipes that emptied into the harbour, including the stream sewer that ran under the Lobster Pot Restaurant. This was delicately known as 'the asshole of Mousehole.' The new pipe ran right around the harbour, underneath the Old Quay to a pipe that ran out into the sea for about 200 yards, approximately 90 metres. This did sort of work but quite often the sewage drifted back into the harbour. This first and oldest system can still be seen as the concrete that runs around the top of the harbour has several manhole covers on it. The only time it really worked was near low water, then it discharged with a vengeance with its accompanying smell, but it was quite a good place to catch bass and mullet. What was surprising is they never connected the sewer pipe that came out by what is now the pumping station, maybe it had something to do with the marvellous display of Arum Lilies that grew by the outlet in the harbour wall each year, I think the car park man, Roy Smith, counted 40 blooms one year in the 80's. This system lasted until 1994.

SECOND SEWERAGE SYSTEM

In 1994 South West Water started 'Operation Clean Sweep' in Mousehole. The amount of equipment used was quite staggering for a small harbour. Three JCB type diggers, a large drilling machine, numerous large water pumps and lorries. Everywhere you looked there were large 6 foot reinforced concrete pipes, you could walk through the pipes without bending, and a huge stack of steel reinforcing rods. I took a series of photographs from when the work started until it finished and even now when I look at the pictures it is amazing how much heavy plant was used. The whole harbour was taken over.

Their first job was to divert the stream that runs out by the monument. Once that was done they built a large dam of harbour material from where the pumping station now is to the monument. Looking at the photographs this dam was at least 6 foot (2 metres) high, this was built to stop each incoming tide filling in the very deep trenches they were digging. One picture clearly shows a digger up to its cab top in one trench, another I took at high water spring tide clearly shows how well their dam worked with still a metre above the sea level. I was taking photographs when I noticed a large lump of rusty looking sand and shingle. I asked the digger driver to give it a tap with his bucket. When it fell apart there was a black looking cannon ball which I took across and put on the stream outlet concrete. Within half an hour it was reduced to a smelly black heap of decomposed metal grains. Two other cannon balls were found but all ended up the same as the first one. The black stain left by the rotten metal was visible on the concrete for a long time.

The new pipes were slowly laid from what is now the pumping station and connected to the old system by the stream. A new larger manhole cover was then installed. As each section of pipe was laid then it was filled in and slowly the dam got shorter. The last section by the stream was not completed until 1995.

During the pipe laying the large drilling rig was slowly digging out a very deep sump for the pumping station. When it couldn't drill any deeper a 'Powder Monkey' (explosives expert) was brought in to blast the rock away, this expert was a young lady. Monitors were put in properties near

164

the site and the first explosion took place. There were men with walkie talkies stationed around the village for this stage of operation. I happened to be at home when the first explosion took place, and did my house shake. Things fell off the walls and the place was full of disturbed dust. I rushed out and told the man to stop the blasting. They put a monitor in my house and did a test fire. The monitor nearly went off its readings. Several people including the explosives expert came to my house for a chat. I explained that my place was built on top of a blue elvin carne that was just over an inch (3 centimetres) below the concrete. I pulled the carpet back and showed them the hole where a plumber had tried to put some pipe in. The hole is still there but now filled up with dust. The lady explosives expert said they would have to use small shaped charges from now on. She did that and the monitor they kept in my house only registered about a quarter of the way up on its scale.

There used to be several large storm drains that emptied into the harbour. These were part of the original quay when it was built. Some of the older photographs in my collection show these large openings in the quay walls. There were three of these emptying into the harbour near where they built the pumping station. The engineer explained to a group of us that all storm drains would be incorporated into the new system. We all voiced concerns that the pumping station would not be able to cope. We had all seen these drains in operation over the years during periods of heavy rain. They would shoot out into the harbour some 2 or 3 metres in a square shape and dig a large trench right down through the mud to the gaps if it was low water. At a guess I would say the openings were between 12 and 18 inches (30 to 45 centimetres) anyway they cut granite blocks and filled the openings in. The pumping station cannot cope and so far the large covers have blown off at least three times filling the harbour with hundreds of gallons of raw sewage. The smell and gases make your eyes water when this happens. They eventually put steel bars over the large covers. This made all the other manhole covers around the harbour blow their tops – these were eventually steel barred and covered in cement. Now during periods of heavy rain the excess sewage gets ejected through the old system to a pipe that runs some 100 yards from the Old Quay. I still find it very hard to understand why engineers always assume they and their computers know better than the local people who know what happens during certain times.

We still have a lot of trouble during times of heavy rain with escaping sewage. The large pump is changed on average about 2 or 3 times a year. All the grit and sand washed down by the storm drains wears some of the working parts and blocks up the filters. From Mousehole this gets pumped via Penzance to the main sewage treatment works at St Erth.

There is one job I would not like to do which I have seen twice. The large pipes between the pumping station and monument have to be cleaned to remove thick deposits of fat that have built up over the years. A man dressed in a tight fitting divers suit is lowered into the pumping station. He has breathing apparatus, a radio, high pressure hose, scraper and attached to a rope. He then walks along the pipe cleaning them as he walks towards the big manhole cover by the stream. He is in constant communication with men at both ends. Once he has finished he is winched to the surface of the pumping station and hosed down by two men before he is allowed to take off any clothing. This can only be done once the large pump has been removed.

There are warning lights and hooters on the station that start up when either too much liquid is present or a build up of gases. We regularly hear these hooters maybe three times a year. Sometimes men come over and work inside the building to relieve the situation, I think there is also an automatic system installed. It is not perfect but the best our village can hope for at the present time.

The weather situation is changing with more really heavy rain over the whole country. From talking to some of the workmen and foreman it appears that the storm drains will be reinstated at some period to help the pumping station. In all probability they will come out at the back of the New Quay.

Bank Car Park

FOR HUNDREDS OF years what is now the Bank Car Park was a rubbish tip used by all the builders and households in Mousehole to dump everything. Old furniture, cardboard boxes of things not used or wanted anymore and garden waste. The builders dumped granite, stone, slates, bricks, chimney pots, rubble, old doors, windows, timber and old Cornish kitchen ranges when modern cookers were put in. It was never a firm, stable bank and southerly gales invariably washed it away, sometimes just a little bit other times the whole bank would be gone. As mentioned before it was a mecca for finding old coins, medals and numerous bronze screws and fittings.

This all stopped in the 1980's after a storm washed away most of the bank. Then the first of the granite boulders were built up with a large JCB. I took a couple of photographs when this was being done. The boulders were not exactly large lumps of rock and the whole job was hurriedly completed. Even so it lasted for twenty odd years but each successive storm was moving the boulders and spreading them along the shore or washing them out to sea.

Then in 1998 it was decided that the bank had to be reinforced properly. It was a massive operation involving a lot of heavy machinery and a large landing craft. Three very large JCB type diggers were involved plus some heavy-duty six-wheeled dumper type trucks. The granite came from Penryn Quarries and two or three hundred ton was loaded onto the landing craft. At high water the barge got as close to the shore as was possible then a large JCB on the barge just threw the one ton plus block of granite over the side as easily as if they were tennis balls. Once the barge was empty it returned to fill up again.

At low water another large digger would pick up the rocks and load them aboard the truck. These would be driven to the top of the bank and tipped up. Another even larger digger would be placing the large rocks in position or throwing them down the slope. Both diggers had caterpillar tracks and could climb up and down the granite slope to securely place the lower boulders. The barge digger had tyres. It took nearly all summer to finish this job and luckily it was flat calm with no ground sea that year. I took a series of photographs of work when I was in from sea. The Bank Car Park is as you see it today and so far none of the granite boulders have moved, even after several storm force 10's. In 2002 the first otters were seen using the granite boulders to make a safe holt (home).

Refreshment Rooms

MIXED UP AMONGST all the fishing, barking and building entries there are several pages that make interesting reading as they show the prices of wines, spirits and beers. From the ledger it would appear that John S. Tregenza had at least three 'Refreshment Rooms,' Truro, Penryn and Penzance. It must be admitted though that these 'Refreshment Rooms' sound more like Taverns.

Stock taken July 22nd 1871, Refreshment Rooms, Penzance

	£	s	d
Stout, small bottles, 9 dozen and 3	1	17	0
Ale, small bottles, 12 dozen and 2	2	8	0
Soda water, 207 bottles	1	15	8
Lemonade, 17 bottles		5	8
Sherry in jar, ½ gallon		9	2
Brandy pale, 7 bottles of 1 pint	2	2	6
Gin, 8 bottles of ½ pint	1	13	4
Rum, 7 bottles of 1 pint	1	9	4
Scotch whiskey, 7 bottles of 1 pint	2	2	6
Irish whiskey, 4 bottles of 1 pint	1	2	0
Sherry wine, 5 bottles of 1 pint	1	2	8
Port wine, 6 bottles	1	4	0
Bitters, 6 bottles	1	4	0
Holland, 6 bottles	1	13	0
Champagne, large bottle		7	6
Soda water and lemonade, 95 bottles	1	11	8
Ginger beer, 198 bottles	1	13	0
Brown brandy, 1 bottle		4	0
Small bottles ales, 6 bottles		2	0
Stout, small bottles, 21		7	0
Cigars, Kings, 350	2	18	4
Cigars, 4d, 32		10	8
Cigars, 3d, 125	1	11	3
Cigars, 3d, 100	1	5	0
Ales in cellar, 2 firkins	2	8	0
3 kills			
Beer 2 kills	7	4	0
Porter, 2 gallons		2	8
Cider to be returned, nil			
total stock	£40	15s	11d

It seems rather strange that John Samuel Tregenza should have anything to do with alcohol as he was the leader of the Temperance Society in Mousehole. He also dealt in butter which was sent down by rail from Mr Stephen Whethem, West Allington, Bridport and a Mr N.T. Whethem, West Street, Bridport. The butter arrived in large pots each holding between 22 and 32 pound which cost 1s per pound. From the ledger it appears that these 'pots' cost between 2s 6d and 3s 6d each, the wicker baskets they were in cost 1s each. These pots would probably be thick stoneware jars with the wicker basket for protection. These jars were always returned to Bridport. One load of butter he bought in 1879 was 345 lb in weight.

He was selling mackerel and pilchard nets for £1 10s per net. Rope for longlines was 1s 1d to 2s 2d, a skein of horsel twine for tying on hooks 1s 3d, 'line hooks 6d per 100,' it does not say what type or size these hooks were. He also sold cork, skin buffs, dahn poles, lead, baskets at 6d each, candles at 6d per pound and everything else to do with the fishing industry. Salt was 1s per hundredweight (112 lbs) or 6d per basket. Potatoes were also 6d per basket.

He bought vast quantities of pilchards and hake at 6d per basket, and there is one entry in the ledger for 10,000 pilchard 2s 6d. The pilchards would be salted but what he did with all the hake is not mentioned. There would be too many landed to sell as fresh so perhaps the hake were dry salted.

From the records it appears that John Tregenza was the largest buyer of pilchards in Mousehole although by no means the only curer. He was undoubtedly the largest importer of salt because the records show that he supplied large quantities to other people in the village besides what he needed himself. In one account from 1876 he bought 600 large baskets of pilchards and 10,000 fish. A large basket held 112 lb (8 stone) of potatoes so it must be assumed that each basket held at least that weight in pilchards. That would mean 600 baskets was about 4,800 stone, 96 hogsheads. Whether this was the total amount he bought is unclear, it could very well have been more because the old ledger has several pages missing.

The number of hogsheads exported from Mousehole between 1850 and 1900 varied between 600 and 850 per year, the average being just over 750. The 'loading dues' or export dues were 6d (2½p) per hogshead. The records do not show how long it took these sailing vessels to reach Italy but they do state that all the boxes and hogsheads were made and imported from Italy with the buyers names already stamped onto them.

The last pages in the ledger are nearly all to do with the rent paid on property that he owned in Mousehole, a considerable number, and the rent on each of these was £5 per year.

Amongst these pages there is a character reference written for a young man who was seeking work elsewhere. It was not dated but the dates around the reference indicate it was written between 1876 to 1880.

This is to certify that Samuel Thomas is a very steady industrious young man of unblemished character and have worked all his time in my district and his work has been such as to recommend him to any employer who requires his services very capable to work in any part of the world.

John Samuel Tregenza
Builder
Mousehole

Mousehole Christmas Lights

THE IDEA OF providing a form of festive illumination was first proposed and funded by Mrs Joan Gillchrest, a resident of Mousehole, for the 1962 Christmas. She donated £200 for a string of lights along the Wharf and a little way up the Old Quay. This was the start of the now world famous Mousehole Harbour Lights, and was the first place in Penwith to put up Christmas lights.

This simple display has been improved upon each year to one that encompasses the highest parts of hills surrounding our village right down to the lower levels including in and around the harbour. They follow a Christmas theme wherever possible and are all made by the volunteers in our village. Some displays are so large that they have to be mounted on scaffolding which is built to accommodate a specific set piece. A good example being the Merry Christmas/Happy New Year display which is 160 foot long (15 metres) and 12 foot high (4 metres). Since these displays are so large it is not possible for them to be left erected between Christmases so they are dismantled and stored until next season.

There are about 50 or more set pieces, some of which are varied each year as well as the individual strings of lanterns which link any gaps in the display. All the roads, streets and lanes near the harbour have lights in them connected to private houses electricity supplies. In 2004 they used approximately 6,500 15 watt coloured bulbs and the estimated length of cable if laid end to end was just over 5 miles. This display takes about three months to erect by a voluntary group of men and women. A lot of the work is carried out at weekends. The lights are supported entirely by voluntary donations and in 2004 cost £6,000 in running expenses. Local residents also supply electricity free of charge and permit the use of their property for the erection of displays. It is also a huge financial benefit to our village with the thousands of people spending money in the pubs and restaurants. The 2010/11 lights was basically a disaster due to snow and icy roads with very few cars and no coaches showing up.

In future years safety legislation will become mandatory for very low wattage bulbs and new cables to fall in line with EEC regulations. Such a conversion will have to be phased in over a number of years and this has already been started. In 2004 the estimated cost was between £40,000 and £50,000 to replace everything and that is a lot of money to come from purely voluntary contributions.

Newlyn Harbour

IT MIGHT APPEAR strange giving a history of Newlyn harbour in a book about Mousehole but the two villages are linked purely by the fishing industry and the demise of Mousehole harbour as a major fishing port. Once Newlyn harbour was constructed that was the beginning of the end regarding Mousehole as a major fishing port in Mounts Bay. Newlyn had everything that Mousehole did not have, permanently floating berths, large fish market and ample room ashore for the expansion of fish buyers, fish merchants, fishermen's lofts, boatbuilders and all other industries that are involved with fishing. Mousehole could not compete in any way with Newlyn after their new harbour was built. By the early 1900's the number of 1st and 2nd class fishing vessels based permanently at Newlyn increased. They still came to Mousehole when changing over nets, painting up or laying up but overall they made Newlyn their main port. They had to go there to land fish and being afloat at all states of the tide meant they could leave when they wanted not when the tides dictated it.

Newlyn harbour is the youngest in Mounts Bay, the oldest are Marazion and Mousehole. These were just rough stone jetties and probably built for the tin trade at Marazion and Mousehole for water and trading some 3000 years ago. Mousehole was the only place with unpolluted water at that time, tin streaming polluted all the other streams with arsenic which turned the waters red, hence the number of Red Rivers in this area. *(see Mousehole – Its Name.)* Strange when you considered that Mounts Bay was still covered in a forest back then.

Newlyn's first jetty, as it was called in those days, was constructed in 1435 instigated and paid for by a Bishop Lacy. The records do not say how large it was and in all probability was just a wide flat granite arm used for unloading stores and fish. This is the old harbour inside the present day construction and known by all the fishermen as the 'Grave Yard.' The reason it has acquired this name is due to old vessels being laid up there and forgotten, they invariably sink and rot. Every few years the Harbour Master has to put a notice in the *Cornishman* newspaper saying that unless the harbour dues are paid and the vessels put in some sort of order they will be towed out to sea and sunk. Nowadays they are in fact broken up and burnt. The top coping on the old harbour was added at a later date.

It was not until August 1873 that the first meeting was held concerning the building of a harbour at Newlyn large enough to give some shelter to the fishing boats. Penzance was the main port for Newlyn vessels and where they moored up during bad weather. In those days their fish was landed on the beach at Newlyn by small rowing boats that ferried the fish from luggers anchored in Gwavas Lake. A famous Stanhope Forbes painting clearly shows how this was done. During the mackerel season boats landed at Penzance close to the railway station where trains took the majority of the catch away, although there are references to small amounts being landed at both Mousehole and Newlyn. This meeting regarding a new harbour came to nothing and it was nine years later that this subject was broached again.

On 23rd November 1882 a large meeting was held in the Institute Reading Rooms, Newlyn, at 6 o'clock in the evening regarding a new pier for Newlyn.

> Mr S. Payne stated there had already been a lamentable loss of life in running for Penzance harbour in a south-south-east or south-east gale and he felt certain that what had happened would happen again. Penzance harbour was little better than a common chip shop for Newlyn boat owners, and their boats seemed little thought of in there. Why not look after themselves as their Mousehole friends had done. It is estimated there are 1,500 men and lads engaged in the Mounts Bay fishery. The boats and nets of the bay alone was some £170,000 worth of property and most of these boats would seek shelter in a good Newlyn harbour in a south-south-easterly or south-east gale. He would do, and trusted everyone in Newlyn would do, their utmost for a more spacious pier or better harbour.
>
> Friends must be pressed and Government agitated. A pier they wanted and a pier they would have. They would probably only want £10,000, while other places got £500,000 grant, every place except poor old Newlyn.

Mr Samuel Payne was a very good orator and tended to take over any meeting he attended, although at this stage there were no actual appointed officers, but from the records of such meetings it appears he just took over, undoubtedly with the backing of other fishermen.

Another meeting was held on 7th December of the same year and Mr Samuel Payne explained that:

> . . . the new pier is estimated at £25,000, calculated that there will be available revenue of £1,500 per year. With the acquirement of the new pier many fishing boats, notably the east coast boats, would make Newlyn their rendezvous because of the convenience.

Prior to these two meetings they had borrowed the plans used in the construction of Mousehole harbour, it could only have been a guide because the harbour they were thinking about was massive compared with the little harbour of Mousehole.

Civil engineers were contacted in London and they arrived on the 29th March 1883.

They examined, measured and surveyed the proposed site for Newlyn's new pier and they are about to prepare plans. The first plan would just be a rough drawing for the benefit of Newlyn's fishermen, the actual detailed scale plan would obviously have to be done in their offices.

The Civil Engineers did not waste any time because on the 10th April 1883 the report states that:

Newlyn fishermen gather at Paul Hill School to see the new harbour plans drawn up by Mr Inglis the engineer. Starting at the Green Rocks 1,000 feet south of the little harbour. Proposed pier will run out 400 foot to the Outer Gallick Rocks in an east-north-east direction. Then a north-north-east line is taken for the outer arm of 360 feet. A parapet 4 feet high will protect the seaward part of the inner arm, and a parapet 6 feet 8 inches high on the outer arm. Walls, solid granite, filling with concrete and rubble, bonded by more granite courses as it goes seaward. Giving a depth of 14 feet at low water ordinary springs, highest spring tide will yield 32 feet of water.

The whole work would cost £35,000. The Government Loan Commission thought a lesser amount might be granted, so plans were modified to £15,000. After some deliberation the offer of Miss Lemon to sell the Old Pier for £500 cash down and £500 in debentures is agreed to. Messrs Bolitho subscribed £100, committee £36, £35 deposited with the plans with the Board of Trade.

Mr Bolitho said:

. . . the Old Pier has to be bought before any work can start, I venture to suggest voluntary subscriptions to raise the £1,000, (Mr Milton, solicitor, £500 cash, £500 debentures). It is for the committee to say how this money is raised and to show the Government you are serious. Many fishermen are prepared to make a contribution at once and to put their name on paper authorising fish buyers to deduct 2d in the £ until the £1,000 is raised, Mr Bolitho gave £100 towards this.

Mr Ridge congratulated the large number of fishermen and buyers gathered to hear what progress the committee had made.

Mr Johns stated that over half the boats landing fish at Newlyn were Mousehole or Porthleven men and would help to this extent, he also thought the east coast men would agree. Especially as it was also classed as 'a place of refuge' for vessels during bad weather and so a Government grant of £15,000 would be forthcoming.

As happened in Mousehole in 1869, Newlyn first had to raise £1,000 to buy the old pier before any Government grant would be given, then, and only then, would the Loan Commission make available the agreed sum of money.

By 30th October 1884 it is reported that:

> . . . drilling at proposed Newlyn harbour has finished, overseen by Mr Inglis the engineer, who stated that a large thick heavy bedrock amply suited for the proposed pier had been found.

Once the committee, now called Commissioners, had seen the engineer's report they advertised for tenders to construct the piers according to the engineers plans and within the £15,000 price range that had been agreed.

By 18th December of 1884 eleven tenders had been received for the proposed work, all within the engineer's estimate. Examination of the tenders was left to the Chairman Mr T.B. Bolitho and Mr Inglis who would report to the Commissioners at a later meeting.

Mousehole fishermen had been writing to various Government officials and MP's for some 30 years regarding a 'safe harbour of refuge' and a fishing protection scheme without any success. The first documented proof of this was a letter written in the 1850's by Mr Josiah Wright of Mousehole, in all this gentleman wrote three letters. Messrs Joseph Trewavas and William Humphreys senior also from Mousehole wrote letters to London in other years, again with negative results. Now that the proposed Newlyn harbour was about to be constructed, which would be the largest in Mounts Bay, and was classed as a 'safe harbour of refuge,' plus the formation of Newlyn Harbour Commissioners, this added weight to what the Mousehole fishermen had been petitioning for for years – a Mounts Bay Fishing Protection Association. The deciding factor was undoubtedly the proposed construction of Newlyn harbour. A meeting was called on the 6th November 1884 asking all fishermen in Mounts Bay to attend.

> Sir John St Aubyn, MP, and William Bolitho explained to 120 Mousehole and Newlyn fishermen the objects contemplated by the Mounts Bay Fishing Protection Association, an institute now being formed in London. The Reverend W.S. Lach-Szyrma, vicar of St Pauls, Newlyn, was elected President. Mr Barrett, Master of Paul Board Schools, was elected as Secretary and Mr William Payne as Treasurer. The Committee as follows.

> Street-an-Nowan:-   Messrs Bath, A. Sullivan,
>   A. Kelynack, W. Tonkin,
>   and W.O. Strick.

Newlyn Town:-   Messrs T.K. Harvey,
                      James James, Henry Downing,
           William Hitchens senior, Henry James senior.

Mousehole:-   Messrs Joseph Trewavas VC,
           William Barnes, William Humphreys junior,
                Richard Tonkin and William H. Worth.

Porthleven:-   Mr John Symons will ask fishermen of
                 that place to nominate 5 of their number.

As can be seen from the above, the knock on effects from the, as yet unstarted Newlyn harbour, was already having its affect. Little did those involved at this early stage realise that within less than 100 years Newlyn would become the 'Premier Port' in England, a distinction it still holds today.

On 22nd January 1885 a letter was received by Newlyn Commissioners from Mr T. Bedford Bolitho, who had been involved with this scheme from the start, which states:

> . . . that he will advance the sum of £12,000 at 3½% interest, for the construction of the Northern Arm which would give additional safety to boats for the prompt dispatch of perishable goods.

The report does not say whether this offer was taken up because the Commissioners first priority was the construction of the long southern arm.

> The southerly arm was started on Monday last, 29th June 1885, with the laying of foundation stone by the Green Rocks. Photographs of this laying were taken by Mr John Gibson of Market-Jew-Terrace, the likeness were very striking, especially those of Mr and Mrs C.C. Ross.

Mr C.C. Ross was the local MP.

Within 10 months of the above on Saturday 3rd April 1886, it is reported that 'the first fish sold at Newlyn's new pier fetched a fair price.'

On 3rd June 1886 'the first cargo of sand landed at new pier from Porthleven and Mr Runnals shipped out his first shipment of stone on board the same schooner.' The shipment of stone from Penlee Quarry reached its peak during the 1960's when they were loading coasters 24 hours a day. It was quite usual to see several of these small vessels anchored in Gwavas Lake waiting their turn to load. If the tides were correct then two vessels could moor up end to end alongside the 'Stone Boat Pier' as it became known.

A report from the 16th December 1886 states that:

> . . . the new pier is nearly completed and they are now waiting the arrival of the new iron lighthouse what will be erected on the end of the South Quay.

Work started on the construction of the North Pier on March 8th 1888 and a tug and two barges arrived from Plymouth on 10th of May to be used in this work, transporting stone and infill etc.

A report on the 25th April 1889 states that the:

> North Arm is finished except for clearing the end of loose stones, first two schooners arrive, *Mary James* of Penzance discharged coal for the Tolcarne Smelting Works. The steamer *Stockton* took on board 650 boxes of mackerel for London.

The new north pier mentioned above was only half the length of the present day quay and finished where the fixed crane and granite steps now are, on the opposite side of the quay was situated the Customs and Excise station.

On 30th October 1890 it is reported that 'Newlyn is awaiting confirmation of a further £17,000 loan from the Loan Commission for the further extension of the North Arm.' This extension had to be undertaken to protect the vessels inside the very open harbour. During a south-east to southerly gale this very wide gap would allow huge waves to roll into the harbour causing considerable damage to both property and piers, and the vessels moored up inside would be hard pressed to stop the surges parting out mooring ropes with the consequent loss of boats. Synthetic materials hadn't been invented in those days and ropes would have been made from esparto grass or hemp.

It was not until the 8th January 1891 that Newlyn got the go ahead to extend this pier. On 20th August 1891 the:

> . . . first stones of the extension of the Tolcarne or North Arm were laid on Monday. The plans were approved by the Board of Trade and will carry this arm to within 150 feet of the Green Rocks or South Arm.

By the end of June 1894 a brief report stated that:

> Newlyn's new north arm was finally finished and will be celebrated by the laying of a memorial stone on Tuesday 3rd July 1894, there will be water sports, rowing, 4 choirs, a bonfire and food.

The week following the celebrations there was a full two page spread in the *Cornishman* newspaper regarding Newlyn's new harbour. Extracts from this report are included below.

Newlyn now has little need to fear from competition with Penzance as regards harbour accommodation. While Penzance was drowsy or devoting its attention to other matters Newlyn was actively gathering to itself the traffic from all the Mounts Bay fishery. Tuesday saw the celebration of the completion of the north arm of the new pier, which ensures the safety of a large fishing fleet, and enables fish to be landed expeditiously, packed on the pier, and sent off to Penzance en route to the central markets . . .

. . . The completion of the work was deemed of such moment to the hundreds of families who cluster upon the slopes of the hill and stretch towards their fashionable neighbour, Penzance, as far as the outskirts of Street-an-Nowan . . .

. . . Canvassing for subscriptions was vigorously carried out resulting in about £70 being collected. Arrangements were made to have the final stone laid by Mr T. Bedford Bolitho, MP, who has taken such an interest in the extension of the original scheme. A similar batch of commemorative medals struck for distribution among the children as on the former occasion, and other pleasures in the shape of decorations, bands of music, a procession, luncheon, sports, fireworks, sweets, tar barrel etc, so that Newlyn might be en fete and the fisherfolk have a little colour and cheerfulness infused into their sometimes gloomy experiences.

The time for the festival was fixed to enable a large contingent of fishermen to be ashore to enjoy it. Only fine weather was needed to make the ceremony a gratifying success, and this amply favoured Tuesday's proceedings.

The completed harbour has the reputation among Lowestoft, Brixham and Plymouth fishermen of being one of the best, if not the best, tidal harbour in England. It covers 40 acres, and the north arm is 1,400 feet long, 40 feet wide for a considerable length, lessening to 12 feet at the outer point and terminating in a broad round pier head. The harbour holds 14 feet of water at low water spring tides. In making the north arm 10,000 tons of concrete were used. The south pier has a powerful and effective revolving light.

The report goes on to say that every single road in Newlyn was decorated with evergreen firs, flowers, flags and bunting. Arches were made from evergreens spanning all the roads and in several places net arches spanned alley ways, roads and pier approaches, all decorated with flowers. The Tolcarne Inn kept by Mr James Trevaskis was decorated with greenery, Mr William Carter, grocer, had bright flags flying from his house top. Every

181

house had some sort of decoration to celebrate the occasion and as the reporter wrote 'but everywhere there are flags – flags of all nations, tricolour, crescent, star and stripes, Union Jacks, Royal Standards, flags innumerable. What a wealth of colour.' Messrs Chirgwin's shop was decorated with:

> . . . the Crown and Cushion and the Prince of Wales Plume, these are set amongst dainty flags and evergreens, a number of fairy lights are also ready to be illuminated at night.

'From the Union Inn long lines of colour join other lines on the Bank.' The Dolphin Inn occupied by Mr Wearne was 'all bright with rosettes and laurel, banneret and colour.'

According to the reporter Mr B.M. Bradbeer's display in the Strand was the:

> . . . most successful, a large motto *Newlyn's hope fulfilled* in white letters on a pink ground surrounded by the Royal Coat of Arms, neatly set in art fabric of soft and delicate colour, fairy lamps are arranged around this . . .

> . . . In Newlyn Town, naturally, the decorations are less important, for it is the northern arm ceremony proper. But there are three fine arches. One stretches across North Corner, another stands by the Red Lion Inn and a third on the Green Square . . .

> . . . In the harbour the *Lanisly* is dressed rainbow fashion and every fishing boat spreads as much bunting as is obtainable, the Brixham trawler *Conqueror* was gay with bunting and a lavish display was made from the *Alice, Temperance Star, Little Clara* and the *Excellent* and from every mast, outrigger and boom capable of sustaining a flag . . .

> . . . Mr Thomas Badcock's arch was tastefully arranged with bright new net and bore the motto *God bless the harbour-of-refuge* . . .

What a great pity that cameras were not more readily available and an even greater shame that colour photography had not been invented to record such a momentous and very colourful event in the history of Mounts Bay.

After all the speeches a silver trowel was presented to Mr T. Bedford Bolitho by the Reverend T. Norwood Perkins on behalf of the inhabitants so that he could lay the stone. The engraved inscription read: *Presented to T. Bedford Bolitho Esq, MP by the inhabitants of Newlyn on the occasion of his laying the memorial stone of the North Pier, July 3rd 1894.* The handle of the trowel was of ornate ivory, as was the mallet which accompanied it.

And so the harbour of Newlyn was up and running. I don't think in their wildest dreams all those men responsible for this project could have foreseen how large and important their harbour was to become in England's fishing industry – 'The Top Fishing Port.'

Because of the increased number of vessels using this harbour each year the Commissioners were continually making improvements as a report on the 5th April 1894 proves.

> The Newlyn Harbour Commissioners are executing a most desirous improvement on both the north and south quays. Pipes are being laid for the conveying of water to the craft in the harbour, which will be a boon.

Things did not always run smoothly at Newlyn however, in fact at one stage of its history it very nearly turned into a war. All the harbours, ports and coves in Cornwall were Sunday observers and no fishing was done, vessels would leave the harbour at one minute past midnight on Sunday, or rather Monday morning at 0001. During the mackerel season, which ran from January until June, sometimes July, Newlyn harbour was the base for up to 60 East Coast mackerel drifters, they did not keep Sunday observance and were out fishing. This had been going on for years and it finally came to a head on 21st May 1896 as the condensed report below shows.

> A big demonstration by all the Mounts Bay boats at Newlyn against the East Coast boats catching fish on Sunday and flooding Monday markets. 350 soldiers occupy Newlyn in an effort to try and keep peace and the warring fishermen apart. 100,000 mackerel were destroyed on Monday morning by Mounts Bay fishermen. A chain was drawn across the harbour entrance to prevent any boat leaving and local fishermen went aboard all the East Coast boats and threw all their mackerel into the harbour. No damage was done to boats, gear or men by Mounts Bay fishermen, although some were seriously hurt by stones being flung from one East Coast vessel that sailed out of the bay on the arrival of 60 St Ives luggers who had come to join the Mounts Bay boats.

The report goes on to say that some East Coast boats sailed to Penzance but were once again harried by Mounts Bay luggers and fishermen that had travelled to Penzance. There was a lot of fighting at Penzance with several people getting hurt but the outcome of it all was that most East Coast boats sailed for home, those that remained, which only amounted to some six vessels, observed the Sunday rule.

There were of course other events that could affect the fishing industry in disastrous ways, especially severe southerly storms which could destroy large numbers of fishing vessels in the harbour. As in 1880 when 21 fishing boats from Mousehole and Newlyn were lost in one night and twice as many severely damaged. 15 boats were lost in 1899, 13 of these in Newlyn harbour, plus an equal number of damaged vessels. All these vessels were 1st or 2nd class luggers, the smallest being 39 foot and the largest 56 foot.

There were also less damaging disasters, to boats at any rate, as this following report from 17th February 1898 shows.

Influenza has devastated Newlyn and Mousehole, the epidemic has confined over half the population, some say three quarters, to bed. Boats from both ports affected and crews being made up from other boats that are short.

It must be remembered that fishing in Mounts Bay was the major employer of men, women and boys during this period and anything that affected that was widely reported. Influenza was and still is a killer, how many people died during this epidemic was not reported but I expect the number was very high, flu jabs we take for granted these days had not even been thought of back then.

Another setback for the fishing industry was reported on the 29th June 1899. 'Forty fishermen have left Mousehole for yachting and Naval mobilisation purposes, it is said a large number will leave later on for other spheres of labour.' And on 10th August 1899, 'upwards of 200 men from Mousehole and Newlyn are now engaged in yachting, Men-of-War, Naval Reserve or steam boating, leaving a fair number of fishing boats on moorings for lack of crews.' If these numbers reported are correct that would be a disastrous loss of able bodied young men to the fishing industry.

Even with these occasional setbacks the commercial fishing trade at Newlyn continued to grow and the fishing fleet expand. By the early 1970's there were so many fishing vessels using this harbour that they were running out of quay space. The actual selling market was also becoming very congested and they were having to have two markets a day during peak fishing times.

In 1976 Newlyn Harbour Commissioners decided that the harbour facilities had to be enlarged. It was a major development and enlargement programme for the whole harbour which included enlarging the existing fish market. The new quay runs right up through the middle of the harbour, a large fish lorry park was incorporated on the reclaimed land along with fishermen's stores. On the other side a large fishermen's car park was created plus a new inshore lifeboat house. In the far corner a new pier and covered area was built where fishermen can store gear and mend nets. Once all the building work was finished dredging went ahead. This started near the harbour mouth and went right up to the new fish market, down both sides of the new central quay and across to the net mending quay. The depth of water at the new fish market after dredging was 15 foot at low water springs, water depth around the central pier was about 20 foot. This depth is sufficient for the majority of trawlers that use Newlyn.

Newlyn harbour used to run right up to the main Mousehole road and small punts running moorings were let into the rocks alongside this road, very occasionally waves sloshed onto the road during times of extreme weather. Near the old ice works there was an area that filled with water at high tide, this was known as Keel Alley and was part of the harbour. This was also filled in and turned into a grassed park area with trees. As you drive or walk along the Mousehole-Newlyn road by Co-Salt you can easily see how much land was reclaimed with all the car and lorry parks, fishermen's lofts and work sheds, the main lifeboat station and inshore lifeboat house plus the new quay and fish market. The largest fleet of fishing vessels occurred in 1980. The winter mackerel fleet usually left for Falmouth in September and got back in March, the boats ranged in size from 20 foot to 60 foot vessels all engaged in handlining for the large winter mackerel. That year we travelled up as far as Plymouth and got back to Newlyn on 22nd December. 1200 boats were crammed into Newlyn harbour with some tiers up to 20 boats deep from the quays. Not one single fish was landed – they had been overfished by the big industrial vessels that came from all over the world. I took a series of photographs from the top of the old ice works showing all the tiers of boats – it really was outstanding. That was the end of our winter mackerel and 40 years later they have never recovered. Mind you I still think of it as one of the best times, plenty of fish, plenty of money and meeting people in their boats from all over the south coast of England, and I was glad to be part of it, something the younger generation of fishermen will never experience.

Even with all the extra berths that were available by the late 1990's berthing space was once again becoming scarce. To that end the Commissioners built a floating pier with individual berths for boats between the new quay and the fishermen's stores by the road. During really bad storms the local fleet is augmented by French and Belgium trawlers seeking a 'harbour of refuge.' The local fleet has already been enlarged with vessels from Scotland and Ireland now fishing these waters.

Present day Newlyn has already used up all available space inside the harbour and any further expansion can only be done by extending seawards. As can be seen from the foregoing account of the construction and eventual working areas of Newlyn harbour, the ease of loading ice from

185

the plant on the new quay, staying afloat at all states of the tide, plus all the other essentials needed for modern day fishing easily accessible, Mousehole had no chance of competing and gradually lost all her large fishing boats to Newlyn. There are still a few small boats that work out of Mousehole during the summer months, crabbing, netting and handlining, but even these run to Newlyn during times of extreme weather.

Public Works Loan Board

IT APPEARS THE above board and Board of Agriculture and Fisheries were in constant communication with Mousehole Commissioners and queried a lot of their decisions. The following is an exact copy of a letter from the above board relating to the workings of the harbour.

Public Works Loan Board,
Old Jewry, London EC,
14th January 1914.

Sir, I am directed by the Public Works Loan Commission to state that they have been informed by Mr F.R. Blewett, the Harbour Master at Mousehole, that the Harbour Commissioners have given him notice terminating his appointment as from 25th March next, and I am directed to state that the Board would be glad to know under what circumstances the Harbour Commissioners have thought it necessary to take this step and I am to enquire whether Mr Blewett's services and conduct have been in all respects satisfactory.

I am at the same time to enquire whether the full dues authorised in 1909 (vis First Class Boats £2 per annum, Second Class Boats 10s per annum) are now being levied, and paid in ALL cases without any exceptions, as this Board have been informed that this is not the case and that some of the Harbour Commissioners themselves are not paying the proper dues.

Has the Harbour Master been insured under the National Insurance Act? If not, for what reason has this not been done?

I am to point out that no payment has been made by the Harbour Commissioners in reduction of their arrears since December 1910, and, from the Accounts of the Harbour, which have been furnished to the Board, it is observed that certain heavy payments have been made by the Harbour Commissioners from time to time since 1909. I am to request that full information may be given as to what these payments were for. The amounts referred to are as follows; 1910 October 6th, Harvey & Co, £39 7s *1911 July 12th, Harvey & Co, £21 18s *1911 October 30th, Charles Tregenza, £30 12s 6d *1912 January 8th, W.H. Harvey, £20.

*Note. These three amounts make up no less than £72 in one financial year, being equal to half the Gross Revenue of the harbour for the year.

1912 September 10th, Harvey & Co, £7 16s 1913 January 16th, C. Tregenza £13 11s 9d.

I am to enquire whether the C. Tregenza referred to is, as a matter of fact, one of the Harbour Commissioners themselves, and if so, whether the work for which he has been paid was put out to tender and given to the lowest, or how it comes about that C. Tregenza was employed.

187

I am to remind you that no expense beyond the <u>ordinary management</u> of the harbour must be incurred without this Board's *previous approval*, and this will be strictly enforced, and the Harbour Commissioners will be held personally responsible for seeing that it is carried out.

I am to enquire whether it is proposed to make any payment to this Board before the close of the present month.

I am Sir your obedient servant,

G.A. Calder

It must be assumed that the Board kept in constant communication with all other harbours around the coast to the same extent, especially those that had taken out a loan, and that would include Newlyn. Below is an exact copy of Mousehole Harbour Commissioners reply.

Portland Cottage,
Mousehole, Near Penzance
January 31st 1914.

Sir, Mousehole Harbour. In reply to your letter of January 14th. I am requested to state that owing to the income of the harbour being greatly reduced, and consequently the work of the Harbour Master lessened the Commissioners feel it their duty to try if possible to get the work done for a less salary, and under the circumstances they gave notice to the present Harbour Master to terminate his duties on March 25th so as to enable them to advertise for a successor.

The dues authorised in 1909 viz, First Class Boats £2 per annum, Second Class Boats 10s per annum, and for smaller craft dues according to the number of oars, are still in force, and as far as the Commissioners know paid in all cases. With regard to the charges of some Commissioners not paying their full dues I may state that when your communication arrived the Harbour Master was called to explain what he meant by such a statement. He said that a Commissioner present was only paying 5s for his crabber when 10s was the lawful dues, and gave his name. The Commissioner was greatly surprised at the statement, having been only asked for 5s which he understood was the lawful dues, which he readily paid, having a receipt for same. Of course the other Commissioners knew nothing about it, and the Harbour Master never once made a claim for it.

The Harbour Master is not insured under the National Insurance Act, for the simple reason that the Commissioners have been waiting to hear from the Insurance Commissioners in regard to him, he having been waited on by an Insurance Inspector who was told by him the facts of the case.

The amount for 1910 October 6th £39 7s, 1911 July 12th £21 18s, 1912 September 10th £27 16s paid to Harvey & Co were for booms which were required in a harbour like this, and which could not be done without. Mr Harvey's account for £20 was for putting rails round the pier and slipway, repairing chain ladders and other iron work which the Commissioners were compelled to do to prevent accidents.

Now about Mr Tregenza's account; the £30 12s 6d was for lengthening the slipway, and the £13 11s 9d for work carried out in stopping weak places in the pier.

I may say that Mr Tregenza is a Commissioner, and when the slipway had to be extended for the benefit of the fishermen to get their fish carted over it. Mr Tregenza offered to do the work for £30, and take the money in instalments, which all present thought exceptionally reasonable, consequently he had the work. No one considered his eligibility but were entirely ignorant of anything preventing him from carrying it out, if such was the case, otherwise it would not have been given him, and I am sure Mr Tregenza himself did not think there was any bar to him being employed to do the work.

I may say that no unnecessary expense has been incurred, nor would the Commissioners think of doing anything elaborate without your Honourable Boards previous approval.

In conclusion let me state that the Commissioners are always anxious to be as economic as possible, and to attend to the Harbour work to the best of their ability.

I am, Sir, your obedient servant,

Bruce Wright, Secretary

As can be seen from the above letter Mousehole's harbour dues and landing dues had been drastically reduced now that Newlyn Harbour was up and running, and it would only get worse as more boats made Newlyn their main port.

The above letter also started a flurry of other letters from the National Health Insurance Commission, extracts of interest are recorded below.

3rd Jan 1914

From enquiries made with reference to the insurability of Mr F. Blewett, Harbour Master, Mousehole, it would appear that he is employed under a contract of service with the Harbour Commissioners and that the employment is whole time.

In these circumstances he is compulsorily insurable under the National Insurance Act 1911 and a contribution is therefore payable in respect of him each week since 15th July 1912.

I shall be glad to receive emergency cards duly stamped.

As the rate of remuneration does not exceed 1s 6d a working day the amount of the weekly contribution is 6d, the whole of which must be paid by the employer.

H.N. Bromby,
National Health Insurance Commission

There were also letters from the Public Works Loan Board regarding paying harbour dues and that 'all persons pay their proper dues.' Also about the National Insurance of the Harbour Master Mr F. Blewett and, 'this should be cleared up at once and steps taken by the Commissioners to this end.' And that 'no work should be carried out on the harbour without previous approval, in writing, to this Board.' This letter was from G.A. Calder, secretary, Loan Board.

At the Annual General Meeting on Saturday 7th February 1914:

> . . . it was proposed by Mr R.T. Harvey that the Secretary get emergency cards in respect of the Harbour Master Mr F. Blewett from 15th July 1912 and have them duly stamped, seconded by Mr J. Matthews and carried.

On 10th Feb 1914:

> Enclosed please find emergency cards each stamped with a 6s.6d. stamp as requested for the contributions of Mr F.R. Blewett.

On 7th March 1914 Mr Obediah Reseigh was elected as the new Harbour Master.

On 7th March 1914:

> . . . the owners of a property overlooking a flight of steps by the Ship Inn the Harbour Commissioners had built are trying to claim these as their own.

10th March 1914 the Public Works Loan Board sent a copy of a map to the Commissioners which showed the steps as belonging to the Commissioners. They had to ask the Loan Board permission to build them. So the person claiming these steps had no chance of claiming them, even today people who buy that property still think they belong to them, but as before there is proof enough that they don't.

Mousehole Wildlife Sanctuary

THE BIRD HOSPITAL that overlooks the village from Raginnis Hill was started by accident in 1928 by three Yglesias sisters. Phyllis (known as Pog) was a woodcarver, Dorothy a flower grower and Mary a taxi driver in Goldsithney, and it was in this village that the Mousehole Wild Bird Hospital, as it was then called, was really started.

The landlord of the Trevelyn Arms, one of the two public houses in Goldsithney, found a Jackdaw with a broken wing in his backyard. Not wanting to kill the bird he put it in Mary's garden knowing that she would help the unfortunate Jackdaw. She eventually found it hiding in a drain pipe and named it Jacko. Mary also had a cat and it was this that decided her to take the bird to her two sisters who lived in Mousehole. This was the start of the Wild Bird Hospital, a pure accident. When the Jackdaw arrived at Mousehole Pog fixed a branch and a small box in the corner of the hut where she was doing a woodcarving. The birds wing was so badly shattered that it had to be removed. Jacko recovered and soon settled down making such a nuisance of itself that a cage had to be built so the carving could be finished. Their second patient arrived a few weeks later. One of the local people found another Jackdaw with a broken wing and knowing of the other Jackdaw took this one to the two sisters, they called this one Muffin. When the wing had healed they introduced it to Jacko. The following spring they mated and Jacko produced five eggs, none of which hatched. Muffin, who could now fly, was later released but never left the hospital or Jacko and spent the rest of his life in and around the hospital. The following spring two baby Jackdaws were brought over from Prussia Cove for the two sisters to rear. Dorothy, Pog and Jacko the Jackdaw were becoming well known and the influx of immature and injured birds gradually increased reaching its climax in the 1967 *Torrey Canyon* disaster which saw the hospital deal with thousands of birds. By this time they had taken on more staff and they worked 24 hours a day during the oil spill.

Both sisters are now dead but the work they started still goes on, looking after hundreds of injured or baby birds each year. They rely solely on the generosity of the public in donating money for the day to day running expenses. The hospital is open to the public and well worth a visit. They do get a lot of rare birds due to Lands End being first or last place during migration. Back in the 60's a beautiful Bittern was taken in. It had flown into wire at Marazion Marshes, its wing had to be amputated. When it recovered this bird was taken to a sanctuary where it was hoped it would breed.

Pog was quite a character with hair that stuck straight up in the air and in later years looked vaguely like a halo, or a cartoonist's idea of a mad professor. One thing she did have more than Dorothy was a rapport with wild birds that quickly became very tame. Some of the older residents like Jimmy the Carrion Crow, a Magpie and some Jackdaws did manage quite a few words as they mimicked Pog and other wardens.

Pog was also a very good woodcarver, her usual work was large carvings from whole tree trunks. She was asked to do a large carving of Christ on a cross which took her several months to complete. I think it was for Sancreed church. When they came down to see the finished work they turned it down immediately. When Pog asked them why they didn't want it they didn't speak but just pointed. It was a beautiful carving but she had given Christ a rather large penis with a semi-erection. I believe she did offer to cut it off or make it smaller but the church was not very impressed with that idea either. What eventually happened to the carving, I can't remember.

St Clements Isle

ST CLEMENTS IS a rocky island just off Mousehole harbour which protects the village during south-easterly gales and is a haven for all types of seabirds and seals. All the seabirds nest there and the seals have pups there each year. Visitors spend a lot of time with binoculars or the harbour telescope looking at both. At half tide there is normally a seal basking on a rock in a banana shape, head and back flippers in the air, it stays there until the flowing tide floats it off. This is one of the first stops for tripper boats during the summer months and there must be thousands of photographs taken of seals on this rock.

There is very little earth left on the island these days as winter gales regularly sweep large waves the length of the island. Gulls carry grass and weeds to build nests in the spring and there is normally a covering of sparse grass and weeds on the north-eastern end on the low flat area during the summer. Back in the 1100's there are plenty of references to Mousehole people going to the island once a year to have a party and picnic under the trees. They have long since gone but even in the 50's and 60's there were a few scraggly bushes and brambles growing there. They disappeared during the Ash Wednesday Storm.

During all my research on our village I have never found any proof that the island was ever inhabited or had a building on it. The earliest record I have found about village people going for a party/picnic on the island was in the 1100's, they mentioned trees but no building. Although the report was only a few lines I feel certain if there had been any sort of building it would have been mentioned. From the records it is clear that village people went to the island once a year, whether it was to celebrate any special occasion it does not say, but it certainly happened from the 1100's until the late 1800's. Maybe it had something to do with the 1099 floods because there is no mention of this happening before the 1100's.

There have been several instances of boats running aground on the island over the years, but all the people have been rescued by fishermen from the village. One common thing that does occur on quite a regular basis is people swimming to the island and not being able to swim back. It is a lot further than it looks – quarter of a mile. If there is a north-west wind getting there is easy but swimming back against the waves is not.

I remember one time I was coming back from a day's fishing and just about to enter the harbour when people started shouting and pointing. I stopped the engine and was told that three or four young boys had swum out to the island and could not get back against the north-west wind. I arrived at the island just as the helicopter arrived. They lowered a winchman who had a long chat with the boys then he walked them across the island to where my boat was. They swam the few yards to my boat where I dragged them aboard, they were very cold and appeared quite frightened. The winchman gave me a shout and wave before I took them back into the harbour to some very worried angry parents. They were all village boys and had often listened to their fathers saying how they used to swim to the island and back. Pity they didn't tell them about a north-westerly wind.

Another time I was standing on the cliff talking to Dave Redhead by his newsagents when I noticed someone on the island waving. I pointed this out to Dave and he got his binoculars. It was a grown man giving the distress wave so I phoned the Lizard Coastguards and they sent out the inshore lifeboat. We both watched the man trying to get into the sea but each time he tried he was attacked by a large seal. Anyway the inshore boat picked him up and landed him in Mousehole. The Coastguard phoned me up a bit later, laughing. He said it was Mousehole's amorous seal going for the man who had a black wetsuit on. The Coastguard said he thought the seal had taken a fancy to the black suited man and was trying to mate with him. He didn't actually say mate but you can guess what he did say. Anyway it was a rather red faced man that walked up the quay.

Another time a young man and woman who both worked in the Lobster Pot Restaurant went out for a row in someones punt. Again it was a north-west wind. Somehow they lost an oar. The young man trying to impress his lady friend jumped in the water thinking he could touch the bottom. He couldn't swim and started sinking. His girlfriend jumped into the water and kept him afloat. Luckily someone ashore noticed what was happening and Jack Worth and myself jumped into my boat and went out to them. The young man was unconscious from nearly drowning and hypothermia and the young lady was nearly the same. I dragged them aboard one at a time and we raced back to Mousehole where an ambulance was waiting. Jack Worth gave the man artificial respiration and kept that up until the medics took over. It was a very lucky escape for both of them. After that I went and towed in the punt that had now blown some three miles out to sea in the fresh north-west breeze. Jack Worth was Penlee Lifeboat coxswain at the time and he received a velum for that rescue. I didn't get anything which upset a lot of the fishermen, not that I was worried.

Someone once asked me how many people I had saved over the years. I did try to total it up once for the family, I'll have to really put my mind to it and think back over the years, but at a rough guess it must be about thirty.

During the 60's and early 70's there were a lot of divers working around the Runnel Stone diving for Crawfish. I used to take some out in the 60's. They were often swept away from their boats to drift into the bay or towards the Longships. The number of times I was going to sea when you heard a high pitched whistle. You knew immediately that it was lost divers but finding them in amongst the waves when only their head is showing was not easy. One day I do remember picking up seven divers three miles off Lamorna Cove. They had been diving at the Runnel Stone during a spring tide. Their boat man was still sitting in their boat smoking a cigarette. They had been missing for two and a half hours. Most times it was two or three divers that went missing but sometimes only one. I'm fairly certain I picked up fourteen divers during those years.

Another time there was a family of three, a man and his two sons. They bought an inflatable raft thing from a local shop. I shouted down to them not to go outside the harbour because of the north-west wind. The man said he knew what he was doing – he didn't. Three other fishermen also gave them this advice but he ignored them as well. We watched the man get to the island quite easily, then he must have noticed the wind but there was no way he was going to row that back. I started my engine and waited. Once he was a mile back of the island I went out and picked them up, the young boys were crying and very frightened. Once they were aboard I slashed the dinghy with my filleting knife and dragged that aboard. Their mother rushed down the steps to comfort the boys when their father turned round and shouted at me about paying for the rubber dinghy I had ruined. His wife was worried and very annoyed with his outburst and gave him a smack in the mouth and shouted at him to thank me. She did come back later that day and gave me a bottle of rum.

On 22nd June 1983 Billy Kneebone and myself picked up six German students and their teacher that were stranded at Penlee Point just below the old Coastguard Station. There was quite a swell running and we had to get into a little gully to pick them up. Billy was using my broom to keep the boat clear of the rock side. We told them to come aboard one at a time. The first two did that then the rest just jumped into the boat knocking Billy down. My boat, *Butts,* was washed against the rocks but luckily I was coming hard astern and she didn't turn over. We took them back into Mousehole where we were met by Frank Wallis the Harbour Master. The seven of them just ran up the steps without saying thank you. I ran the boat up on the beach to check for damage. Luckily the only thing that happened was a long chunk taken out of the bilge keel. 'Cod' now owns the *Butts* and I expect the bilge keel still has that gouge in it.

195

Henry Hamblin who worked aboard my boat *Butts* was also involved in two or three rescues of people stranded or lost between Lamorna and Mousehole. One that comes to mind was quite funny in a strange sort of way. We had just come in to land fish when a perspiring lady rushed down the quay to say her young daughter was missing along the footpath between Lamorna and Mousehole. We turned around and slowly went along the shore. Just this side of the trees I heard a shout, stopped the engine and looked. We had to ask her to wave her hands because we couldn't see anything. We did finally see her hands but that was all. I radioed through to Lizard Coastguard to call out the LSA (Life Saving Apparatus, now called Coastguard Volunteers) and told them where to go. I put Henry ashore who soon disappeared amongst the brambles and gorse. I stayed put in the boat to mark the place for the LSA. Between them they finally got the girl to the footpath. I went back to the harbour and waited for Henry. He was laughing when he told me the young girl was only wearing a bikini and her body was 'cut to rags' by the brambles. I think she was taken to hospital by an ambulance. The grateful parents presented Henry and myself the next day with a bottle of rum each.

There were several other rescues carried out by me and other crew members, but to remember all of them is not for this book.

The reason why I did so many rescues is quite simple. I was a volunteer Coastguard watcher at Penlee Point for 28 years and have a long service medal to prove it and I also volunteered myself and my boat for any shore work rescue. Any call-out which entailed my boat was covered for damage by the Coastguards but I never actually claimed in all those years.

There is an old legend that involves St Clements Isle that is worth relating. Mrs Baines from Chapel Street in Penzance was condemned to weave a rope of sand from St Michaels Mount to St Clements Isle but as the sea keeps washing away the sand she labours in vain. She was sentenced to this endless task for haunting her own home!!! Mrs Baines owned a large house, which is now a restaurant in Chapel Street. This house also had a large orchard and to protect her apples she employed a guard. Suspecting that the guard was sleeping every night she decided to rob her own orchard and teach the guard a lesson, but the guard was awake and he shot Mrs Baines who of course died. Mrs Baines was so annoyed by this that she haunted her own house for several years. So effective was her haunting that no one could live in her house for several years until it was exorcised by a priest who condemned her to weave a rope of sand. So as long as the Mount, St Clements and of course the sea are present Mrs Baines' haunting days are over.

Section V

Coastguard Lookout & Coastguard L.S.A.

MOUSEHOLE COASTGUARD STATION was situated at Penzer Point and was on the highest part of the coast between Mousehole and Lamorna. It was known as Penzer Point Coastguard Station. If you take the coastal footpath towards Lamorna from the top of Raginnis Hill you can still see the concrete base of where it used to be.

There used to be three Coastguard Stations in Mounts Bay. They were Treen, near Porthcurno, Penzer Point and Rinsey on Cudden Point – they have now all closed down. Lands End is now a voluntary Coastguard station manned by volunteers. Falmouth Coastguard Station is situated on the end of the Lizard. The last station to close down in Mounts Bay was Penzer Point which was closed about 1990 along with the LSA, Life Saving Apparatus. I was a volunteer Auxiliary Coastguard at Penzer Point for 28 years, you did get paid for each 6 hour watch, although not very much. My number was PZP29 and after 25 years I received a long service medal. If they hadn't closed the lookout I would have received a bar to the medal for 30 years service. I saw a lot of changes during those 28 years. The three types of rockets used were – flash and sound to warn vessels they were in danger – red star to let a boat know you had seen their distress signal – and parachute flare for searching the cliffs or lighting up the sea near a wreck. These rockets had to be put together before being used. A six foot notched stick was pushed into two fastenings on the rockets side until they clicked, the rockets themselves were about 2 foot long and heavy. Once the stick had been placed into the cemented-in pipe and positioned to go in the right direction you pulled a cone-shaped piece of wood attached to the rocket body off. Then pulled the waterproof tab off the rocket bottom. Using this cone-shaped match thing you scraped it across the rocket base. It didn't hiss or give any warning but just shot off into the air in a shower of sparks and an almighty 'whoosh'. You did have gloves to do this but they were invariably missing or hiding somewhere. You also ended up with a completely hairless hand after firing one of these, that seemed to be the worst thing that happened.

I was walking out towards the lookout to relieve Willie Cornish just before midnight on one watch and could see lights from a boat very close to the shore during a south-easterly gale. Next moment a rocket left the watch house and went streaking inland and out of sight followed by a flash and sound. When I arrived Willie was shaking like a leaf in a gale, rockets always frightened him but he was unhurt. The wind had spun the rocket around. With Willies help we made up a new rocket which was jammed in the pipe with paper to stop it moving then I fired it towards the boat. This time it worked and the vessel steered clear of the rocks. At 0200 I heard the sound of fire engines somewhere at the back of the watch house, going outside I climbed the path up to the field and then onto the stone hedge. I could see a large red glow in the sky and lights from two fire engines making their way towards the glow. It turned out a hayrick was on fire which was right in line with the watch house, Willie's rocket that went inland had probably landed on the hayrick. I don't think they ever found out how that fire started.

The rockets were eventually changed in the 70's to hand held ones that were smaller and easier to use. The smoke flares that had always been white were changed to red at the same time. I used the old white smoke flares for rabbiting after that but you did need half a gale. Light the smoke flare and push it down a rabbit hole, the wind would blow the smoke right through the warren and rabbits would come out downwind coughing and sneezing and rubbing their eyes which made it easy for the dogs to pick up, sometimes. During the late 60's we did Atomic training which was rather a laugh considering what we were supposed to do. According to the gentleman giving the lecture the main targets during the cold war were Goonhilly Satellite Station, Culdrose Air Base on the Lizard, and Penzance telephone exchange. Cable and Wireless at Porthcurno was also mentioned. The telephone exchange in Penzance was the biggest in the country and all foreign calls were routed through here to Porthcurno Cable and Wireless. The old telephone exchange was the largest building in Penzance back then and stretched the whole length of one road. It went from Chapel Street to New Street level with the main Penzance centre road, Market Jew Street. It has now been turned into studios and offices and is in the first road on the left-hand side when you walk down Chapel Street. Porthcurno Cable and Wireless station is now a museum open to the public and well worth a visit. Goonhilly and Culdrose are still operational although Goonhilly Satellite Station appears to be winding down.

We were shown several things we had to use in case of an atomic blast. One was like a fountain pen that you held up at the blast which told you how big the bomb was by measuring the brightness of the flash and how high the mushroom cloud was. Then you had another strange looking thing that told you how much radiation was being emitted. You also had a badge to pin on that told you how much radiation you were receiving, there were another two things you were supposed to do as well, after that you picked up this red telephone which was already installed in the watchhouse. This put you through to an underground atomic blast-proof station where you read off the readings on all your instruments. The instructor did say that in all probability it would only be one big bomb that would take all those installations mentioned. I asked him how long would we live considering Goonhilly was only about 12 miles away across the bay right opposite our lookout. His reply was until your lapel badge goes red, maybe two or three seconds. When I asked him how we were supposed to carry out all those tests and phone the answers through in two or three seconds he couldn't answer, he stood there blank faced. I said well it will give us something to do before we turn into a melted glowing radiation blob on the floor. He didn't seem very pleased with what I said, perhaps being in the Ministry of whatever took his sense of humour away, if he had any to start with.

There were of course lots of other funny things that happened during those 28 years but without the Coastguard ledgers to jog my memory I can't remember them. The same applies to all the emergencies that happened during that time, some ended up good, others did not with boats and lives lost.

During the 60's and 70's Penlee Quarry worked 24 hours a day crushing and loading stone onto coasters of all sizes and it was nothing unusual to see up to 8 vessels waiting to be loaded. During that period the horizon between Lizard and Lands End was a mass of coaster's lights travelling in both directions at night. It looked like a town that was lit up, when you look towards the western horizon now you are lucky to see one vessel's lights. During one very bad north-west storm that lasted several days I counted and logged 64 coasters of all sizes sheltering in the bay just off Newlyn and Mousehole. It was a very busy time for the lookout up until about 1980/90. Once Penlee Quarry closed down this constant traffic of coasters calling in for stone stopped. The Coastguard Stations around the coast were closed down by the government because there were better communications aboard, plus radar and Decca, now its GPS. I often wonder if people who make these rules have ever been to sea. One thing you cannot beat though is a pair of eyes looking out over the bow, nobody who makes their living on the sea would disagree with that. Rinsey Point Coastguard was closed just after WW2.

Mounts Bay was notorious before the 1600's to mid 1900's for the loss of life from all sea-going vessels. It was often written and quoted that for every foot of coastline between the Lizard Point and Lands End in Mounts Bay there is a dead seaman, and after forty-five years research I can well believe that quotation is correct. The number of sailing craft lost that have been recorded from way back in the 13th century comes to several hundred, and those are the ones recorded. Even in the 1800's there was sometimes only a small paragraph in the local papers that read '. . . great quantities of lumber washed ashore at . . .', followed by '. . . the number of bodies recovered . . .'. Other times it simply stated that a sailing vessel was seen trying to fight her way out of Mounts Bay, last seen off such and such a point, presumed lost. This was probably the commonest report in newspapers of the day, it did not say whether any wreckage or bodies were found because it was such a common occurrence. Most unnamed bodies were buried on the cliff top or dunes above high water mark, to ensure a decent burial seamen took to wearing a gold ear ring to pay for their final resting place. Skeletons are often recovered when the sea erodes cliffs or dunes away, they are then reburied in a graveyard with a simple inscription, 'Unknown Seaman.' It just shows how cheap human life was in those days for seamen. When a passenger vessel went ashore the loss of life could be counted in the hundreds because they all tended to be large sailing vessels. Most of these wrecks happened on the Lizard Peninsula. They were often sailing from or going abroad to other countries. They did get reported and recovered bodies usually buried in a churchyard.

During severe south-westerly gales or storms Mounts Bay was a death trap for sailing vessels that ended up inside the Lizard-Lands End headlands line and was often reported as such by local papers. Once inside that line it took a very good skipper to get back to the open sea again, they didn't have a long enough run, 'reach,' between the Lizard and Lands End to make sea way, 'wear away,' against a south-west gale. These are not my thoughts but taken from a paper I saw. Whoever wrote that had to be a seaman because the language used in his report was in general use by men that were used to sailing vessels in the 1600's to 1900's, unfortunately it was not signed or dated.

Due to the huge loss of life in Mounts Bay groups of people were formed in various locations around the bay for the sole purpose of rescuing people from wrecked vessels. They were then called 'Rocket Crew,' later becoming the LSA, Life Saving Apparatus. They were named Rocket Crew because they fired a large rocket carrying a light line to a stranded vessel. This was pulled in until a thick rope was aboard the vessel. Once that was made fast then it was pulled up tight and made fast ashore. Once that was done they could take people from the wreck in a breeches buoy, one person at a time. There were probably hundreds of lives saved using this method, it is still used today in certain circumstances but helicopters now save more people than the LSA from wrecks. The LSA is now known simply as the Coastguards, or Cliff Rescue. Regardless of what they are called Mousehole LSA did their fair share of rescues over the years, not all of them ended happily though.

In all probability the first lookouts came into being 400 or 500 years ago, whether it was the Customs and Excise or Coastguards is unknown – the Customs and Excise did spend a lot of time on cliffs looking for smugglers etc so they were usually the first to raise the alarm.

Mousehole LSA did practices once a month in various locations, never the same place, it was to get us used to different types of terrain. Each time we did different training depending on where we were – Penlee Quarry was cliff rescue, lowering volunteers over the cliff edge and then pulling them back up. Allan Johns was in charge of our LSA, Cyril Torrie was the rocket man and I was the radio man, the rest of the crew all had their various jobs under the guidance of Allan. The Coastguard in charge during any practice or call out was Don Buckfield, a full-time Coastguard Officer. My job was being lowered out on a rope until I was level with the cliff top and could see down the cliff face and direct any operations via the radio. The man I trusted my life to was Basil Torrie, Cyril's brother, he always tied me on and lowered me out until I was level with the cliff edge. We did most of our practices at Lands End when the weather was fine. Once a Culdrose rescue helicopter turned up and we had to be hoisted up to the hovering craft then back down again. You either had to close your eyes or turn your back until the chopper was right over head, if you didn't your eyes would be full of dust or other particles kicked up by the very strong wind coming from the rotors, once the helicopter was right overhead the wind eased. One of the scariest things I did was again a practice at Lands End. Cyril fired a rocket across a bay that was marked on the charts as Sandy Cove. Why it was called that I don't know because there was nothing but rocks below. Once the main hawser was pulled across and made fast the breeches buoy was clipped on. If I remember right it was 400 foot above sea level. Anyway I was pulled across and its surprising what goes through your head, the thick hawser suddenly looks very thin, especially when you get half way across and the hemp rope has been stretched out in a deep curve by your weight. Then you are looking skywards at the cliff edge. I have never examined anything that closely before, every single rope and knot, including the massive brass pulley on the buoy, by this time I was well over half way and wondering if there were any weak points. It took me a long time to realise what I was looking at hundreds of feet below. It was a colony of seals, and they really looked minute from that height. Once I was pulled up over the cliff edge by four men I found my legs had gone a bit weak, well jelly-like really. I decided to walk back with the others around the cliff top of the bay. Only two of us did that breeches buoy, me and Coastguard Don Buckfield, once was plenty enough for me.

The other place we used fairly regularly was Lamorna Cove – cliff rescue and breeches buoy training. This one particular time Cyril fired the rocket from the end of Lamorna pier across the bay to the cliffs opposite. It was the middle of a very dry summer. Anyway we successfully managed to catch the bracken and gorse on fire across the bay as the rocket burnt itself out. Needless to say a fire engine had to be called out to stop the whole cove going up in flames. Strangely enough that was the last time we used Lamorna Cove for training. The actual rocket was made of metal and very heavy and extremely powerful, it had to be to battle a gale of wind. There was a long metal loop on the rocket tail where the light line would be clipped on. If that rocket ever hit anyone it would kill them instantly. It was fired from a 'rocket launcher' that reminded me of mortars during my army days, it was mounted on a calibrated swivel tripod, there was no stick just a long metal rocket.

Wreck of the *Baltic*

THE *BALTIC* WAS a ketch rigged London barge carrying cement from Cowes to Newlyn to be used on Newlyn pier. She was wrecked on St Clements Island, Mousehole, on 1st November 1907 during a south-east gale, the crew of five were all saved and nobody was hurt. Below is a *Cornishman* newspaper report from 7th November 1907.

Soon after 7.00 on Friday night some boys at Mousehole observed a bright light in the vicinity of the island and at once informed the Coastguard. Another flare was seen and a rocket signal was at once fired to call the rocket brigade together and in a very short time arrived on the scene, soon after Commander Cartwright from Penzance arrived, by this time some 700 or 800 people had congregated. There was a very strong south-east wind blowing and the harbour baulks were down. Mr George Laity's 15 foot crabber, *Lady White*, was placed at the disposal of the crew, Messrs William Stanley Drew, Richard Thomas, Luther Harvey, Harry Harvey, Richard Harry and Charles Harry, all fishermen except Richard Thomas. One of the crew, Charles Harry, stated 'there was no difficulty in getting a crew to man the boat. We experienced great difficulty in getting to sea and had to hoist the boat over the pier. Sea terrible, we rowed with all our might until we reached the island where they could hear shouting. 'We are here' shouted Stanley Drew, 'are you on the island or in the rigging.' We could not hear their reply because of the wind and sea. When we got closer we heard a voice shouting 'we are ashore.' We knew that some of the crew was on the island. We tried to land on the western side of the island but found that impossible because the seas were breaking over it, finally got in on west part of island (presumably the belly of the island which would be sheltered from a SE wind). Stanley Drew, at great personal risk, landed but was knocked into the water by a wave. We threw a rope to him which he managed to catch and get ashore. Drew took the lantern that we had on board onto the island and one of our crew, Richard Harvey, followed him. After some time Drew shouted back they had found some of the crew and that the party consisted of two ladies and three men. At this time it was blowing hard and the seas were washing over the island. We managed to get on shore and found the boat, the crew were all clinging together and in a shivering state. We took them onto our small boat and it was with great difficulty that we managed to get back. The rocket apparatus was made ready in case it should be needed. Both piers were crowded with people from all parts and on the old pier the crew were landed by means of a rope ladder over which they came up the quay. One by one they were landed amidst rounds of cheers and applause and taken to various homes by Mousehole folk who were willing to give food and lodging to those in trouble. The Captain and his wife were taken to Captain Sincock's house, Owen Trembath and wife looked after the Captain's daughter. The two seamen were taken to the homes of Francis Blewett, Harbour Master, and Burton Williams.

Charles Harry said they had left Salcombe at 0600 Friday morning bound for Newlyn with cement, we passed the Lizard at 5.30, the weather was worse, we did not see or hear any danger until the vessel went aground. We lit flares and two blankets, then clambered over the bowsprit and onto the rocks after seeing the rocket (signal rocket to called out Rocket Apparatus Crew).

On November 11th 1907 over 400 people crowded into the Wesleyan Day School to see the six crewmen presented with medals for their heroic rescue. The Penzance lifeboat took nearly an hour to get afloat because the carriage was stuck in the mud. Ten horses were used but it was not until a large number of other people waded into the shallow water and mud to push the carriage that they finally got the lifeboat afloat. By then it was 9.00 and when she reached Mousehole the rescue was completed.

This was not the first time that there had been trouble launching the Penzance lifeboat and this incident added to the chorus of voices calling for the lifeboat to be housed where she could be launched at any state of the tide. In 1913 Penlee Lifeboat station was constructed which allowed the vessel to launch at any state of the tide and in any weather. This station is still capable of taking a slip boat but is basically a memorial to those lost on the *Solomon Browne* Lifeboat and was closed in 1983. The new lifeboat is now permanently stationed at Newlyn Harbour.

One of the rescued seamen from the *Baltic* was Adam Torrie who married Francis Blewett's daughter Janie, they lived in Ireland for a time before coming back to Mousehole. They had eight children, George, Hilda, Jack, Edwin, Cyril, Leslie, Basil and Marrack. I personally knew five of them. George who was blind, Cyril worked for a large construction company and ended up a digger driver, he was also a volunteer Coastguard up at the watchhouse the same as me and in the LSA (Life Saving Apparatus). He also worked several meadows up at the Crackers growing flowers. Basil was a fisherman and also had meadows, he was also in the LSA and was my 'anchor man' for cliff rescue work. Marrack was a fisherman and later worked for Trinity House, Leslie I still occasionally see either at Newlyn but usually Mousehole (2011).

The *Baltic* was the last large vessel to be wrecked on St Clements but there was another some 40 years early that was lost on the island. She was an iron boat built at Robert's Yard, Newlyn named *Maggie Maxwell* and was skippered by Captain Nankervis from Penzance. Over the early years several fishing boats have hit the island but from the records it seems that most of these were not seriously damaged and were floated off again and managed to reach Mousehole Harbour.

The 'Gallant Six,' as the crew became known, was suddenly reduced to five by a Mr William Nicholls of Penzance in his poem written just after the rescue in 1907.

In the midst of raging billows
Thro' the darkness of the night
Struggling hard with hoary Neptune
Towards the glaring danger light
Five Cornish fishers onward sped
Thinking nought of dread or dangers
Nor of those they'd left on shore
Only of the sails out yonder
Round whose ship the waves did roar
And those hearts were filled with dread
With their little lantern flickering
On they went through storm and rain
Now flung high on raging billow
Now down out of sight again
But slowly nearing the goal ahead
Reached the ship all strained and quivering
At the sea's rapacious shocks
Heard the tearing grinding noises
Caused by sharp and ragged rocks
Her crew spent and almost dead
They gave help and gently took them
In their little broad beamed boat
Waiting on the tumbling water
Her extra burden to take afloat
Then again they shoreward sped
Where, with hearty hands and willing
They dragged up on the strand
And the cheering, soaring upwards
Greets each one of that brave band
As the rescued forth are led
With drooping heads and haggard mien
The heroes now their duty done
Smiled with happy consciousness
Of a fearful fight and a fight well won
Old Neptune, cheated of his dead.

The poem mentions five fishers so presumably the writer did not think that Richard Thomas, a mason, knew anything about fishing or sea-going. I find this rather strange when you consider the conditions prevailing on the night of the rescue. A SE gale at half tide is not the place someone who did not know the sea would want to be. There is one other thing that William Nicholls did not take into account or know and that is Richard Thomas, a mason, also owned a 29 foot lugger of 7 ton, PZ376 *Secret* from 1906 until he sold her in 1908. He was the owner and skipper of this vessel and he also had a 14 foot crabber/tender for his lugger. The *Lady White* was also a registered fishing boat PZ357, 14.8 foot, 1½ tons built in St Ives in 1900 with a 5ft beam. These punts were heavily built and used as fishing vessels lifeboats.

Richard Thomas's grandson, Norman Wilcock, was a registered firearms officer in the Met Police CID Division. He met and married a Mousehole girl in London and when he retired they both returned to Mousehole where they now live, his wife Janet is a magistrate.

Torrey Canyon

THE 18th MARCH 1967 saw the world's first massive pollution at sea from a tanker. The *Torrey Canyon* ran aground on the Seven Stones reef a few miles off Lands End where she ripped open her hull allowing millions of gallons of oil to escape. She was the biggest tanker afloat at that period of time. The prevailing westerly wind blew massive quantities of crude oil into Mounts Bay. This was the first major oil disaster at sea and nobody knew how to deal with it.

The army was called in to help with the clean up but they were poorly clothed for the cold wet weather we were having at that time, three or four soldiers died due to hypothermia. All the fishing boats were called in to spray the oil and each had a soldier aboard. I felt really sorry for those men because they were not equipped with the correct clothing for sea going, they all ended up very cold and wet the first day. The next day most boats brought extra sea oilskins for them to wear and also plenty of food. I used to take home the soldier from my boat and give him a large hot cooked meal before he returned to his camp at Eastern Green. In fact the vast majority of the fishing boats were doing the same. The detergent was in fifty gallon drums which had to be loaded aboard by cranes that had been brought into Newlyn. We were issued with the most ridiculously small garden spray pumps to use with the fifty gallon drums. The weather was atrocious with a westerly force 6 in driving rain and most of the soldiers were horribly seasick. They were supposed to pump the stuff overboard once we got into the oil. Added to all that was the strong nauseating smell of crude oil and the detergent that burnt your eyes when it was blown back aboard. Not only that this detergent was so strong that it melted tar, pitch and paint on the boats but also brought out a troublesome itchy red rash if it got onto your skin. How more soldiers and fishermen did not die during that period I do not know. This spraying was stopped after about two weeks because they found out it did not disperse the oil but just made it sink to the seabed.

There were nine Mousehole boats involved in the spraying and we basically guarded our village. Any oil that approached the harbour gaps promptly had fifty gallons of spray dumped on it. It was also a lot more comfortable because you were out of the worst weather. The Harbour Commissioners had also put a type of boom across the baulks to stop any oil getting into the harbour but the westerly wind tended to blow most of the oil eastwards. Even so oil did creep along the shore with each flood tide.

They eventually bombed the wreck and set it on fire. The smoke that drifted across the bay was very thick and black and in Mousehole, midday was like twilight. I managed to get a series of photographs from a Culdrose airman who was photographing the bombing raid and the whole incident from the very first day. I have framed them and still have the complete series.

Divers regularly survey the wreckage of the *Torrey Canyon* and film the whole thing, the last was in 2008. This is done because there are two of the vessel's tanks full of oil and they have now started leaking. From what they were saying there is very little that can be done at the present time. When those tanks get eroded away and become brittle then there will be another large oil spill from the *Torrey Canyon*. On the last film you can see globules of oil leaking from the tanks and floating towards the surface, it is only a matter of time now before they rupture. Then we'll have another major disaster.

The exact number of birds and animals that died will probably never be known but it was in the thousands. The vast majority of these birds were taken to Mousehole Wild Bird Sanctuary to be cleaned or put down if they were badly infected with ingested oil which just burned their stomachs and intestines causing a slow painful death. The worst affected were Razorbills, Guillemots and Puffins but Shags and Gulls were also coming ashore in large numbers. As before they had no knowledge of dealing with oiled birds on such a scale and it was a case of experimenting with various detergents. Once the birds were cleaned they had to be kept for another two or three months to let their natural oils waterproof their feathers again. Letting them go too early would be a death sentence because they would die from hypothermia once the sea water touched their bodies. Considering the huge number of birds taken to the hospital very few survived to be released. That was the start by scientists to find the best way of treating oiled birds including force-feeding to inhibit the serious damage caused by swallowing oil as the birds tried to clean their feathers by preening. At the present time the majority of oiled birds brought in do survive.

Seals were another species seriously affected and most of those ending up on beaches were blind. How many died at sea is unknown. It was believed that oil and detergent being sprayed caused this blindness.

Badgers and foxes scavenging for dead or dying seabirds were also badly affected. The thick oil that gathered on their paws and picked up sand and pebbles was the cause, along with eating oiled seabirds. They tried to clean their feet by licking and chewing the mass of sand and oil which ended up being swallowed and causing a slow agonising death. Domestic cats also had this trouble but their owners were able to help by cleaning with warm water and detergent, even so several had to be treated by vets but they invariably died within the year. When fishing along the shore we regularly saw otters swimming between Mousehole and Lamorna, that stopped after the *Torrey Canyon*. It is only in the last fifteen years, 1990's onwards, that otters have been seen in Mousehole harbour near the stream lifting rocks looking for eels. One year they actually had a breeding holt under the Bank car park amongst the boulders and successfully reared three pups. They used to walk down the new quay then down the granite steps into the harbour around midnight, often watched by people.

Several of us in the village were privileged to see an experiment carried out by two scientists in a rock pool near the concrete walk. They calculated the amount of sea water in the rock pool by measurements. Then wrote down everything living in that pool and put in some small fish and crabs. Scooped out a container of water and added a small amount of measured detergent then put that in the pool and swished it around. The results were dramatic. All the crabs scuttled out of the pool and everything else just keeled over and died. They did this experiment in several rock pools slowly reducing the amount of detergent, they finally both agreed that even the smallest amounts of this type of detergent was lethal to sea life, but by then it was too late because the spraying was finished. Back in the early 60's, an experiment was carried out by marine biologists along the low water mark off the concrete walk. They seeded the area with ormers, a type of large edible sea snail which thrives in the Channel Isles. Their shells are used for making jewellery and known as Mother of Pearl, the flesh is expensive and a delicacy. They disappeared after the spraying as did another common leathery shellfish called chitons, these are slowly making a come back after 40 years. Barnacles and limpets that cling to tidal rocks also disappeared for a year, killed off by detergent, but made a swift recovery. How many other types of small shore shellfish suffered is unknown. Even in 2010 the oil that sank is causing problems for trawlers in certain areas, with huge balls of oil containing sand, shingle, corals and starfish contaminating trawls and fish.

School Bus & *Golden Corn*

BACK IN THE 1960's and 70's there used to be a private coach company that picked up children from Mousehole, Newlyn and Penzance and take them to Heamoor School. The coach always parked in the same place just past the Coastguards Hotel facing downhill towards Newlyn. This particular day the driver was chatting to garage staff waiting for children when the bus brakes failed. It ran down the hill, across the road, through the steel mesh fencing on the path, down the slope leading to the sea, bounced off the concrete walk to land on the beach rocks still in an upright position. Luckily the tide was out and more importantly nobody was in the coach. A large crane from MacSalvors arrived to drag and finally lift the coach onto a low-loader. Looking at the state of the coach I would imagine it was scrapped. I took several photographs of the coach on the rocks but was at sea when the recovery took place.

GOLDEN CORN

In the early 1970's I got up at 0330 to go fishing. My dog called 'Peter Dog' and 'Toby Jug', my tame Magpie, normally woke up as I made up my sea bag. They were always interested in what I was doing and both hoping for some food. As the Magpie used to sleep on top of the dog it always woke up when the dog woke and used to fan its tail and say 'Peter Dog walkies.' The dog never took any notice after he got used to the bird mimicking my voice. This morning the dog collapsed with a heart attack – he had two more before the vet arrived. He was examined, the vet said there was nothing he could do for the dog so I had him put down.

Just after the vet left I was called out because a fishing boat had gone ashore just past the Bank car park. She was the *Golden Corn*, a 20 foot east coast beach boat used in the mackerel handline industry. Her engine failed and she was blown ashore in the south-easterly breeze. The owner jumped overboard and waded ashore, he was wet but unhurt. The vessel filled up with water but surprisingly there was no damage to her hull, she had landed on a flat area of rock. I took some photographs of her when she was high and dry. She was later towed off at high water.

Conqueror & the Bountious

AT 0600 ON the 28th December 1977 the LSA were called out to attend a trawler that had run aground to the south-west of Mousehole. We loaded up the lorry with life saving gear and arrived at the wreck just as day was breaking. She was a large Grimsby midwater trawler engaged in the mackerel fishery named *Conqueror* GY1364.

The lifeboat *Solomon Browne* was already in attendance as was a tug that had secured a towing wire to the trawlers stern. She could have been towed off quite easily at that stage because only the bulbous bow was on the rocks, the rest of her was afloat. I was talking to the First Mate and explained that she was right over the top of two large sharp pointed rocks that I used to work with lobster pots. I said that if they let her ground she would never come off because they would hole her bottom. They had about three hours to make up their minds but for some reason the owners in Grimsby decided against trying to save her. I took a series of photographs from daylight until she grounded and was holed, they were used at the subsequent inquiry. She became a total loss and what is left is now a favourite haunt for divers during the summer months. A great pity because it was a fine ship and could easily have been saved that morning.

There was very little pollution because she used light diesel oil for propulsion. The biggest threat came from the tons of mackerel that were rotting away in her holds but as she broke up they washed away into the sea and the smell of rotting fish abated.

They had been processing fish that had just been caught and were steaming on tick over towards the lee of the land. Penzer Point sticks out clear of the general coastline just there and because there are no lights between Lamorna and Mousehole they misjudged the distance from land. If she had been travelling faster then half the vessel would have beached itself on the rocks instead of just the bulbous bow, about three to four foot of her rested on rocks.

Two local divers, Bob and Hazel Carswell, decided to 'rescue' all the electronic equipment as the vessel was then a write-off and nearly on her side. They succeeded in taking off everything and took it all home. In due course they did, of course, have to hand over everything to the Customs and Excise Receiver of Wrecks. Some of the iron work, shaft, propeller and most brass work was salvaged before the vessel sank below the waves.

BOUNTIOUS

Scottish pair trawler *Bountious* was working about three miles to the back of Mousehole Island with her sister ship on 4th January 1980 when she sank with the loss of three lives. The bodies were never recovered.

They were pair trawling for mackerel at night, but unbeknown to either skipper there was a very narrow pointed rock known as the 'Shannock' that rose up from the seabed by some eight to ten fathoms (60 foot, 18 metres or so). It was a well known fishing mark for me and all other local inshore boats and always yielded a good catch of pollock. I once took Bob Carswell out to dive on it. He said the bottom around the rock was paved with fishing leads and when he dived down this rock just appeared before he could see the seabed. Anyway the midwater trawl caught in this rock causing the *Bountious* to overturn and sink immediately. This pinnacle of rock does not exist anymore because her nets broke the rock off near the bottom. At the inquest the sister ship skipper said 'one minute we could see her lights and then there were none.' She had completely disappeared.

She was eventually raised and brought into Newlyn harbour where I took a series of photographs. She looked a sorry sight, gunnels were just above the water and the midwater trawl was draped right over the top of her mizzen and foremasts, and she was full of rotting mackerel. They had hoped to find the missing crew but didn't. She was cleaned up, pumped out and taken to Penzance floating harbour. She was there for quite a long time and there was talk of turning her into a luxury yacht but whether this actually happened I do not know.

Lady Catherine, Waratiki
and the Grey Flamingo

ON 13th DECEMBER 1983 the Mousehole LSA were called out to the fishing boat *Lady Catherine* PZ633 that went ashore in a fresh south-easterly breeze three quarters of a mile south-west of Mousehole towards Lamorna. She was a 28 foot wooden boat and in good condition. She was also a lovely boat to look at with good lines and a fine sea boat. She was bringing in her fishing nets (tangle nets) for the winter when she apparently lost engine power and went ashore. All the crew were safe. It was the only stretch of coastline between Lamorna and Mousehole that had a long low rocky foreshore, anywhere else and she would be under cliffs. Within a few minutes of the LSA arriving she was lying on her side full of water. An hour later she started to smash up as the waves rolled her from side to side. What was left of the boat was covered in nets, buoys and ropes, a total write-off. If anything was salvaged I do not know but I would say it was very doubtful. I took a series of photographs from when we arrived until when we left. A great shame as she was a pretty boat to look at but at least no one was injured or worse still killed.

WARATIKI

On 9th August 1989 the *Waratiki* from Penzance hit a rock on the corner of the island while trying to show a boat load of trippers seals. She sprang a plank and was filling up with water. Two other boats from Penzance took the passengers off and lashed the *Waratiki* between them and managed to get her into Mousehole harbour. She was patched up at low water and then went to Penzance for an overhaul. Quite an experience for the passengers and would probably make a good talking point for years afterwards.

GREY FLAMINGO

24th November 1989 the beam trawler *Grey Flamingo* sank 2½ miles off Lamorna. Her beams had become entangled with another beam trawler and when she tried to haul them up she turned over and sank within 3 seconds. 3 of her crew were swept overboard, 2 were picked up by the other trawler, the other one was picked up by helicopter but died of hypothermia later. The skipper went down with his boat trapped in the wheelhouse. Numerous fishing boats, the lifeboat and two helicopters searched until dark for the skipper's body, but he was never found.

Solomon Browne & Union Star

19th DECEMBER 1981 started off a normal day with the Christmas festivities under way. The harbour Christmas lights brightened up the village and at 7.00 in the evening the Royal British Legion was full of people getting ready for the Christmas turkey darts competition that I used to run every year. There must have been about 50 or 60 people there because we were using four dart boards. The competition was well under way when we heard three maroons go off – a signal that both lifeboat crew and LSA were required. It was a foul night with a south-south-west storm 10 and torrential rain. The lifeboat crew and LSA crew walked or jogged down to the harbour – the lifeboat crew to waiting cars and the LSA crew up to the LSA hut by the Coastguard Hotel. We loaded up the lorry and set off for Lamorna. As we left Mousehole the lifeboat was just passing the island.

Once we reached Lamorna, Richard, Dug Hoare and myself being radio man, were sent along the coastal path towards the lighthouse to try and find the exact place where the *Union Star* had gone ashore. Visibility was very poor that night. After we had struggled for a quarter mile in the wind and driving rain Duggie said he couldn't go any further. I radioed back to Lamorna and they sent some men to pick Duggie up. Richard and myself carried on. Once we got round the corner it was even worse with sea water running down the path, a tree had blown down and the only way past was underneath the tree trunk. I went first and sea water running down the path just ran straight down my neck. Richard came next. The radio was the big old-fashioned type with massive rechargeable batteries that only lasted for about twenty minutes talking.

We got further along the path when we saw the lifeboat lights right off the lighthouse between the Buck Rocks and shore. I heard a very feint crackly voice say they had four people from the *Union Star* aboard and then a broken message about damage and returning to station. Just after that the lights disappeared and both Richard and myself were covered in diesel. I radioed through to say we had seen the lifeboat lights and could smell diesel and that we were covered in it. The time was 9.45. We did not see the lifeboat again and assumed she had returned to Newlyn.

I was having trouble with the radio so changed the battery. When we arrived at the cliff the rest of the LSA crew were present looking at the

Union Star under the cliff. Don Buckfield, HM Coastguard, asked me to do my cliffhanging bit with the radio while he went down and searched for survivors. Basil Torrie tied a rope around my waist and lowered me out over the cliff until I was parallel with the cliff face looking straight down and in contact with Don Buckfield as he searched along the shoreline and among the rocks. Nothing was found. Basil held me in that position for three quarters of an hour until Don Buckfield was once again on the cliff top, then several of the LSA crew pulled me upright.

The only thing that ached was my right arm from holding the heavy radio next to my ear. It had to be there because the noise of the waves and wind would have made it impossible to hear anything otherwise.

We were stood down about midnight and had just returned to the LSA hut and unloaded when we were called out again to look for the lifeboat. Back at Lamorna huge amounts of lifeboat wreckage was coming ashore along with body parts. We searched every rock from Lamorna to Mousehole that night but found nothing. Daybreak we were once again at Lamorna doing more searches, but in our hearts we knew there would be no survivors. Both the Lizard and Sennen lifeboats were also searching.

I took a series of photographs during the next week of the *Union Star* and lifeboat wreckage. Also of all the LSA crew forking back seaweed looking for bodies, we did that for four days. These photographs were used at the final inquest. Two bodies were found amongst the seaweed – one young girl from the *Union Star* and Nigel Brockman, my neighbour, from the lifeboat, plus one leg that was later identified as belonging to Charlie Greenhaugh from the lifeboat who was also the landlord of the Ship Inn in Mousehole.

At the inquest both Richard and myself gave evidence that we had seen the lifeboat lights at 9.45 and that I had reported that along with being covered in diesel and the message I heard. The last message that Lizard Coastguards received was at 9.15 and they assumed that was when she was lost. I was asked why nobody else had heard that message and that I couldn't answer. It was not until a week later that I learned there was a very short distance radio aerial welded onto the lifeboat wheelhouse. It was known that the lifeboat lost its radio mast when she slid off the *Union Star* deck just after nine. I'm not sure that the lifeboat inspectors believed Richard and myself when we both said she was steaming and under control, not drifting, at a quarter to ten, but that is the truth. She was still afloat and manned at that time. Not smashed up under the *Union Star*. Richard and myself were the last people to see the lifeboat that night.

In the New Year Don Buckfield called for me and said they had divers going down to search for lifeboat wreckage around the *Union Star* and would I go up with them. The divers were Bob Carswell and his wife Hazel. They nearly used up a tank of air looking and found a lifeboat door – that was it, nothing else. I asked them to go where I had last seen the lifeboat and was certain she had foundered just under the lighthouse. Mainly because of being covered in diesel just after we lost sight of her and because I had been up in my boat and noticed a large rock where barnacles had been knocked off over a large area, plus blue lifeboat coloured paint on the rock. I directed Bob and his boat to where I thought she was lost which was about 2 or 3 hundred yards from *Union Star*. He said there was only two minutes air left so they couldn't do a real search, I remember saying it won't take that long. Hazel went down and was up again in less than a minute. Bob radioed back to say they had found all the aluminium engine room plates, an engine and prop shaft and propeller from the lifeboat. The other engine was found by pleasure divers between the lighthouse and Buck Rocks that summer. It was a great pity that we did not know this when the final inquest was carried out.

On the 20th December the *Union Star* was upside down straddling a gully and surprisingly she still had her lights burning. The sound of metal grinding on rocks made some people's teeth go on edge, this sound was overlaid by the booming crash of waves that hit the underside of the vessel, each time a wave hit the ship you could see the whole vessel shudder. A day later she broke in half. By the end of December she was in three pieces. Great lumps of her iron sides were missing and that made it easier for the waves to do the damage. By mid January only bits of the *Union Star* could be seen at low water.

Now there is nothing left to show that any shipwreck had ever been there. That is the power of waves on mere man-made metal.

Dolfyn

ON 30th NOVEMBER 2000 I was sitting at home watching a film when this roaring noise finally made me get up and go outside. The time was 11.00pm. I walked across to the Bank car park and looked down. There was a large ship that had run up the shore and was going hard astern, near the boats stern was our lifeboat that had already taken some of the crew off. The ship was going nowhere because she must have been going quickly for half of her hull to be up on the beach. Midnight the skipper stopped the engine and went aboard the lifeboat.

The following morning I went out with my camera and took a couple of pictures. I took photographs until well into January as she broke up. By 2nd December she was starting to break up in the heavy seas. She was painted green and was an Irish vessel being used to guard cable-laying in progress off Lands End. Down both sides of her in very large white letters was the word GUARD. Someone from the village said 'they didn't know Mousehole had a cable running under the village that needed guarding.' This caused a lot of laughter from the assembled crowd.

By 5th December she broke in half and huge pieces of her metal sides were just ripped away. She was soon in four very large pieces and there were arguments about getting someone to cut up the *Dolfyn* and take the metal away, and who was going to pay for this. It must have been sorted out because Mojo Marine got the contract to cut up and remove every scrap of iron work from that area of the beach. They started work the first week of January 2001. They used acetylene and electric cutters as well as a large JCB type digger to cut her up and load the bits onto a landing craft to be taken away for scrap.

She was all cut up and the beach cleared of every bit of iron by midsummer. At the inquiry the skipper said they had been to Newlyn for water, fuel and food and were setting off. For some reason they decided to return to Newlyn and mistook the island and Mousehole quay for Newlyn harbour and ran her aground by the Bank car park. How anyone could make that mistake I do not know because the island does not have any lights on it like Newlyn quays.

Section VI

Rising Sea Levels

GLOBAL WARMING AND rising sea levels are now an everyday topic of conversation which will eventually affect every living thing on planet Earth, but because it does not affect us directly at the moment we tend to pretend it isn't happening, or going to happen, or change our way of life. But it most certainly will change and affect everything.

For those who think it is not happening then there are two things that may just change your mind that can be seen in and around Penzance. Firstly I have a large photograph taken at low water of the construction of Mousehole Harbour in 1870. No living person has ever seen the tide that low. From the gaps to the waters edge is about 20 yards, nowadays the water hardly leaves the gaps, even at spring tides. Seaweed that only grew to the gaps in 1870 now grows halfway along the quays. The other photograph shows St Michaels Mount with the water just about reaching the outer edges of the Mount, this was again taken at low water in the 1870's, both photographs can be seen in Morrab Library. The other thing which is plainly visible are the foundations of fishermen's cottages that can only be seen in their full extent at low water. If you walk along the cycle/foot path from the Tolcarne in Newlyn towards Wherrytown and look down at the beach you will see large granite blocks that have been polished white by the pebbles that were once fishermen's cottages, now all that is left are the foundations. They start from under the Tolcarne car park and sea wall and run nearly halfway to Lidl's in Wherrytown. Both of these things are easy to see and should convince even the most disbelieving that sea level is rising.

The weather is changing and anyone who thinks it isn't are wearing blinkers. Since 2000 hardly a year has gone by without a disastrous flood happening in some part of Britain, it has now become a common thing. Heatwaves that kill thousands of people around the world each year are now more common. These same heatwaves cause famine as the ground dries up and crops die. Other countries are having biblical floods on a regular basis which kills thousands, either from drowning or destroying food crops. Skin cancer from sunlight is increasing at an alarming rate each year, often with fatal results. Rising sea levels have already claimed numerous small islands in the Pacific Ocean resulting with the people being rescued and given new homes in New Zealand, Australia and other countries in that area.

Rising sea levels from melting glaciers and ice caps happens on a slower scale and would not be so noticeable except to people living on the coast. Places at risk in Mounts Bay would be Loe Bar, Porthleven, Praa Sands, Perranuthnoe, the coastline from St Michaels Mount to Newlyn, especially Marazion, parts of Mousehole and Lamorna, St Loy Bay and Porthcurno. On the north coast Sennen, St Ives, Hayle and Godrevy Sands.

What will have to be decided is where to build a sea wall. Will it get undermined by beach erosion, how high to build it and would it be financially feasible, or do we let nature take its course in that area. In Penwith there is only one area that is already below sea level and could possibly fall into this category, that is the land between Hayle Estuary and Marazion Marshes large parts of which are permanently under water. If it ever did break through then the strong tides in the Bristol Channel that now go around Lands End would in all probability take the shortest route and soon gouge out a wide deep channel between Hayle and St Michaels Mount. At some stage Penwith Council will have to face this problem, you can only build a sea wall so high before it becomes unstable. Then the resulting flood would be devastating for property and people's lives. That is why some councils in Devon, Somerset and Dorset have already decided to let nature take its course in some areas. There have been some interesting experiments on the east coast of England in areas that have already been reclaimed by the sea that could possibly apply to the Hayle/Marazion scenario if the sea broke through. On either side of deep channels large expanses of reed have been planted to form massive reed beds. It is cheap, self-perpetuating, reduces tidal wave surges, slows down erosion and in the thickest reed beds collects silt deposits very much like the equatorial mango swamps. The next large area to be flooded will undoubtedly be the Somerset Levels and reed beds will be used here for the reasons stated above.

A rise of one foot (30 centimetres) in sea level does not sound very much and most people just measure that amount above the tideline. Unfortunately this is not the case, on a quay wall it would only be 30 centimetres but on a sloping beach it would be a lot more. Depending on how much sand has been dumped the main Cliff Beach of Mousehole varies between 10 and 15 degrees slope. A 30 centimetre rise in sea level would mean the tidemark would be 2 metres higher on a 10 degree slope. This would put a lot of properties in and around Mousehole harbour in the danger zone for flooding with each tide. Some scientists predict a 10 foot (3 metre) rise within the next hundred years. If that happened the tideline would be 60 foot (20 metres) higher than at present on a 10 degree slope. It all depends on the gradient of the beach how far inland the water would reach *(see diagram)*. Such a rise would be disastrous not only for Mousehole but the whole country.

If you are one of those people who think nothing like that could possibly happen remember the examples given earlier that are easy to see. Other more dramatic evidence can be seen on the Isles of Scilly. On some of the smaller islands there are stone hedges that run down the side of one island, then underwater to reappear on another island. When the water is clear you can easily pick out these old stone hedges by the line of dark seaweed against the sand. These are the remains of ancient fields that once grew crops or held cattle. These old underwater hedges have been well documented and filmed by divers and have appeared on local television programmes several times. Proof enough that sea levels are rising.

A one foot (30 centimetre) rise in sea level would increase the high water mark for the following beach gradients.

5 degree beach by 11 foot,	3½ metres
10 degree beach by 6 foot,	2 metres
15 degree beach by 4 foot,	120 centimetres
20 degree beach by 3 foot,	90 centimetres
25 degree beach by 2½ foot,	75 centimetres
30 degree beach by 2 foot,	60 centimetres

The highest a natural beach can form is 45 degrees. Pour a bucket of dry sand onto a flat surface and the slope will be a natural 45 degrees.

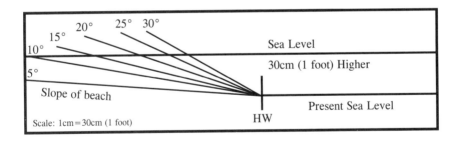

229

Storms

MOST REALLY BAD storms seem to happen at night when it is impossible to get any photographs, but one storm, Force 9 to 10, happened during the daylight hours on 18th December 1983.

It was a spectacular southerly storm with waves going some 80 to 90 foot, (30 metres) in the air when they hit the old quay, 4 times the height of the old quay wall. I used up a whole film, 36 exposures, with my OM10 camera and used both a telephoto and a wide-angle lens to capture some impressive and mighty waves crashing into the quays from all angles. Some of the best were taken from around the Gurnick showing the back of the old quay. I had to buckle myself to a telegraph pole to keep from being blown away and keep the camera steady, but it worked and they are probably the best storm photos taken in Mousehole. I do remember having to clean with fresh water both my camera and lenses to remove the salt spray.

Each huge wave was dumping hundreds of tons of sea water onto both quays and the noise was rather impressive to say the least. Several boats pulled up onto the car park for the winter were damaged, some smaller ones were washed into the harbour where they became smashed up. Several cars were smashed up as well, some repaired others scrapped. Wind was carrying the heavy spray right over the village and several properties were flooded. Others lost all or part of their slate roofs which again let in gallons of heavy spray. Sea water was running along Cliff Road past the newsagents to the monument and then down the slip. Seaweed being thrown up as the waves hit the quays was being blown right over the village to end up at Paul, Paul Lane looked very similar to a beach with so much seaweed on it.

Every single baulk was broken during that storm, the photographs show the broken ends, not worn away but completely broken. Our harbour was then left open to whatever the sea could throw at it and there was some slight damage to the Wharf Quay and houses. It was not until the middle of summer that new baulks could be found that were large enough and long enough to replace the whole lot. Then the blacksmiths took over and made new shoes to fit the ends that slid up and down in the harbour groove and also fitted two lifting hooks to each baulk. It was all completed and ready for use before the winter storms again battered our village.

Storm Damage & Wolf Rock Lighthouse

THERE IS ONE force in nature that is unstoppable, it changes the shapes of continents, it moves countless millions of tons of earth, sand and shingle every day and deposits it miles away. It does all this in calm weather, during severe storms this amount can be increased by at least ten fold. This unstoppable force is water. Be it river, sea or ocean it continually erodes away at whatever it comes into contact with and nothing can stop it. Even the small village ponds are victim to this erosion, they soon develop small banks on their edges caused by ripples created by wind. With all his ingenuity man has tried over the centuries, and failed miserably each time, to hold back the waters and stop erosion.

All his large beach defences and harbours only stay intact because they are constantly being repaired. So what causes all this destruction. Not a simple question to answer because there are really three elements involved and they all work with each other to wear away and weaken any structure.

To explain this further we will look at one of the hardest natural structures in the world, the tall granite cliffs of Cornwall, and explain how they arrived at their present shape. Water alone would not create such a diversity of shapes. All rock has weak points and faults caused by either cooling down faster in one place than another or intrusions of other materials during volcanic activity. In the case of sedimentary rock the weak points are caused by different layers of materials being laid down. Whatever the cause it is these weak areas that get eroded away first. During severe storms the huge waves can weigh several hundred tons and mixed up with all that weight of water is sand. Sand is one of the best natural abrasives known and it does not take that long before a small fissure appears in these weaker areas. Once that happens then the third element comes into play, air. It is air, compressed by the huge weight of water in large waves, that does the most damage. It gradually turns a small fissure into a larger one and, if the weaker rock runs parallel, into a cave. Over a period of time this constant hydraulic effect splits and loosens rocks which are then dislodged by the waves. Areas that have no faults in them are eroded more slowly and so you get this marvellously picturesque cliff coastline around Cornwall.

Bearing in mind the above it is easy to see why harbours that are open to the full force of any storms are constantly getting damaged and constantly need repairing, such as Mousehole. Each join between the granite stones is

233

a fault line which is exploited by both the air and waves during a storm. Mousehole harbour is protected during a south-east storm by the island and by Penzer Point headland during a south-westerly storm, but during a southerly storm there is no protection whatsoever and that is when all the damage is done. The Lizard Point is due south-east from Mousehole, and Penzer Point is south-west, enough for protection as the harbour is set back in a natural inlet caused by the two streams that empty into the harbour.

The history of Mousehole goes back about 4,000 years but the skill of reading and writing, which we all now take for granted, was only practised by academics and the gentry at that time, and the most prolific writers 1,000 years or more ago were the monks and others connected to the church. Consequently surviving records are few and far between and they tended to concentrate on very important issues. Some of the events that we would consider as important only warranted a few lines way back then.

For example, 'In 1313 Muzel (Mousehole) used to hold a seven day fair beginning on the Festival of St Bartholomew.' Exactly what type of fair or what happened during those seven days is not mentioned, a brief description from 'Morley's Memoirs of this fair' might give some idea though.

> Bartholomews Fair was held annually on 24th August from 1133 until 1855 when it was abolished as being a nuisance. It was the main cloth fair in the country and an important market for cattle, pewter and leather. A great feature of the fair was the large number of exhibitions, shows, performers of all kinds and quack doctors, which combined to make it one of the most popular fairs of its kind.

Another brief mention was 'in 1392 Mouzel (Mousehole) quay was extended by 60 foot.' Between this date and 1414 there must have been a very bad storm which did considerable damage because:

> Mosal (Mousehole) had once a chapel dedicated to the Virgin Mary. It was ruined by the sea. It had long been a useful landmark and saved many lives. Bishop Stafford in 1414 asked the good and humane to restore the chapel.

This is the earliest documented evidence I have come across regarding storm damage to Mousehole.

During Mousehole's long history there must of course have been other instances of storm damage that have not been recorded. If it had not been for the loss of the chapel in 1414 then in all probability this would not have been mentioned, and for a chapel to get washed away it must also have done considerable damage to the quay and Mousehole.

Storms are something that all harbours have to live with, after all they are only built to protect boats, and the longer the quays are that are open to the sea, the more damage they will sustain during severe weather. This was proved when the old quay was extended and the new quay built at Mousehole.

Prior to 1869 the old quay ended where the granite steps lead down to the harbour and during southerly storms there was only this short length open to damage. From the records it appears that this short length of quay had a charmed life, or maybe it was just constructed correctly, because there are very few mentions about any damage. That all changed after the extension and construction of the new quay.

During storms it was not always harbours that suffered, sailing vessels were also lost and usually with considerable casualties. Between 1700 and 1900, when sailing vessels peaked in numbers carrying cargo and passengers, it has been estimated that for every fifty yards of coastline in Mounts Bay a boat was wrecked and for every foot of coastline there was a corpse during those 200 years. Not all the corpses came from shore wrecks, vast numbers of boats were lost crossing the bay from the Lizard to Lands End, and to add to this collisions were a common occurrence, even more so when steam boats first made their appearance on the seas.

During the 1860's this loss of life was so great that Mr Josiah Wright from Mousehole wrote to the Right Honourable Sir George Gray, Bart, GCB, Secretary of State of the Home Department in London regarding 'the construction of a floating harbour of refuge in Mounts Bay. From Penlee Point in an easterly direction about three fifths of a mile.' This was Mr Wrights third time of writing about a breakwater to make a harbour of refuge and it was done because 'of the fearful loss of life from ships passing from the Lizard to Lands End with no shelter to run into.'

On 10th June 1867 a petition with 160 fishermen's signatures was sent to Mr A.G. Berdett Coutts, MP, 1 Stratton Street, London W, once again asking about a 'harbour of refuge' for Mounts Bay. It was once again deemed as 'not practicable' and that was just after two naval 'Ships of the Line' were lost with all hands trying to shelter in Mounts Bay.

It was about this time that Mousehole decided to enlarge its harbour to accommodate its ever increasing fishing fleet of luggers. It was started in 1869 and finished in spring of 1872.

The new quay was only eight months old when it suffered its first damage during a storm. The outside wall of the quay subsided due to insufficient foundations and this caused the stones to move and the paving on the quay top to also subsided. This was the start of a long legal battle between the Commissioners and Messrs Freeman and Sons that was not finally settled until the 1880's. The sum involved was £400 which was being withheld until the new quay was 'done to specifications.' The new quay was never finished or 'done to specifications' and the engineer, James Douglas, refused to sign the completion document, it was never ever signed.

So the first damage occurred in November 1872 mainly due to infill being earth and rubble instead of rocks and this same problem exists to the present time with the paving stones subsiding on a regular basis as the lighter infill gradually washes out. The last major subsidence of the paving stones was in 1998 and civil engineers came over and took up several of the paving stones along the pier. The infill that I saw was just sand and when this was tested with an eight foot iron bar it sank in up to the workmans arm without any effort. According to the engineer the only way to do the job properly and make it perfectly solid was to pump liquid cement under pressure into the interior of the quay. The bill for doing the whole of the new quay would in all probability run into hundreds of thousands of pounds, and that amount of money the Commissioners most certainly don't have, but about 30 foot near the gaps was done with liquid cement.

During August 1875 there were more heavy gales from the south which did considerable damage to the new quay and also washed away some of the roadway 'leading down to the south quay (old quay).' At this period of time the bank, (where the car park now is) was used by boatbuilders and the area closest to the harbour was where the smaller pilchard drivers used to be hauled out for the winter, much as todays boats are. So the roadway that was washed away must have been the one leading down to this area.

The southerly storm of February 1880 did an enormous amount of damage to the harbour and also fishing boats. All the harbour entrance baulks were broken and the paving slabs in the harbour mouth were all ripped out. The new harbour lights and mast was broken beyond repair. The crane was completely demolished and there was a very large breach in the back of the new quay.

The damage sustained was very severe and widespread. Twelve 1st class fishing vessels were wrecked and more than that again seriously damaged. Nearly all the vessels lost nets and footlines, some lost everything. Mr Runnalls was allowed to store 'up to 100 tons of stone on the quay for shipping out.' All these were washed into the harbour damaging boats. The estimated damage to Mousehole as a whole was put at £5,000. This was so serious for the village, harbour and fishermen that help was sought from the Government. A relief fund was also set up and was well supported from the other ports around the country. It took most of 1881 to get the repairs done, but the breach in the new quay was still not completed when in 1882 another southerly storm ripped the back of the new quay wide open again. Mr John Tregenza, who was doing the repairs, was instructed by the Commissioners to fill in the cavity 'with concrete of cement and that he order three tons of cement.'

After the bad storms in the early part of 1895 there was considerable damage done to both piers and the Commissioners met in the harbour to inspect the same. The work was put out to tender and it was finally agreed that Charles Tregenza's tender for £65 be accepted and that the 'work to commence at the earliest possible date, continued and finished as quick as possible.' The whole job was completed by the middle of November and after inspection Mr Charles Tregenza was called over and asked to finish of pointing the old pier, do the plot and rectify the slipway 'with a mixture of sand and cement in equal parts as to the former agreement.' This he agreed to do for £25.

Pointing was done on both the inside and outside of the new quay as well as the paving on the pier top. This was done in an effort to try and stop the infill from washing out and weakening the quay. It also made the quay a lot more hygienic and easier for the fish buyers to keep clean, it also prevented the cotton nets from dropping between the paving stones and getting torn. Regardless of how clean any fish buyer was there would always be a certain amount of blood and fish offal that managed to drain down between the cracks in the paving. The pointing would reduce this happening.

Severe storms once again did considerable damage to the back of the quays during the early part of 1905. The Commissioners decided that 'a practical man be employed to look at the back of the piers to see what could be done to the same.' The 'practical man' was a Mr Caldwell, architect from Penzance, who was asked 'to come and give his opinion on the same during the next spring tides.'

After inspection, plans and specifications where drawn up by Mr Caldwell for the repair to the back of the old quay. Tenders were to be invited for the work and the following notice was to be 'posted as well as inserted in the *Cornishman* and *Cornish Telegraph* newspapers.'

MOUSEHOLE PIER AND HARBOUR

Tenders are invited for the repairing of the back of the old quay. Plans and specifications of the work may be seen in the Harbour Office. Tenders must be sent to the undersigned on or before Saturday noon 2nd September 1905.

The lowest or any tender not necessarily accepted.

Bruce Wright, Secretary to the Commissioners.

Three tenders where received:

Messrs Harvey and Waters	£320
Mr John Tregenza	£220
Mr Charles Tregenza	£170

Mr Charles Tregenza's tender for £170 was accepted. Mr Caldwell was informed of the decision and was asked 'to inspect the work at intervals when it was proceeding to see that it was carried out according to plans and specifications.' From this we can determine that the Commissioners where definitely going to see that the work was carried out as Mr Caldwell specified.

One thing I have noticed during my research is the vast difference in prices tendered by contractors regarding various work to be done in the harbour. No reasons are given why some are twice the price, one must assume that they either had a larger profit margin or were prepared to take their time and do a more substantial job of work.

During the beginning of 1912 a severe southerly storm did considerable damage with,

> . . . the south pier (new extension) which was exposed to the full force of the waves received such a shaking that on a survey it was found that in some parts the foundations had shrunk several inches. The Commissioners, who have no money at their disposal, are at their wits end fearing that unless something is done very quickly there will be quite a breach made.

The above extract was part of a letter sent to Sir Clifford J Cory, Bart, M.P. asking for help in securing a loan to pay for the repairs.

A survey was carried out by Mr Hooper and Mr Greenway who where in charge of work being carried out at Newlyn Harbour. After inspecting the old quay they 'found it in a very bad state and in making out the specifications the amount required to put it in thorough repair would amount to a good sum, which the Commissioners must be prepared to ask for from the Treasury.' The amount the surveyors recommended on their specification was £4,000.

By a strange coincedent the civil engineer who drew out the plans and specifications for this work was Mr William James Douglas, the son of James, later, Sir James Douglas, who drew up the original specifications for the new quay in 1869. His son William became a Ministry Inspector for all work carried out in Cornwall.

All storms do some damage to a lesser or greater degree but the storm which caused the most wide spread damage during the last 100 years occurred on Ash Wednesday 1962. It was a very severe southerly storm come hurricane with winds recorded at 138 miles per hour during gusts. The damage front in Mounts Bay extended from Lands End around the coast to Praa Sands. A considerable amount of ground was lost to the sea for ever along this front.

At Porthgwarra and Penberth the steep slipways of these two coves was broken up and washed away, some cove boats were also damaged. In St Loy Bay the coastline was cut back by 100 yards in some places and the trees, which are a feature of St Loy, where devastated. Great swathes where flattened and uprooted.

Between St Loy and Lamorna large areas of the softer earth and boulder cliff face fell into the sea and were washed away as the large waves and wind forced tons of sea water onto the cliff tops. On the western side of Lamorna Cove there were, and still are, a considerable number of caves, most of these collapsed in on themselves cutting the actual cliff face back by some 200 yards in certain places. The same thing happened on the western side of Penzer Point where the Coastguard station used to be, this is between Lamorna and Mousehole. The end of Lamorna quay was broken off and their slip washed away.

In Mousehole the old quay was badly damaged and the top coping washed away. The wooden crane that was on the end of the old quay was also badly damaged and it even lifted the whole crane out of its iron pivot that was set into the quay. The new quay was breached and undermined and the force of the air inside the quay compressed by the huge waves lifted up several of the paving stones. The wind was so strong and the waves where so large that they were going right up the slip road at the end of the new quay, and the water was running along the Cliff Road and pouring back into the harbour down the slip by the monument. Seaweed torn from its anchorage on the rocks was being blown all over the village and at Paul pub and the church, about a mile inland up the hill, they were also being blessed with seaweed.

The car park at the end of the old quay was inundated and at the end of the cement slip there was a drop of about three foot to the sand caused by the amount of water coming over the quay and pouring down the slip. The car park at the end of the new quay just disappeared completely and was taken down to the bedrock. The houses backing this car park were undermined by about six foot and hanging in the air, all the doors and windows were broken. The road that led up to the car park ended some twenty foot in the air. Round the corner from here the sea walls protecting those properties was badly damage and the Coastguards Hotel wall was basically washed away, just the bottom layers of stones remaining. Round the corner from here there was no protective wall and some twenty foot of earth and stone was washed away. The zig-zag path leading to the main road had also disappeared except for the top two turns. The concrete walk was breached in several places allowing the sea to erode the soft ground away behind it, this in turn caused the main road to subside in one area.

There was also a considerable amount of flooding to properties around the harbour, especially on the western side of the village where several cottages had to be evacuated. At the Ship Inn water was coming in through the back door and running out through the front door, but it did not stop anyone from drinking, it used to be a fairly regular occurrence during a very bad southerly. All this flooding is caused by the waves hitting the quays and sending tons of water up into the air which would then be blown by the storm force winds all over the village, this still happens during every southerly storm.

There were breaches in all the sea walls between Mousehole and Newlyn which let the sea into the soft ground behind causing more erosion. Newlyn was very badly damaged with considerable flooding up to three foot deep around the Tolcarne area. All the properties from the old Newlyn bridge to the Tolcarne Inn lost back walls and roofs and one commercial property was flattened. Inside the harbour boats were sinking from the amount of water coming over the quay, others kept parting their moorings and were then blown into other tiers of boats which smashed up in the heavy surges running up the harbour. Several of the larger vessels started their engines and as they parted rode out the storm in the middle of the harbour with just enough speed to keep them in one place. Several of the smaller boats where completely wrecked and one even ended up being washed onto the fish market, undamaged.

Wherrytown, between Newlyn and Penzance, took a real battering and lost some 400 yards of ground to the sea, right back to the main road which was also damaged. Some of this land was reclaimed, and is now a car park. Opposite used to be the Western National bus depot and this building was very badly damaged losing most of its roof and some of its walls, these in turn collapsed onto some of the buses. The gardens and bowling green could not be seen as they were buried under about six foot of sand and shingle, this dammed up the stream which caused even more flooding.

Penzance promenade and band stand where demolished from Wherrytown to the bathing pool. The sea wall and promenade had completely disappeared as far back as the road. All the shops, hotels and private houses along the prom had all their windows broken and in some cases the roof had lifted off. Stone, sand and shingle covered the road to a depth of three feet and all the gardens as well, all where flooded. The bathing pool suffered a major crack and there was damage to the floating dock gates. Penzance harbour was also damaged. Penzance railway station was flooded to the depth of the platforms and the line was also undermined where it runs along the sea front.

240

Marazion sea defences where breached in several places and there was also considerable flooding, the causeway leading to St Michaels Mount disintergrated and washed away.

At Perranuthnoe the waves carved away some 200 to 300 yards of the softer cliff and their small slipway leading to the beach was also carried away leaving a six foot drop to the sand. Praa Sands suffered the same type of damage which left the beach showing the old peat bog which was some twelve inches above the remaining sand.

The cost of repairing all the damage during the Ash Wednesday storm must have run into several millions of pounds.

It is not only structures that are affected by storms but also the boats that ply their trade around the oceans of the world, even those vessels moored up in harbours are not necessarily safe as the following shows.

On Monday 12th February 1883 a southerly storm lashed Mounts Bay which put a boat and crew in danger whilst moored up in Mousehole harbour.

> The schooner *Victoria* of Penzance, Captained by Mr Gunn, took a severe beating and Master and crew had a narrow escape from hurt. The schooner was laden with road stone from Mr James Runnalls quarry and had been at Mousehole some three weeks. The harbour entrance baulks were smashed and the sea rolled over the northern arm of the quay onto *Victoria*. Her bulwarks were smashed, punt washed off the deck, galley smashed, her anchor washed from port to starboard side and she parted her forward warp.
>
> Captain and crew had to take to the rigging but even here it was dangerous and they called for help. The waves were now so big and heavy that three large granite blocks of the quay pavement were washed away and the schooner now had over six feet of water in her. The 'Rocket Apparatus' was about to be fetched to rescue the men when a heavy shower came on. The fishermen said that this and the falling tide would soon calm the sea. When the tide receded the work of repairing began.

During this storm houses along the wharf were also flooded and 'furniture was moved from flooded houses to neighbours houses, fires were lit, and there was much bailing and mopping up, with wet things laid out to dry.'

Mounts Bay and ship wrecks appear to go together and to mention them all would be virtually impossible, no one will ever know the exact number of vessels lost in the bay and in so many cases the only report was 'wreckage washed ashore at.' The reason why there has been so many wrecks is quite simple in general terms. Mounts Bay was, and still is, classed as a 'safe anchorage and shelter from storms from all directions except when the wind is from the south.' From my research it becomes apparent that over 99% of all wrecks occurred from vessels that had taken shelter in the bay when making passage from the Lizard to Lands End, these vessels were all bound up channel for Wales or the Liverpool area. Some of the accounts mention that when they '. . . took anchor the wind was from the west, or south west, and after three days the wind came south, the Master tried unsuccessfully to beat out the bay but went ashore at . . .' Other accounts state that '. . . the schooner . . . tried to make passage past Lands End to safer waters but the strong southerly gale drove her back into the bay where she went ashore at . . .' A lot of these incidents were also accompanied by the loss of all crew, but this was not always the case as an eye witness account by the Reverant Thomas Stanley, a Wesleyan Minister, proves.

In February 1797 there was a most dreadful storm which proved fatal to several vessels and their crews near Penzance. Among other vessels that were driven ashore was a Brig from Cardiff bound for London. The Captain, though a young man, acted with the greatest prudence. When his vessels appeared round Penlee Point she was much shattered. With lifeboats and rails washed away and her sails torn to shreds, one man only appeared on deck and he was at the helm.

When about half a mile of Penzance the man threw over a small barrel to which one end of a rope was tied, the other end being fastened to the Brig. Instead of running the vessel in he brought her round with her head to the wind and let her drive in stern first. This method prolonged the time so much that the barrel, with rope attached, reached the shore, and the anxious crowd on the beach rejoiced in the possession of it. Once the barrel reached the shore the Captain and five of his crew appeared on deck. Each man instantly fastened himself to the end of the rope which was on board and plunged into the raging sea and were all soon dragged through the angry waters to dry land, where they were most joyfully congratulated by their deliverers who had so miraculously saved them from drowning. The Captain informed me that this was the second time he had been saved by throwing a barrel overboard.

The following account shows how difficult it must have been for sailing boats to beat out of the bay during a southerly gale.

On 20th April 1880 a vessels could be seen beating up and down the bay in a south gale, trying to make sea room in an attempt to pass Lands End. All day the fisherman watched her sail fearing for her safety. As well they might for on 21st April they noticed the craft had been driven closer inshore and some time around midday she struck the Great Cudden Point and sank 100 yards eastwards of the extreme point. All her crew where saved. She was a German Galliot named *Emmanuel* from Emden of 72 ton gross.

It was not always sailing boats that where affected by a southerly storm and got blown off course as the following shows.

On 1st April 1880 the SS *Dawlais* carrying 1,500 tons of iron ore was on passage from Bilbao to South Wales, she was blown off course, struck the Runnel Stone and sank during a southerly gale. There where 19 men on board, 17 of whom where landed at St Ives and two were lost.

It is quite possible that this vessel also damaged the Runnel Stone Buoy, although this is not mentioned, because on the 7th July 1881 'a new buoy was placed at the Runnel Stone, 30 to 40 foot long, 10 to 12 foot wide, the bell is fixed in the centre and struck by four iron balls that run in grooves.' Even with all the buoys and lighthouses that were being constructed around the coast could not really help any vessels during storms. Even the mighty Royal British Navy had to bow down to the weather as the following extract shows.

On the 18th July 1910 a large fleet of nearly 200 British warships assembled in Mounts Bay for a review, and remained there until the 24th. Great preparations were made for this event. Shopkeepers took in extra stores and provisions for the crowds who would come to purchase their viands. To grace the occasion the celebrated airman of the day, Graham White, came west, and on the 23rd made circuits over the fleet in his aeroplane, he was the first aviator to fly over Mounts Bay. This was a great achievement and crowds of people watched with great excitement from every point of vantage along the coast as the daring airman slid just over the castle of St Michaels Mount and circled over the fleet of ships and back again. The flight was a subject of much comment for a good while after.

Unfortunately the review did not take place. The weather during the week was fine but towards the end it changed. On Sunday a gale from the south made it insecure for the ships to remain in Mounts Bay. On Sunday evening disappointed crowds watched the ships weigh anchor and steamed around the Lizard to more peaceful waters. While shopkeepers and vendors were left with large stocks of provisions on their hands.

If a southerly gale can move 200 warships from the bay then it gives you some idea what sailing ships had to put up with. There are many references concerning sailing vessels trying to beat out of the bay during southerly gales, in 1874 there is an article concerning a schooner that was seen beating across the bay for six days trying to make herself some sea room. It was never established whether she made it round Lands End but during the next two days wreckage came ashore between Penzance and St Michaels Mount. The name of the schooner or wreckage was never discovered, maybe they where one and the same, this seems more than probable as the last line stated 'The wreckage was new and not long in the water.'

A lot of southerly storms are accompanied by torrential rain which in itself causes problems for property ashore as well as fishing boats. During very heavy rain fall there are numerous references to boats sinking 'due to extremely heavy rain.' From the reports it appears that the vast majority where pumped out and refloated without to much damage.

This would not be the case of property on the land as the following shows.

> On 22nd November 1894 floods in Mousehole caused untold damage, everywhere rivers overflow and streets turned into new rivers, all drains blocked, all bolts filled with stone, grit and dirt. Messrs Gibson and Sons from Penzance spent the day taking photographs.

It is a great pity that the reporters of the day did not go into more detail. If they had then it could be compared with the floods that devastate the village at the present time. During the last few years, 1996-2000, there have been several severe floods which have caused untold damage to householders. In 1997 the council put several skips around the village for householders to dump ruined carpets, curtains, fridges, furniture, televisions in after one severe flood. It also took the council three days to remove all the stones, shingle and mud from the roads and unblock the storm drains and clear the blocked streams. Early 1999 they made a start on flood defences by putting in larger storm drains in an effort to transport the water from the hills and streams instead of it rushing down the back streets during heavy rain storms. Unfortunately they could not dig up peoples houses so these very large storm pipes some four or five in diameter lead down to the middle of the village and then have to be reduced into a normal very much smaller sewer pipe. As yet they have not been severely tested and some of us who saw these pipes being laid wondered what will happen when we get a torrential downpour or cloud burst, will they be able to cope or block up, back up, when the water reaches the smaller pipes. Only time will tell.

When South West Water put in our new sewer system in 1994/95 several of us voiced our concerns regarding the storm drains which they incorporated into the main sewer which leads to the pumping station. *(see Sewer system)*.

WOLF ROCK LIGHTHOUSE

The authorities where trying their hardest to make the sea a safer place by marking all the reefs that were claiming so many vessels and even more lives. Even though they could do very little about the extremes of weather they could at least mark these dangerous areas with buoys or lighthouses.

On 18th June 1861 Mr James Douglas and staff formally started work on Penzance quay to build the Wolf Rock lighthouse. On 17th March 1862 they first landed on the rock to prepare the foundations. The first foundations stones were laid on 6th August 1864 2 foot 4 inches above low water spring tide. They spent 267 hours on the Wolf Rock during this year. In 1865 they worked on the Rock for 248 hours. High water mark was reached on 24th July 1866 after 224 hours work that year. In 1867 they worked for 313 hours on the Wolf Rock and 276 hours during 1868. Sir Fredrick Arrow fixed the capstone on the lighthouse on the 17th July 1869. The total cost of the whole construction, including the lantern, came to £62,726 and it took 1,736 hours 50 minutes work to complete the whole work from start to finish.

There appears to be a slight discrepancy in the dates of starting and the date that Mr James Douglas designed the lighthouse of one year, which he is credited with in 1862. Even so when you consider that there was only sail power to transport all the granite stones the 16 miles to the Wolf Rock from Penzance, and a lot of the work was restricted by tides and of course the vagaries of the weather. Then 8 years does not seem to long a time for this work, especially when taking into account that only a few men would be able to actually work there due to restricted space and all the work would be done by hand. No horses or steam cranes to help with the heavy work, just pulleys and muscle power.

Summer Storm Damage

OCCASIONALLY WE GET severe southerly summer storms, force 9 to 10 during the summer months. These nearly always cause a lot of damage in the harbour and on the quays. I have photographs that show the slip by the monument covered from top to bottom with broken and smashed punts that have been pulled up there so as not to cause more damage in the harbour. The last bad storm was in 2002 where some twenty small punts were severely damaged or just smashed up. Some of these were just small pieces about a metre long, mixed up amongst the seaweed. The slip looked just like a tip scene full of broken wood and fibreglass punts. These were all taken away by lorries to be dumped at special sites. How much monies worth of punts were lost I don't know but it must have been up to £10,000 if they were all going to be replaced, probably a lot more money than that, I don't know the price of punts not having every brought one.

Years ago farmers would come down with their tractors and trailers to collect seaweed to use as fertiliser on their ground. This stopped in about 1950-60. I have one photograph showing seaweed being collected.

The amount of sea water coming over the quays during a southerly storm can be measured in tons and this causes a lot of damage to any car that has not been moved. Back in the 60's some six or seven cars on the New Quay got caught in a southerly storm one day. They were all written off with one car being washed through the railings and into the harbour. The roof of the car had been pushed down below the level of its seats by the weight of water hitting its roof. It bent the single harbour railings up to get through, and it only took one wave to push it under the railing. The number of cars that have been written off must be well over a million pounds worth over the years.

In the 90's there were three brand new cars on the old quay, a new BMW with less than three hundred miles on the clock took a real pounding. Every window was broken, the roof was pushed down below the seat level and all its door were buckled. Inside the car was full of shingle, sand, seaweed and sea water, the owner was in the pub trying to sell his new BMW for £10 – there were no takers. It was finally towed away to St Erth scrapyard and put through their car crusher.

Another car was a brand new large Volkswagon that suffered the same fate as the BMW, that had less than five hundred miles on its clock. He tried to sell it in the pub for £10, same as the other man. Once again no takers. Altogether some nine or ten cars were destroyed during that storm. The last such storm was in 2004 and this time there were sixteen cars involved. Some of them new, I took photographs of some. Both quays were affected and any vehicle on either quay was severely damaged or written off. One such was a new Landrover, no windows, bent roof, buckled bonnet and full of sand and shingle. The owner came down in the morning jumped in and started it up, then drove it to the local garage to be mended. Others had to be towed or winched clear as they were jammed under the harbour railings, some went straight to the scrapyard. It is only a matter of time before it happens again. A sign is always put up before the storm arrives but for some reason visitors either can't read or ignore the sign. Now the Harbour Master chains off the quay to stop cars going down.

When there is a lot of heavy rain the stream that empties into the harbour under the monument gushes into the harbour in a stream of liquid mud that dredges a wide deep channel right down through the beach towards the gaps. Over the years several gold sovereigns have been found after such an event. The last one to my knowledge was found by a visitor in 2009. The coin was just resting on a lip of the stream outlet in full view, I watched him pick it up from the Cliff Road. I had thought of going down with my metal detector but gave up because the whole family were busy searching the dredged gully. Whether they found any more I don't know because I gave up and went home.

If there is a really heavy downpour of rain up at Paul then the little stream that runs under the village to the monument can become blocked at the top end. When that happens the flood water gushes down Duck Street. The worst I've seen was in the 90's when it came down there about two or three foot deep. When that happens the Cliff Road is blocked by large rocks, stones and earth washed down Duck Street as the water rushes across the road into the harbour. Very little damage is done to properties in this street because it's flowing so fast. All the flower pots, grow bags and wheelie bins end up in the harbour, the bins and grow bags floating, one grow bag was happily floating around the harbour with its flowers intact. Our village could be in real trouble if a cloudburst with two or three inches of rain happened up at Paul. One day it will happen, hopefully not on a Boscastle scale.

Ash Wednesday Storm
27th February 1963

TO FIND THE direction of wind in Mousehole is really simple. If you stand in front of the village clock facing the Cenotaph and look at the Lizard Point that is due south-east, turn around and look at our clock and you are facing north-west. When coming home in my fishing boat once you breast the Lizard Light wind the wheel around until the compass reads North West and you will end up at the back of Mousehole Island. The only wind to affect Mousehole really badly is from the south. A point halfway between the Lizard Point and the harbour buildings is roughly south and wind coming from that direction has thousands of miles of Atlantic Ocean to cross before it hits Mousehole. That is why a storm from the south always has and always will cause damage to our village.

One of the worst storms for well over 100 years happened on Ash Wednesday 1963. Mousehole, Newlyn and Penzance were all badly damaged – the worst affected was undoubtedly Penzance. Mousehole also suffered badly with both quays sustaining severe damage. The Old Quay (South Quay) lost a lot of its top coping stones and the back of this quay had lots of its large rocks displaced. The old wooden crane used to lower and lift the wooden baulks was lifted up and out of its iron pivot but all the chains and wires kept it from washing away. Numerous wooden baulks were also smashed up like matchwood. The New Quay (North Quay) had several large stones washed out of the back to leave a very large hole with some of the paving stones on the quay surface being displaced. The Bank car park just disappeared leaving the slip road ending up in mid air some 12 foot (4 metres) above the shore. All the houses facing the car park lost their doors and windows and several houses were left with the outside wall hanging in mid air. The local children spent days collecting money, medals etc that had washed out of the bank and gathered in rock pools. Several gold sovereigns were also found which prompted a few grown men to search the area. There was also an unbelievable amount of bronze screws and large nails left in the pools which children collected by the bucket full and sold to either shipwrights or antique shops along with bronze door knockers and letter boxes. One such bronze letter box is now fixed firmly into my door although it is rather narrow for today's larger mail. I also have a bronze window opener from this period which is used most days, unfortunately the little pins are modern material not bronze.

Severe damage was done to the Gurnick area with houses also flooded and evacuated, as were the houses alongside the harbour by the south car park. The concrete walkway past the Bank car park that goes nearly to the old lifeboat station was breached in several places which let the waves wash away the earth and rubble up to the road. Two areas on the main Mousehole Newlyn road collapsed, one went half way across the road the other affected just the pavement. Engineers deemed the road unsafe and a one way system was introduced until they could backfill then resurface both the road and pavement. The village of Paul was covered in seaweed that had blown up the hill, the graveyard was covered in weed and people were taking that away in wheelbarrows. I walked from Mousehole along the coast to Penzance taking photographs. A friend of mine called Julian Pender decided to go in on his motorcycle, he got as far as the quarry when a gust of wind blew him and his bike against the quarry wall breaking both his legs.

Newlyn was another disaster area with numerous vessels sinking or breaking up in the weather. Those that broke adrift were washed against the fish market and smashed to pieces. The Fishermen's Mission was also badly damaged and flooded as were all the houses in and around the Tolcarne. The Tolcarne pub and some engineering premises next to it were flooded and some places lost their roofs.

At Wherrytown it was a job to recognise some places. Where Lidl's now stands used to be the main bus depot for Penwith. Not one bus left there because that area was flooded to a depth of eight foot (2½ metres) and had shingle washed into there which was over 3 foot (1 metre) deep. In front of the depot across the road there used to be a large park with old ruins and tall coniferous trees going out some 200 to 300 yards (approx 250 metres) into the sea. That was all gone and there was not one single bit of tree left to show they grew there, it had been washed away right to the road. It has since been built out a little way with quarry spoil and a tall sea wall, it now has a skateboard arena where trees once grew. The bowling greens were buried under 3 foot (1 metre) of shingle and it took nearly two years to re-open. They had to remove shingle, then the soil, which was salt laden, bring in new earth and reseed the whole area, hence the long gap before it could be used properly for bowls.

From Wherrytown to Penzance bathing pool there was nothing left of the sea wall, bandstand or prom, it was just smashed up. The road was like a shingle beach 3 foot (1 metre) deep. All the hotels and houses along the prom were evacuated and there were no windows left anywhere and very few doors and their gardens buried under shingle. Not one single building escaped along the prom but the bathing pool stood firm, it just filled up with sand and shingle. All the major hotels were closed for about three months as repairs and drying were carried out, some of the houses took even longer. Restoration work on Penzance prom took all summer and was only just finished in time for the winter gales.

Lands End Coastguard Station and Culdrose Airbase on the Lizard recorded winds of up to 130 miles per hour. This was by far the most damaging storm since 1880 – force 12 on the Beaufort Scale which is classed as a hurricane. We regularly get storms and severe storms as when our lifeboat was lost but nothing on the scale of the Ash Wednesday storm of 1963. A lot of ground was lost to the sea during that storm – just washed away. From Newlyn to Penzance bathing pool there is now a new sea wall that is hoped will deal with such a thing again. Even so Penzance prom is often closed during bad storms to prevent people and cars getting damaged or washed away. It still takes a day or so for diggers and mechanical road sweepers to clear the sand, shingle and seaweed after a southerly storm, and there is very little that can be done to stop that happening once or twice a year.

They could of course build a higher sea wall but when you see waves of 12 foot (4 metres) hitting the quay and shooting up in the air how high would it have to be? I feel sure that nobody would like to see a wall that high along the prom. It might save the road and property but unless the pavement was higher you wouldn't be able to see the sea. Something will have to be done in time because of rising sea levels.

Earthquakes

MOST PEOPLE ASSOCIATE earthquakes with other places not in England but we do get them. The most active area in the UK for earth movement is a place called Sticklepath Fault in Devon which has sliced off a large part of Dartmoor Plateau on the eastern side of the moor. This fault is in constant movement and the deep fault line is full of seismic measuring devices. I walked up the fault in the 1960's and it really is a strange feeling and sight because Dartmoor Plateau rises vertically for hundreds of feet above your head. When you drive along the bottom edge of Dartmoor, I think its the A38 road, it rises straight up just like its been cut with a large knife. As long as this large long fault line keeps moving there should not be any earthquakes, if it does stop then after a few years there would be a massive earthquake.

Mousehole suffered a very bad earthquake in the early 1970's which effected a large area of Penwith and Helston. It happened at night and various reports from people driving cars on the A30 towards Penzance reported seeing a large flash of light followed by a huge bang. My own experience is as follows. I was asleep when I heard the bang and getting up found it hard to walk across the floor because everything was shaking which turned out to be lucky for me. I had been in earthquakes abroad so knew what it was. There was a sudden crash and a small part of my roof collapsed near the cooker, there was also a huge crack in the chimney breast. The roof and skylights were mended the next day but it took me another day to clear the cooker of grit and dust as well as all my books and floor. The chimney breast never did get mended and was still like that when the building was pulled down in the 90's. Other people in the village reported things falling off walls or windows breaking and nearly all said their house was full of floating dust particles. It was quite a good shaking I can tell you. The *Cornishman* reported damage over a wide area. At St Just windows were broken, St Michaels Mount also suffered but it appeared the worst was Helston. They had just finished building a full size swimming pool which was due to be opened the next day but a huge crack had appeared across the bottom and sides of the pool.

When asked what could be done about it the engineers said fill it in and start again somewhere else, whether this actually happened I do not know. There was also a good picture in the *Cornishman* showing the Headmaster of Helston School standing in a large crack. Needless to say the school was closed down while repairs were carried out.

The epicentre was put out in Mounts Bay and various reports on the magnitude varied between 3.5 to 5 on the Richter Scale. The epicentre also varied slightly from Mounts Bay, the Wolf Rock Lighthouse or beyond but they all did agree that it was near Mounts Bay under the sea, there was no tsunami.

I have discovered a couple of interesting facts since the earthquake, although there is no documented proof. Firstly that a piece of very rough ground that rises up quickly to within a few fathoms of the surface a couple of miles off Lands End is very, very, slowly rising. This was reported to me by a man who worked on the Trinity House vessel that serviced the various lighthouses. This piece of ground is known as Carn Base and has a horrendous tide race but it is also a very good place for catching fish and shellfish. I used to work this area with gill nets in the 80's up until 2000 when I retired, but because of the tide race it was only possible to work that area during neap tides. I have found no documented proof that this is happening and whether it is rising or how fast.

The other regards nuclear submarines. It was a TV programme back in the 80's that was talking about American and Russian nuclear submarines that were missing at sea, and going by this programme there appeared to be quite a few. Anyhow one American submarine went missing somewhere off Lands End in the same year that we had our earthquake, maybe it blew up which could account for the bright flash reported by car drivers. Both countries are very secretive about losing nuclear submarines for obvious reasons so whether it was lost where the programme claimed is another matter, or for that reason whether in was actually lost.

We have had lots of small tremors since the big one, the last tremors were in 1999 when two occurred fairly close together, since then nothing.

Tornado

HERE'S SOMETHING ELSE that is only associated with other countries but happened in Mousehole on Sunday 11th February 1990. One of the longest and hardest winters for continuous storms with the wind seemingly shifting every day to another direction started on the 11th December 1989 and didn't really let up until 2nd March 1990. When you read the following some of you will remember national newspaper headlines and recall television programmes relating to this period. Some of you will have lost friends or relations because the total count was some 53 people killed in the south of England between the above dates. The following accounts are all taken from my own personal diaries.

Monday 11th December, south-south-east storm force 9 blowing, barograph reading 29.3. Mousehole taking a beating from waves.

Tuesday 12th December, southerly storm force 9 blowing, barograph 29.2. Again damage to Bank car park and both quays awash.

Wednesday 13th December, south-west storm force 9 with heavy rain, barograph 28.9. Very big ground sea with island awash. Very large earth slide at Penlee Quarry that I hit in my car causing damage, car up on two wheels, rocks, stones and mud about 15 to 20 foot high across road. Police car arrived and helped me, they blocked off road with signs saying road closed, diggers and lorries coming to clear the road.

Thursday 14th December, south-south-west storm force 9, barograph 28.7.

Friday 15th December, southerly storm force 9-10, expected shortly.

Saturday 16th December, southerly storm force 9-10, barograph 28.0. Culdrose Air Station and Lizard Coastguard recorded gusts up to 100 miles per hour. Huge great seas smashing into harbour, Bank car park washed away with lots of damage to parked cars, some written off from stones and boulders landing on them. Mousehole Harbour Christmas Lights smashed up. Huge waves sweeping whole length of both quays. 5.30 harbour entrance baulks being broken, gang of fishermen with helpers worked until 9.30 roping and securing baulks which Graham Moore, shopkeeper, towed up the slip with his Landrover. Newlyn badly flooded and damaged, Penzance prom closed with paving stones washed out.

Sunday 17th December, southerly storm force 9, barograph 29.0. Bank car park washed right away during night, both quays had huges rocks several feet across washed up onto them. Lots of damage to houses in the village, roofs, chimneys, windows and flooding. Lots of boats smashed up.

255

Newlyn badly flooded, old Newlyn bridge severely damaged, Fishermen's Mission also damaged, boats in Newlyn harbour damaged or smashed. Penzance prom severely damaged with breaches in sea wall. Praa Sands lost its beach cafe, slipway and fourty foot of cliff, all washed away. Porthleven took a real battering with huge waves going right over the top of some houses, saw that on television. Gusts up to 120 miles per hour recorded at height of storm, now classed as a hurricane. Scillies also took a battering with St Mary's lighthouse washed away. National news, south-west took brunt of hurrican with 17 people killed, mostly by falling trees.

Monday 18th December, south-west storm force 9, barograph 28.5. No let up.

Tuesday 19th December, south-west gale 8, barograph 29.1.

Wednesday 20th December, south-west gale 7-8, barograph 29.5.

Thursday 21st December 1989 until 22nd January 1990, only force 6 with odd gale.

Tuesday 23rd January 1990, forecast is for severe gales again, barograph 29.5.

Thursday 25th January, westerly storm force 10 blowing, barograph down to 28.5. I got up 0300 because of the noise. Could hear slates flying around and windows breaking. The village took a real battering, lots of back roads closed because of flying slates, cars damaged with slates and chimneys falling down. Electric went off at 0900 and didn't come back on until 9.00 in the evening. According to the local builders a third of houses in Mousehole were damaged, whole roofs or part roofs gone, chimney stacks gone or badly cracked. Electric company said pylons at Camborne had blown down, also mains relay at Camborne had been damaged. On north coast some houses were blown down. Lands End was also closed. Sleet and snow fell during the afternoon and most of the night.

Friday 26th January, westerly gale 8 now, barograph 29.3. Sleet and snow all day. South-west took brunt of hurrican, papers saying 37 people killed yesterday, most from branches or trees blowing down but also from flying slates and chimney stacks. Still no television, relay station badly damaged. It did come back at 8.00, now saying 54 people killed, several school children when their school blew over. Electricity still intermittent. Bad thunder and lightening storm in afternoon. My roof leaking but builders can't do anything until wind eases. Still sleeting and snowing at 5.00 but it is melting. Local news saying villages on north coast still no electricity and probably will not be until Monday at earliest, all the pylons have been blown down.

Saturday 27th January, southerly storm force 9 blowing, barograph 28.4. A lot of thunder and lightening, sleet and snow. Electricity went off again, lightening struck the transformers, might be back on by Monday.

Another night of paraffin lights, getting used to lighting those this winter. Another wild night with no television.

Sunday 28th January, south-west gale 8, barograph 29.3. Sleet and hail showers all day. Electricity came back on midday, we are lucky because places on north coast still have no power.

Monday 29th January, southerly gale 8 with heavy rain, barograph 28.8. Roof still leaking, found I had lost all my diaries from 1960 until 1982, 20 years of Mousehole history lost, hadn't noticed that they were sitting in water and all the ink had run and turned the pages bright blue, builders can't do anything until wind and rain eases. Turning out to be a horrible winter with storms and deaths.

Tuesday 30th, Wednesday 31st and 1st February, southerly storm force 9 blowing, barograph 28.8 for 3 days without moving. Radio Cornwall saying Culdrose Airbase recording winds to 100 miles per hour for last three days. Village and quays taking another pounding, more of the Bank car park has disappeared, very little of that left now. Lots of roofs have yet to be repaired, weather against any person working on high roofs.

Several power lines that had just been mended have blown down again, they have had people repairing lines and pylons from all over the country in the south-west for the last week or so, now some have come down again, Mousehole alright at the moment.

Friday 2nd, Saturday 3rd, Sunday 4th, Monday 5th and Tuesday 6th February, south-west gale 8 non-stop, barograph between 29.4 and 29.5. So many places flooded in the whole country with continuous heavy rain, seems most rivers have burst their banks and flooded towns. Trawlers and other fishing boats have not been out to sea since early December now and crews must be getting short of money, don't see many out drinking now. Reports coming in of several people dying during the floods. One pub landlord caught a 13 pound salmon in his car park 2 miles from the river. Local news showing lots of places in Cornwall flooded. Forecast is for another south-west storm with severe flooding and structural damage.

Wednesday 7th February, south-west storm force 10 blowing, barometer 29.1. Radio Cornwall saying wind at Lizard and Culdrose gusting to 100 miles per hour. All emergency services again on standby, including troops that were sent down to help out for the last few weeks, don't think they have really been stood down this winter. Very big ground sea running, both quays taking another battering with waves sweeping both of them from end to end, good job it's not a southerly storm with those seas running. More damage to buildings in the village, can't be many places that don't have new roofs now, expect house insurance will go up after this winter. On television it showed extent of flooding with just trees and buildings sticking up above the water, lots of farm animals drowned as well. They are saying it's the worst spell of weather ever recorded, including the floods, several people reported dead. Noise of waves hitting quays very loud and continuous.

Thursday 8th February, south-south-west storm force 9 blowing, barometer 29.5. Several baulks broken during night and this morning. One broken baulk jammed in between others in the gaps. We managed to get a rope around that and made fast to a ring bolt on the quay, the other we pulled up the slip – well Graham Moore and his Landrover did. Quays really taking a battering again, there has to be structural damage to those after the last couple of months.

Friday 9th and Saturday 10th February, southerly force 6 to 7 blowing, barograph 29.7. At last the winds have eased. The national news for these two days was showing storm damage along the south coast which has been taking the worst of each storm or hurricane since December. Also swathes of flattened trees in the south of England, so many trees lost this winter they are saying it will take 20 years just to replace them. Government is considering doing a large scale planting operation for five years. They are saying a fifth of all trees in England have been lost this winter, around the ten million mark. Seems a lot of trees to me but when you watched the television with whole woods wiped out perhaps they are right. Forecast is for another severe storm this weekend. Insurance companies are talking about 2 billion to settle claims so far.

Sunday 11th Febrauary 1990, westerly force 8, barograph 28.8, a big drop, hail and sleet showers during morning with thunder and lightening. It was just after midday on a Sunday and I walked to the end of my alley to go down to the Ship Inn for a few drinks. I stopped and looked out to sea and couldn't believe what I was seeing. I will always remember what I was thinking – no it can't be, it doesn't happen in this country. It was a whirlwind. Just as it hopped over the old quay wall hailstones the size of ten-penny pieces started falling. I rushed back into my place and looked out of the windows. I could hear slates coming off my roof then the building lurched. Jimmy Richards was doing work on a house just across the way from me when I saw the scaffold boards go whirling away along with slates and bits of paper. When it got out over the sea by the Bank car park it just collapsed. I walked down the alley over slates and bricks, looked up and down the street then went back and phoned the police telling them what had happened and to get an ambulance. The whole Cliff Road from the shop by the village clock to the last house on the bank was completely devastated with the road full of slates and broken glass. A police car arrived and I went up and introduced myself. They just stood there open-mouthed. They had those very large old-fashioned radio sets which had to have their aerials pulled out before they would work. Anyway they called for reinforcements and two fire engines, two ambulances and six police cars turned up, the police closed every road into our village. I had to go through all those properties with the police to make certain nobody was hurt. Graham Moore, the shop owner, was the only person who got hit by flying slate, a badly cut lip and he lost 2 teeth, no one else was injured. The Chief Fire Officer took charge and ordered his men to pull down any chimney that was unsafe and any overhanging roofs. They went from the shop by the village clock to the bank houses making everything safe for the general public. All the local builders were there with their lorries, plus some council lorries shovelling slates from off the roads and gardens. Not one single house along the harbour front survived the tornado without serious damage. My place where I used to live lost some slates and a chimney had to be pulled down. It was like a mighty bomb had exploded, most windows were smashed in or cracked and every building had to have new roofs and most places new chimneys. The Ship Inn next to the shop was untouched. Once the council took over the local builders were busy boarding up windows and doors and covering bare roofs with tarpaulins. I would say that nearly every person in the village turned out to help clear up. I never did get a drink that lunch time. My biggest regret was never taking some photographs of the street and all the damage. The first time I had not done that when a disaster hit our village. All the rubble, slate and glass was tipped over the edge of the Bank car park to build that up after the winter storms. That was the local tip for years until it was finally stopped in the late 80's when the first large granite blocks were placed there.

It was twelve months before all the damage was repaired and the street clear of scaffolding and builder's lorries. Surely the storms will stop sometime, I think our village has taken enough beatings and batterings for one winter.

From Monday 12th February to Saturday 17th February a south-east wind force 6-7 blew, barograph varied from 29.1 to 29.6. Chilly but no storms. Just clearing up rubbish and storm damage with builders working non-stop repairing damage.

Fairly fine weather until 25th February, another severe storm forecast. Only one pub open along Penzance prom at midday and that was the Yacht Inn. Had lunch and a pint there. Rest of pubs still clearing up after storm damage.

Monday 26th February, southerly storm force 9 blowing, barograph 29.5. Baulks breaking again, went down 3.00 and we managed to lasso some of them and pull them inshore where Graham Moore towed them up the slip. Winds to 104 miles per hour recorded. Really heavy rain everywhere. Stream that comes out by the monument overflowed and poured down Duck Street about 2 foot deep. Roads in village covered in mud and stones washed down from the hills. Council lorries clearing it up, several houses also flooded, flower pots and grow bags washed into the harbour. Village once again a real mess. On the news 14 people died in storms today. 2,000 people evacuated in Wales from flood water and high tides, several other places also being evacuated including places in Cornwall. Sea defences being breached in numerous places including Penzance, Newlyn flooded again with several houses being evacuated. Wind dropped away to a force 4 by March 2nd, hopefully that's our winter storms over.

Tuesday 27th March diggers and lorries started building up the Bank car park with granite to make an armoured defence, not certain it would cope with this winter's weather.

Wednesday 28th March they started work on mending the concrete walk just past the Bank car park that was also severely damaged and washed away. They are using a crane to lower huge skips of concrete down, never seen one with such a long arm before, think they said it came from Plymouth.

Saturday 31st March, south-easterly breeze and chilly, took baulks out this morning, a sod to get out after the winter's beating, most of those that are left are also badly damaged on their ends, most will have to be replaced.

Thursday 5th April, new diggers finally back at work, the old one is still broken down on the beach where it's been for the last few days, dumper trucks didn't stop bringing in rocks though and they are piled high all over the place.

Sunday 27th May, watched the time trial from Penzance to Paul then up Raginnis Hill for the Bicycle Milk Race, surprised how fast they cycled up Raginnis Hill.

So the worst weather for storms, rain, flooding, structural damage and deaths for one winter is finally over. 154 people died this winter from storms and floods, and I don't think all of the deaths made television or the newspapers, so it could be more.

Mousehole Blizzard

VISITORS OFTEN SAY that we don't get any snow, not real snow like we do up country. Well they are most certainly wrong but thankfully it does not happen very often.

On 12th January 1987 about 7.00 in the evening it started snowing with a strong southerly wind, not just a few flakes but a blizzard. By ten that evening it was over three foot (1 metre) deep in most places with drifts up to six foot (2 metres) in some areas. The village was cut off for two days until the local people using ash from their fires finally managed to grit the whole of Parade Hill, the lowest hill out of Mousehole. I walked into Penzance to pick up a prescription for my neighbour Mrs Roberts and found there was no snow at all in Penzance and Newlyn only had a slight scattering. The blizzard only hit the Lizard Peninsula and from Mousehole westwards – the further west the deeper the snow with the Scillies coming off the worst. They lost a lot of their exotic plants on Tresco due to that. Once again the local people turned out and shovelled every road clear of snow within the first day and using ash from their fires gritted every road and alley in Mousehole. On the harbour front snow was piled up higher than the old railings. I managed to take a series of photographs from 9.00 in the evening during the blizzard up until the 17th January when traffic and buses could once again use the village roads.

The worst affected areas during this blizzard was the Lizard Peninsula which was cut off for nearly 10 days before they cleared the roads. St Just was cut off for about a week and they built a very large snowman with a huge erection in their village square. From the photographs I've seen it appeared to have a six foot penis. In the Scillies the snow was reportedly six to eight foot deep.

Section VII

Fishing Boats

THE FIRST TYPE of vessel ever used for fishing some million years or so ago would in all probability have been just an old log from which fish were speared. Not a very stable platform so the next obvious step would be to lash two or three logs together. There are still three log rafts in use at the present time by Indians in various remote forest rivers in South America. These rafts would gradually get larger as more logs were added until they became substantial stable floating platforms capable of making sea journeys.

When the first log was hollowed out to form a canoe is not known but probably originated in estuaries where they would be more manageable than rafts. The very first logs were hollowed out by using fire, there are still a few very remote islands that use this method even today.

It was the discovery of iron smelting and the consequent manufacturing of iron woodworking tools that led to the boat building industry. Wooden boats have now been superseded by steel and fibreglass vessels. It is possible to trace the evolution of boats from their humble beginnings as a hollowed out log to today's modern high performance craft.

Regarding fishing vessels in Mounts Bay the earliest records are very sparse regarding the actual type and size of boats used in this industry. Because of the abundance of large untouched fish stocks the boats would not have to travel far in their search for pilchards, herring, mackerel etc, so in general they would probably be smaller vessels that could be pulled above high water mark by horses. By the late 1400's some of these boats were obviously quite large as there are records that show fishing vessels from Mounts Bay sailing to Ireland following the herring shoals. During the 1500's the largest were making the long dangerous Atlantic crossing to Newfoundland to catch cod. There are obviously records somewhere that give the type and size of these vessels, especially the Newfoundland fleets, but as yet I have not come across them.

In the 1700's the luggers from Mousehole, Porthleven, Newlyn and St Ives were regular visitors to the Irish coast and usually arrived there in July. From the records it is clear that there was a very large fleet of Mounts Bay boats engaged in this fishery. The size of these vessels was about 35 to 40 foot in length. The Customs and Excise registration forms for this period are missing, extensive enquiries in the Penzance libraries, Redruth Cornish Studies Centre and the County Records at Truro have failed to turn up any evidence of these so it must be assumed that they have been destroyed. These forms would have given useful information regarding the size and number of vessels registered for each of the Mounts Bay ports. It would also give the boats name, number and the owners name, at this period in time all the Penzance fishing vessels carried the letters PE. It was not until 1st January 1869 that all Penzance registered fishing boats had to carry the now familiar PZ letters. The Customs and Excise forms from this date up until 1940 are readily available at the County Records Office in Truro. So it is really only possible to get a true picture of the number, size and types of vessels employed in the fishing industry from this date onwards. The old newspaper reports from the 1700's do not give actual numbers or sizes of vessels and most details are rather sketchy to say the least.

The old records do show however that the most popular type of rig for fishing boats was the 'dipping lug.' This type of sail was ideal for the fishing industry because there was very little rigging and virtually no mast stays for nets to get caught up in. It did have one major disadvantage though and that was the sail had to be lowered and the huge heavy boom passed around the mast each time the vessel changed tack, and this operation might have to be carried out every few minutes if the wind was in the wrong direction and the boat was trying to beat into the bay. Conventional luggers on the other hand did not have this problem, their bottom boom was fixed to the mast and the top boom slid up the mast when the sail was hoisted. They did however require a lot more rigging and stays.

Other types of riggings used in the fishing industry were ketch, schooner, cutter, dandy, yawl and spritsail. By 1900 engines were increasingly being fitted to fishing boats, 'Kelvin' petrol paraffin engines were far and away the commonest engine used. Some vessels had steam engines fitted and these were entered in the register as S.S. boats. I always thought that S.S. stood for 'Steam Ship' but in the Customs and Excise documentation it was always written down as 'Steam Screw.'

The total number of registered fishing vessels of all classes for each of the coves and ports in the Penzance area between 1869 and 1944 are as follows: Porthleven 788, Newlyn 758, Mousehole 627, Penzance 277, Sennen 168, Penberth 130, Prussia Cove 70, Mullion 62, Marazion 61, Porthgwarra 49, Gunwalloe 45, St Michaels Mount 38, St Just 33, Pendeen 27, Lamorna 11, Rinsey 11, Perranuthnoe 10, Long Rock 9, Praa Sands 1.

There were numerous other vessels stationed around the country that retained their PZ registration.

The figures above are the exact numbers that were actually registered but taking into account that there were also a large amount of seine boats that did not have registration numbers then the actual number of boats employed in the fishing industry would be a lot higher. For example not one single seine boat was ever registered for Sennen Cove but it is known that this cove had a large fleet of seiners. There is the possibility that during the seining season they stripped down some of their other vessels to use in this fishery. Gunwalloe had the largest number of registered seine boats with 22, Mullion 11, Penberth 10 which traded under the name of Penberth Fishing Company, Porthleven 6, Mousehole 6, Newlyn and Prussia Cove 2, Longrock, Lamorna, St Just and Praa Sands 1 each. All seine boats were 3rd class vessels ranging in size from 16 to 43 foot in length and propelled by oars. The largest boats had a crew of 21, one steering and the rest would be either rowing or shooting the seine net. Fishing boats were, and still are, divided into three classes which has nothing to do with their actual size. 1st class vessels were fully decked and ranged in size from 38 foot to 60 foot, 2nd class vessels were half decked and from 16 foot to 48 foot, 3rd class vessels were open boats between 12 and 50 foot, the very largest were always seiners, although several of the larger ones were also used as barges for transporting stone.

The early registrations, from 1869 to the late 1890's, must have been rather confusing when boats were landing fish, and undoubtedly there must have been mistakes made in crediting fish to the wrong vessel. The reason being that until the late 1890's each number could have three vessels registered to it at the same time, e.g., PZ1, 1st, 2nd and 3rd class all with the same number and some of these with the same name.

There are numerous examples of up to 10 boats all registered at the same period with the same name, the favourites being *Annie*, *Lily*, *Dove*, *Emily*, *Gleaner* and *Bessie*, very confusing when you had two boats with the same name and number but a different class. At this period of time there was no ruling on how the numbers and letters were painted on the boat so it became an accepted unofficial rule to put PZ1 for 1st and 3rd class boats and 1PZ for 2nd class vessels. This all changed in the very late 1890's when the ruling on the registration forms stated that the port letters would be followed by the number, e.g. PZ1. At the same time it also stated that the registration port, Penzance, had to be painted on the stern and not the home port, e.g. Mousehole, Newlyn, Porthleven etc., and that a name could only be entered once in the register until that registration was cancelled. It took nearly 20 years before each boat had a different name. They just waited for the registrations to be cancelled until there was only one *Annie*, *Lily*, *Dove* etc. left on the books. Some boats names reflect religion while others such as *Narrow Escape*, *Lost and Found* and *Try Again* might indicate their owners previous experiences. Then of course there are the humorous names, *Pantaloon* and *What's That To You* being just two. The name

267

Pantaloon makes the mind boggle, or perhaps it meant something different in those days. Famous battles and topical names such as *Telephone*, *Telegraph* and *Railway* were also used as were famous people, usually General someone and *Samuel Plimsoll*. He was the gentleman who worked out the safe 'load line' on cargo vessels, hence 'Plimsoll Line.'

The largest number of privately owned Penzance registered fishing vessels between 1869 and 1944 in Mousehole was the Humphreys family with 31 boats. Thirteen 1st class vessels and eighteen 2nd class. A lot of these were jointly owned by other members of this large family, on the registration forms there are 8 men and 3 women listed in this family who owned or partly owned boats between them. All the men skippered a boat and the others had Masters to run them.

Another Mousehole family of eight men owned 15 fishing vessels between them during this period. Three of them, Charles, Henry and James Pezzack were Channel Pilots and they had a lugger built at Mousehole called *C.H.J.* which was used for this purpose. She was a 2nd class boat, 33.5 foot long of 10½ tons, registration number PZ97, they finally broke her up for firewood in 1908 after nearly 40 years of work. Another of their pilot boats, PZ283 *Heroine*, a 32 foot lugger, was completely smashed to pieces in Mousehole harbour in 1890 during a severe southerly storm. The pilot boat *Nautilus* PE15, (later PZ15) parted her moorings under St Clements Isle and sank between island and shore on 10th January 1866, she was a new boat worth £200. She was refloated and after repairs continued working until 1893 when she was again damaged during a storm, this time the boat was broken up and used as firewood.

Obtaining a Channel Pilot Licence in the mid 1800's entailed a lot of training and knowledge of a considerable amount of the English coastline. Every five years they had to take a test which was carried out by inspectors from London who arrived at Mousehole by boat. The pilot would go aboard and be told where to go by the inspectors. One report states that Charles Pezzack piloted the boat to Bristol, from there to Liverpool, then back to Milford Haven and from Milford to London. The report does not state how long this test took but he obviously passed as he was still classed as a Channel Pilot. Most of the tests involved taking a vessel to Bristol or London. Anyway Charles, Henry and James Pezzack held these licences until they retired.

During the 1800's Porthleven had the largest boat building industry in the south-west, these are the only records I have regarding the actual number of boats built but this industry goes back a lot further as there are references from the 1600's regarding boat building at Porthleven. The largest boat builders up until 1900 were the Kitto's, Bawden's and Bowden's. From the records it appears they just built boats and got someone to work them until sold, they did not wait for a specific order before building. There were of course just as many built to order for various ports around the country as well as Mounts Bay.

Mousehole also had a thriving shipwright industry but not on the same scale as Porthleven and all vessels built at Mousehole were to order. The two main areas where they were built was the large car park by the old quay, which was known as the South Bank, and the raised car park near the new quay which was called the North Bank. There are also records which show the area behind the monument was used to construct small boats up to 20 foot in length, this was before the harbour offices were built.

The North Bank was also used for the construction of carts and carriages and for this privilege the carpenters had to pay 6d per year. This caused friction between them and the boat builders who were charged 5s per year. The carpenters were then asked to pay the same as boat builders but they complained bitterly pointing out that 'they (boat builders) do take more room than we with their large piles of timber and tis not fair that we should pay the same for less space.' This was finally overcome when it was agreed that boat builders pay £1 for each keel laid up to 30 foot in length and £2-10s for every keel over this length. Peace then reigned until the Commissioners were called upon to settle disputes regarding someone who had 'borrowed a piece of wood' which it was always claimed had been 'thrown away.' The Commissioners decided what the wood was worth and the 'borrower' either returned the wood or paid what the Commissioners deemed a 'fair price.' During the 1800's the 'Mousehole Harbour Board of Commissioners' were called upon to settle all manner of disputes in the village regarding a very wide range of complaints. It could be anything from property boundary to rights of way or water supplies, they always managed to sort it out to the satisfaction of everyone without recourse to the courts. Anyway, back to the boat building. One surprising fact that has emerged from my research is the large number of Mousehole fishermen that actually built their own boats. Some of them being 1st class vessels up to 52 foot in length.

A report from 15th February 1894 states that:

> Mr John Bodinner, 80 years old, does not lack in energy, he has just laid the keel of a new boat which he is building, she will be 35 foot long.

In actual fact the boat ended up with a registered length of 41 foot, a 1st class lugger, PZ556 *Iverna* which was worked by William Bodinner until she was sold to France in 1912. The records show that John Bodinner built at least 7 boats, the last one being in 1905 when he was 91 years old. She was a 2nd class lugger, PZ307 *Hyacinth* with a length of 25.8 foot, she was sold in 1922 to St Ives. His most famous boat was PZ592, a 2nd class lugger of 25.7 foot called *Pantaloon* which he built in 1896. She was freely admitted as being the fastest vessel under 30 foot in Mounts Bay and only lost one race in 20 years before being sold to St Ives in 1916. Considering the number of lugger races that used to take place during the 1800's until about 1920 this was some record. There were yearly lugger races at Penzance, Marazion, Porthleven, Newlyn, Longrock and Mousehole all with cash prizes to be won, the winners usually raced for a prize between £10 and £5 with the 2nd and 3rd placed boats receiving decreasing amounts. This was a considerable amount of money in the 1800's and all the boat class races were keenly contested.

There were of course periods when fishermen had no time to build a new boat and this was usually after losing their working vessel, then they would invariably buy another and in most of these cases from one of the Porthleven shipwrights. From the records it appears that most fishermen built a new boat during their spare time between fishing trips. During the severe southerly storm on 7th October 1880 there were 9 fishing boats lost in Penzance harbour and another 12 either completely wrecked or severely damaged in Mousehole harbour in one day. During another severe north-westerly storm 13 fishing vessels parted their moorings in Newlyn and blew out of the harbour on 7th April 1899. Out of these 13 boats only three were saved. These boats would obviously have to be replaced and from the records it shows that several were obtained from Porthleven.

The chapter on fishing boat wrecks gives all the details on vessels from the Penzance registration area that have been lost up until 1940.

Those were the unfortunate ones but not all ended so, as this report from the 10th January 1866 shows.

6 Mousehole fishing boats left Falmouth for Mousehole on Tuesday, when off the Lizard they ran into a storm. 3 boats arrived Mousehole at 11-00 Wednesday and 2 at Penzance, the 6th boat *Jason* of 32 foot could not work into the bay so shaped her course for Lands End and anchored. She parted her anchor warp and drifted out to sea, the crew rode out the storm 6 miles south of Scilly. The poor men suffered very much from exposure. The boat had been feared lost but she finally arrived at Mousehole on Friday at 0700.

Exposure was a common occurrence amongst fishermen during the days of sail due mainly to the fact that there was no shelter of any description for them to rest in. No dodger, wheelhouse or cabin to break the wind or

reasonable 2nd class lugger around 30 foot, or 7,200 pints of beer at 1d per pint. The comparison with todays prices I will leave for you to work out. On 24th January 1884 Mr Berryman, an auctioner,

> . . . held a sale of seine boats, nets etc at the Three Tuns Inn, Newlyn.
> Lot 1. 3rd class seine boat *Union*, 31 foot, seine, warps, anchors, etc, was bought by Mr William Trehair, Newlyn, for £64.
> Lot 2. 3rd class seine boat *Good Templar*, 20 foot, seine, warps, anchors, etc, was bought by John Harry, Mousehole, for £53.
> Lot 3. Seine only, was bought by Mr Eddy, Porthleven, for £27.
> Lot 4. Warps, anchors, tarpaulins, etc, was bought by Mr William Trehair, Newlyn, for £8.

As can be seen from the above the most expensive part of seining was not the boat but the actual seine net, then add on the anchors, warps, tarpaulins etc and together they amounted to more than the boat itself. A lot of seine boats where in fact 2nd class luggers that were stripped down for the seining season, once that was over they would be remasted and used for crabbing or handlining.

A report from 2 February 1884 states 'that a large mackerel driver is being built at Newlyn by Richard Warren for Messrs Ladner of Mousehole.' She was a 1st class lugger of 50 foot and 30 tons and named *Fleetwing* PZ322, owned by Elizabeth and Richard Ladner. She was sold to Anne and Nelson Ladner in 1895, who then sold her to Adelaide and Francis Blewett in 1907 who changed her name to *Ibex*. In 1917 they sold her to Arklow, in County Wicklow, Ireland.

An even larger boat was built in Mousehole by Mr Williams for Thomas and Charles Harvey in 1900, she was the 51.4 foot 37 ton 1st class lugger *Morning Star* PZ45, she was sold in 1912 to France.

These larger vessels were used in the longline fishery and herring drift net fishery. The following report from 21st August 1884 shows how far Mousehole vessels were willing to travel in pursuit of their calling.

> Mousehole boats fishing at Aberdeen were eminently successful during the last two weeks, some boats realising £100 per week with the *Percy* PZ30, a 50 footer owned by George Laity and William Pezzack, *Humility* PZ415, of 47 foot, owned by William Worth, both making £80 a week. The *Matchless* PZ517, a 1st class lugger of 41 foot owned by John Madron making £70 a week, *Golden Fleece* PZ107, a 2nd class lugger of 42 foot owned by William Rowe and Josiah Trembath making £60 a week. All the others doing very well, prices 25/- to 30/- per cran for herring.

Not all the Mousehole vessels were doing well though as this report from 4th September 1884 indicates.

Mousehole boats at Whitby and Scarborough are having splendid catches but they are worthless because the herring are 'black gutted' and are sold for 8d to 1/- per 1,000. Most are throwing their catches back into the sea.

It appears from reports that once the boats at Whitby and Scarborough heard about the success at Aberdeen they sailed up to that port arriving towards the end of September. If ship's radios were available in those days just think of the time those east coast boats would have saved.

Another report from the 22nd April 1886 regarding the fishing of three Mousehole vessels illustrates the varying success of this fluctuating industry.

The *Fleetwing* PZ322, the second largest boat, caught 700 very fine mackerel 60 miles NNW of Lands End, finest fish caught this season and made 47/- per 100. *Sunbeam* PZ383, of 53 foot, the largest Mounts Bay boat, 80 miles NW of Lands End had 1,500 mackerel in two nights. *Wesley* PZ472 tried her luck in another direction and shot her nets 4 leagues west of the Bishop for 400 very fine fish. Thus our boats dot the fishing grounds from Plymouth to Kinsale.

The *Sunbeam* was a 1st class lugger of 53 foot and 36 tons built in Mousehole by William Williams in 1885 for William Rowe and C.C. Ross MP. She was sold in 1889 to Lowestoft. The *Wesley* was a 1st class lugger of 48 foot and 26 tons built in Penzance in 1878 and owned by Thomas Richards and Rebecca Williams, she was broken up for firewood in 1909.

Occasionally the fishing boats had a welcome bonus that had nothing to do with fishing as was recorded on 23rd April 1891.

The owner and crew of the fishing boat *Bonnie Lad* PZ251 received £100 for the services they rendered to the *Charles Sundbland* after the collision in which she was crippled off the Lizard.

It is a great pity this report does not go into more details regarding the collision and what part the *Bonnie Lad* played after the accident. The *Bonnie Lad* was a 1st class lugger of 50 foot and 29 tons built at Porthleven in 1885 for William and Stanley Drew of Mousehole, she was sold to Howth in 1916.

Steam cargo ships were becoming increasingly common and could and did cause a lot of damage, sometimes with a great loss of life. Then again these steam boats also helped out some of the luggers as this report from 20th September 1892 shows.

Most Mousehole boats have or are returning from the North Sea, the *Onward* PZ510, leading the way having been towed by a friendly steamer from Lowestoft to the Lizard.

The *Onward* was a 1st class lugger of 44.8 foot and 25 tons owned by Philip Worth, she was built in Newlyn in 1871 and finally sold to Plymouth in 1907.

The report goes on to say that:

> . . . these boats then went on to Plymouth on the 27th October for the herring and pilchard fishery. *Vesta* PZ155, took 50,000 fish (5 last) of herring and had to cut away 5 nets, she made £60 that night and the *Ganges* PZ156 made £25. The majority of Mousehole boats now have steam capstons fitted.

The *Vesta* was a 1st class lugger of 47 foot and 25 tons owned by William Ladner and built for him at Newlyn in 1878, she was finally broken up in 1915. *Ganges* was a 1st class lugger of 42 foot and 16½ tons owned by William Pezzack and George Laity, she was broken up in 1901 for firewood.

There were other factors which affected Mousehole boats over the years from following the shoals of herring. One such happened in August 1893 which curtailed the Mousehole fleet from sailing to the North Sea as the following shows.

> Cholera outbreak in the district laid some boats low of crew and other boats fear going to the North Sea because of the same disease.

This outbreak was not an isolated occurrence and from the records it appears that cholera was a regular visitor to fishing ports around the coast.

Occasionally skippers did make mistakes during fishing which in most instances was the last one they ever made as most mistakes proved fatal. Luckily for the four men in the following account this was not the case.

> On Friday 1st December 1893 the *Unity* PZ286 a 2nd class lugger of 40 foot and 12½ tons owned by Edward Trembath from Mousehole was taking herring from a seine at Mullion, 7 last of fish, (150 stone to a last, so she would be carrying just under 6 tons of fish) it was a strong wind and she could only carry a 50 yard sail foreward. As she was shipping a lot of water they had to ease her off a lot of seas. This caused such leeway that Mousehole could not be fetched on a tack from the eastern land. Finding the boat foundering the crew of four took to the punt they were towing when the *Unity* was 200 yards back of the island. The crew made shore at Spaniards Point. The loss of the *Unity* was made worse because 19 herring nets were aboard. The *Unity* was insured for £70 with the Mounts Bay Mutual Insurance Society.

The above must be classed as good luck for the four man crew, the following can only be classed as bad luck.

21st June 1894. Two Mousehole boats, both owned by William John Humphreys, were in collision. *Bessie* PZ522 a 1st class lugger of 47 foot and 25 tons was entering Newlyn harbour and was run into by a Newlyn fishing boat. The *Minerva* PZ72 a 1st class lugger of 46.6 foot and 26 tons was rammed by Plymouth trawler *Myra*, both travelling at about 6 knots, it was found that *Minerva* had half the stem of bow knocked away, but they kept her afloat and were towed into Mousehole by another Mousehole boat.

The *Minerva* was built in Mousehole in 1878 for William Humphreys. The following was not dated but it was probably in the mid 1800's because it mentions Longfellow who died in 1882 at the age of 75. The way it is written does suggest a date in the 1600's or 1700's. Staff at the Cornish Studies Centre did say that some reporters incorporated very much older text in their reports so perhaps this is a combination of two such reports.

Some of the Mousehole mackerel fleet during the week returned from Ireland where they met with no success for the summer. Never before have our men been compelled to give up a season in this manner. Last year mackerel in the Irish waters were abundant and a good season this year was anticipated, but we are sorry to say it is a hope deferred which maketh the heart sick. Much depression is felt among the people on account of this chill penury that represses their noble rage and freezes the genial current of their sole. Still we hope that a rift will soon be made in the dark cloud which at present hangs over the village and that our people, so long tired, will be in the position of Longfellows Blacksmith who 'Looked the whole world in the face, for he owed not any man'.

When Mousehole harbour was full of vessels there was always plenty of fish that had to be discarded due to damage caused by the drift nets, these poor quality fish were invariably just thrown in the harbour and sank to the bottom. This large amount of fish that lay on the bottom proved a bonanza to others. Gulls can only eat a certain amount and they could only get at these fish when the water was low enough, this abundance of daily fresh food did not go to waste though, other fish soon learned that Mousehole harbour was a laden dining table. The rights to net the harbour were always let out by tender which had to be applied for each year. The main quarry was always mullet and these came into the harbour to feed on discarded fish in great numbers as reported on 22nd December 1906.

A large shoal of mullet was netted in Mousehole harbour by two men who caught some 2,000 fish which sold for 4/- per score on Christmas Eve. Several years ago another large shoal was caught in the harbour but then the rights were let by tender. This had lapsed and now the question arises again about the rights to fish.

Other fish regularly caught in and around the harbour were bass, red bream, hake, pollack, turbot and halibut, sadly those days have long since gone although bass, pollock, flounder and plaice are still caught in and around the harbour today.

This report from 30th April 1930 gives some indication of how many boats and men could have been saved if ships radios where available in those days.

But for the prompt appearance of the *Boy Willie* PZ602, from Mousehole then the Newlyn fishing boat *Bona Fide* PZ339, would have sunk along with all her crew.

Boy Willie was proceeding to the fishing grounds and when 32 miles WSW of Mousehole found the *Bona Fide* sinking. Her crank shaft, propeller shaft had broken and the propeller dropped off and she was filling with water. *Boy Willie* took her in tow and her crew went aboard *Bona Fide* to help pump out. She was towed to Newlyn. The *Bona Fide* had no small boat with her so all would have perished.

The *Boy Willie* was a 1st class lugger of 51.6 foot and 25 tons owned by James Pender, built at Newlyn in 1896 and sold to Falmouth in 1940. The *Bona Fide* was a 1st class lugger of 44.9 foot and 26 tons owned by Edward Tonkin who had two steam engines of 26 and 13hp fitted in 1909, she was condemned as unseaworthy in 1939.

The Board of Trade was trying to tighten up on safety regulations and cut the number of both boats and lives lost in the fishing industry, but the biggest drawback to these new ideas that were being issued was the basic fact there were no radios or reliable distress flares available. The matter of navigation lights however could and was rigorously enforced as the following shows.

Our Lizzy PZ109 a 1st class lugger of 51 foot and 26 tons owned by Richard Worth was rammed by the *Water Lily* PZ146 a 1st class lugger of 38.6 foot and 18 tons owned by Richard Nicholls and Alex Bond. *Our Lizzy* sank off Penlee Point at 0300 hours but all the crew were picked up by the *Water Lily*. There was a court case regarding the lack of lights on both vessels. *Our Lizzy* had only a masthead light while the *Water Lily* had no lights at all and had just come from the Scillies fishing grounds 50 miles away. It was stated that the foremast light should be visible for 5 miles and port and starboard lights 2 miles. Charges brought by Captain Charles Chester Cartwright OBE, Nautical Surveyor of the Survey Branch of the Mercantile Marine Department of the Board of Trade against both boats. Both skippers were fined £5. The Magistrate issued a warning that if any similar case came again a heavier penalty would be imposed. The Clerk of the Court, Capt C.E. Venning, stated that the maximum penalty was £100 or not more than 6 months imprisonment.

The Second World War was being fought across Europe and safety equipment for fishing vessels would obviously take second or even third place in priorities at this time. So fishermen made do with what was available as the following shows.

> Mr Joliffe had been fishing off the Runnel Stone all day but his lines fouled his propeller. He attracted a passing steamer who towed him into Mounts Bay. Thinking he could make Mousehole from this position he hoisted sail, but ended up on the back of the island. Soon as the boat touched he grabbed a tin of petrol and stepped ashore without getting wet, the matches in his pocket remained dry.
>
> He tore up his coat, soaked it in petrol and lit it. The flames were seen from the harbour and Mr Joseph Madron, Harbour Master, and Mr Ben Jeffery got into their boat and rescued Mr Joliffe bringing him ashore without even getting his feet wet from start to finish.

The war was beginning to take its toll on the fishing industry as the following reports indicate.

> On 1st February 1940 the east coast drifter *Celita* was machine gunned by German planes as she was returning to port. Bullets went right along the deck and through bulkheads, no one was hurt.

This was by no means an isolated incident to Mounts Bay fishing vessels and from the records it appears that fishing boats were regularly attacked. On 20th June 1940:

> All night fishing was banned by an Act of Parliament. No craft shall be out before sunrise or out after sunset. There was a lot of opposition from fishermen to this saying they knew all the boats from other ports and if anything suspicious were about they would be the first to notice it. The Fishery Officer, Mr W.H. Barron, said that the whole thing was very much in the hands of the Admiralty.

This ban was in force for most of the war. On 4th July 1940:

> British soldiers dressed in a weird array of clothing arrive at ports along the South Cornish coast in small boats of all descriptions, some having taken 7 days to cross the Channel. Channel Islanders also arrive in fishing boats.

A lot of these small boats were 16 foot French luggers punts and there are still a few of them left in some of the harbours, there is one left in Mousehole.

The following is a message sent by King George VI to the fishermen of Mousehole and Newlyn in December 1940.

278

This second wartime Christmas finds the members of the British Merchant Navy and Fishing Fleets pursuing their calling through the 7 seas and I wish to send them a personal greeting.

You were the first of our civil population to suffer the merciless attacks of our enemy.

Your courage and daring has been an inspiration to your fellow countrymen who are now facing the same brutal assault. In their name, I thank you and I send you all best wishes for Christmas and a good landfall.

George R.I.

When the King's speech was read to the fishermen of Mousehole and Newlyn they spontaneously sang 'God Save Our King' in a stirring scene. At Mousehole the choir was assembled and they too sang the National Anthem.

This message was so much appreciated that the following reply was immediately sent.

The fishing fleets of Newlyn and Mousehole are deeply conscious of your kind message and would like to assure your Majesty of our loyal and unremitting efforts to defeat this brutal and merciless enemy.

Our tradition will be a safe standby in our endeavours to carry out our calling throughout the 7 seas.

Your Majesty can rest assured that the destinies of this England that we love so much will be taken care of by the Merchant Navy and the Fishermen of Newlyn and Mousehole.

The Scilly Isles, St Ives, Newlyn and Penzance were regularly bombed throughout the first half of the war and fishing boats bombed and machine gunned. The following are a few reports from 1941.

Feb 6th, enemy planes dropped a number of bombs on a fishing village (Newlyn) then machine gunned fishing boats off a neighbouring village (Mousehole), a vessel near the fishing boats was bombed and appeared to have two direct hits, the plane was seen to crash into the sea opposite the neighbouring village (Mousehole). No official confirmation or denial of this story has yet been made.

(This wreckage was a well known fishing mark about three miles SE of Mousehole Island. When a Culdrose Navy boat was looking for this aircraft they asked me if I knew where it was. When I finished doing that tier of nets I took them across to it. Their divers recovered most of the aircraft that was salvageable in the 1970's).

'South West fishing ports again bombed by German planes in February'. 'St Ives bombed again, several houses wrecked and damaged but no casualties, fishing ports bombed again in March.' '28th August 1941, two

279

people killed in Scillies air attack, Sylvia Jenkin and Dorothy Paice killed by direct hit on their house'.

And so the reports went on, but luckily nothing lasts for ever.

A public meeting was held on Monday 21st April 1851 for the purpose of establishing a lifeboat in Mounts Bay to help combat the terrible loss of life incurred in and around the bay from shipwrecks. Mounts Bay has proved a death trap to countless thousands of vessels since it was formed, especially during those years prior to 1940 when the only means of propulsion was the wind, very few vessels had engines compared with those that used sails. It was not until after the war that engines were fitted in all boats, mostly petrol paraffin jobs, diesels did not become widely available for small boats until the 1950's.

The number of vessels known to have been lost in Mounts Bay is probably a very small fraction of the total number lost over the last 1,000 years. Someone estimated that for every foot of coastline in the bay there was a drowned seaman, I don't know how they arrived at this figure but I expect that it is not very far from the truth. There are numerous references to passenger sailing vessels passing the Lizard but not making Lands End. There are also countless references of fishing boats classified as being 'lost at sea,' this could be one of several causes, swamped by heavy seas, dismasted and damaged or being run down by another vessel. The last mentioned was a common occurrence due mainly to the fact that most boats did not have any lights and those that did tended to be very dim paraffin lamps. There was no electricity aboard sailing vessels in those days.

It had to be a very big ship or a very important one before it rated much in the line of reporting. Small fishing boat losses of three or four men hardly ever got mentioned, life was cheap, unless it was your own, and paper expensive. One report from the 1500's just states that 'a large number of fishing boats are lost in Mounts Bay during a storm.' It does not say how many or if people were drowned. It does not even give the wind direction.

Even in the 1700's and 1800's a lot of the reports just state that a fishing boat is 'lost at sea,' no details about the boat or crew members. Then there are other reports that simply say 'a lot of newly broken wood is strewn along the shoreline from St Michaels Mount eastwards.' In most of these cases the report goes on to say 'that it could be wreckage from a sail that was battling into the bay.' If no name plate or other distinguishing feature is washed ashore then identifying such craft is virtually impossible.

The same applies to bodies that have been washed up on a beach, in most instances the report just says 'an unidentified body was found at . . . and interred at . . .' In the very early years, 1400's to 1700's, a lot of these unidentified bodies were buried on the beach above high water mark or on the cliff tops. Skeletons are quite often uncovered by erosion on certain cliff tops around the south-west of Cornwall and the Scilly Isles.

It is not until the late 1800's that a more detailed report was filed on boat losses at sea or shipwrecks, prior to this it had to be a big loss of life or a large important boat before any real details were recorded.

A report from 17th October 1866 gives some idea of how unimportant small boat losses where considered in that period.

Fishing boat *Cyrus* from Porthleven was run down by a barque bound for Amsterdam with salt, 1 drowned, Edward Cotton aged 20 years.

That was all this incident merited in the local newspapers, no other details were forthcoming regarding the rest of the crew, and no other information relating to the boat as to whether she sank or not. This was how some fishing boat losses were reported.

A more detailed account was given to an incident that occurred on 15th March 1871.

Porthleven fishing boat *Desire* PZ335 a 2nd class lugger of 38.6 foot with 7 men and a boy aboard was run down by steamer *Corlic*. Drowned were owner John Strict 40, his two sons James 17 and John 13, John Hockin 63, John Thomas James 26, William Allen 19, Thomas Matthews 19. The only survivor was Thomas Toy 19, who was landed a week later at Liverpool with a broken leg.

There was no report of any enquiry.

Death was and still is a constant shipmate with those who go to sea, especially in the fishing industry. The sea is a very unforgiving element and in most instances your first mistake is usually your last, and it can even happen in the quiet of a harbour as the following shows.

5th September 1878, drowned at Aberdeen, William James Richards 20, from Mousehole, fell overboard while the boat was in port and drowned.

Two other mistakes which both proved fatal were:

PZ18 *Mary Ann* 2nd class lugger of 32 foot, owner Thomas Ellis Vingoe drowned whilst hooking a chain onto the anchor during a gale of Whitby on 23rd September 1879 . . .

. . . and on the 28th April 1880. . .

William Charles White 15, from Mousehole, sculled out in a punt to be taken in tow by a mackerel boat, once the rope was made fast he forgot the jerk, fell overboard and drowned before the big boat could come about.

281

The practice of incoming mackerel boats picking up and towing a punt to Newlyn that was manned by a boy was known as *Yawling*. Each mackerel boat had its own yawler and the boys were paid about 2/- per week. The following extract tells the story clearly.

At an early hour large numbers of yawlers could be seen just off Mousehole harbour, sculling about anxiously awaiting the arrival of their boats. Sometimes many hours were spent in this way. When the lugger came near the yawler a rope was thrown and made fast. The punt was then towed to Newlyn which was the main market for mackerel. The catch was put into the punts and taken ashore where mounds of fish were laid out on the beach ready for auction. This presented a very busy scene with scores of punts laden with mackerel, fishermen in oilskins and seaboots, counting up the fish and loading wagons for Penzance to catch the early trains for up-country markets. The people on shore were always anxious to know the catches of mackerel and the following method was adopted. Some person on shore would take off his hat and hold it high, this sign meant how many mackerel have you. One of the crew on the lugger would lift his hat high and bring it down once for each hundred fish. If the catch was 1,000 then the hat would be swung around his head once for each 1,000 fish.

A similar way of signalling regarding the number of stone of mackerel caught is still used by the small handlining boats today, even though they all have VHF radios.

A radio would have been very handy to:

. . . the crabber *Mur* which put to sea with two elderly fishermen, Edward Grenfell and Edward Quick from Mousehole on 21st September 1882. The wind increased and they could make no headway, in fact they were being blown seawards. A four man gig pulled out of Mousehole and towed them into the harbour.

It would have been nice to know the gig crew but the report does not mention their names.

The two old fishermen above could be classed as lucky and I suppose the following could also be said to be the same as the disaster could obviously have been a lot worse.

On 11th January 1883 the *Banner* PZ91, a 1st class lugger of 47 foot owned by Richard Cary, arrived Falmouth at 10.00 and reported losing two men overboard, Richard Cary and Fredrick Davies of Mousehole, both drowned of the Deadman. (Dodman). They left Plymouth 8.00 and encountered heavy seas, bulwarks stove in, ballast moved, pumps choked and full of water.

Valetta PZ49 a 1st class lugger of 47 foot owned by Nicholas Cornish of Mousehole arrived having lost her punt, following boats and crews arrived here safe. *Golden Fleece* PZ107 a 2nd class lugger of 42 foot owned by William Rowe of Mousehole, *Wesley* PZ2 a 1st class lugger of 44 foot owned by Thomas Pentreath of Mousehole, *Agamemnon* PZ17 a 1st class lugger of 42 foot owned by Joseph Trewavas VC of Mousehole, *Saxon Spirit* PZ4 a 1st class lugger of 42 foot owned by James Klynack of Newlyn, *Weatherall* PZ1 a 1st class lugger of 48 foot owned by James Pezzack and Martin Matthews from Mousehole, *Alacrity* PZ84 a 2nd class lugger of 39 foot owned by Abednigo Harvey of Mousehole, *Emulator* PZ265 a 1st class lugger of 48 foot owned by James Blewett of Mousehole, *Triumph* PZ93 a 1st class lugger of 48 foot owned by William Johns of Mousehole and *Messenger* PZ79 a 1st class lugger of 47 foot owned by Daniel Richards of Mousehole.

The above fleet were returning from the herring fishery, the report does not mention whether it was the North Sea or Western Approaches fishery, to change over their nets for the mackerel season.

The *Alacrity* PZ84 owned by Abednigo Harvey had another lucky escape a few years later as this extract from 24th May 1888 indicates.

Alacrity PZ84 struck a rock while entering Scilly and with an ebbing tide stayed there aground. When the tide had ebbed she was on a rock five foot wide and fourteen foot long and was lying on her side. Some 200 hand stripped her of nets, footlines, ballast etc, after that they raised her so she was nearly upright. She floated off on the next tide with no damage. All the gear was then put aboard again.

I wonder if you would get that much help in today's enlightened world. It was not only the fishermen that occasionally got into trouble because,

On the 19th July 1883 Chief Officer at Mousehole Coastguard Station, Mr Beckerleg, his two sons William 15, Thomas 14 and another Coastguard went out fishing. When off Carn Dhu they were struck by a squall which capsized their boat. Beckerleg grabbed one of his sons but Thomas, the youngest, disappeared and was drowned. The other three were rescued by Pilot Cutter *Pill* who had seen the accident.

This ending could well have been a lot worse but for the Pilot Cutter. It was not only sail powered vessels that were lost as on the,

8th March 1888 the Steam Screw Schooner *Dream* PZ153 of 50 foot powered by a 15hp steam engine sank near the Wolf Rock Lighthouse, there were no casualties. On board were Captain Martin Guy, Anthony Jane engineer, George Williams and two visitors.

The *Dream* was owned by Joseph Legg and she was mainly used to take sightseers around the bay from Mousehole and Penzance, she was also used in the longline fishery, presumably when there was a shortage of visitors.

It was not all doom and gloom with the fishing fleet though. There were some 8 to 10 lugger sailing races each year around the bay and these were always very keenly contested by the luggers proud owners. All these races went by keel length and most lasted nearly three hours. Mousehole's first regatta-water-harbour sports was on Saturday 27th July 1889 and the first three in the larger class to finish were *Magnet* PZ40 owned by William Humphreys in 2 hours 48 minutes, *Temperance Star* PZ427 owned by John Tregenza in 2 hours 55½ minutes and *Amy Pratt* PZ327 owned by Nicholas Praed in 2 hours 58 minutes, prizes were £4 10s, £3 and £1. One vessel *Louie* PZ160 owned by Joseph Johns sprang her forward mast while leading and had to retire. There was also rowing, sculling, swimming etc. Mousehole's second regatta was an even bigger event with vessels from all around the bay sailing, as well as entering in the rowing, sculling and swimming events.

Even in these fun times during sailing races, death was never far away as an incident at Porthleven regatta shows.

2nd class lugger *Daisy* PZ496 a 24 footer and only 2 years old, owned by Joseph Pascoe and William Bawden sank while racing at Porthleven regatta on Saturday 11th August 1894. She was carrying too much sail in very poor weather. 6 men on board, 5 rescued, Captain Joseph Williams was drowned.

Not all disasters ended in tragedy although the next account could very well have done so except for prompt action from the shore.

On Tuesday 28th January 1890 two Mousehole fishing boats, *Kite* PZ130 a 1st class lugger of 42 foot owned by John Trewavas and Richard Murrish, and *Boy Tom* PZ22 a 2nd class lugger of 30 foot only one year old, owned by George Polgrean, were returning from the Plymouth herring fishery. They both missed the warping stays off Mousehole pier and in the confused seas (frightfully high) and tempest of wind from the NE went ashore opposite the Gerrick. The crews from both vessels were rescued by boats from the shore and both boats were total wrecks. Lord be praised that both crews were returned to their families safe and well.

One of the major fishing boat disasters to affect Mousehole was the loss of the *Arethusa* PZ65 a 2nd class lugger of 39 foot and 8 tons owned by William Ladner. It was not the actual loss of life which made this such a disaster but those it left behind, four widows, one of whom was pregnant, and 16 children aged between 9 months and 16 years. All those lost were from one family, two brothers and two brother-in-laws.

> The Commissioners held a special meeting and immediately set up a public relief fund with the aid of the local church ministers and Bolitho's Bank. Letters were sent to all the major fishing ports where Mousehole fishing boats were known as well as all the big buyers. The response was very good with lots of donations coming in from all sorts of people.

The following people were asked to help in raising a fund for the dependants. Rev. R.W. Aitkin vicar of Paul, Rev. G.F. Rose vicar of Newlyn, Mr W.E. Bailey Esq. Lynwood, Paul, Mr Foster Esq. Stablehobba, Mr J.W. Julian Mayor of Penzance, Mr M. Wright of Mousehole, Messrs Peacock & Co Newlyn, Mr Thomas Richards fish salesman, Mr Benjamin Ridge fish salesman, Mr Thomas Strick of Porthleven and Newlyn Harbour Commissioners. The following evening there was another meeting in which all boat owners were present and they contributed £1 per boat. From the records it appears that every vicar from around the neighbourhood was also present. The Rev.'s Perkins, Faraday and Hooper were cooperating with the Newlyn Commissioners. Mr T.B. Bolitho Esq. MP, would be the general treasurer. William Wright was elected secretary and Messrs Bolitho and Carnes Banks were also involved. All the ministers in churches and chapels said 'they would make a collection in each place of worship.' Rev. Aitkin said he would take to the country to collect and Rev. Rose would do likewise in the Methodist papers.

The report goes on to say that on the,

> 31 January 1895 the Mousehole fishing boat *Arethusa*, was presumed run down at the back of Mousehole island, drowned were Captain Richard Ladner, William Maddern Ladner 46, Thomas Cotton 42, and Henry Harvey. She had shot some nets for bait to go longlining and was never seen again. All they found the next morning was a sail floating in the water. They found the wreck 1½ miles off Mousehole cave, they grappled up some nets but bad weather stopped them getting the boat up. The Penzance diving boat *Chase* will try to get the boat up.
>
> Mousehole, Paul, Newlyn, Penzance, Porthleven, Helston and other places on the Lizard are or have all held concerts in aid of the appeal, plus all the other donations coming in from around the coast.

A report in the *Cornishman* newspaper of 13th December 1900, 5 years after the tragedy, gives an idea of what actually happened that night.

> The drowning of Willie Ladner on Wednesday morning naturally carried the minds of all Mounts Bay seafarers back to the loss of the *Arethusa* when the crew perished off Mousehole a few years ago.

285

On that occasion many theories were advanced for the loss of the craft. It was premised by most people that she had foundered after a collision. But how that collision came about was a mystery. No incoming craft at Penzance or Falmouth reported a casualty. No outward-bounder ever gave the least clue to the cause of the sad loss.

But the writer has a story to tell which will bear the closest scrutiny and which gives an explanation to the loss of the fishing boat.

Although it is a fo'c'sle story it is certainly not that of a sea-lawyer, here it is.

Among the crew of one of Messrs Hain's ships, commanded by a local Captain whose name for the present we will suppress, was a seaman who made a bosom friend and confidant of another young seaman belonging to Penzance.

One night, before 'turning in' time he confided the story of the loss of the *Arethusa* to our townsman. He stated that on the night of the loss (it was a squally night in the latter part of February or early part of March) he was on a ship called the . . . , bound from Liverpool to London. At the Longships, the Captain who was a Penzance man, whose name it will not be necessary to give here, left the bridge in charge of the Mate with instructions that he might be called when near the Lizard.

As the steamer crossed the bay there were four hands on deck, the officer of the watch, the wheel man, the lookout and the seaman who tells us this remarkable story.

The lookout man reported a light, but the Mate was asleep and made no response. Again the lookout reported the light and again there was no reply. By this time she had crashed into the little *Arethusa*.

With the flares from the fishing boat and by the lights of the steamer the number and name could be clearly observed. In a moment the frail Mounts Bay boat was crumpled under the bows of the vessel and all was over.

By the time the sleeping officer was awake, and half dazed at the terrible catastrophe, he begged his companions to keep silent on the matter. Even the Captain was never made aware of the awful culpability.

Having heard this story from his friend our young townsman gave it publicity and the Customs authorities arranged for him to make certain depositions on the matter. This he has done, and every detail given here can be thoroughly substantiated as to names and dates. Why the matter has got no further the writer does not know.

But it seems a most remarkable thing that such statements have not led to a court of inquiry and some compensation for those bereaved on that lamentable occasion.

The *Arethusa* was lost at the end of January 1895 but I suppose that after five years a 'young seaman' could have got the month wrong as it was the last day of January. Vessels rounding Lands End would, and still do, come right into Mounts Bay when making for the Lizard if they are small or underpowered or during poorish weather. Coming into the bay, especially if they have to push a strong tide, saves both time and money, it must also be remembered that steamers during this period were very often well underpowered.

On 2nd February 1905 'the trawler *Eliza* PZ20 a 1st class dandy rigged vessel of 50½ foot and 25 tons owned by Horatio Pollard of Newlyn was towing (trawling) in Lamorna Bay when they hauled up the tack hook and stem of a small boat. This proved to be part of the *Arethusa* which sank just over 10 years ago.'

The *Eliza* was built in Newlyn in 1885 and finally sold to Yarmouth in 1907.

The public relief fund did very well with donations coming in from all over Cornwall and other fishing ports around the coast. Numerous letters were received by the various organising bodies involved and some of these were reprinted in the local press, one of which is below.

> Blue Bells, St Ives, Cornwall. February 7th 1895.
>
> Dear Mr Trewavas,
> Please accept the enclosed, I wish it were more, put it down to me who was saved from collision in the Baltic Sea.
> Wishing you may be successful in raising a large sum for the widows and orphans.
> Believe me, yours truelly,
>
> W.J. Hoolethwaite.

Another Mousehole fishing vessel was run down in the same year as the *Arethusa* on 18th April but this time there was no loss of life.

> On 18th April 1895 the Mousehole fishing boat *Gleaner* PZ139 a 1st class lugger of 49 foot and 28 tons was run down by a barque on Friday. Considerable damage was done to the *Gleaner* and the Captain of the barque gave the *Gleaner* £20 for repairs and £5 to the fishing boat *Telephone* PZ230 of Mousehole to tow her home. Repairs were started straight away and she was soon back fishing.

The *Gleaner* was owned by John Hicks, she was built in Mousehole by William Williams in 1880, she was finally sold to Polperro in 1916. The *Telephone* was a 1st class lugger of 48 foot and 26 tons built in Penzance in 1878, she was owned by Richard Pentreath of Mousehole and was finally condemned as unseaworthy in 1916 after 38 years of service.

1899 was one of the worst years on record for storm damage during the early part of the year and a lot of fishermen around the coast of Britain lost their lives. It has been calculated that 1899 saw the biggest loss of all types of vessels and lives during peace time. The exact number of vessels lost during the April storm will never be known as most cargo and passenger vessels were just listed as missing. Of those posted as missing the authorities had no idea where they were lost and the records just say, 'missing on passage between .... and ....'

From the reports it becomes clear that the storms started at the end of January 1899 and, with slight lulls, continued for some 3 to 4 months, these were not just gales as they were all listed as 'severe storms.' One report from 23rd February 1899 gives some idea of how high the sea was running.

> Severe storms during the past week have caused some major damage to Mousehole quays. Some 30 foot of coping has been washed away by the storm, several baulks smashed and others fractured, the old quay has also been fractured.
>
> The seas were so high that they continually swept over Cairn Louge, the highest part of the island, old fishermen say they have never seen that before.
>
> Hundreds of tons of debris tipped from the quarry at Penlee Point has been washed away leaving a great vacancy where there had been a large plot made.

The only time this century that a storm of this ferocity has been recorded was the Ash Wednesday storm of 1963. During the height of this storm Mousehole island was completely buried under the huge waves that continually swept in from the south. The wind speed during this storm has not been matched this century, gusts to 138 miles per hour were recorded, although the wind force of 7th April 1899 storm appears to have been even stronger going on the reports for this period. A condensed account taken from the records of what happened is as follows.

> 7th April 1899. The Mounts Bay fleet returned to Newlyn harbour due to increasingly severe weather, they moored up at Newlyn and went home. Sometime during the night several boats parted moorings and blew out of the harbour during the severe NNW storm. Five were wrecked on the eastern side of the bay, four others were reported to have got round the Lizard. *Florence Edith* and *Alpha* had but a single man aboard. *Florence Edith* was wrecked at Porthleven but the owner was saved. The *Alpha* was seen going round the Lizard with William Treneer, 70, at the tiller, Cadgwith lifeboat was launched but only found the derelict *Alpha*, no one aboard.
>
> HM Gunboat *Leda* went out searching for the craft which had escaped the Lizard.
>
> A telegraph arrived from Gravesend from William Treneer where he had been landed by another boat.
>
> The *Progress* was found and towed into Plymouth and the *Alpha* was towed into Brixham. 3 of the 13 boats swept away had been recovered, the rest lost.

The *Thistle*, by a smart piece of plucky seamanship had been run to St Michaels Mount by owner William Henry Tonkin and a friendly Porthlevener or two. (John Thomas, Andrew Mitchel and William Henry Pascoe). *Florence Edith* and *Sir Wilfred Lawson*'s gear was found and saved.

A list of the 10 vessels lost that night are as follows.

PZ3 *Sir Wilfred Lawson* a 1st class lugger of 43 foot and 16 tons owned by C.C. Ross MP wrecked at Trenow Cove east of St Michaels Mount.

PZ41 *Dart* a 1st class lugger of 40 foot and 16 tons owned by William Bone of Newlyn foundered off Cudden Point.

PZ49 *Valetta* a 1st class lugger of 47 foot and 21½ tons owned by Nicholas Cornish of Mousehole wrecked Predannack Point.

PZ161 *Cygnet* a 1st class lugger of 47½ foot and 18 tons owned by Richard Harvey of Newlyn, foundered off Cudden Point.

PZ234 *Dewdrop* a 2nd class lugger of 40 foot and 14 tons owned by Richard Pollard, Newlyn, foundered off Cudden Point.

PZ257 *Onward* a 1st class lugger of 47 foot and 19 tons owned by Francis Bawden, Porthleven, wrecked Polurrian near Mullion.

PZ366 *Come On* a 1st class lugger of 44 foot and 20½ tons owned by William Maddern, Mousehole, foundered off Cudden Point.

PZ388 *Queen of the Bay* a 1st class lugger of 47 foot and 18½ tons owned by Nicholas Klynack, Newlyn, wrecked at Rinsey.

PZ512 *Excell* a 1st class lugger of 48 foot and 28½ tons owned by William Barnes, Mousehole, wrecked at Church Cove.

PZ557 *Florence Edith* a 2nd class lugger of 34 foot and 12½ tons owned by Thomas Wallis, Mousehole, sank at Porthleven.

Only 3 of the 13 boats that blew out of Newlyn harbour were saved. PZ441 *Thistle* a 1st class yawl of 47 foot and 18 tons owned by William Tonkin, Newlyn, the 3 Porthleven men already mentioned managed to row out and board her, then sail her into St Michaels Mount. PZ85 *Alpha* a 1st class lugger of 44.8 foot and 24½ tons owned by James Hosking, Newlyn, only man aboard was William Treneer, 70, who managed to steer her around the Lizard, he was taken off by a steam boat and landed at Gravesend. The *Alpha* was found full of water and nearly sinking, she was towed into Brixham. PZ134 *Progress* a 1st class lugger of 47 foot and 26 tons owned by Charles Chapple, Newlyn, she was found full of water and just floating, she was towed into Plymouth. PZ391 *Mizpah* a 1st class lugger of 44 foot and 21 tons owned by William Pascoe, Porthleven, was also lost in this storm, she sank off Plymouth.

In Mousehole harbour during this storm several of the small boats were smashed up and the *Emeline* PZ392 a 1st class lugger of 53.8 foot and

26½ tons owned by Abraham Madron of Mousehole suffered with a badly damaged keel, this was repaired within a few days.

Then during another storm on the 27th April 1899 the,

Emeline and *Jonadab* PZ299 a 1st class lugger of 46 foot and 25 tons owned by Nicholas Humphreys of Mousehole were blown onto the island. The *Jonadab* had her bottom smashed in but using empty barrels she was finally floated into Mousehole Harbour. The *Emeline* suffered very little damage.

By the 11th May 1899 *Jonadab* was repaired, relaunched and started fishing.
'During May of this year Mousehole held a series of concerts with all funds going to the Mounts Bay and East Coast Fishermen's Relief Fund for those lost during the April storms.'
The Mousehole fishing boat *Emeline* had suffered twice with damage during April but worse was to come.

On 30th October 1899 the *Emeline* left Lowestoft bound home to Mousehole after the herring season had finished. She was observed passing Dover under full sail on 1st November, this was the last time she was seen. Some of her sails were washed ashore at Folkstone and Hythe, nothing else was ever found of the *Emeline*. Drowned were Captain owner Abraham Madron 30, brothers John and Charles Pollard 16, Benjamin Harvey 27 and Richard Polgrean, there were no survivors.

The reason for the loss of the *Emeline* was never established but it was assumed that she was run down by a steamship.
The number of sail driven fishing boats that were run down by steamships during this period was quite appalling and the loss of life was so great that the government were always introducing new laws to try and prevent these accidents. But all the laws laid down are as nothing if there is not a competent man on watch, even at the present time fishing vessels are still regularly run down by cargo vessels and always with great loss of life. Too much reliance is placed on electronics with alarms that should warn approaching cargo vessels of the possibility of collision, but these obviously do not work in all cases otherwise collisions would not happen, but they do. There is nothing to beat a man on watch with a good pair of eyes. Things have moved on since the loss of the *Arethusa* though, very few vessels can get away after a collision these days, there is always a far reaching enquiry and for those vessels that do not report such an accident there is still little chance of getting away with it. Marine accident investigators worldwide now collaborate with each country when an unreported accident happens. Scientists can now match paint samples taken from

suspect vessels to those of the craft lost, if proven the courts around the world come down very hard on both the vessels owners and the Captains who invariably lose their job.

Some collisions take a lot of understanding on exactly how they came about as the following shows.

> On 23rd October 1907 the *Orlando* PZ495 a 1st class lugger of 48 foot and 27 tons owned by Richard Jenkin of Mousehole was on her way back from Plymouth when she fell in with another Mousehole boat which had lost her foremast in the gale, this boat was the *Emblem* PZ575 a 1st class lugger of 50 foot and 35 tons owned by John Hicks. *Orlando* took her in tow. At the height of the gale off Lamorna the *Orlando* came about to change tack and the *Emblem* somehow rammed her nearly cutting the *Orlando* in half. She sank almost immediately. All the crew of the *Orlando*, Captain owner Richard Jenkin, John Worth, George Hall senior and junior plus a boy Richard Brownfield were picked up by the *Emblem*, there were no casualties.

I would imagine that the atmosphere aboard the *Emblem* on their way back to Mousehole could have been cut with a knife after that accident.

Seven years after the above incident the *Emblem* was once again in trouble only this time it was one she lost.

> On 25th March 1914 during a severe storm several fishing boats broke their moorings in Mousehole harbour. Most were saved but the *Emblem* was carried out of the harbour with the surf. She was immediately driven ashore by the Coastguard Station in Mousehole (where the North Bank car park now is). She had just had £300 spent on a new engine. John Hicks senior and junior and another hand gave chase in a jolly boat but the waves, which were mast high, prevented them reaching her. The *Emblem* was completely wrecked but all the village people helped to salvage all the nets, footlines, sails and the engine.
>
> The surf was so bad with huge waves coming through the gaps that boats were one minute aground then floating.

After the loss of the *Emblem* John, Edward and Richard Hicks with David Sleeman went to Porthleven and bought a boat that was just being built, she was a 1st class dandy rigged vessel of 40.8 foot and 22 tons. They had their 30hp engine installed that was rescued from the *Emblem* earlier in the year. Their new boat was PZ26 and called the *Emblem*. In 1920 they had her lengthened at Newlyn so she now measured 53 foot and 32 tons, they also had Gardener 30hp and Kelvin 26hp engines fitted.

After being lengthened she worked happily until the 4th June 1930 when,

. . . at 1.00 on Wednesday afternoon an explosion in the engine room caused fire to spread rapidly through the whole boat and the crew abandoned her in the boats punt. The fire burnt for three hours and at one stage the flames were mast high. At 4.00 the crew approached the burning *Emblem* and put a large hole in the side of her to scuttle the boat. Half an hour later she sank.

The fishing boat *Orion* was two miles away and saw what happened, she steamed across and picked up the crew after the *Emblem* had sunk and took them back to Mousehole. No one from the *Emblem* was injured.

The name *Emblem* and the Hicks family did not seem a happy combination but at least in the three incidents they were involved in not one person was even injured.

As well as fishermen the small village of Mousehole also produced the largest number of sea captains per head of population than any other port. In the 1600's, 1700's and 1800's when men were applying for merchant or navy seafaring jobs, the name Mousehole was like an academy name. This also applied to Channel Pilots and those men who went yachting during the latter part of the 1800's. One report from the *Cornish Telegraph* in the 1850's said 'that every merchantman afloat had a Mousehole man aboard and those that didn't knew or had been shipmates with a Mousehole man.' I think that perhaps this report is rather exaggerated to say the least but it does give some idea about the number of men from this village that sought their livelihood on the oceans of the world. As in the present time it appears to be only the sad news that makes the papers as the following few extracts from the *Cornish Telegraph* shows.

20th April 1870. A list of Mousehole seamasters who have died in the last few years either at sea or in foreign ports. Captains Benjamin Pentreath, William John Wright, Richard Pezzack, 3 brothers Charles, Obediah and Roulle Cary, Captains Richards, Carolan, Bosustow, Thomas, Richard Gruzelier, James Willis, Charles Harvey and others. We regret to record the death of Captain George Gruzelier aged 34 who died in Mobile. He commanded the ship *Dorest* out of Liverpool. Mrs Gruzelier was with her husband when he died. His brother brought the ship back to Liverpool.

On 26th July 1871 Joseph Pentreath 19, was killed when he fell from the Royal Yards on the *Aconeagua* while in Valparaiso. His brother Benjamin Pentreath was the Captain, both men were from Mousehole.

September 6th 1871. Sidney Wright of Mousehole, on a voyage from Jamacia to London when he fell from the Main Yard and ended up overboard, he was never seen again.

On September 14th 1882 Capt. Maddern lost with all hands on the SS *Cardiff*. He was the main instigator of the relief fund for the fishing vessel *Jane* lost with all hands off Penzance Harbour.

These are just a very few extracts from the records relating to Mousehole men that sailed the oceans of the world and never made it back to their beloved village. The actual numbers of men from Mousehole that were employed in the Merchant and Royal Navys during this period of time is not known but the majority of them did get back to retire in the village. These well travelled gentlemen, sea captains, took a very active part in the running of Mousehole and its harbour.

Those men that stayed at home to persue their living by fishing not only had the weather to contend with but during the latter part of the 1800's and early 1900's large numbers of Mousehole men took to crewing the large ocean-going racing yachts. This put an extra strain on boat owners that suddenly found a shortage of crewmen. The following report shows this clearly.

July 22nd 1897. A large number of Mousehole young townsmen are engaged in yachting this year. Boat crews so short for the pilchard fishery that a lot of owners have taken on young people who go 'pleasuring' in the evenings.

Pleasuring was the name given to those who sailed small boats purely for pleasure. Young people meant just that and their ages ranged from 8 to 14 years old.

Because Mousehole was a very tightly packed community any infectious disease could and did sweep through the inhabitants with devastating results. These again could affect the availability of crew for fishing boats. The following might not actually involve the crewing of boats but in all probability it would have some knock on effect for certain vessels.

29th May 1884. Whooping cough is raging severely among the children of Mousehole. One or two deaths have occurred this week. A reckless policy by some parents of sending their children to school is communicating this disorder to other children. This especially applies to a Dames School in the Gurnick which some 12 to 14 attend in which 3 or 4 have whooping cough very badly.

On 19th March 1873 the *Cornish Telegraph* published the following.

Death rates of 1872 in Mousehole, 39, 8 more than 1871. 25 males, 14 females, average age for men 33 to 76, females 37 to 86. 12 above 70, 5 between 50 - 70, 7 between 30 - 50, 3 between 20 - 30, 2 between 10 - 20, 5 between 1 - 10 and 5 under 12 months. 3 died from smallpox, 6 from fever, 2 from consumption, 1 from cancer, 1 from jaundice, 7 from fits, 1 from heart disease, 1 burnt to dead, no other details for the rest.

The census form showed that the population of Mousehole was 1,602 in 1894. 100 years later the population of Mousehole was just over 500, taking into account that the total amount of living accommodation has nearly trebled, due to the conversion of all the fish cellars and net lofts plus the construction of the new estate and other houses, it gives some indication of how many people were living in one cottage during that time. It must also be remembered though that during the present time there are a considerable amount of second homes and holiday lets which also accounts for the drop in permanent residents. 100 years ago Mousehole must surely have been a very busy, congested and exciting place to live.

In 1894 there was no running water in the village, it all had to be collected in buckets from the 'shutes' and taken to each house, so certain luxuries that we now take for granted did not exist, such as showers and baths. The following extract from 5th April 1894 shows this was easily overcome. 'Several fishermen and others were seen in the enjoyment of a sea bath between Mousehole and Newlyn last week.'

Another report from 18th July 1895.

> Friday saw a large number of people on the island enjoying a sea bath in the sea breeze, there was a large bonfire, food and other entertainment for the enjoyment of Mousehole inhabitants.

Going by the number of reports in a similar vein to the above these sea baths, bonfires, food and entertainment were a regular feature of life in Mousehole until the early 1900's. Then they appeared to have just faded out. I can only assume that once mains water was piped into all the dwellings there was not so much need for those sea baths and BBQ's.

As can be seen from all the foregoing pages the men of Mousehole paid a high price in lives for those who made their living out at sea. So much in fact that a paragraph in the *Cornishman* on October 25th 1900 sums it all up.

> A singular fact – it is said with every appearance of truth, that since one man drowned from Newlyn, 50 persons have perished by drowning from the neighbouring village of Mousehole.

Mousehole Fishing Boat Wrecks

THIS LIST OF fishing boats wrecked between 1871 and 1940 is undoubtedly incomplete as there are numerous entries on the Customs and Excise registration forms which just state 'cancelled.' Unless they were actually informed that a vessel was wrecked then cancelled would be entered. Casualties were never recorded on the registration forms. The *Western Morning News, Cornish Telegraph* and *Cornishman* reported the larger fishing vessel disasters and in most cases gave considerable detail, the earlier reports tended to be rather sparse though, and in some cases there was no report at all. That is why some of the recorded wrecks are very short on detail. The same applies to those men that were lost overboard either during storms or in harbour, I have only included those reports which give their name and some detail regarding what actually happened. Between 1800 and 1900 the number of Mousehole men lost overboard from fishing boats was approaching 300. During the 1700's and 1800's there was a much quoted and publicised report that stated 'for every Newlyn man lost at sea 50 were lost from Mousehole.' The report failed to say that for every Newlyn fisherman at sea there were 50 Mousehole men between the 1400's to the early 1800's which puts the above report into some perspective.

PZ101 *Gideon Curly* – 2nd class lugger, 39.5 ft, owner Martin Wright, ran into back of Mousehole quay in fog, went ashore and broke up, no casualties, 22nd March 1871.

PZ106 *Monarch* – 2nd class lugger, 42 ft, owner Joseph Trewavas VC wrecked back of Mousehole quay in fog, 22nd March 1871, no casualties.

PZ515 *Cornish Girl* – 1st class lugger, 41 ft, 16 tons, owner Nicholas Cornish, wrecked during gale in 1873, no casualties.

PZ85 *Robert Young* – 2nd class lugger, 41 ft, (was PE247), owner John Trewavas, missed harbour warp in gale and smashed up on Mousehole beach 1875, no casualties.

PZ26 *Jane* – 2nd class lugger, 45 ft, 14 tons, owner John T. Wallis, sank entering Penzance harbour in a southerly storm, she was on her way home from Newhaven to Mousehole, no survivors. Lost were John T. Wallis, John Williams, John Jacka Harvey 15, Fredrick Curtis 22, Nicholas Richard Downing 24, William Tonkin 19, Philip Worth 17. The married men's widows, Mrs Wallis and Mrs Williams received five shillings per week for life and 2/6 for each child until they were 14, 7th October 1880.

PZ221 *Why Not* – 2nd class lugger, 31 ft, owner Thomas Wright of Mousehole, broke moorings in Penzance harbour during southerly storm and smashed up, no casualties, 7th October 1880.

PZ77 *Daring* – 2nd class lugger, 38 ft, owner Richard Bodinner, parted moorings in Mousehole harbour during southerly storm and smashed up, no casualties, 7th October 1880.

PZ283 *Heroine* – 2nd class lugger, 32 ft, owner Charles Pezzack, parted moorings in Mousehole harbour during southerly storm and smashed up, no casualties, 7th October 1880.

PZ2 *King Arther* – 2nd class lugger, 40 ft, owner Charles Humphreys, badly damaged in Mousehole harbour during southerly storm, 7th October 1880, repaired and sold to Isle of Man in 1885.

PZ130 *Kite* – 1st class lugger, 42 ft, owner Richard Murrish, very badly damaged in Mousehole harbour during southerly storm, 7th October 1880, repaired and returned fishing.

PZ420 *Nyanza* – 2nd class lugger, 28 ft, owner John Pentreath, badly damaged in Mousehole harbour during southerly storm, 7th October 1880, repaired and returned fishing.

PZ100 *Pimento* – 2nd class lugger, 39 ft, owner William Drew, very badly damaged in Mousehole harbour during southerly storm, 7th October 1880, repaired and sold to Isle of Man 1885.

PZ143 *Rodney* – 2nd class lugger, 38.9 ft, owner William Harvey, just returned from Scarborough herring fishery, parted moorings in Mousehole harbour during southerly storm and smashed up, 7th October 1880.

PZ377 *Market Maid* – 2nd class lugger, 29 ft, owner Andrew Mitchell, smashed up in Mousehole harbour during southerly storm, 7th October 1880.

PZ144 *Sarah Hills* – 2nd class lugger, 29 ft, owner Thomas Pentreath, smashed up in Mousehole harbour during southerly storm, 7th October 1880.

PZ282 *Water Lily* – 2nd class lugger, 30 ft, owner William Trembath, badly damaged in Mousehole harbour during southerly storm, 7th October 1880, repaired and returned fishing until broken up in 1890.

PZ201 *Primitive* – 2nd class lugger, 39 ft, owner Richard Trembath of Mousehole, wrecked at Whitby, 7th October 1880.

PZ22 *Boy Tom* – 2nd class lugger, 30 ft, 6½ tons, only 8 months old, owner George Polgrean, returning from the Plymouth fishery with *Kite* during a NE gale, both vessels missed the warping stay into Mousehole harbour, were blown ashore and wrecked, Tuesday 28th January 1890, no casualties from either vessel.

PZ130 *Kite* – 1st class lugger, 42 ft, owners John Trewavas and Richard Murrish, (see *Boy Tom* above for details), Tuesday 28th January 1890.

PZ286 *Unity* – 2nd class lugger, 40.2 ft, 12½ tons, owner Edward Trembath, sank 200 yards back of Mousehole Island carrying 7 'last' of herring from a Mullion seine to Newlyn in a NE gale, the four men made Spaniards Point in a punt which was also wrecked, no casualties although they were all badly injured, Friday 1st December 1893.

PZ420 *Nyanza* – 2nd class lugger, 28 ft, (was PE166), John Pentreath of Mousehole, sank at sea Friday 1st December 1893.

PZ65 *Arethusa* – 2nd class lugger, 39 ft, 8½ tons, (was PE89), owner William Ladner, shot nets off Mousehole cave for longline bait, run down by steamship which did not stop, next day they found a sail, floating nets and finally the sunken boat 1½ miles off the Mousehole cave. Penzance diving boat *Chase* tried to raise her but she was too badly damaged, drowned were Captain Richard Ladner, William Maddern Ladner 46, Thomas Cotton 42, and Henry Harvey, two brothers and their two brother-in-laws leaving four widows and 16 children between them, there were no survivors, 31st January 1895.

PZ49 *Valetta* – 1st class lugger, 47 ft, 21½ tons, built in Mousehole by owner Nicholas Cornish, parted moorings in Newlyn during NW storm, blew out of harbour and wrecked at Predannack Point, no casualties, 7th April 1899.

PZ366 *Come On* – 1st class lugger, 44 ft, 20½ tons, owner William Maddern of Mousehole, parted moorings in Newlyn during NW storm, blew out of harbour and foundered off Cudden Point, no casualties, 7th April 1899.

PZ512 *Excell* – 1st class lugger, 48 ft, 28½ tons, owner William Barnes of Mousehole, parted moorings in Newlyn during NW storm, blew out of harbour and wrecked at Church Cove, no casualties, 7th April 1899.

PZ557 *Florence Edith* – 2nd class lugger, 34 ft, 12½ tons, owner Thomas Wallis of Mousehole, parted moorings in Newlyn during NW storm, blew out of harbour and sank at Porthleven, no casualties, 7th April 1899.

PZ392 *Emeline* – 1st class lugger, 53.8 ft, 26½ tons, owner Abraham Madron of Mousehole, left herring fishery at Lowestoft on 30th October 1899 bound for Mousehole, last seen off Dover on 1st November 1899, sails picked up at Folkstone and Hythe, no survivors. Drowned were owner Captain Abraham Madron 30, brothers John and Charles Pollard 16, Benjamin Harvey 27 and Richard Polgrean, believed to have been run down by a steamship.

PZ13 *Vanguard* – 1st class lugger, 45 ft, 19 tons, (was PE196), owner Richard Jacka of Mousehole, run down and cut in half by East Coast steam drifter *Berry Castle* 2 miles off the Buck Rocks, no casualties, February 1903.

PZ495 *Orlando* – 1st class lugger, 48 ft, 27 tons, built Newlyn 1881, owner Richard Jenkin of Mousehole, on passage from the Plymouth fishery to Mousehole, found another Mousehole boat, *Emblem*, dismasted off the Lizard in the gale. She was taken in tow by the *Orlando* and when changing tack off Lamorna the *Emblem* surged forward and cut the *Orlando* in half which sank immediately, no casualties. Saved were owner Captain Richard Jenkin, John Worth, George Hall snr and jnr, boy Richard Bromfield and another, 23rd October 1907.

PZ1 *Weatherall* – 1st class lugger, 47 ft, 26 tons, owner William Polgrean of Mousehole, returning from Bristol Channel fishing grounds was run down 4 miles off the Longships by Lowestoft sailing trawler *Trevone*. *Weatherall* sank within 20 seconds at 0600 hours on 8th February 1911, one casualty, Paul Humphreys 17, was drowned.

PZ293 *Minnie* – 2nd class lugger, 30 ft, 5½ tons, built Porthleven 1883, owner James Harvey, parted moorings in Mousehole harbour during severe storm, washed out of harbour and smashed up on beach, 25th March 1914.

PZ575 *Emblem* – 1st class lugger, 50 ft, 35 tons, built Porthleven 1895, owner John Hicks, parted moorings during severe storm and carried out of Mousehole harbour by surf, went ashore by the old Coastguard Station, (where the Bank car park now is) and was completely wrecked, salvaged were her new £300 engine, sails, nets and footlines, 25th March 1914.

PZ334 *Agnes* – 2nd class lugger, 31½ ft, 11 tons, built Porthleven 1885, owner Edward Downing of Mousehole, wrecked Boscowan Point in Mounts Bay, 1925.

PZ26 *Emblem* – 1st class lugger, 53 ft, 32 tons, (built Porthleven 1914, 40.8 ft, 22 tons), lengthened Newlyn 1920, owners John, Edward and Leslie Hicks of Mousehole, destroyed by fire near the Wolf Rock after explosion in engine room while fishing, scuttled two hours later, crew picked up by fishing boat *Orion*, 4th June 1930.

PZ84 *Ivy* – 2nd class lugger, 25.5 ft, 6½ tons, built St Ives 1902, owner James Pender, wrecked Mousehole harbour during southerly storm and burnt, 1935.

PZ621 *Dashing Spray* – 2nd class lugger, 24.8 ft, 4½ tons, built Porthleven 1898, owner Richard Cornish of Mousehole, lost at sea 1940.

There were undoubtedly a lot more lost overboard than were actually reported by the newspapers of the day but these were the only ones that actually made the papers.

5th September 1878. William James Richards 20 from Mousehole fell overboard from a fishing boat in Aberdeen harbour and drowned.

23rd September 1879. Thomas Ellis Vingoe from Mousehole drowned at Whitby during a gale while hooking a chain onto an anchor for his boat.

28th April 1880. William Charles White 15 from Mousehole fell overboard from a punt being towed by a mackerel boat and drowned near the island.

11th January 1883. Richard Carey, owners son, and Frederick Daniel, both from Mousehole, washed overboard and drowned from their fishing boat *Banner* PZ91 during a severe storm off the Dodman. The boat reached Falmouth although very badly damaged.

19th July 1883. Thomas Beckerleg 14 was drowned after the lugger capsized off Carn Dhu. Three others were picked up by the pilot cutter *Pill* and landed in Mousehole.

These are just a few of the wrecks and casualties – to list them all would fill a book. The worst storm to hit Mounts Bay occurred on 7th October 1880 when winds up to 140 mph lashed the bay from the south. It was estimated that 40 to 60 fishing vessels were lost during that period between Porthleven and Sennen from Penzance and Mousehole harbours and all the slipways around the bay. Considerable damage was done to property and a lot of the coastline was washed away, much like what happened during the Ash Wednesday storm on 27th February 1963.

Boats Built in Mousehole

BELOW IS A list of some boats that were known to be built in Mousehole between 1869 and 1944.

PZ36 *Gleaner* – 2nd class yawl, 22.5 foot long, 2 tons, date unknown.

PZ45 *Morning Star* – 1st class lugger, 51.4 foot, 37 tons, built by William Williams 1900.

PZ49 *Valetta* – 1st class lugger, 47.2 foot, 21½ tons, built by Nicholas Cornish 1879.

PZ53 *Bolinder* – 2nd class lugger, 21.4 foot, 2 tons, built 1931 by Nicholas Cornish

PZ63 *Velox* – 1st class lugger, 47 foot, 27 tons, built 1901 by William Williams.

PZ66 *Kate* – 3rd class lugger, 13.4 foot, 1 ton, built 1900.

PZ72 *Minerva* – 1st class lugger, 46.6 foot, 26 tons, built 1878.

PZ75 *Coronation* – 1st class lugger, 52 foot, 24 tons, built 1902.

PZ87 *Niagra* – 1st class lugger, 48.3 foot, 27 tons, built 1878 by William Williams.

PZ90 *Jason* – 2nd class lugger, 22.5 foot, 2 tons, built 1931.

PZ94 *Martha* – 2nd class lugger, 31½ foot, 8½ tons, built 1886.

PZ96 *Valourous* – 1st class lugger, 48.3 foot, 27 tons, built 1878.

PZ97 *C.H.J.* – 2nd class lugger, 33.5 foot, 10½ tons, built 1869.

PZ131 *Edgar* – 1st class lugger, 54 foot, 36 tons, built 1902.

PZ139 *Gleaner* – 1st class lugger, 49 foot, 28 tons, built 1880 by William Williams.

PZ154 *Alga* – 2nd class motor boat, 18 foot, 1 ton, built 1932 by William Cornish.

PZ173 *Kate* – 2nd class lugger, 28 foot, 7 tons, built 1903.

PZ187 *Magic* – 2nd class lugger, 27.3 foot, 7½ tons, built 1903 by John Bodinner.

PZ189 *Margaret* – 2nd class lugger, 28 foot, 7 tons, built 1903.

PZ197 *Boy Philip* – 2nd class lugger, 27 foot, 6½ tons, built 1903.

PZ198 *We'll Try* – 2nd class lugger, 31.4 foot, 8½ tons, built 1903.

PZ198 *We'll Try* – 1st class lugger, 40.6 foot, 16½ tons, lengthened 1921.

PZ199 *Puritan* – 2nd class lugger, 28 foot, 7 tons, built 1903.

PZ227 *Sarnia* – 2nd class motor boat, 15.4 foot, 1 ton, built 1933 by William Cornish.

PZ261 *Marion* – 3rd class rowing boat, 10.7 foot, ½ ton, built 1906.

PZ266 *Bessie* – 2nd class lugger, 23 foot, 5 tons, built 1886 by William Williams.

PZ302 *Faithful* – 2nd class lugger, 25.5 foot, 6 tons, built 1905.

PZ310 *Mur* – 2nd class lugger, 24½ foot, 5 tons, built 1880.

PZ314 *Mary Lizzie* – 2nd class lugger, 35 foot, 11½ tons, built 1887.

PZ347 *Return* – 2nd class lugger, 24.1 foot, 5 tons, built 1884.

PZ381 *Breeze* – 2nd class lugger, 29.9 foot, 7 tons, rebuilt 1907.

PZ383 *Sunbeam* – 1st class lugger, 53 foot, 36 tons, built 1885 by William Williams.

PZ410 *Village Bride* – 3rd class lugger, 13.8 foot, 1 ton, built 1890.

PZ415 *Humility* – 2nd class lugger, 47 foot, 27 tons, built 1877.

PZ556 *Iverna* – 1st class lugger, 41 foot, 22 tons, built 1894 by John and William Bodinner.

PZ571 *Rising Sun* – 1st class lugger, 39.6 foot, 21 tons, built 1895.

PZ573 *Ben-My-Chree* – 1st class lugger, 51 foot, 33 tons, built 1895.

PZ592 *Pantaloon* –2nd class lugger, 25.7 foot, 6½ tons, built 1896 by John Bodinner.

PZ603 *Primrose* – 1st class lugger, 40 foot, 21 tons, built 1896 by J. Bowden.

PZ612 *Jubilee* – 2nd class lugger, 26½ foot, 5½ tons, built 1897.

PZ631 *Reaper* – 2nd class lugger, 25 foot, 5½ tons, built 1902.

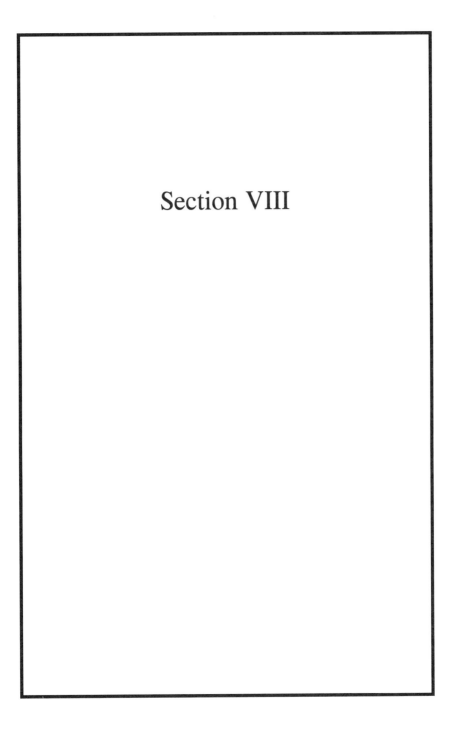

Section VIII

A Few Strange Happenings

A SHOPKEEPER CALLED Jim Caslake who is a very good friend of mine kept ducks, geese, chicken, pigs and bees. He had several bee hives and the honey he sold in his shop along with crabs and lobsters he caught in his pots through the summer. When he retired he went to live In St Mary's on the Scilly Isles.

Anyway A couple of his ducks flew down to the harbour and made that their new home, both were females. They lived there for over a year before being caught by Chris Cass and taken back to Jim where he clipped their wings. A year later one duck flew back to the harbour to be joined by a wild female mallard duck where they lived quite happily. Five o'clock one morning Dave Redhead, he kept the newsagent and general stores on the harbour front, and myself were chatting when a male mallard flew into the harbour and made advances towards the two females with his mating display. To our amazement both females attacked the male and drove it away. This happened every morning for a week before the male finally understood that the two females did not like males. They were a bit strange because they often mated with each other. Mousehole must have been the only place in the UK with 'Queer Ducks'!!! They lived quite happily in our harbour for about two years and then both disappeared a few days before Christmas! We did wonder if someone had killed them for Christmas but they would have been tough. Maybe a fox or badger took them, both these animals are regular visitors to the harbour each night.

* * *

Talking about badgers reminds me of something. I live in Abbey Place and right opposite my door under the steps of another flat is a badger sett. Back in the 90's three lived there permanently and became very tame. All I had to do was shout down the hole and they would come out to see if there was any food. Local school children used to crowd into my house to watch them when I called them out with food. The hardest thing was teaching the children to talk in a normal voice or shout, if they whispered the badgers would back off into their sett, they were frightened when people whispered. They would be out about five in the evening wandering around looking for food, if I hadn't fed them they would come into the house and stare at me or scratch the door if it was closed. I took numerous photographs of them and my cat feeding from the same bowl. Judy and Paul Joel, who live next door to me, couldn't believe how tame they had become and when we had a barbeque the badgers would be hanging around waiting for sausages or chicken bits along with my cat. Lots of visitors saw and photographed the cat and badgers and all said the same thing, its the first time I have seen a wild badger, the wild bit was strange because they would take food from my hand. Then the cat would be purring and rubbing its body against my arm until the badger backed off, then it would sniff my hand, but I found out my cat did not like peanut butter sandwiches. They left when the building opposite was gutted and rebuilt as holiday flats. The sett is still there and used occasionally but there are no permanent badgers now although they do come back most nights along with foxes all looking for food. A farmer and his family staying in the flats watched and photographed a badger and said it was the first time he had seen one and thought they looked very smart and bigger than he expected. My cat lived in the harbour as a feral cat for several years after its owner died. Then one winter's day during a southerly gale it wandered up to my place and took over. It only took the cat a month to train me to do what it wanted and make friends with the badgers and foxes, which it had often seen while living in the harbour.

THE FOX

Talking about foxes reminds me of something else that happened in our village which caused a lot of laughter when it was finally all over.

There were, and still are, a lot of local characters who seem to liven the place up as soon as they enter the building or join your company, and of course there are those who are or were 'loveable rogues.' The definition of the word loveable depending on whether you were the butt of their roguish activities.

One of these characters, long since dead, had a 'thing' about mullet, that's a type of fish that usually swims in large shoals and it was also worth a 'bob or two.' If there was one mullet swimming between the island and shore it was said that he knew about it. Anyhow he had a friend who also saw a school of mullet as a shoal of swimming pound notes, trouble is they have to be caught and mullet don't like being caught, they are the Houdini's of the fish world. They tried all the conventional ways with nets, but mullet have this nasty habit of jumping over the head rope or finding some small hole that nobody knew about and escaping. So putting their war experiences into practise they obtained some dynamite and detonators, and full of expectations the two of them sailed away to make a fortune. The dynamite in all probability came from Penlee Quarry where nearly half of Mousehole used to work in the 50's. The quarry closed down in the 90's.

Well the first try was not very successful. They primed and threw in two sticks of dynamite and promptly turned the shoal of mullet into fish fingers – too much explosives.

The next attempt was equally dramatic. They only caught one fish – not enough explosives. Eventually they got it right but inevitably had to stop as this type of fishing was, and still is, illegal.

One of them was also a great hunting man and dearly loved rabbiting during the winter. The farmers at Paul village were quite happy for him to hunt their grounds and get rid of rabbits which were a pest. This was before myxomatosis nearly wiped out the rabbit population. The farmers were losing quite a few chickens and a fox was blamed, all the local lads had a go at trapping this fox and all failed. The fox would get into the chicken runs, take a chicken or two and be away avoiding all the different and ingenious traps and devices set to ensnare it. The local paper reported on the Paul fox and its plundering.

At the local pub, the Kings Arms, this was the main topic of conversation and usually centred around other clever foxes and how they were eventually caught, but this one seemed to be craftier than any previously known. Eventually of course it was caught, and what a fox it turned out to be. The local paper's headlines summed it up best. 'Paul Fox, Mousehole Fisherman'. Seems like the old boy liked chicken as well as rabbit and mullet. After that he was often referred to as 'The Fox'.

Diary Dates

THESE INCIDENTS ARE taken from my own personal diaries. Unfortunately I lost my diaries between 1960 and 1980 when my place was flooded. They were all written in ink and the ink just covered each page in a blue colour washing away any writing. I now only use pencil which does not wash away when it is wet. There are also other gaps caused by my various bypass operations since 1980. 13 bypasses and one amputation, which again means I might have missed some events. The last one being December 2009 until March 2010 when the village experienced its hardest and longest spell of freezing weather. That was for an amputation, so I don't have any records for that 10 weeks. I have not included every flood that occurred only what I considered to be the worst according to what I say in my diaries. I think most of what I have included will jog peoples memories, especially the dates. Most people can't believe it was that long ago when certain things happened. A lot of the earlier incidents from 1960 onwards I have covered in more detail so those below are only from 1993.

MONDAY 1st MARCH 1993, first wheelie bins in Mousehole.

WEDNESDAY 9th JUNE 1993, 3 inches of rain fell overnight, all village flooded, roads covered in mud and stones, fire engines pumping out houses, council clearing roads.

MONDAY 21st JUNE 1993, new cement and iron guides fitted in harbour mouth for baulks.

SATURDAY 5th NOVEMBER 1995, first firework display on St Clements Island.

NOVEMBER 29th, 30th, 1st DEC 1995, Severe southerly storm for 3 days, everything covered in oil, quays, driftwood, netting, rope etc, lots of dead seabirds.

FRIDAY 19th JANUARY 1996, Mousehole fishing boat *Renovelle* PZ177, decommissioned and broken up.

SUNDAY 10th NOVEMBER 1996, strong earth tremor 0900, local TV and radio saying 3.8, epicentre near Epsom Shoal in Mounts Bay and lasted 8 seconds, strongest since 1966, Bark House severely damaged, slates, windows and chimneys fell down. Structural engineer gives owners 2 days to make it safe.

FRIDAY 13th DECEMBER 1996, large spectacular meteor display between 11.00 and 0100.

THURSDAY 2nd JANUARY 1997, another earth tremor at 10.30 in morning, not so strong.

THURSDAY 20th to 24th MARCH 1997, Hale-Bop comet visible from Mousehole from 20.00 hrs.

SUNDAY 31st AUGUST 1997, Princess Diana killed in car crash.

FRIDAY 7th NOVEMBER 1997, cloudburst over village at 3.00. Rocks and mud 3 foot deep on roads. Lobster Pot, Cornish Range and Ship Inn flooded and full of mud, all closed, some 50 cottages also flooded and filled with mud, furniture, carpets and electric goods ruined, police cars blocked every road into village, several fire engines pumping out houses all night, council workmen clearing roads of boulders, suction pumps being used to clear mud, Saturday and Sunday workmen still clearing up and putting up sandbag barriers, didn't stop raining until Tuesday 11th November.

WEDNESDAY 28th JAN 1998, first barge arrives with 750 tons of granite for Bank car park.

SATURDAY 20th JUNE 1998, everything covered in fine red sand, believed from Sahara, Mousehole artist Jack Pender died in Penzance hospital during afternoon.

SUNDAY 30th MAY 1999, artist Nigel Hallard opens his new gallery.

MONDAY 9th AUGUST 1999, Carnival week and phosphorous bomb washed up on Bank car park rocks, police cordoned off area and bomb disposal blew it up at 0100.

WEDNESDAY 11th AUGUST 1999, total eclipse of the sun at 11.11am, birds totally confused, strong wind 5 minutes before eclipse, total eerie silence, dark in 10 seconds, thousands of winking flash bulbs all around Mounts Bay, 10 seconds to get light again, from start to finish about 20 minutes.

FRIDAY 24th to 26th DECEMBER 1999, village once again flooded, Ship Inn flooded but didn't stop anyone drinking, we just wore wellingtons, vast majority of Christmas lights around harbour fused, but most working again before the New Year.

WEDNESDAY 10th MAY 2000, severe rain storm and village once again flooded, mud, rocks, wheelie bins being carried down Duck St by flood water 2 to 3 foot deep, pumping station covers blew off with water pressure and filled harbour with raw sewage, shooting 3 foot into the air, job to breathe, roads into village flooded, 2 fire engines pumping those clear before starting on cottages, some roads and alley ways leading from mountains ripped up.

THURSDAY 24th AUGUST 2000, village once again flooded, not helped by southerly gale, pumping station covers and manhole covers once again blown off filling the harbour with raw sewage, roads 1 to 2 foot deep in mud and stones, took council 2 days to clear up.

MONDAY 11th SEPTEMBER 2000, fishing boats leaving Newlyn to blockade ferry ports in Plymouth against rising fuel prices.

TUESDAY 12th SEPTEMBER 2000, on local news vast majority of petrol stations in Cornwall out of fuel, those that have fuel they are queuing for over 2 hours, village very quiet with hardly any traffic, only half of buses running.

THURSDAY 30th NOV 2000, guard vessel *Dolfyn* ashore in southerly gale *(see Dolfyn)*.

SUNDAY 31st DECEMBER 2000, some 20 cars smashed up on both quays during southerly storm 10, including new Rover, Volvo, BMW and Mercedes, 2 baulks also broken.

FRIDAY 5th JANUARY 2001, replaced broken baulks in southerly 6 to 7, waves coming over both quays, we all got soaked but finished the job.

SUNDAY 7th JANUARY 2001, bottom half of zig-zag path from far beach to main road washed away during southerly storm, large landslide with nearly 30 foot of first car park lost, huge cracks in cliff. Friday 16th Feb 2001, another large area of cliff fell down.

TUESDAY 9th JANUARY 2001, total eclipse of the moon at 8.00pm.

THURSDAY 1st MARCH 2001, all footpaths, moorland parks, zoos etc, closed in Cornwall due to Foot and Mouth outbreak, by 24th April 1,480 farms infected.

MONDAY 19th MARCH 2001, work started on building a sea wall near the zig-zag path where the cliff is falling down.

SATURDAY 24th MARCH 2001, 4 new baulks towed up from Newlyn, £1,000 each.

THURSDAY 26th APRIL 2001, Mousehole Post Office held up and robbed by two men, one with a gun the other a knife, about £10,000 stolen.

TUESDAY 31st JULY 2001, barge taking first lot of scrap metal away from *Dolfyn* wreck, yacht tried sailing between barge's mooring buoy and got caught up in hawser, towed clear and into Penzance for repairs.

TUESDAY 26th MARCH 2002, salvage boat clearing up last scrap metal from *Dolfyn*.

TUESDAY 15th OCTOBER 2002, southerly storm force 9 to 10, huge waves sweeping both quays, 100 plus pots, ropes, nets washed into harbour, car trailer washed off quay, cars damaged or written off, numerous boats damaged or lost, scaffolding for new baulk slides twisted up like spaghetti, new pier head railing twisted and broken, took over a week to clean up the harbour area.

THURSDAY 14th NOVEMBER 2002, Radio Cornwall reported 2 inches of rain fell in 6 hours during south-west gale 8, Mousehole once again severely flooded, mud, rocks, flower pots and wheelie bins banging their way down Duck St all night, lots of houses flooded, all village roads closed by mud and rocks, Newlyn, Penzance, Marazion all flooded, St Ives worst affected with 6 to 8 foot of water which caved in shop fronts and flooded houses, people stuck in cars or sheltering in farm houses.

WEDNESDAY 27th NOVEMBER 2002, southerly storm force 9 to 10, village once again flooded during heavy rain, took council workers 2 days to clear all the roads.

MONDAY 2nd DECEMBER 2002, southerly storm force 9 to 10, coaster escorted into Penzance by Coastguard tug *Anglian Princess*, deck cargo of wood had moved and she was listing very badly with her port side under water, from the shore it looked like she was on her beam ends.

WEDNESDAY 1st JANUARY 2003, lightening bolt hit electricity pole in Abbey Place, melted the wires, electricity off, computers and phones melted and damaged around village.

THURSDAY 20th MARCH 2003, Iraq war started.

FRIDAY 25th JULY 2003, south-west 4 to 5, very heavy rain, some cottages flooded, pumping station tops blew off again with water pressure, harbour filled with raw sewage.

SATURDAY 16th AUGUST 2003, yacht went aground back of new quay trying to make harbour, ebbing tide, inshore and offshore lifeboats, Coastguards and fire engine standing by, people taken off before she went over on her beam ends, floated off at 4.00pm and escorted to Penzance harbour for repairs.

FRIDAY 22nd AUGUST 2003, carnival BBQ, helicopter, both lifeboats, Coastguards and police called at 9.00pm, 2 men missing on a small surf sail board, helicopter found them several miles back of St Clements Isle, inshore lifeboat towed them back to Mousehole at 10.20pm, both men very cold and shaken up.

WEDNESDAY 3rd SEPTEMBER 2003, a funny incident that could have ended tragically. Dave Redhead and myself noticed a man waving his arms on the island, I got my binoculars, 3 large seals were following him around the island and attacking him every time he tried to get into the water, I phoned up the Coastguards and the inshore lifeboat took the man off, the Coastguards phoned me back later and they were laughing, his exact words were, 'your local amorous seals took a fancy to him or his aftershave and was trying to mate with him, kept going for his nether regions when he tried getting into the water, there is no way he could have swum back ashore without losing his dangly bits.'

FRIDAY 2nd JULY 2004, strong westerly gale force 8, start of the Sea, Salt and Sail 3 day festival, only one vessel made Mousehole, 20 storm-bound in Falmouth and 6 in St Ives.

SUNDAY 8th AUGUST 2004, tail end of Hurricane Alex hit today, carnival events cancelled.

MONDAY 16th AUGUST 2004, Boscastle hit by flash floods, village swept away, no lives lost due to helicopters rescuing people.

MONDAY 20th SEPTEMBER 2004, a large articulated lorry got stuck on Parade Hill, it couldn't turn the corner and it was too heavy to reverse up the hill, the road was black with burnt rubber, the driver tried for about two hours to reverse out but couldn't, it was stacked with palettes of two inch thick slates and timber, he unloaded these into Tremayne Courtyard but it made no difference, a large recovery vehicle finally arrived from Scorrier and towed the artic out backwards and parked by the Coastguards Hotel, another crane had to pick up his load and transfer that, the artic had also crashed into Jack Matthews house and damaged that, structural engineers examined that, the road was basically closed for another two days while the building was made safe.

WEDNESDAY 27th OCTOBER 2004, southerly storm force 10 to 11, Mousehole, Newlyn and Penzance put on Red Alert for flooding and storm damage, some Gurnick houses evacuated, 3.00pm half tide those houses were being buried by waves and spray, it was going right over the top of houses, 6.00pm high tide it was no better, lots of damage and flooding to those properties, 12 to 15 boats in harbour reduced to matchwood, Christmas lights very badly damaged, some not repairable, island was completely covered by huge waves, rafts of Shags were in harbour sheltering, approximately 50 to 60, they ended up roosting on window sills, walls, gardens and Lobster Pot balcony that was being turned into flats, in fact anywhere that they could shelter for the night, several killed as they were blown into harbour walls. 6.00 high water huge waves in harbour coming right up into Cliff Road by newsagents, bad storm but still not as strong as Ash Wednesday storm. 0715 next morning a lot of us turned out to pull all the pieces of boats etc up onto the slip, massive hole 200 yards plus opened up on main Mousehole Newlyn road, police and council cordoned off half of road to make single file traffic. Gurnick sea wall washed away, in some places back to footpath, council had to take down part of old quay and build a concrete road along shoreline rocks before they could start building a new sea wall at Gurnick.

MONDAY 1st NOVEMBER 2004, new ITV channel started this evening.

SATURDAY 4th DECEMBER 2004, council diggers and lorries finally moved all the smashed up boats etc from October storm.

TUESDAY 14th JUNE 2005, proposed new Marina model for old unused Penlee Quarry on display at Sunday School, looks very good.

THURSDAY 7th APRIL 2005, 2 people stuck on Merlin Rock taken off by inshore lifeboat.

FRIDAY 3rd FEBRUARY 2006, large fire in evening at bottom of Cherrygarden St, whole street evacuated, Steven Lashbrooke's house gutted, 5 others badly damaged, road melted in heat, lucky it didn't sweep up the whole street.

THURSDAY 14th SEPTEMBER 2006, power cut at 9.00 in evening, heavy rumbling and banging that shook houses, large underground electricity cable bottom of Duck St blew up creating large hole in road, flames shooting up 6 to 7 foot, Dave Ingram from newsagents using fire extinguisher until police and fire engine arrived, houses nearby evacuated. Electricity company worked all night with angle grinder and jack hammers, power back on at 0600 next morning. Number 1 Duck Street lucky not to catch on fire, all flower pots melted, scorched windows and railings damaged, sewer pipe broken during explosion, electricity company and SW Water finally finished and road tarred by Tuesday 26th September.

TUESDAY 24th OCTOBER 2006, not much wind, southerly 5 to 6, but massive ground sea, 7 cars on New Quay and 8 cars on Old Quay smashed up or jammed under railings, half of them write-offs, tail end of Hurricane Gordon blamed.

WEDNESDAY 27th DECEMBER 2006, southerly 6 to 7, 13 canoeists from Falmouth and Scotland rescued 1 mile off Lands End, 2 lifeboats, 2 helicopters and a fixed wing aircraft involved in rescue, all saved.

THURSDAY 18th JANUARY 2007, WSW storm 10, container ship *Napoli* started breaking up in heavy seas off Lizard, 26 men rescued by 2 Culdrose helicopters, Coastguard tug *Anglian Princess* towed *Napoli* to Branscomb Bay where she was beached. Looters raided every container that came ashore. *Napoli* finally unloaded of containers and on Monday 9th July floated off for inspection, nearly split in half so decided to leave her there and scrap her. She was finally cut in half with explosives, the two halves floated then taken to breaker's yards.

MONDAY 22nd JANUARY 2007, NE 8 to 9, Newlyn trawler *Algarie* had wheelhouse smashed in by huge wave, escorted into Newlyn by Penlee Lifeboat.

SUNDAY 5th AUGUST 2007, 0100 hours helicopter, police, ambulance and Cliff Rescue called to Mousehole Cave, local man Adam Torrie fell over cliff onto rocks, flown to Treliske Hospital, Truro, with head and back injuries.

TUESDAY 14th AUGUST 2007, S 8 to 9, Fastnet Race again a disaster. (Nothing like the 1979 Fastnet Race disaster when 15 people lost their lives, most of the fleet had damage, some yachts sank others dismasted, local trawlers spent a week looking for abandoned yachts and towing them to Newlyn for the salvage money, Culdrose helicopters spent several days rescuing people from disabled yachts).

FRIDAY 7th to SUNDAY 9th DECEMBER 2007, Westerly 10 to 11, lots of damage to roofs in village, builders very busy battening down roofs with plastic sheets to keep rain out, 2 roads into Mousehole closed by fallen trees.

SUNDAY 28th APRIL 2008, bus company ran an old bus from 40's and 50's that used to run into Mousehole, conductor and driver both wore the old uniforms and the conductor even had an old-fashioned wind up ticket dispenser, there was no charge for using the bus.

SATURDAY 13th JUNE 2009, injured badger was discovered hiding behind skiffs on the beach, we called the Badger Rescue Group who caught her, badly infected back from fighting, treated and released 3 months later.

WEDNESDAY 8th JULY 2009, Digital TV changeover day.

SUNDAY 12th JULY 2009, our village does get its fair share of strange people. For the last couple of days a man has been round the village dressed up like a Jedi Knight, he really believed he was a Jedi, tattoos all over his body of Jedi and some Star Wars characters, he was up the legion this Sunday and told everyone up there he could open a bottle of beer with his penis and kept offering to show us, he was told to keep his trousers on or get out, another man a few years ago dressed and thought he was Zorro, and he even had a sword, he stayed for a few months before leaving.

FRIDAY 13th to 14th NOVEMBER 2009, south 9 to 11, a very stormy gusty 2 days, lots of damage to houses with chimney pots, cowling and TV aerials being blown down, a lot of cars damaged or written off, wheelie bins being blown around roads with some ending up in the harbour, rafts of Shags sheltering in harbour each evening.

SATURDAY 11th SEPTEMBER 2010, a large red Penzance catamaran full of wildlife trippers lost its mast, several people hurt and boat leaking, lifeboat took people off and inshore lifeboat towed catamaran back to Penzance for repairs.

MONDAY 15th NOVEMBER 2010, lifeboat picked up a body one mile off the back of St Clements Isle 10.00 in the morning.

SATURDAY 27th NOVEMBER 2010, Paul Church hit by lightening bolt, electricity intermittent all night, lots of computers and telephones fried.

SUNDAY 28th NOVEMBER to FRIDAY 3rd DECEMBER 2010, 6 days of hard frost and snow, didn't settle on village roads, all schools in area closed, no buses or deliveries, everything frozen, worst hit areas Cornwall and Scotland, snow line stretched from Helston to Penzance and St Ives upwards into Devon.

TUESDAY 1st MARCH 2011, main sewer pipe between Mousehole and Newlyn broken at Penlee Quarry with sewage running down the road, lorries pumping sewage from pump house in harbour for the next 48 hours, night and day, until pipe mended.

Old Sayings

WAY BACK IN the days of sail there used to be usually rhyming sayings for things to do with the weather and fishing. It is always easier to remember something that is in rhyme. The old fishermen of sailing days found it easier to remember a rhyming saying than one that didn't rhyme and remember there were no ship's radios or engines in those days aboard fishing boats, just the wind and sails to propel your boat along. There were no radios, fish-finders, radar or GPS' in those days, just a watch and compass and of course charts. That is all I had in those early days. Towards the end of the 60's VHF radios became available along with the paper echo sounders and fishing marks were done by day marks on shore. I have often regretted not writing down some of those sayings during my early days of fishing, they are now probably gone forever. I was 75 in 2011 and the old memory box is not so good as it used to be. I can remember some of the older fishermen from the 60's and they all had their sayings about certain aspects of fishing and they all had nicknames. A few I can still remember. 'Sleepy John,' 'Dim Tonkin,' 'Pasties,' 'Long John,' 'Long Tom,' 'Chuggy,' 'Smoker,' 'Hurricane Hutch,' 'Black Jack,' 'Squeaky,' 'Leftie,' 'Pups,' 'Shrimpy,' 'Doga,' 'Restless.' I was always known as 'The Boy' or 'Butts.' A couple of the local lads worked my boat for a fortnight when I was off sick and when I was recovering I'd be out on the bank with older fishermen and they would say, '. . . ah, boat coming, ah 'tis Butts on his way in.' never the name of the boat. When I had my last boat built in Penryn in 1980/81 I named her *Butts* PZ584. She is still being worked full-time fishing from Mousehole under the same name by a local man called 'Cod.'

A lot of the old sayings came from Jack Worth who was cox of the *Solomon Browne* lifeboat when I was on her, I retired from the lifeboat a year after Jack did. I have an old photograph taken in the 60's of the lifeboat and crew doing an exercise off Penzance prom. I sure do look young in that, most of those in the picture have all passed on now. On calm nights when we were steaming off on a Medico we had lots of time to talk and he would relate various fishing tales from the 30's and 40's, nearly always accompanied by the old sayings. Those I can remember are below.

'When the corn is in the shocks the fish are on the rocks.' This was harvest time in the fields and when the fish are in closest to rocks for feeding on the abundance of small baitfish (baby fish born that summer).

'Shocks' are three sheaves of corn stood upright to dry that have been cut with a binder, this was before combine harvesters were invented.

Just after WW2 and before lighthouses lights were upgraded there was another saying, 'Plymouth light is hard to mark flashing two dim and one dark.' Probably because the two light flashes were hard to see, dim.

Back in the early 60's Ben Pender and several old fishermen were talking about pilchard drifting and they all came out with several sayings regarding that part of their trade but only two come to mind. 'Gulls a sitting on the sea there'll be fish enough for you and me.' When you see a patch of gulls sitting quietly on the surface there is invariably a shoal of fish right below them. 'Gannets circling overhead there's fish enough to go with the bread.' Gannets are plunge divers and if they are circling high up it means they have spotted a deep shoal of fish.

The commonest saying which is regularly used even today is this, 'The easterly wind is like a kite, up by day and down by night.' An easterly wind will freshen as the sun rises and blow all day, then die away as the sun sets.

Another saying about easterly winds is this, 'An easterly wind is a lazy wind and goes through you instead of around.' I think everyone knows what that means.

Another old fisherman named Jack Wallis used to come out with this, or something very close to it, back in the 60's. He said it was an excuse for not going to sea. It might not be word perfect but it's the best I can remember. 'If the candle blows out it's too windy for a shout, if it stays alight the sails can't take flight, so its back to the missus for the rest of the night, in the lee of bum island you snuggle up tight.'

There were and are lots of one-liners regarding certain aspects of life, a few of those are below.

'Dark as a dogs guts,' referred to a black moonless and starless night.

'Calm as a clock,' referred to a flat greasy calm with no wind.

'As ugly as a bag full of assholes,' referred to something or someone that was ugly.

'As rough as a sack full of nails,' referred to something or someone that was rough or untidy in appearance.

'Porthleven built,' Porthleven boats nearly always had a wide stern and this remark usually refers to a lady with a large posterior.

'As hard as a begger boys heart,' refers to someone with no or little feelings.

One saying I came across in some old diaries from the early 1800's is rather strange and I have no idea what it means or refers to, 'Sharper than a serpents tongue,' I am only guessing this saying applied to someone who was vindictive.

There are of course some funny ones as well, I made this one up after losing my left leg in 2009, and it's very appropriate for some people. 'He's as fast as a one legged man running up a hill.' Refers to a person who is slow at doing everything.

'COLD ENOUGH TO FREEZE THE BALLS ON A BRASS MONKEY'

How many times have you heard that during a cold winters day? How many people know what it means and where the saying comes from?

Like so many old sayings it is nautical, some are readily recognisable as being nautical such as 'Three Sheets to the Wind' when a person has had too much to drink, others like the one above are not. The vast majority date back hundreds of years to the time of square-rigged sailing ships. Ships of the Line were square-rigged fighting vessels and by their very nature had no or very little deck shelter of any kind. Deck space was taken up with masts, ropes for sails, stays, ladders, sail winches and large anchor winches. What little space was left was used for cannons, so the top deck was just an open fighting platform open to whatever the weather was doing. Lower decks were afforded some shelter from the elements, cannon and musket fire.

The upper or top deck was open to whatever the weather threw at the boat, cannons, men and cannon balls would undoubtedly freeze during cold winter days with spray flying onboard. Cannon balls would be stacked in a pyramid shape close to each cannon and to stop them rolling around in heavy seas they were stacked in a brass tray called a 'Monkey.' During very cold weather this pyramid of cannon balls would all freeze together making them unusable, hence the saying, 'Cold enough to freeze the balls on a brass monkey.' It was the Powder Monkey's job to provide and keep gunpowder dry for the cannons and also to fetch warm water to free the frozen cannon balls. Today a Powder Monkey usually applies to a person employed to use explosives.

Communications aboard the early sailing vessels to ensure all the men worked or pulled together was a major problem especially during strong winds. The earliest documented accounts state that a large bass drum was used to beat out a certain rhythm for a specific job, each hauling job required a different beat. So the drummer had a very important job that ensured a sail or whatever was hauled up efficiently and as quickly as possible so saving time. As time progressed and ships got bigger the Port or Starboard Watch took to shouting 'haul' every few seconds or so to raise anchors or sails. This gradually turned into Sea Shanties for each job aboard a sailing vessel where men were required to hoist sails or anchors. Each shanty had a different tempo so that the men knew when to pull. A good shanty man was essential for the efficient running of a sailing ship in those days and was rewarded with an extra few pence each month in his wages. The drummer was now basically redundant and only used to beat men to quarters during periods of conflict.

Hayle Causeway

TRAVEL BETWEEN THE towns of Penzance and Redruth up until 1820 was a difficult and dangerous adventure. There were three ways of travelling between these towns, walking, horseback or horse-drawn carriages. Carts or carriages would appear to be the best and fastest way of travel but that was not the case. To get from Penzance to Redruth entailed a very long uncomfortable days journey in a draughty coach along the coastal road through Marazion to Helston and then on to Redruth. The more direct route followed by those on horseback or walking entailed crossing the Hayle river estuary with its marshes, quicksands and mud filled pools for just over a mile. To help travellers to cross this dangerous area whitewashed posts and balls were erected to indicate the most favourable area for crossing, but even with these markers the records show that numerous people were drowned attempting to cross, including people from Mousehole. One report states that a local Lord of the Manor was crossing the estuary in a two horse carriage when it got bogged down in the mud.

Fearing the worst he picked up his box of gold coins and set off towards the shore. He then got stuck in mud and had to drop his gold in order to save his life. The two horses were saved but it did not state what happened to his carriage or the gold. If his gold was recovered then it was kept very quiet by the finder, or it could still be buried in the mud or underneath the modern Hayle Causeway. Presumably this happened somewhere near the Hayle River. In daylight with a good horse the crossing was reasonably easy, providing the tides were right. At night it was extremely dangerous especially around half tide with the strong currents and ever changing mud filled pools. It appears from the records that those who knew the estuary really well preferred to stop off at the Royal Standard Inn to wait for high tide. Undoubtedly they would partake of a few glasses of brandy or rum before swimming their horses across the estuary. They knew that a warm welcome awaited them at the Lamb and Flag tavern in Canonstown plus a hot meal of beefsteaks cooked on hot tin ingots from the Rose-an-grouse smelting works nearby. The records give the estuary crossing as being one mile in length but for a great number of years large areas of the estuary marshes were being filled in with spoil from the mines and dross from the smelting works. The Causeway of Hayle was first built in 1820, it has been widened and upgraded several times since then. This Causeway gave a direct route between Penzance and the rest of Cornwall.

Nelson's Blood

THIS IS INCLUDED because a lot of Mousehole men were in the Navy at that time. In the 1600's to the late 1800's Penzance was a busy thriving port full of merchants, importers, exporters, smugglers, privateers and fishermen with a very large Jewish population. It is said that the Jewish population of Penzance was one of the largest, if not the largest, in the country. Penzance also has the largest Jewish cemetery in the country. The name of the main street of this town indicates how important this community was to the prosperity of Penzance by being named Market Jew Street. The facades of the older buildings in some of the roads leading towards the quay and the main street, plus of course all the very large mansions and manor houses that dot the countryside around Penzance give an indication as to how prosperous this town used to be.

The Squires, Lords of the Manors and merchants were all businessmen but they all had fingers in lots of different schemes that made money, not all of these enterprises were legal *(see Privateers in South-West Cornwall and Smugglers & Excisemen).*

The main meeting place for these merchants and other businessmen was the Dolphin Tavern next to Penzance harbour where goods brought in by large sailing vessels were sold and then transported to their final destinations. One such merchant was a Jew named Parness Rav Lemmie bar Eliezer who imported sugar, tea, wines and spirits. He had warehouses in Quay Street, Queens Street and Parade Street. He was known by the local inhabitants as Mr Hart, Mr Lemon Hart.

In 1804 he started a distillery at the top end of Jennings Street which was named Lemon Hart & Son. He produced a very high quality rum which was said to be 150 proof, 90% proof by volume, which is very nearly pure alcohol. Trying to drink that neat must have burned the back of anyones throat, presumably it was watered down before consumption. It was marketed under the name of Lemon Hart Rum.

On 15th March 1851 Lemon Hart was awarded the contract to supply the Royal Navy with 100,000 gallons of their rum each year. Unfortunately Mr Lemon Hart died in 1845 so did not benefit or see the sudden financial increase to the company he started in 1804. Up until 1824 every man in the Navy was issued with ½ pint of rum a each day, that is half a bottle of normal rum today but today's rum is not 90% proof, it varies between 38 and 45% proof, and that is a lot weaker than Lemon Hart's original rum he supplied the Navy with.

In 1824 it was reduced to a quarter pint, one gill, per man each day. On 1st June 1951 the ration was halved again. On 30th July 1970 the 'Tot of Rum' ceased to be issued to Royal Navy personnel and so a long-standing tradition was finally brought to an end. There are lots of speculative reasons put forward for giving rum to naval sailors during those days of sail but in all probability we will never know the real reason. It could have been to keep them half drunk so they wouldn't get annoyed with their conditions aboard a very smelly cramped boat, but considering they had to climb rope ladders to alter sails day and night as well as doing it in gales of winds or pouring rain it does make you wonder whether it was a good idea.

Lord Nelson was killed in the battle at Trafalgar in 1805 and his body was preserved in a barrel of rum and brought back to England. Even this is unclear because some historians claim it was a barrel of brandy, the only thing which is certain is that it was a barrel of alcohol. Once he reached England and his body was removed from the barrel some sailors found the half empty cask and promptly drank the contents, that is how rum became known as 'Nelson's Blood.' The thought of drinking something in which a dead body had been preserved for four or five months does not really bear thinking about, but I suppose if it was 90% proof there would not be many bugs left alive and those that were would be horribly drunk. I would also imagine there would be a thick layer of sludge near the bottom of this barrel.

Mr Lemon Hart died on 13th October 1845 and was buried in Penzance Jewish Cemetery which is the largest and oldest Jewish cemetery in the country, it did fall into neglect for several years but is now well looked after and maintained.

Although he was a Jew he was also a Cornishman at heart. When the French threatened to invade Cornwall and England he raised a volunteer army and equipped them with weapons. He used his own money to do this and was their leader and Captain. This army was known as the 'Ludgvan Volunteers.'

Penzance and the surrounding districts owe a lot to the Jewish settlement in this town. When I bought my present cottage in 1980 I took six months off from fishing to do the place up and make it comfortable and draught-proof. I did what I was capable of and got builders in to do the rest. For several years I had noticed a small piece of angled wood attached to the outside door frame which I thought was some sort of holding device for a porch or suchlike. One day I unscrewed it and was surprised to find it was a sealed hollow piece of wood. Inside was an old parchment type piece of paper with strange foreign writing. I sent this off to Bristol University for them to decipher and explain what is was and why it was where I found it. A few weeks later I got their reply and was rather surprised. They could not decipher the paper but told me it was in old Jewish writing and was to keep the house and occupants free from evil spirits and make it a happy place to live. I have since sealed and put the original writing and wood back where it always was. The only thing I regret is not getting a photocopy of the writing, if I had then it's quite possible I would now have a transcript.

The Gourmatiser

NOT EVERYTHING WAS doom or gloom that got reported. Occasionally there were reports which showed the lighter side of the Cornish character as the following extract shows.

21st April 1887. A labourer at Newlyn said he could eat ten mackerel at one sitting. This was heard by some fish buyers who made a 5s bet, one said he couldn't, the other backed the man. He was agreeable so they all went to the Red Lion Inn where it was to be carried out. The 5s stakes were to be handed to the man if he was successful.

Large numbers of other people hearing the bet had arrived to watch and place side bets.

Both the fish and man were ready and he vigorously attacked the first fish. Mackerel after mackerel disappeared down the capacious gullet, and with the ninth he also had some bread. The last fish he divided into four parts, which vanished in a few movements of his fork. More ale and bread and the gourmatiser declared he was not half full and could demolish a pound of beef steak if they would supply it. That was not available but the sympathetic landlady gave him a pasty to fill up the empty corners.

The losing fish merchant remarked that if there were such appetites for fish it would pay to despatch mackerel to London or other good markets.

The victor was desirous of trying his powers on a leg of mutton on the same terms.

It is a great pity that the above report does not give any names. There was no other mention regarding the leg of mutton so presumably the fish merchants thought better of trying our 'gourmatiser' with this bet.

Some of the reports relating to Mousehole and Paul Parish are very brief indeed and consist of just a few lines as so. 'Hutchens' Charity' at Paul was started in 1709 'for the aged of the Parish to provide a refuge' by a Captain Stephen Hutchens RN with a bequest of £500. Captain Stephen Hutchens died in Port Royal, Jamaica in 1709, his will was dated 1707. Hutchens House, just past Paul church, is still going strong and still does the job it was originally started for. It was looked after by a retired Mousehole fisherman and his wife, Joseph and Hilary Madron until the 2000's.

Appendices

Appendix I
Mousehole 'PE' Registered Fishing Boats

PRIOR to 1869 all the Penzance fishing boats were registered as PE. After 1st January 1869 they all had to be registered as PZ as there were already fishing boats with a PE registration at Poole in Dorset. Several other fishing ports around the country also had to change their registration letters for similar reasons. Penzance Customs and Excise registration ledgers for all PE boats have either been lost or destroyed and Truro County Records Office only have the PZ registration ledgers from 1869 until 1945. After that date the ledgers were kept at Swansea Customs and Excise right up to the present time. Perhaps one day they might be given to Truro County Records Office where researchers like myself will be able to see them. I didn't think there would be any chance of getting any PE boats but I made enquiries around the village for any ledgers or books kept by Harbour Masters from the 1800's. Tommy Rowe's grandfather used to be a Harbour Master back in the 1850's and he still had his little notebook which he kindly leant to me. This is the only source of PE registration fishing vessels I have been able to find along with some census forms from that period. Some of them I have matched up with the PZ vessels from 1869 as can be seen below.

PE3	*Whisper*	PZ50	PE25	*Wasp*	PZ85	
PE12	*Diamond*		PE25	*Victory,* Howell Richards, b. 1785		
PE13	*Albion* PZ243 Abraham Jacka			*ONO,* John Johns, b. 1792		
PE13	*Excelsior*	PZ67	PE26	*Mayflower*	PZ16,	
PE14	*Industry* PZ102, Will Harvey, b.			William Mann, b. 1789		
		1795	PE27	*Jason,* Charles Mann		
PE15	*Nautilus*	PZ15,	PE29	*Banner*	PZ91	
	Chas. Pezzack, b.1822		PE29	*Peterel,* Henry Richards		
PE17	*Packet*	PZ61	PE31	*What You Will*	PZ82,	
PE19	*Jason*	PZ95		John Harvey		
PE20	*John*	PZ436	PE33	*Gideon Curly*	PZ101	
PE20	*Briton*		PE34	*Flora*	PZ453,	
	John Rich. Wright, b.1801			Rich. Humphreys, b.1813		
	Enterprise, Rich. Trewavas, b.1802		PE35	*Pearl*	PZ157	
			PE36	*Speed*	PZ414	
	George, Richard Harvey, b.1789		PE39	*Susan Mary*	PZ14	
			PE40	*Gregor,* John Blewett, b.1809		
PE21	*Rovenna*	PZ159	PE41	*Richard Watson*	PZ79	
PE22	*Clementina*	PZ88	PE42	*Britannia*	PZ145,	
PE23	*Triton* PZ70, Edwin Mann, b.1825			Richard Tonkin		
PE24	*Nile* PZ270, John Pentreath.		PE43	*Mary*	PZ162	

PE44	*Fearless*	PZ150
PE44	*Mary Ann*	PZ153,
	John Madron, b.1802	
PE45	*Providence*	PZ218
PE46	*Liberty*, Will Beadon	
PE47	*Betsey*, Ben Harvey, b.1825	
PE48	*Brothers*,	
	Nicholas T. Mann, b.1785	
PE49	*Selicia*	PZ148
PE50	*Pomona*	PZ72
PE52	*Polorus*	PZ220
PE55	*Emily*, William Richards, b.1809	
PE60	*Glide*	PZ71
PE66	*Hope*	PZ76
PE67	*Warrior*	PZ160
PE67	*Barbados*, Edwin Quick	
PE75	*Seabreeze*	PZ86
PE80	*Waterlily*	PZ282
PE82	*Surpass*	PZ90
PE82	*Charles Wesley*,	
	Chas. Wright, b.1791	
PE83	*Harmony*, Ben Harry, b.1806	
PE84	*Saundershill*	
PE85	*Return*,	
	William Blewett, b.1793	
PE85	*Godild*	PZ94
PE86	*Warbler*	PZ86
PE89	*Arethusa*	PZ65
PE89	*Three Brothers*, Will Ladner	
PE90	*Jasper*	PZ154
PE95	*Mariner*, Nicholas Praed	
PE96	*Evince*	PZ104
PE107	*Brilliant*	PZ161,
	Richard Angwin, b.1822	
PE116	*Two Brothers*	PZ3,
	John P. Richards, b.1826	
PE122	*Cornish Girl*	PZ93
PE166	*Nyanza*	PZ420
PE187	*Gleaner*	PZ163,

	Elias Glasson, b.1796	
PE189	*Wanderer*	PZ142,
	Richard Pentreath	
PE196	*Vanguard*	PZ13,
	William Jacka, b.1796	
PE200	*Cornwall*	PZ92
PE203	*Briton*	PZ89
PE207	*Vivid*, Thomas Matthews	
PE215	*Daring*	PZ528,
	Richard Bodinner	
PE216	*Rodney*	PZ143,
	Elias Glasson, b.1820	
PE225	*Nonpariel*	PZ411
PE226	*Zephyr* PZ190, John Ash	
PE231	*Amity*	PZ147,
	William Humphreys	
PE232	*John Wesley*	PZ9,
	Thomas Pentreath	
PE236	*Edwin*	PZ158,
	John Harvey, b.1811	
PE246	*Charles Wesley*	PZ343
PE247	*Robert Young*	PZ83,
	John Trewavas, b.1799	
PE259	*Weatherall*	PZ1,
	Richard Pezzack, b.1794	
PE260	*Why Not*	PZ128
PE261	*Cygnet*	PZ430
PE262	*Trinity*	PZ146
PE281	*Dove*	PZ413
PE311	*Mystery*	PZ7
PE321	*Telegraph*	PZ87
PE320	*Sarah Hills*	PZ144
PE335	*Gratitude*	PZ74
PE339	*Joseph*	PZ217
PE349	*Matchless*	PZ152
PE360	*Ariadne*	PZ222
PE365	*Dart*	PZ80
PE366	*Stativa*	PZ151

Appendix II
Mousehole 'PZ' Registered Fishing Boats

BETWEEN 1869 AND 1920 there were fifty-seven registered seine net boats in Mounts Bay that were basically used for catching pilchards when they came in close to a sandy beach. They were between 18 and 32 foot in length and powered by oars, the largest at 32 foot was PZ493 *James Francis* owned by Messrs Rowe of Mousehole. There were undoubtedly a lot more seine boats than the 57 that were registered and the majority were owned by groups of people, large families or land owners. The following is where all the seines were in Mounts Bay. Gunwalloe 20 boats, Mullion 11 boats, Penberth 10 boats, Porthleven 7 boats, Mousehole 3 boats, Prussia Cove 3 boats, Long Rock 1 boat, Newlyn 1 boat and St Just 1 boat. Between Sennen and St Ives there were just as many.

When the PZ registration came into force in 1869 the rules were very lax and also confusing. For instance an owner who had three vessels could, if he wanted, name all three vessels with the same name providing they were in different classes, 1st class, 2nd class and 3rd class. There are examples of this in the ledgers. Fishermen took to painting in their registration numbers as a way of classification. 1st class boats were PZ followed by the number, 2nd class the number followed by PZ. This was unofficial and banned in the 1900's at the same time only one boat could have a certain name, each vessel had to have a different name regardless who owned them. There are lots of funny stories how boats got their names and as you read the following you may well wonder why. The definition of vessels classes, 1st class boats were fully decked, 2nd class were half or partly decked, 3rd class were completely open with no decking, it had nothing to do with a boats size as some people thought. The largest 3rd class I have read about was a seine boat of 60 foot in length. The Customs and Excise inspected fishing boats each year, if a vessel was found to be unseaworthy they would impound it and deregister that vessel. Mousehole had 627 fishing boats registered, the following is a list taken from the Customs and Excise registration ledgers of some Mousehole fishing boats between 1869 and 1945.

PZ1 *Weatherall* – 2nd class lugger, 42 foot long, owners James Pezzack & Martin Matthews, was PE259, in 1875 classed as unseaworthy. The same owners then bought another vessel of 47 foot and 26 tons in 1875, they kept the same name and number, she was built in Penzance

In 1869. They sold her to William Polgrean of Mousehole in 1900, he had her until she sank after a collision in 1911.

PZ2 *King Arther* – 2nd class lugger, 40 foot long, owned by Charles Humphreys who sold her to the Isle of Man in 1885.

PZ2 *Wesley* – 1st class lugger, 44 foot long, owned and skippered by Thomas Pentreath, he had her from 1877 until 1885 when registration was cancelled.

PZ3 *Daisy* – 2nd class lugger, built Newlyn 1930 motor fitted, 16.3 foot long, 6 foot beam, owned and skippered by Richard Oliver from 1934, sold to Newlyn 1941.

PZ7 *Mystery* – 2 class lugger, was PE311, 38 foot long, owned and skippered by Nicholas Cornish, sold to Ireland in 1877.

PZ7 *Undine* – 1st class lugger, 46 foot long, 25 tons, owned by Richard Tonkin & William Rowe from 1878 to 1889 sold to Newlyn, skipper Richard Tonkin.

PZ9 *John Wesley* – 2nd class lugger, 40 foot long, was PE232, owned and skippered Thomas Pentreath, sold Plymouth 1883.

PZ9 *Lydia* – 1st class dandy, 40 foot long, 12.5 foot beam, 20 tons, built Porthleven 1897, two 13hp Kelvin engines fitted, owned and skippered William Blewett from 1919 until 1925 sold to Porthleven.

PZ13 *Vanguard* – 1st class lugger, was PE196, 45.1 foot long, 19 tons, owned and skippered by Richard Jacka, 1903 run down by east coast steam drifter.

PZ14 *Susan and Mary* – 2nd class lugger, was PE39, 39 foot long, owners Ben Harvey & John Rowe, skipper Ben Harvey, 1886 broken up.

PZ14 *Fairy* – 2nd class lugger, 32.8 foot long, 10.2 foot beam, 10 tons, built Penzance 1885 for Charles & Henry Pezzack, skipper Charles Pezzack, sold Porthleven 1919.

PZ15 *Nautilus* – 2nd class lugger, 40 foot long, 14½ tons, was PE15, owners Charles Pezzack & Martin Matthews, skipper Charles Pezzack, broken up 1893.

PZ17 *Agememnon* – 1st class lugger, 42 foot long, 16½ tons, owned and skippered by Joseph Trewavas, 1872 until 1898 sold to Lowestoft.

PZ22 *Boy Tom* – 2nd class lugger, 30 foot long, 6½ tons, owned and skippered by George Polgrean, 1885 until 1890 wrecked Mousehole.

PZ22 *Energy* – 2nd class lugger, 37.3 foot long, 10 tons, owned and skippered George Polgrean, from 1890 to 1897 sold to St Ives.

PZ23 *Water Lily* – 2nd class lugger, 22.2 foot long, 2 tons, built Porthleven 1884 for John Wills, sold to Prudence & Richard Bryant, Mousehole in 1902, they sold her to Arthur Williams, Mousehole in 1912 when she was finally broken up in 1919.

PZ26 *Jane* – 2nd class lugger, 45 foot long 14 tons, owned and skippered John T. Wallis, from 1879 until 1880 when she sank entering Penzance harbour with the loss of 7 lives.

PZ26 *Emblem* – 1st class dandy, 40.8 foot long, 13.1 foot beam, 22 tons, built Porthleven in 1914 with 30hp motor for John, Edward and Richard Hicks and David Sleeman, skipper John Hicks, sold to John and Edward Hicks in 1917, lengthened at Newlyn 1920 to 53 foot, 13.9 foot beam, 32 tons, Gardener 30hp and Kelvin 26hp fitted, sold to John, Edward and Leslie Hicks in 1925, destroyed by fire and sunk in 1930.

PZ30 *Percy* – 1st class lugger, 49.9 foot long, 25 tons, built Penzance 1878 for George Laity & William Pezzack, skipper George Laity, broken up in 1907.

PZ33 *Rock* – 3rd class open seine boat, 25 foot long propelled by oars, owner and skipper William Madron, 1869 to 1878 cancelled, seine boats did not have PE registration.

PZ33 *Lady Smith* – 2nd class lugger, 17.5 foot long, 6.2 foot beam, 1½ tons, built Porthgwarra 1900 with 3½hp Kelvin, owner and skipper John Rowe, bought 1928, 1938 sold to William Stone of London, skipper Everett Lugg, this boat was still in Mousehole harbour up until the late 1960's early 70's, can't remember who owned her then.

PZ34 *Keniha* – 3rd class open seine boat, 24.6 foot long, owner and skipper Richard Pentreath, 1869 to 1874 when she was broken up.

PZ36 *Express* – 1st class lugger, 44 foot long, 22 tons, built Newlyn 1870 as 2nd class boat, owner and skipper Thomas Wallis, Mousehole, had her fully decked when bought in 1901, she was broken up in 1907.

PZ36 *Gleaner* – 2nd class lugger, 37.4 foot long, 11.1 foot beam, 10½ tons, built Looe 1901 with 7hp and 26hp Kelvins, bought in 1929 by Thomas Jenkin owner and skipper, sold in 1937 to Obediah Prouse, Mousehole, he sold her to Newlyn in 1943, she was worked through the war by L. Decrop who, I was told, came from Belgium.

PZ38 *Our Boys* – 2nd class lugger, 31 foot long, 9.8 beam, 9½ tons, built Porthleven in 1904 for William and Richard Humphreys, in 1912 they had 7hp and 13hp Kelvin engines fitted, sold in 1915 to John H. Cary, Mousehole who sold her to Plymouth in 1931.

PZ39 *Porth Ennis* – 2nd class lugger, 26.1 foot long, 8.4 beam, 6½ tons, built Porthleven 1904, bought by owner skipper Stephen Blewett in 1930, he sold her to Joseph Madron in 1937, he sold her to Newlyn in 1942 where she worked through the war, she did eventually come back to Mousehole in the 50's and was owned and skippered by Jack Worth, Penlee Lifeboat coxswain, until he retired in 1969/70, she was then sold to a company to be used as a mould for making fibreglass pleasure boats, I think he told me it was the Cornish Crabbers Company.

PZ40 *Magnet* – 2nd class lugger, 33 foot long, 12 tons, built Porthleven 1886 for owner skipper William Humphreys, sold to Newlyn in 1913.

PZ41 *Ranger* – 2nd class lugger, 26.2 foot long, 8.7 beam, 6½ tons, built Porthleven 1909, James Bodinner & Paul Humphreys, skipper James Bodinner, bought her in 1927, sold to James Bodinner and George Waters in 1930, sold to Newlyn in 1933, she eventually ended up at Milford Haven.

PZ45 *Apapa* – 2nd class lugger, 15.6 foot long, 6 beam, 1½ tons, owner skipper Ernest Beare bought her in 1935 and fitted an engine, sold to William Thurban, Mousehole, in 1937, he changed her name to *Reaper*, he sold her to Alfred Jago, Mousehole in 1943.

PZ46 *Internos* – 1st class lugger, 52.2 foot long, 14.8 beam, 22 tons, built Porthleven 1930, 12hp and 50hp Bolinder engines, for owners David and Edward Sleeman, skipper David Sleeman, she was used for air/sea rescue and other jobs during last war, she did return to long lining and was sold in the early 1960's.

PZ49 *Valetta* – 1st class lugger, 47.2 foot long, 21½ tons, built in Mousehole by owner skipper Nicholas Cornish in 1879, foundered in a storm off Cudden Point, Mounts Bay, in 1899.

PZ51 *Rosalind* – 2nd class lugger, 34 foot long, 11½ tons, owner skipper Joseph Johns bought her in 1883 sold her to Guernsey 1895.

PZ51 *Rosalind* – 2nd class lugger, 29.7 foot long, 9.8 beam, 10½ tons, built Porthleven 1899, owners Josiah & James Pawlyn, Richard Richards, bought her in 1919, skipper William Richards, sold to Fowey in 1922.

PZ53 *Bolinder* – 2nd class lugger, 21.4 foot long, 6.6 beam, 2 tons, built Mousehole in 1931, 4hp Britt and 3½hp Kelvin fitted for owner skipper Thomas Hicks, he sold her to John James Johns in 1934 who changed the name to *Ceres*, if I remember correctly she was still in Mousehole until the very early 60's.

PZ55 *Garelable* – 2nd class lugger, 41 foot long, originally a PE registration, owner skipper Thomas Tonkin, she was broken up in 1881.

PZ55 *Mary Jane* – 3rd class dandy rig, 15.2 foot long, 5 beam, 1½ tons, bought by owner skipper Richard Sampson in 1929, sold as pleasure boat 1936.

PZ61 *Packet* – 2nd class lugger, 32 foot long, was PE17, owner skipper William Barnes, broken up in 1884.

PZ63 *Velox* – 1st class lugger, 47 foot long, 27 tons, built Mousehole 1901 by William Williams for Abraham Madron, sold 1912 to Joseph Johns, Mousehole, he sold her to Sir Thomas Freake in London in 1913.

PZ64 *Boy Dick* – 3rd class lugger, 16.4 foot long, 5.4 beam, 1½ tons, owner skipper Richard Sampson bought her in 1915, broken up in 1918.

PZ65 *Arethusa* – 2nd class lugger, 39 foot long, 8½ tons, was PE89, owner skipper William Ladner, she was run down by a steamer on 23rd January 1895, about 2 miles off Mousehole Cave, no survivors, 2 brothers and 2 brother-in-laws, all from the same family lost.

PZ66 *R.M.P.* 2nd class lugger, 32 foot long, originally PE registration, owner Richard Pezzack, skipper Ben Pender, sold to Porth Madoc 1874.

PZ66 *Aurora* – 1st class lugger, 46.8 foot long, 25 tons, built Newlyn 1875 for John Trewavas & Thomas Glasson, skipper Thomas Glasson, sold to John Matthews and Thomas Glasson in 1876, sold to George Polgrean & Rosetta Glasson in 1878, broken up in 1907.

PZ66 *Kate* – 3rd class lugger, 13.4 foot long, 4.8 beam, 1 ton, built in Mousehole 1900, owner skipper Richard Ash bought her 1915, broken up in 1920.

PZ67 *Excelsior* – 2nd class lugger, 40 foot long, was PE13, owners John Humphreys & Mortimer Trewavas, skipper John Humphreys, sold in 1887.

PZ68 *Lily* – 2nd class lugger, 26 foot long, was PE registered, owner skipper Michael Bennetts, broken up in 1876.

PZ69 *Princess Marina* – 1st class lugger, 37.2 foot long, 12.2 beam, 16 tons, built Looe 1926 with a motor, owner skipper Richard B. Humphreys bought her in 1935, sold to Dartmouth 1936, originally PH59 *Waterlily*.

PZ70 *Triton* – 2nd class lugger, 39.5 foot long, was PE23, owner William Mann, skipper John Mann, broken up in 1890.

PZ71 *Glide* – 2nd class lugger, 40 foot long, was PE60, owners Henry Harvey and Fredrick Wright, skipper Henry Harvey, broken up in 1887.

PZ72 *Pomona* – 2nd class lugger, 34 foot long, was PE50, owner skipper Francis Richards sold her to Ireland 1877.

PZ72 *Minerva* – 1st class lugger, 46.6 foot long, 26 tons, built Mousehole 1878 for owner skipper William Humphreys, cancelled registration 1908.

PZ72 *Dorothy* – 3rd class lugger, 11.8 foot long, 4.8 beam, 1 ton, built Penzance 1895, owner skipper Richard Pentreath bought her in 1915, broken up in 1920.

PZ73 *Galilee* – 2nd class lugger, 32 foot long, was PE registered, owners William Humphreys and William Reseigh, skipper Thomas Reseigh, broken up in 1890.

PZ74 *Gratitude* – 1st class lugger, 49 foot long, 21 tons, was PE335, owners John and William Humphreys, skipper John Humphreys, broken up in 1901.

PZ76 *Hope* – 2nd class lugger, 38 foot long, was PE66, owner skipper John Pentreath, sold to Plymouth in 1880.

PZ77 *Daring* – 2nd class lugger, 38 foot long, was PE215, owner skipper Richard Bodinner, smashed up in Mousehole harbour during storm of 1880.

PZ77 *Rippling Wave* – 2nd class lugger, 26 foot long, 6 tons, built St Ives 1902 for Joseph Johns, skipper John Harry, sold to Falmouth 1918.

PZ78 *W.J.* – 2nd class lugger, 33 foot long, was PE registered, owners William Pollard and Henry Richards, skipper Henry Richards, broken up in 1883.

PZ78 *Narrow Escape* – 2nd class lugger, 31 foot long, 6 tons, owner Nicholas Cornish bought her in 1887, skipper Fredrick Wright, sold to St Ives 1891.

PZ78 *Early Dawn* – 2nd class lugger, 25.5 foot long, 6 tons, built St Ives 1902 for Joseph Johns, skipper Abraham Johns, motor fitted 1923, sold to Padstow 1926.

PZ79 *Richard Watson* – 2nd class lugger, 33 foot long, was PE41, owner skipper Richard Trewavas, sold to Isle of Man 1877.

PZ79 *Messenger* – 1st class lugger, 47.8 foot long, 27 tons, owner skipper Daniel Richards bought her in 1878, sold to Richard, Joseph and John Harry in 1901, skipper Richard Harry, broken up in 1905.

PZ79 *Western Land* – 2nd class lugger, 26 foot long, 7.8 beam, 3 tons, built Belfast 1920, motor fitted, owner Patricia Cardell bought her in 1936, skipper E.B. Williams.

PZ80 *Dart* – 1st class lugger, 43 foot long, 16 tons, was PE365, owner John Bodinner, skipper William Bodinner, broken up 1894.

PZ81 *White Heather* – 2nd class lugger, 24.5 foot long, 5½ tons, built St Ives 1905 for Thomas and Mathew Matthews, skipper Mathew Matthews, sold to Thomas Matthews 1913, sold to Falmouth 1919.

PZ81 *Lyonesse* – 1st class lugger, 51.8 foot long, 15.1 beam, 26½ tons, built Porthleven 1930 for Jack, Sydney & Benjamin Pender, 50hp, 33hp and 3½hp engines fitted, skipper James Pender, WW2 service, went back to longlining after war, Ben Pender then skipper, sold in the early 1970's.

PZ82 *What You Will* – 2nd class lugger, 40 foot, was PE31, owners George Waters and Samuel Harvey, skipper George Waters, broken up in 1887.

PZ83 *Robert Young* – 2nd class lugger, 41 foot long, was PE247, owner John Trewavas, skipper James Harvey, wrecked back of Mousehole quay 1875.

PZ83 *Eugenie* – 3rd class lugger, 15.7 foot long, 5 beam, 1 ton, owner skipper Luther Oliver bought her in 1915, broken up in 1918.

PZ83 *Girl Stella* – 2nd class lugger, 40.6 foot long, 13 beam, 14 tons, built Porthleven 1896, 13hp & 26hp Kelvins fitted, owner skipper Edwin Madron bought her in 1924, sold to London 1931, originally named *Primavere*.

PZ84 *Alacrity* – 2nd class lugger, 39 foot long, 14 tons, was PE registered, owner skipper Abednigo Harvey, registration cancelled in 1890.

PZ84 *Ivy* – 2nd class lugger, 25.5 foot long, 8.8 beam, 6½ tons, built St Ives in 1902 for owner skipper James Pender, burnt in Mousehole Harbour 1935.

PZ85 *Wasp* – 2nd class lugger, 35.6 foot long, was PE25, owner skipper William Pezzack, broken up in 1871.

PZ86 *Seabreeze* –2nd class lugger 42 foot long, was PE75, owner skipper Samson Roberts, Obediah Reseigh was skipper from 1880, registration cancelled 1890.

PZ87 *Telegraph* – 2nd class lugger, 29 foot long, was PE321, owner skipper Stephen Blewett, broken up in 1878.

PZ87 *Niagara* – 1st class lugger, 48.3 foot long, 27 tons, built in Mousehole by William Williams in 1878 for William Rowe and Henry Pender, skipper Henry Pender, broken up in 1910.

PZ88 *Clementina* – 1st class lugger, 46.7 foot long, 28 tons, built in Hayle 1862, was PE22, owner skipper Francis Blewett, stopped fishing 1907.

PZ88 *Kia-Ora* – 2nd class yawl, 24.8 foot long, 6.7 beam, 3 tons, owner skipper William Rogers bought her in 1915, sold to Thomas Eddy, Mousehole, in 1916, sold to Newlyn in 1920, she was finally wrecked on the Buck Rocks in 1928.

PZ89 *Briton* – 2nd class lugger, 39.6 foot long, was PE203, owner skipper John Wright, broken up in 1871.

PZ90 *Surpass* – 2nd class lugger, 33 foot long, was PE82, owner skipper John Blewett, broken up in 1885.

PZ90 *Theodore* – 2nd class lugger, 28.1 foot long, 6½ tons, built St Ives 1884, owners Nicholas and John Cornish, skipper Nicholas Cornish, bought in 1885, sold to John Cornish in 1915, broken up in 1919.

PZ90 *Jason* – 2nd class lugger, 22.5 foot long, 6.8 beam, 2 tons, built in Mousehole for owner skipper Edward Downing in 1931, 7hp Kelvin and 7hp Austin engines fitted, sold to John Cotton in 1941, worked through WW2.

PZ91 *Banner* – 1st class lugger, 47 foot long, 20 tons, was PE29, owner skipper Richard Cary, sold to Plymouth in 1892.

PZ92 *Cornwall* – 1st class lugger, 43.9 foot long, 17½ tons, was PE200, owner skipper Benjamin Trewavas, broken up in 1900.

PZ93 *Cornish Girl* – 2nd class lugger, 37 foot long, was PE122, owner skipper Nicholas Cornish, broken up in 1871.

PZ93 *Triumph* – 1st class lugger, 48 foot long, 29 tons, built in Newlyn 1878 for owner skipper William Johns, broken up in 1909.

PZ94 *Godild* – 2nd class lugger, 38 foot long, was PE85, owner skipper John Wallis, sold to Carnarvon as a barge in 1879.

PZ94 *Martha* – 2nd class lugger, 31½ foot long, 8½ tons, built Mousehole in 1886 for owner George Laity, skipper William Laity, sold to Newlyn in 1910.

PZ94 *Morning Star* – 2nd class lugger, 30 foot long, 8.3 beam, 4½ tons, built Chatham 1916, motor fitted, bought by Arthur Worth in 1936, skipper Benjamin D. Worth, sold to Benjamin D. Worth, Mousehole 1938, worked WW2.

PZ95 *Jason* – 2nd class lugger, 30 foot long, was PE19, owners John Richards and Benjamin Downing, skipper John Worth, broken up 1892.

PZ96 *Isis* – 2nd class lugger, 40 foot long, was PE registered, owner skipper William Humphreys, sold to Ireland 1878.

PZ96 *Valourous* – 1st class lugger, 48.3 foot long, 27 tons, built Mousehole in 1878 for owner skipper William Humphreys, sold to Thomas Matthews and Robert Oliver in 1900, skipper Robert Oliver, broken up in 1915.

PZ97 *C.H.J.* – 2nd class lugger, 33.5 foot long, 10½ tons, built Mousehole 1869 for owner skipper Charles Pezzack, broken up 1908, quite often referred to as *CHI*.

PZ98 *Pioneer* – 2nd class lugger, 32 foot long, was PE registered, owner skipper Nicholas Smith, sold to Ireland in 1877.

PZ98 *Pioneer* – 1st class lugger, 46 foot long, 25 tons, built Newlyn 1877 for owners Nicholas and William Smith, skipper Nicholas Smith, registration cancelled in 1907. There was a *Pioneer* in Newlyn the same length owned by Henderby, during war service she had a 5hp steam engine fitted and used to bunker in Falmouth, she went back fishing, trawling, after the war. A diver named Gascoin bought her in the 70's for wreck diving, when he sold her I understand she was converted back to sailing as a pleasure craft.

PZ98 *Leader* – 2nd class lugger, 18 foot long, 6.1 beam, 1½ tons, built St Just in Falmouth 1914, motor fitted, was FH82, owner Richard Maddern bought her in 1936, skipper John T. Worth, sold to John T. Worth in 1940, worked through WW2, then bought by Mousehole Harbour Master Clarence Williams crabbing until he sold her to shipwright Dudley Penrose in the 1970's. She is still crabbing and can be seen in Mousehole Harbour usually moored on the new quay.

PZ99 *Eason* – 2nd class lugger, 41 foot long, was PE registered, owners John Richards and Benjamin Downing, skipper John Richards, registration cancelled in 1889.

PZ100 *Pimento* – 2nd class lugger, 39 foot long, was PE registered, owner skipper William Drew, sold to the Isle of Man in 1885.

PZ101 *Gideon Curly* – 2nd class lugger, 39.5 foot long, was PE33, owners Martin Wright and James Rouffegace, (known as Roughneck), skipper Martin Wright, ran into back of Mousehole old quay during heavy weather and sank in 1871.

PZ101 *Reaper* – 1st class lugger, 49 foot long, 30 tons, built Penzance in 1885 for Mary and William Harvey who was also the skipper, registration cancelled in 1915.

PZ102 *Industry* – 2nd class lugger, 39 foot long, was PE14, owner skipper John Madron, sold to Ireland in 1873.

PZ102 *Mur* – 2nd class lugger, 20 foot long, 4 tons, bought by owner skipper John Gruzalier in 1874, registration cancelled in 1878.

PZ103 *Freedom* – 1st class lugger, 39.6 foot long, was PE registered, owner skipper Nicholas Humphreys, registration cancelled in 1893.

PZ104 *Evince* – 2nd class lugger, 31 foot long, was PE96, owner Richard Jacka, skipper Fredrick Johns, broken up in 1891.

PZ104 *Wee Pal* – 2nd class dandy rig, 15.3 foot long, 6 beam, 1½ ton, built St Ives 1912, motor fitted, owner skipper Vivian Johns bought her in 1931, sold to Clarence Williams in 1937, broken up in 1942.

PZ105 *Robert* – 1st class lugger, 43 foot long, was PE registered, owner skipper Charles Trewavas, sold her to Thomas and Joseph Johns in 1885, they sold her to Plymouth in 1887.

PZ105 *Boy Sid* – 2nd class lugger, 27.6 foot long, 7 tons, owner skipper John Sampson bought her in 1910, Kelvin engine fitted 1919, sold to London in 1930.

PZ106 *Monarch* – 2nd class lugger, 42 foot long, was PE registered, owner skipper Joseph Trewavas Jnr, wrecked in Mousehole harbour during storm in 1871.

PZ107 *Golden Fleece* – 2nd class lugger, 42 foot long, was PE registered, owners William Rowe and Josiah Trembath, skipper William Rowe, registration cancelled in 1891.

PZ107 *Renovelle* – 1st class lugger, 54.4 foot long, 14.7 beam, 26½ tons, built in Mousehole in 1902, 25hp and 35hp Kelvins fitted, was PH202, owner skipper Edwin Madron bought her in 1931, did WW2 service, eventually broken up in Mousehole Harbour when new *Renovelle* acquired, PZ177, in early 50's.

PZ111 *Veracity* – 2nd class lugger, 30.6 foot long, 9.8 beam, 10½ tons, built Newlyn 1902, 7hp Kelvin engine fitted 1917, bought by owner skipper Paul Humphreys in 1929, sold to Mark B. Humphreys in 1938, worked through WW2.

PZ112 *Boy Jess* – 2nd class dandy rig, 21 foot long, 4 tons, built Porthleven 1901, bought by owner skipper William Cattran in 1902, broken up in 1916.

PZ115 *Mermaid* – 2nd class lugger, 25 foot long, 5.7 beam, 2 tons, motor fitted, bought by owner skipper William Lyne in 1931, sold to Scilly Isles 1933.

PZ117 *Moonbeam* – 2nd class dandy rig, 21.5 foot long, 5.4 beam, 1½ tons, motor fitted, owner skipper John M. Blewett bought her in 1936, worked through WW2, last time I saw her was in the early 60's in Mousehole Harbour.

PZ122 *Daisy* – 2nd class lugger, 23 foot long, 4½ tons, built Penzance 1887, owner Thomas Matthews and Robert Oliver bought her in 1904, skipper Thomas Matthews, sold to Thomas and Martin Matthews in 1908, sold to Thomas Matthews in 1913, sold to Thomas Symons in 1921, he had motor fitted 1921, broken up in 1928.

PZ126 *Sweet Promise* – 2nd class lugger, 30.7 foot long, 11 tons, built Porthleven 1902 for owner skipper William Madron, sold to Baltimore in 1917.

PZ126 *Harvester* – 2nd class lugger, 38.9 foot long, 11.4 beam, 10½ tons, built Mevagissey 1886, motor fitted, bought by owner skipper John H. Cary in 1928, WW2 service.

PZ127 *Diadem* – 2nd class lugger, 25.8 foot long, 8.8 beam, 6½ tons, built St Ives in 1902 for owner skipper William Polgrean, motor fitted 1920, sold to Francis Hawke 1927, broken up in 1929.

PZ128 *Why Not* – 2nd class lugger, 27 foot long, 4½ tons, owner skipper Francis Blewett bought her in 1893, broken up in 1903.

PZ130 *Kite* – 2nd class lugger, 42 foot long, was PE registered, owners Richard Murrish and John Trewavas bought her in 1878, skipper Richard Murrish, wrecked back of Mousehole old quay trying to enter harbour in heavy weather in 1890.

PZ130 *Nellie Jane* – 1st class lugger, 54.2 foot long, 16.1 beam, 41 tons, built Porthleven by J. Kitto in 1902, bought by owner skipper William Worth in 1907, sold to William, Benjamin and John Worth in 1912, 26hp and 60hp Kelvins fitted in 1912, sold to Sunderland in 1938.

PZ131 *Edgar* – 1st class lugger, 54 foot long, 36 tons, built Mousehole 1902 for George and Percy Laity, skipper George Laity, 55hp Kelvin engine fitted in 1909, sold to Plymouth in 1928.

PZ133 *Speed* – 2nd class lugger, 26.3 foot long, 6½ tons, built St Ives in 1905 for Richard, Joseph and John Harry, skipper Richard Harry, broken up in 1930.

PZ134 *Ocean Pride* – 2nd class lugger, 36.7 foot long, 13.1 beam, 13½ tons, built Newlyn 1920 for Joseph and Richard Brownfield, skipper Joseph Brownfield, 26hp and 13hp Kelvins fitted, sold to George Pezzack and Ann Tripp in 1937, skipper George Brownfield, WW2 service, returned to fishing, crabbing with Chuggy Downing and sons until 70's. Sold and worked out of Hayle tangle netting. Finally bought by the landlord of Dock Inn, Penzance and returned to a sailing lugger. She can be seen in Penzance Floating Harbour.

PZ138 *Boy Sam* – 2nd class lugger, 18.4 foot long, 5.8 beam, 1½ tons, built Porthleven 1928, motor fitted, owner Patricia Cardell bought her in 1938, skipper Thomas Tonkin, sold to Newlyn in 1941.

PZ139 *Gleaner* – 1st class lugger, 49 foot long, 28 tons, built in Mousehole 1880 by William Williams for himself, skipper Richard Jenkins, sold to John Hicks in 1892, sold to Polperro in 1910.

PZ140 *Phillises* – 2nd class lugger, 34 foot long, 8 tons, owner skipper Richard Humphreys bought her in 1880, sold to St Ives in 1893.

PZ142 *Wanderer* – 2nd class lugger, 39 foot long, was PE189, owner skipper Richard Pentreath, registration cancelled 1890.

PZ143 *Rodney* – 2nd class lugger, 38.9 foot long, was PE216, owner skipper William Harvey, smashed up during storm in Mousehole Harbour 1880.

PZ144 *Sarah Hills* – 2nd class lugger, 29 foot long, was PE320, owner Thomas Pentreath, skipper Henry Pentreath, smashed up during storm in Mousehole harbour 1880.

PZ145 *Britannia* – 2nd class lugger, 37 foot long, was PE42, owners Richard Tonkin and Charles Cary, skipper Charles Cary, broken up in 1876.

PZ145 *Britannia* – 1st class lugger, 45.5 foot long, 24 tons, built in Penzance 1877 for owner skipper Charles Cary, sold to Hedley, Richard and Phillip Cary in 1912, broken up in 1917.

PZ146 *Trinity* – 2nd class lugger, 31 foot long, was PE262, owner skipper William Humphreys, broken up in 1878.

PZ147 *Amity* – 2nd class lugger, 39 foot long, was PE231, owner skipper William Humphreys, sold to Plymouth 1874.

PZ147 *Velox* – 2nd class lugger, 31 foot long, built St Ives 1893, motor fitted, was named *Thomas*, owners Joseph and Edwin Madron bought her in 1920, skipper Edwin Madron, sold to St Ives 1925.

PZ148 *Selicia* – 2nd class lugger, 30 foot long, was PE49, owner Harvey Williams, skipper Nicholas Richards, registration cancelled in 1871.

PZ149 *Dido* – 2nd class lugger, 32 foot long, 7 tons, was PE registered, owner skipper Richard Worth bought her in 1873, sold to Scilly in 1892.

PZ150 *Fearless* – 1st class lugger, 44 foot long, 21 tons, was PE44, owner skipper John Madron, condemned by Customs & Excise in 1901.

PZ151 *Statvia* – 2nd class lugger, 39 foot long, was PE366, owner skipper Richard Worth, broken up in 1891.

PZ152 *Matchless* – 2nd class lugger, 32 foot long, was PE349, owner skipper John Madron, broken up in 1871.

PZ153 *Mary Ann* – 2nd class lugger, 27 foot long, was PE44, owner John Madron, skipper Henry Worth, sold to Polperro 1884.

PZ153 *Alaska* – 2nd class lugger, 22.9 foot long, 5 tons, built in Penzance in 1880, owner skipper Charles Cary bought her in 1884, sold to Newlyn in 1918.

PZ154 *Jasper* – 2nd class lugger, 31 foot long, was PE90, owner Charles Mann, skipper Richard Tonkin, broken up in 1889.

PZ154 *Daring* – 2nd class lugger, 26.8 foot long, 7 tons, built in St Ives 1902, bought by William Humphreys in 1903, skipper William Mann, sold to Porthleven in 1913.

PZ154 *Alba* – motor vessel, 18 foot long, 5 beam, 1 ton, built in Mouse-hole as a motor boat by William Cornish for himself in 1932, sold to Penzance in 1933.

PZ155 *Jane* – 2nd class lugger, 27 foot long, was PE registered, owner skipper Henry Richards, broken up in 1878.

PZ155 *Vesta* – 1st class lugger, 47 foot long, 25 tons, built in Newlyn 1878 for owner skipper William Ladner, sold to James Ladner in 1906, broken up in 1915.

PZ156 *Ganges* – 1st class lugger, 42 foot long, 16½ tons, bought by William Pezzack and George Laity in 1872, skipper Richard Pezzack, broken up in 1901.

PZ156 *Girl Joyce* – 2nd class lugger, 40 foot long, 12.5 beam, 13½ tons, built Porthleven in 1920 for owners Thomas Glasson and Thomas Oats, 26hp and 13hp Kelvins fitted, skipper Thomas Glasson, sold to Carnarvon in 1937, she was sold in 1941 to the Air Ministry.

PZ157 *Pearl* – 2nd class lugger, 32 foot long, was PE35, owner Martin Wright, skipper Richard Murrish, sold to Carnarvon in 1871.

PZ158 *Edwin* – 2nd class lugger, 35 foot long, was PE236, owner skipper James Harvey, broken up in 1871.

PZ159 *Rovenna* – 2nd class lugger, 38 foot long, was PE21, owner skipper Robert Harvey, sold to Belfast in 1879.

PZ160 *Warrior* – 2nd class lugger, 36 foot long, was PE67, owner skipper Benjamin Harvey, sold to Henry Wright in 1878, broken up in 1886.

PZ160 *Louie* – 2nd class lugger, 29.4 foot long, 7½ tons, built Porthleven in 1886, owner skipper Joseph Johns bought her in 1888, sold to Falmouth in 1907.

PZ161 *Brilliant* – 2nd class lugger, 33 foot long, was PE107, owner skipper Richard Angwin, sold to Plymouth in 1878.

PZ161 *Boy Kenneth* – 2nd class lugger, 17.2 foot long, 6 beam, 1½ tons, built Porthleven 1907, motor fitted 1929, owners George Maddern and Benjamin Wallis bought her in 1936, skipper Benjamin Wallis, fish salesman B.J. Ridge owned at various intervals, probably to do with unpaid bills, they owned her from 1938 onwards, worked through WW2.

PZ162 *Mary* – 2nd class lugger, 32.7 foot long, 6½ tons, was PE43, owner Richard Angwin, skipper William Drew, sold to Francis Blewett, Mousehole, 1891, broken up in 1893.

PZ162 *Fraternity* – 2nd class lugger, 29 foot long, 8½ tons, built Newlyn 1903, owner skipper Joseph Johns bought her in 1914, motor fitted in 1919, sold to Vivian Johns in 1921, sold to Fowey in 1924.

PZ162 *Three's Company* – 2nd class lugger, 25.3 foot long, 7 beam, 3 tons, owner Richard Tudor Lewis bought her in 1938, skipper Irwine Carne, worked through WW2.

PZ163 *Gleaner* – 2nd class lugger, 36 foot, was PE187, owners Robert Humphreys and Josiah Trembath, broken up in 1871.

PZ164 *Billikin* – 2nd class motor boat, 20.2 foot long, 6.2 beam, 1½ tons, built Southampton 1914, owner skipper Joseph Virgo bought her in 1925, sold to William Hitchens in 1938 who changed her name to *Swiftsure*, worked during WW2.

PZ166 *Nonpariel* – 2nd class lugger, 26½ foot long, 5½ tons, built St Ives 1905 for owners Richard, Josiah and John Harry, skipper John Harry, broken up in 1931.

PZ171 *Enterprise* – 2nd class lugger, 18.9 foot long, 6 beam, 2½ tons, built St Ives 1903, motor fitted, George Eddy bought her in 1933, skipper William Cornish, sold to owner skipper John Cotton in 1934, sold to owner skipper Edward Tregenza in 1938, sold to Marazion in 1940, worked during WW2.

PZ172 *Olive* – 2nd class lugger, 28 foot long, 5½ tons, built Porthleven 1869, owner skipper Richard Humphreys bought her in 1893, sold to owner skipper Richard Cary in 1904, broken up in 1920.

PZ173 *Katie* – 2nd class lugger, 28 foot long, built Mousehole 1903 for owner skipper Nelson Ladner, 12hp Kelvin fitted, sold to Newlyn in 1919, name changed to *Plethora*.

PZ175 *Maureen* – 2nd class dandy rig, 18 foot long, 6 beam, 2 tons, built Porthleven 1926, 3½hp Kelvin fitted, bought by owner skipper William Jefferey in 1933, worked WW2.

PZ178 *Golden Sunset* – 1st class lugger, 37 foot long, 12.2 beam, 15½ tons, built Newlyn 1920 for Ministry of Agriculture and Fisheries, 22½hp Gardener and 13hp Kelvin fitted, skipper William Richards, sold to William, Richard, Arthur and Frank Richards in 1923, sold to Plymouth in 1931.

PZ181 *J.C.* – 2nd class lugger, 29 foot long, 6½ tons, built in Porthleven in 1869, owner skipper William Drew bought her in 1893, sold to Fowey in 1906.

PZ181 *Girl Leana* – 3rd class lugger, 14 foot long, 5 beam, 1 ton, bought by owner skipper George Pomeroy in 1921, registration cancelled and used for pleasure in 1933.

PZ182 *Asthore* – 1st class lugger, 44.4 foot long, 13.9 beam, 18 tons, built Porthleven 1926, 13hp, 26hp Kelvins and 3½hp Britt engines, bought by owners Edward Downing and James Jenkin in 1928, skipper Edward Downing, WW2 service, back fishing, longlining and handlining in winter mackerel season until early 1970's.

PZ183 *Eden* – 2nd class lugger, 22.4 foot long, 4 tons, built 1886, owners Richard Sampson and Mike Wakfer bought her in 1919, skipper Richard Sampson, sold to London owner in 1920, Richard Sampson continued as skipper until she was broken up in 1925.

PZ183 *Kathleen* – 2nd class motor boat, 16 foot long, 5.3 beam, 1½ tons, built in Yarmouth, owner skipper William Hall bought her in 1939, worked WW2.

PZ184 *J.T.* – 2nd class lugger, 30.2 foot long, 5½ tons, was PE registered, bought by owners George Laity and William Wroath in 1892, skipper William Wroath, broken up in 1902.

PZ185 *Elizabeth* – 2nd class lugger, 30.6 foot long, 9 tons, built Porthleven in 1872, owners William Madron and Charles Cattran bought her in 1886, skipper Charles Cattran, condemned by Customs and Excise in 1906.

PZ187 *Magic* – 2nd class lugger, 27.3 foot long, 7½ tons, built in Mousehole by John Bodinner in 1903 for himself, registration cancelled in 1912.

PZ188 *Myrtle* – 2nd class lugger, 29.6 foot long, 6½ tons, built in Porthleven in 1886 for owner skipper Richard Jacka, sold to St Ives 1919.

PZ189 *Margaret* – 2nd class lugger, 28 foot long, 7 tons, built in Mousehole in 1903 for owner skipper John Worth, sold to Falmouth in 1924.

PZ193 *Carn Dhu* – 1st class lugger, 37 foot long, 12.2 beam, 15½ tons, built in Newlyn 1921 for Ministry of Agriculture and Fisheries, 15hp and 31hp Kelvins fitted, skipper Richard Humphreys, sold to owner skipper Richard Humphreys in 1923, sold to Folkstone in 1931.

PZ194 *Boy Jack* – 2nd class lugger, 26½ foot long, 6 tons, built St Ives 1905 for owner skipper John Pender, sold to Newlyn 1914.

PZ197 *Boy Philip* – 2nd class lugger, 27 foot long, 6½ tons, built in Mousehole 1903 for owner skipper William Worth, sold to King Harry in Falmouth 1924.

PZ198 *We'll Try* – 2nd class lugger, 31.4 foot long, 8½ tons, built in Mousehole 1903 for owner skipper Francis Blewett, he had her lengthened in Mousehole in 1921, 2 Kelvins and Britt engines fitted, now a 1st class lugger of 40 foot long, 11.4 beam, 16½ tons, sold to Newlyn in 1941, then Conway in 1944.

PZ199 *Puritan* – 2nd class lugger, 28 foot long, 7½ tons, built in Mousehole 1903 for owner skipper Richard Ash, sold to owner skipper Edwin Harvey, Mousehole, in 1908, motor fitted 1914, sold to Plymouth in 1924.

PZ200 *Annie* – 2nd class lugger, 22.5 foot long, 4½ tons, built Penzance 1872, owner skipper Joseph Trewavas bought her in 1884, sold to owner skipper William Pender, Mousehole, in 1900, broken up in 1909.

PZ201 *Primitive* – 2nd class lugger, 39 foot long, was PE registered, owner Richard Trembath, skipper James Harvey, wrecked in storm at Whitby in 1880.

PZ209 *Doreen* – 2nd class lugger, 19 foot long, 6.3 beam, 2 tons, built in Looe 1930, motor fitted, bought by owner skipper Kenneth Jolliffe in 1933, worked WW2, was in Mousehole harbour until 1960's.

PZ212 *Salacia* – 2nd class lugger, 30 foot long, was PE registered, owner Harvey Williams, skipper Nicholas Richards, sold to Ireland 1874.

PZ212 *Daffodil* – 2nd class lugger, 23.2 foot long, 7.5 beam, 3 tons, built Porthleven in 1926, 6hp Kelvin fitted, owner skipper Francis

Blewett bought her in 1942, worked WW2, sold to Falmouth in 50's, owner skipper Mike Buttery (that's me) bought her in 1970, renamed her *Carn Dhu*, Coventry Victor 9-11hp diesel and 15hp Lister diesel fitted, worked her until 1977, sold to Newlyn 1978, smashed up during storm on Canners Slip, Newlyn the same year.

PZ214 *Two Boys* – 1st class lugger, 45.8 foot long, 13.6 beam, 28½ tons, built Newlyn 1927 for owners Fredrick and Edgar Richards, 13hp Kelvin, skipper Fredrick Richards, two 24hp diesels fitted in 1942 for WW2 service, went back fishing after war, ended up in Newlyn harbour in the 60's.

PZ217 *Joseph* – 2nd class lugger, 41 foot long, was PE339, owner Joseph Hocking, skipper Philip Worth, broken up in 1887.

PZ218 *Providence* – 2nd class lugger, 28 foot long, was PE45, owner William Angwin, skipper Thomas Blewett, for some reason she was remeasured at 32 foot long and given a new registration number PZ491, she was last registered in 1880.

PZ219 *Wellesley* – 2nd class lugger, 32 foot long, was PE registered, owner skipper John Pentreath, broken up in 1897.

PZ220 *Pelorees* – 1st class lugger, 40 foot long, was PE52, owner skipper Benjamin Harry, sold to Belfast in 1888.

PZ220 *Darling* – 2nd class lugger, 16.3 foot long, 5.3 beam, 1 ton, owner skipper Joseph Sleeman bought her in 1933, worked WW2.

PZ221 *Why Not* – 2nd class lugger, 31 foot long, was PE registered, owner skipper Thomas Wright, smashed up during storm in Penzance harbour 1880.

PZ222 *Ariadne* – 2nd class lugger, 40 foot long, was PE360, owners Michael Pender and Francis Praed, skipper Francis Praed, broken up in 1888.

PZ223 *Rosezillia* – 2nd class lugger, 31 foot long, 8½ tons, owner James Rowe, skipper William Rowe, sold to St Ives in 1900.

PZ223 *Bethel* – 2nd class lugger, 28.6 foot long, 7 tons, built Porthleven in 1897, owner skipper John Hicks bought her in 1914, sold to St Ives in 1919, hit Carn Dhu Point near Lamorna and sank in 1924.

PZ224 *Rosetta* – 2nd class lugger, 14½ foot long, owner William Rowe bought her in 1884, skipper John Sampson, registration cancelled in 1890.

PZ227 *Sarnia* – 2nd class motor boat, 15.4 foot long, 5.6 beam, 1½ tons, built in Mousehole by owner skipper William Cornish for himself in 1933, she was sold the same year.

PZ228 *Little Francis* – 2nd class lugger, 30 foot long, 7½ tons, built Porthleven 1886, owner John Trewavas bought her in 1886, skipper John Humphreys, sold to George Polgrean & William Hicks in 1898, skipper George Polgrean, broken up in 1917.

PZ230 *Telephone* – 1st class lugger, 48 foot long, 26 tons, built Penzance in 1878, owner skipper Richard Pentreath bought her in 1889, sold her to John Pentreath in 1906, condemned by Customs and Excise in 1916.

PZ231 *Onaway* – 2nd class lugger, 19 foot long, 5.1 beam, 1 ton, motor fitted, bought by George A., George W. and Henry R. Pomeroy in 1933, skipper George W Pomeroy, broken up in 1944.

PZ236 *Wanderer* – 2nd class lugger, 32 foot long, 9½ tons, owner skipper William Humphreys bought her in 1892, sold to St Ives in 1899.

PZ242 *Emmie* – 3rd class dandy rig, 16.4 foot long, 1½ tons, built Porthleven in 1909, owner skipper Luther Oliver bought her in 1922 and changed name from *Deer* to *Emmie*, registration cancelled in 1925.

PZ243 *Albion* – 2nd class lugger, 45 foot long, 19 tons, owner skipper Thomas Treleaven bought her in 1878, broken up in 1901.

PZ247 *Good Templar* – 2nd class lugger, 20 foot long, owner skipper John Harry bought her in 1884, broken up in 1888.

PZ250 *Come On* – 2nd class lugger, 21.2 foot long, 6.5 beam, 2½ tons, motor fitted, owner skipper Josiah Richards bought her in 1921, sold to Newlyn 1924, she was eventually sold to Isles of Scilly.

PZ251 *Bonnie Lad* – 1st class lugger, 50 foot long, 29 tons, built Porthleven 1885 for owner skipper William Drew, sold to Stanley Drew in 1916 who sold her the same year to Howth.

PZ254 *Smiling Morn* – 1st class lugger, 50 foot long, 32 tons, built Porthleven for owners Jane and Joseph Johns in 1887, skipper Richard Johns, sold to Joseph Johns and John Harry in 1914, skipper John Harry, 26hp motor fitted in 1914, sold to Plymouth in 1928.

PZ261 *Marion* – 3rd class rowing boat, 10.7 foot long, 5 beam, ½ ton, built in Mousehole 1906, owner skipper Joseph Rowe bought her in 1915, registration cancelled in 1923.

PZ262 *Heather Glen* – 1st class lugger, 44.5 foot long, 14 beam, 19½ tons, built in Porthleven in 1928 for owner skipper William Hall, 13hp, 30hp Kelvins, 3½hp Britt engines fitted, registration cancelled in 1939.

PZ328 *Guide* – 2nd class lugger, 29 foot long, 6 tons, was PE registered, bought by owner skipper Richard Ash in 1894, broken up in 1898.

PZ329 *Jubilee* – 3rd class lugger, 16.6 foot long, 1½ tons, built St Ives in 1890, bought by owners Richard Wright and Joseph Ash in 1909, skipper Joseph Ash, sold to Michael Wakfer, Mousehole, in 1919, registration cancelled in 1922.

PZ330 *Quo Vadis* – 2nd class lugger, 21.4 foot long, 7.1 beam, 2½ tons, built Porthleven 1922, bought by owner skipper Henry Eddy in 1932, sold to owner skipper Richard Sampson, Mousehole in 1936, worked WW2, she was bought by Chris Tyler, Mousehole, in 1964 for handlining mackerel, he worked her until the early 70's.

PZ332 *Charles* – 2nd class lugger, 29.9 foot long, 6 tons, built Porthleven 1869, bought by John Edmunds in 1882, skipper Thomas Cary, sold to Charles Tregenza in 1895, skipper Stephen Downing, sold to Abraham Madron in 1905, skipper Joseph Madron, sold to Joseph Madron in 1912, broken up in 1913.

PZ333 *Kittywake* – 3rd class yawl, 14.9 foot long, 5 beam, 1 ton, bought by owner skipper Robert Harvey in 1915, sold to Penzance in 1916.

PZ334 *Agnes* – 2nd class lugger, 31½ foot long, 11 tons, built Porthleven 1885 for owner skipper Edward Downing, motor fitted 1914, wrecked on Boscowan Point, Mounts Bay, in 1925.

PZ335 *Lost and Found* – 2nd class lugger, 28.9 foot long, 5½ tons, bought by owner skipper Joseph Hocking in 1883, broken up in 1905.

PZ336 *Come On* – 1st class lugger, 47.2 foot long, 20½ tons, bought by owner skipper Henry Richards in 1873, last registered in 1892.

PZ341 *Mary* – 2nd class lugger, 28.9 foot long, 8½ tons, built St Ives 1911 for owner Percy Laity, skipper Obediah Nicholls, engine fitted 1916, sold to owner skipper Arthur Williams Jnr in 1919, sold to Fowey in 1924.

PZ342 *Meteor* – 2nd class lugger, 23.1 foot long, 4½ tons, bought by owner skipper John Harvey in 1911, sold to owner skipper William Cattran in 1916, sold to owner skipper Benjamin Wallis in 1919, sold to St Austell 1919.

PZ347 *Return* – 2nd class lugger, 24.1 foot long, 5 tons, built Mousehole in 1884 for owner skipper Thomas Wallis, sold to owner skipper John Brownfield, Mousehole, in 1912, motor fitted 1914, registration cancelled in 1917.

PZ348 *Pet* – 3rd class lugger, 16 foot long, 1½ tons, built St Ives 1892, owner skipper bought her in 1906, broken up in 1911.

PZ349 *Willie* – 2nd class lugger, 13.6 foot long, 1 ton, built St Ives 1900, owner skipper William Eddy bought her in 1906, engine fitted 1916, registration cancelled 1920.

PZ350 *R.J.M.* – 2nd class lugger, 14 foot long, was PE registered, owner skipper Robert Matthews, registration cancelled in 1878.

PZ352 *Kaff* – 3rd class dandy rig, 17.8 foot long, 1½ tons, bought by owner skipper Joseph Jeffery in 1906, sold to owner skipper John Sampson in 1907, broken up in 1909.

PZ353 *Activity* – 2nd class lugger, 48 foot long, 26 tons, built Porthleven 1878 for owner skipper Thomas Matthews, broken up in 1912.

PZ354 *Endeavour* – 2nd class lugger, 26.6 foot long, 7 tons, built St Ives in 1911 for owner skipper Nicholas Humphreys, sold to Feock, Truro in 1925.

PZ357 *Lady White* – 3rd class lugger, 14.8 foot long, 1½ tons, built St Ives 1900, bought by owner skipper George Laity in 1906, sold to owner skipper Richard Johns, Mousehole, in 1913, sold to Nelson Ladner, Mousehole, in 1923, registration cancelled in 1924. (1st November 1907 rescued 5 people *see Wreck of the Baltic*.)

PZ359 *Jane* – 2nd class lugger, 27.3 foot long, 4½ tons, built Porthleven in 1897, owner skipper George Laity bought her in 1906, sold to Porthleven 1929.

PZ360 *May Queen* – 3rd class dandy rig, 14 foot long, 1 ton, built St Ives 1894, owner skipper Joseph Johns bought her in 1906, registration cancelled in 1918.

PZ363 *Albert* – 2nd class lugger, 19 foot long, was PE registered, owner William Rosewarne, skipper John Rosewarne, broken up in 1878.

PZ366 *Come On* – 1st class lugger, 44 foot long, 20½ tons, bought by owner Daniel Richards in 1876, skipper Henry Richards, sold to owner skipper William Maddern in 1897, foundered in storm off Cudden Point near Praa Sands in 1899.

PZ368 *Ocator* – 2nd class lugger, 24 foot long, 5 tons, built Penzance 1869, bought by owner skipper Abraham Thomas in 1887, sold to owner skipper James Blewett, Mousehole, in 1893, sold to owners James Harvey and John Sampson, Mousehole, in 1896, broken up in 1907.

PZ369 *Peep of Day* – 2nd class lugger, 28 foot long, 3 tons, bought by owner skipper George Quick in 1888, broken up in 1900.

PZ370 *Mur* – 2nd class lugger, 12½ foot long, 1 ton, built Porthleven 1896, owner skipper John Gruzalier bought her in 1906, broken up in 1916.

PZ376 *Secret* – 2nd class lugger, 29 foot long, 7 tons, built Porthleven 1869, owner skipper Richard Pezzack bought her in 1882, sold her to owner skipper Richard Thomas, Mousehole, in 1906, sold to owners John Pentreath and John Cotton in 1908, skipper John Pentreath, broken up in 1909.

PZ381 *Breeze* – 2nd class lugger, 29.9 foot long, 7 tons, built Porthleven 1869, owner skipper Edward Pezzack bought her in 1889, sold her to Richard and Edwin Pezzack in 1898, skipper Richard Pezzack. Sold to Newlyn in 1907, rebuilt in Mousehole for new owners 1907, owner skipper George Dennis, Mousehole, bought her in 1911, sold to owner John Dennis in 1913, skipper George Dennis, broken up in 1919.

PZ383 *Sunbeam* – 1st class lugger, 53 foot long, 36 tons, built in Mousehole by William Williams in 1885 for owners William Rowe and C.C. Ross, skipper Thomas Jenkin, sold to Lowestoft in 1889.

PZ384 *Larkspur* – 1st class lugger, 47.9 foot long, 26 tons, built Penzance 1879 for owner Samson Roberts, skipper Joseph Brownfield, sold to Joseph Hocking in 1906, skipper John Pender, broken up in 1912.

PZ375 *Onward* – 2nd class lugger, 27 foot long, was PE registered, broken up in 1898.

PZ388 *Olive* – 2nd class lugger, 15.5 foot long, 5.7 beam, 1 ton, bought by owner skipper Thomas Williams in 1911, sold to owner skipper Richard Sampson in 1918, sold to Everett Lugg owner skipper in 1919, motor fitted 1920, sold to owner skipper Garfield Jeffery in 1932, name changed to *Reaper*, sold to owner skipper Benjamin Wallis in 1933, registration cancelled in 1936.

PZ392 *Emeline* – 1st class lugger, 53.8 foot long, 26½ tons, owner skipper Abraham Madron bought her in 1897, left Lowestoft herring fishery returning to Mousehole, lost with all hands, no bodies recovered, believed run down by steamship 1899.

PZ396 *Elizabeth* – 2nd class dandy rig, 26 foot long, 4 tons, built Penzance 1887, owners Elizabeth and John Pentreath bought her in 1906, skipper John Pentreath, registration cancelled in 1917.

PZ398 *Express* – 2nd class lugger, 33 foot long, was PE registered, owner Josiah Trembath, skipper Thomas Matthews, broken up in 1886.

PZ402 *Genesta* – 2nd class lugger, 38 foot long, 18 tons, built Porthleven for owners Robert Oliver and John Richards in 1888, skipper Robert Oliver, sold to Scilly in 1908.

PZ405 *Comfort* – 1st class lugger, 51.4 foot long, 35 tons, built Plymouth 1889 for owner Joseph Rowe, skipper John Waters, sold to Howth in 1917.

PZ410 *Village Bride* – 3rd class lugger, 13.8 foot long, 1 ton, built Mousehole in 1890, owner skipper William Wallis bought her in 1906, broken up in 1920.

PZ411 *Nonpariel* – 2nd class lugger, 28 foot long, was PE225, owner skipper James Harry, broken up in 1882.

PZ413 *Dove* – 2nd class lugger, 28 foot long, was PE281, owner skipper Joseph Wright, broken up in 1881.

PZ413 *Gem* – 2nd class lugger, 37 foot long, 13 tons, built Newlyn 1887, owner skipper Richard Rowe bought her in 1889, sold to owner skipper William Perry 1896, sold to owner skipper Richard Rowe in 1910, engine fitted 1916, sold to Scilly in 1923.

PZ414 *Speed* – 2nd class lugger, 31 foot long, was PE36, owner skipper William Madron, broken up in 1888.

PZ414 *John Redmond* – 3rd class dandy rig, 16.7 foot long, 1½ tons, built Penzance 1890, owner skipper George Quick bought her in 1906, broken up in 1916.

PZ415 *Humility* – 2nd class lugger, 47 foot long, 27 tons, built in Mousehole for owner skipper William Worth in 1877, last registration 1906.

PZ416 *Guide Me* – 2nd class lugger, 32.4 foot long, 10.2 beam, 11 tons, built Porthleven by John Bawden in 1906, owner skipper Thomas Tonkin bought her in 1923, sold to owner skipper Richard Sampson in 1929, worked WW2.

PZ420 *Nyanza* – 2nd class lugger, 28 foot long, was PE166, owner skipper John Pentreath, lost at sea in 1893.

PZ423 *Mary Ellen* – 2nd class lugger, 29.6 foot long, 7 tons, built Porthleven 1872, owner skipper Charles Trewavas bought her in 1880, sold to Thomas Matthews in 1909, broken up in 1918.

PZ427 *Temperance Star* – 2nd class lugger, 31.8 foot long, 8 tons, owner John Tregenza bought her in 1889, skipper Thomas Tregenza, sold to St Ives 1900.

PZ430 *Cygnet* – 2nd class lugger, 29.9 foot long, 5½ tons, was PE261, owner skipper John Bodinner, condemned by Customs and Excise in 1904.

PZ433 *Two Sisters* – 2nd class lugger, 32 foot long, was PE registered, owners Samson Roberts, Orlando and Robert Humphreys, skipper Robert Humphreys, broken up in 1889.

PZ436 *John* – 2nd class lugger, 27.9 foot long, was PE20, owners Charles, Henry and Richard Mann, skipper Charles Mann, broken up in 1877.

PZ437 *Bessie* – 2nd class lugger, 28 foot long, 6½ tons, built Porthleven in 1872, owner skipper Henry Pentreath bought her 1885, sold to Philip Simons and Robert Matthews in 1904, skipper Robert Matthews, broken up in 1915.

PZ445 *Comrades* – 2nd class dandy rig, 15.3 foot long, 1½ tons, built St Ives for owner skipper John Johns in 1912, registration cancelled in 1928.

PZ446 *Valetta* – 3rd class rowing boat, 11.4 foot long, 4.9 beam, 1 ton, owner skipper bought her in 1915, registration cancelled in 1920.

PZ449 *Mizpah* – 2nd class lugger, 34.5 foot long, 14 tons, built Porthleven 1880, owners Nicholas amd Francis Praed bought her in 1890, skipper Nicholas Praed, sold to Kinsale in 1909.

PZ452 *Tipperary* – 3rd class rowing boat, 11.4 foot long, 4.9 beam, 1 ton, owner skipper Louis Hicks bought her in 1915, registration cancelled in 1918.

PZ453 *Flora* – 2nd class lugger, 19 foot long, 2 tons, owners Charles Simons and John Rowe bought her in 1890, skipper Charles Simons, sold to Newlyn 1893.

PZ455 *Monarch* – 1st class lugger, 48.4 foot long, 27½ tons, owners Edwin Ash and Edwin Harvey bought her in 1902, broken up in 1912.

PZ456 *Cesilia* – 3rd class rowing boat, 13.7 foot long, 5.5 beam, 1½ tons, owner skipper Bertram Jenkins bought her in 1915, broken up in 1920.

PZ495 *Forget-me-Not* – 2nd class lugger, 32.7 foot long, 10.6 beam, 9 tons, built Porthleven 1906, owner skipper Stephen Blewett bought her in 1908, 22hp Kelvin fitted, sold her to Newlyn 1942, worked WW2.

PZ460 *Foam* – 2nd class lugger, 38.5 foot long, 10.4 beam, 14 tons, built Mevagissey 1881, 13hp and 7hp Kelvins, 3½hp Britt fitted, owner skipper William Hall bought her in 1922, sold to Beaulieu in 1929.

PZ461 *Sabron* – 1st class lugger, 47 foot long, 26 tons, built Penzance in 1878 for owners Charles and Henry Pezzack, skipper Henry Pezzack, sold to owner skipper Charles Pezzack in 1887, broken up in 1908.

PZ461 *Primrose* – 2nd class lugger, 30.7 foot long, 10.1 beam, 10 tons, built St Ives 1906, owner skipper John Brownfield bought her in 1916, 13hp Atlantic fitted, sold to owner skipper Richard Wallis Johns in 1921, name changed to *Girl Kathleen*, sold to Portsmouth in 1937.

PZ462 *Peggy* – 2nd class lugger, 28 foot long, 8 tons, built Newlyn 1893, owner skipper Alfred Matthews bought her in 1902, sold to Plymouth in 1919.

PZ466 *Little Aggie* – 2nd class lugger, 24.9 foot long, 5½ tons, bought by owner skipper Richard Richards in 1906, sold to Newlyn 1918.

PZ467 *Boy Ben* – 1st class lugger, 39 foot long, 18 tons, built Porthleven 1891 for owner skipper Bendict Trembath, sold to owner skipper John Trembath in 1914, sold Porthleven 1916.

PZ469 *Never Leave Thee* – 3rd class dandy rig, 13.5 foot long, 1 ton, built Penzance 1881, owner skipper John Harry bought her in 1906, registration cancelled 1912.

PZ472 W*esley* – 1st class lugger, 48 foot long, 26 tons, built Penzance 1878, bought by owners Thomas Richards and Rebecca Williams in 1885, skipper John Trewavas, sold to owner skipper Stephen Downing in 1897, broken up in 1909.

PZ478 *Willing Boys* – 2nd class lugger, 35.9 foot long, 14 tons, built Porthleven 1891, owner skipper Richard Humphreys bought her in 1911, sold to Looe in 1912.

PZ479 *Ada* – 2nd class lugger, 27.7 foot long, 6½ tons, built Porthleven for owner skipper Edwin Pezzack in 1906, motor fitted in 1913, sold to Penzance 1916.

PZ480 *Kindly Light* – 2nd class lugger, 26 foot long, 5½ tons, built Porthleven 1906 for owner Joseph Rowe, skipper Richard Johns, sold Porthleven 1907.

PZ481 *Maud* – 3rd class cutter, 16.4 foot long, 1½ tons, built Truro in 1905, bought by owner skipper Henry Trenoweth in 1906, registration cancelled in 1910.

PZ483 *Fly* – 2nd class lugger, 16 foot long, bought by owner skipper Charles Mann in 1876, registration cancelled in 1878.

PZ483 *Zephyr* – 2nd class lugger, 26.4 foot long, 6½ tons, built St Ives 1906 for owners James Piercy and John Klynack, skipper James Piercy, sold to Truro in 1924.

PZ488 *Henry Martin* – 2nd class lugger, 34.6 foot long, 11 tons, built Newlyn 1898, bought by owners Edwin Polgrean, George Richards, George and Robert Hall in 1912, skipper Edwin Polgrean, sold to owners Richard and Peter Cary in 1914, broken up in 1916.

PZ490 *Mary Ann* – 2nd class lugger, 38.3 foot long, 19 tons, built Porthleven 1892, owner William Cattran bought her in 1894, skipper James Drew, sold to Kinsale in 1909.

PZ491 *Providence* – 2nd class lugger, 32 foot long, owner William Angwin bought her in 1870, (see PZ218, mix-up by Customs and Excise).

PZ493 *James Francis* – 2nd class dandy rig, 31.6 foot long, seine boat, built St Ives 1912 for owners Joseph, Edwin and Stephen Rowe, sold to St Ives in 1918.

PZ494 *Fly* – 3rd class lugger, 18.5 foot long, 2½ tons, bought by owner skipper Richard Rowe in 1905, sold to Scilly in 1919.

PZ495 *Orlando* – 1st class lugger, 48 foot long, 27 tons, built Newlyn in 1881, bought by owner skipper Richard Jenkin in 1892, run down off Bucks near Lamorna by PZ575 *Emblem* in 1907.

PZ496 *Early Dawn* – 2nd class dandy rig, 23.2 foot long, 3 tons, built Porthleven 1897, bought by Thomas Treleaven in 1906, skipper Thomas Worth, broken up in 1916.

PZ504 *William* – 1st class lugger, 50 foot long, 23½ tons, built Porthleven 1892, bought by owner skipper Stephen Downing in 1908, 26hp Kelvin fitted in 1916, sold to owner skipper William Richards in 1920, registration cancelled in 1929.

PZ504 *Sea Crest* – 1st class lugger, 49.1 foot long, 14.8 beam, 23½ tons, built Porthleven 1893, 26hp Kelvin fitted, owners William Downing and Charles Chapple bought her in 1929, skipper Charles Chapple, sold to William Downing in 1932, skipper Edward Downing, broken up in 1936, could be same boat as *William*, name change and new owners would mean remeasuring.

PZ508 *Test* – 1st class lugger, 45 foot long, 17 tons, was PE registered, bought by owner skipper William Humphreys in 1871, condemned by Customs and Excise 1906.

355

PZ508 *Our Gracie* – 3rd class rowing boat, 12.2 foot long, 5.1 beam, 1 ton, bought by owner skipper George Quick in 1916, registration cancelled in 1923.

PZ510 *Onward* – 1st class lugger, 44.8 foot long, 25 tons, built Newlyn 1871 for owners Ann and Samuel Wallis, skipper Samuel Wallis, sold to owner skipper Philip Worth in 1887, sold to Plymouth in 1907.

PZ512 *Excell* – 1st class lugger, 48 foot long, 28½ tons, owner skipper William Barnes bought her in 1871, wrecked Church Cove, Mounts Bay, in 1899.

PZ512 *Alice Jane* – 2nd class lugger, 26 foot long, 3 tons, bought by owner skipper Mark Hollow Wallis in 1912, registration cancelled in 1919.

PZ513 *Excellent* – 1st class lugger, 40½ foot long, 17 tons, bought by owner skipper William Williams, boatbuilder, in 1888, sold to Penzance 1893.

PZ514 *Mignionette* – 1st class lugger, 43.6 foot long, 16 tons, bought by owner skipper John Wright in 1871, sold to Shoreham in 1888.

PZ514 *Sweethome* – 1st class lugger, 51 foot long, 14.8 beam, 33 tons, built Porthleven in 1893 for owners Edward and Benjamin Downing, skipper Benjamin Downing, sold to Newlyn in 1916.

PZ515 *Cornish Girl* – 1st class lugger, 41 foot long, 16 tons, owner skipper Nicholas Cornish, wrecked in 1873.

PZ517 *Matchless* – 1st class lugger, 41 foot long, 17 tons, was PE registered, owner skipper John Madron bought her in 1871, broken up in 1888.

PZ518 *Gleaner* – 1st class lugger, 40 foot long, 15½ tons, was PE registered, owner William Williams, boatbuilder, bought her in 1871, skipper Richard Jenkin, sold to Belfast in 1880.

PZ522 *Bessie* – 1st class lugger, 47 foot long, 26 tons, bought by owner William Humphreys in 1893, skipper Thomas Cotton, sold to Newlyn in 1899.

PZ527 *J.H.* – 1st class lugger, 41 foot long, 15½ tons, was PE registered, owner skipper James Harvey registered her in 1871, broken up in 1888.

PZ528 *Seven Brothers* – 2nd class lugger, 22 foot long, owner skipper Daniel Richards bought her in 1871, sold to St Ives 1873.

PZ528 *Daring* – 2nd class lugger, 38.7 foot long, 12.3 beam,14 tons, built Porthleven 1893, 13hp & 26hp Kelvins fitted, bought by owner skipper John Pender in 1913, changed name to *Boy Fred* in 1922, sold to Newlyn in 1931, renamed *Israel Britain*, broken up in 1942.

PZ530 *Volunteer* – 1st class lugger, 38.9 foot long, 13.2 beam, 20 tons, built Porthleven 1893 for owner skipper William Curtis, 15hp and 26hp Kelvins fitted 1913, sold to Newlyn in 1926.

PZ532 *Mizpah* – 1st class lugger, 39.4 foot long, 20 tons, bought by owner skipper William Polgrean in 1894, sold to Newlyn in 1899.

PZ534 *Mistletoe* – 1st class lugger, 38.5 foot long, 20 tons, built Porthleven in 1894 for owners William and James Pender, skipper William Pender, 13hp Kelvin fitted 1915, sold to Newlyn in 1919, converted to coal barge in 1925.

PZ540 *Nellie* – 2nd class lugger, 17 foot long, 6.1 beam, 2 tons, bought by owner skipper William Eddy in 1919, broken up in 1933.

PZ545 *Ben-My-Chree II* – 1st class ketch, 53.7 foot long, 15.8 beam, 40 tons, built Porthleven 1912 for owners Thomas and Lewis Hicks, 48hp engine fitted, skipper Thomas Hicks, sold to Louis Hicks in 1930, last registration 1934.

PZ554 *Gleaner* –1st class lugger, 34.2 foot long, 19 tons, bought by owner skipper Charles Pezzack in 1896, sold to St Ives 1901.

PZ555 *Belle* – 2nd class lugger, 22.5 foot long, 5 tons, built Penzance in 1890, bought by owner skipper Thomas Cary in 1894, sold to owner skipper Joseph Johns in 1895, broken up in 1920.

PZ556 *Iverna* – 1st class lugger, 41 foot long, 22 tons, built in Mousehole 1894 by John and William Bodinner for themselves, skipper William Bodinner, sold to France in 1912.

PZ557 *Florence Edith* – 2nd class lugger, 34 foot long, 12½ tons, bought by owner skipper Thomas Wallis in 1895, wrecked off Porthleven in 1899.

PZ558 *Gertrude* – 2nd class dandy rig, 28 foot long, 7 tons, built Porthleven 1895, bought by owner skipper John Harvey in 1905, sold to Falmouth 1908.

PZ559 *Boy Harry* – 3rd class rowing boat, 10.8 foot long, 5.5 beam, 1 ton, bought by owner skipper Abraham Johns in 1916, registration cancelled in 1920.

PZ564 *Gladys* – 3rd class dandy rig, 15 foot long, 4.7 beam, 1 ton, bought by owner skipper Richard Hicks in 1916, sold to James Virgo in 1916, sold to owner skipper Richard Tonkin in 1918, sold to owner skipper Everett Lugg in 1919, sold to Joseph Sleeman in 1920, broken up in 1927.

PZ566 *Lizzie* – 2nd class lugger, 31 foot long, 9 tons, built Porthleven in 1885, bought by owner skipper Thomas Matthews in 1895, sold to Nelson Ladner in 1918, broken up in 1922.

PZ568 *Belle* – 2nd class lugger, 23.3 foot long, 5 tons, built Porthleven in 1878, bought by owner skipper Charles Cary in 1895, broken up in 1926.

PZ571 *Rising Sun* – 1st class lugger, 39.6 foot long, 21 tons, built in Mousehole 1895 for owner skipper Joseph Johns, sold to Newry 1910.

PZ573 *Ben-My-Chree* – 1st class lugger, 51.6 foot long, 33 tons, built in Mousehole 1895 for owners William Rowe and John Harvey, sold to John and Thomas Hicks in 1901, skipper Thomas Hicks, sold to Thomas and Lewis Hicks in 1910, sold to Dublin 1911.

PZ575 *Emblem* – 1st class lugger, 50 foot long, 35 tons, built Porthleven 1895, bought by owner skipper John Hicks in 1902, engine fitted 1914, wrecked at Penlee Point near lifeboat slip in 1914.

PZ575 *Radiant Morn* – 2nd class lugger, 35.9 foot long, 11.5 beam, 13½ tons, built St Ives 1905, 7hp and 26hp Kelvins fitted, was SS188 *Hopeful*, bought by Vivian Johns in 1924, sold back to St Ives in 1934.

PZ580 *Miranda* – 1st class lugger, 38.8 foot long, 20 tons, built Porthleven 1896 for owner skipper Richard Rowe, sold to Belfast in 1908.

PZ581 *Lily Barber* – 2nd class lugger, 21 foot long, 2 tons, bought by owner skipper James Beckerleg 1896, sold to owner skipper George Francis in 1897, sold to owner skipper William Polgrean in 1898, last registered in 1906.

PZ586 *Pansy* –1st class lugger, 30.9 foot long, 9 tons, built Porthleven in 1896 for owners William and Nicholas Smith, skipper William Smith, sold to owner skipper Nicholas Smith in 1916, sold to owner skipper Richard Richards in 1918, motor fitted in 1918, sold to Plymouth in 1924.

PZ587 *R.C.* – 2nd class lugger, 30 foot long, 10 tons, built Porthleven in 1896 for owner skipper Thomas Cary, sold to owner skipper William Blewett in 1903, sold to Baltimore in 1918.

PZ590 *Favourite* – 2nd class lugger, 26.3 foot long, 6 tons, bought by owner skipper Stephen Downing in 1904, sold to Richard & John Cary in 1919, skipper Richard Cary, motor fitted in 1920, sold to Padstow in 1925.

PZ591 *Benbow* – 2nd class lugger, 23.4 foot long, 5 tons, bought by owners Nicholas Cornish and John Tregenza in 1912, skipper Nicholas Cornish, sold to owner skipper Henry Pender in 1917, sold to owner skipper Edwin Ash in 1920, sold to owner skipper Theodore Cornish in 1921, motor fitted in 1921, broken up in 1923.

PZ592 *Pantaloon* – 2nd class lugger, 25.7 foot long, 6½ tons, built in Mousehole 1896 by John Bodinner for himself, skipper Emanuel Glasson, sold to St Ives 1916.

PZ600 *Sweet Hope* – 1st class lugger, 52 foot long, 26 tons, built Porthleven 1888, bought by owner skipper John Alderman in 1910, broken up in 1919.

PZ602 *Boy Willie* – 1st class lugger, 51.6 foot long, 14.9 beam, 24½ tons, built Newlyn in 1896 by Henry Peak, sold to owner skipper James Pender in 1918, 39hp engine fitted, sold to James Pender Jnr in 1928, sold to Falmouth in 1940.

PZ603 *Primrose* – 1st class lugger, 40 foot long, 21 tons, built in Mousehole by J. Bowden in 1896 for owner William Weaks, skipper Charles Weaks, sold to Mevagissey 1909.

PZ604 *Merlin* – 2nd class lugger, 19 foot long, 6.9 beam, 3 tons, built in St Ives by Paynters in 1896, owner skipper William Eddy bought her in 1931, sold to William Harvey in 1935, worked WW2, owner skipper Mike Buttery (that's me) bought her in 1963, Coventry Victor 9-11hp diesel fitted 1963, new registration issued, PZ337, sold to Porthleven 1976. I last saw her in 1978 moored by Falmouth Yacht Club, tried to buy her back in 1998 but couldn't find where she had gone, was going to put her back to sail, heavily built with 1 3/8 inch pitch pine planking, 3 foot 6 inch keel, very stable sea boat.

PZ605 *Lizzie Ann* – 2nd class lugger, 24.6 foot long 5½ tons, built Porthleven 1897, owner skipper Thomas Treleaven bought her in 1903, sold to Newlyn in 1919.

PZ606 *Emblem* – 2nd class lugger 19 foot long, 3 tons, built by Paynters St Ives in 1897, bought by owner skipper John Humphreys in 1901, sold to Charles and James Rowe in 1906, sold to Calstock 1919.

PZ609 *Jubilee* – 2nd class lugger, ship's lifeboat, 20.4 foot long, 5½ tons, bought by owner skipper John Bodinner in 1905, broken up in 1922.

PZ611 *Emily* – 2nd class lugger, 30.9 foot long, 9.8 beam, 9 tons, built Porthleven by John Kitto in 1897, bought by owner skipper Richard Ash in 1898, name changed to *Girl Eileen* and engine fitted in 1919, 1929 Richard Ash died and vessel to be sold.

PZ612 *Jubilee* – 2nd class lugger, 26½ foot long, 5½ tons, built in Mousehole 1897 for owners John Ash and Joseph Madron, skipper John Ash, Joseph Madron bought out by Richard Wright in 1909, sold to Falmouth 1918.

PZ613 *Hawa Dilli* –1st class lugger, 51.5 foot long, 15.2 beam, 14 tons, built at Newlyn by Peake in 1897, bought by owners Richard and Nicholas Humphreys in 1916, 5hp and 26hp Kelvins fitted, skipper Richard Humphreys, sold to Weston-on-Sea, Essex, in 1935.

PZ614 *Percy* – 1st class lugger, 50.4 foot long, 33 tons, built in Newlyn by Peake in 1897, owners Henry and George Laity bought her in 1906, skipper Henry Laity, sold to Whitby 1916.

PZ618 *Arizona* – 3rd class lugger, 18.6 foot long, 2 tons, built St Ives 1898, owner skipper Benjamin Wallis bought her in 1919, sold to Sennen in 1919.

PZ619 *Childrens Friend* – 1st class lugger, 52 foot long, 15 beam, 25 tons, built Penzance in 1898, owners George and William Dennis bought her in 1906, 13hp and 26hp Kelvins fitted, skipper George Dennis, sold to Kilkeel in 1935.

PZ621 *Dashing Spray* – 2nd class lugger, 24.8 foot long, 8.4 beam, 4½ tons, built Porthleven 1898, motor fitted 1921, bought by owner skipper Richard Cornish in 1935, lost at sea in 1940.

PZ627 *Pet* – 2nd class lugger, 25 foot long, 6 tons, built Porthleven 1898, owner skipper George Hocking bought her in 1903, sold to Fowey in 1919.

PZ631 *Reaper* – 2nd class lugger, 25 foot long, 5½ tons, built in Mousehole 1902, bought by owners David Sleeman and Edward Hicks in 1905, skipper David Sleeman, sold to Newlyn in 1918.

PZ634 *Hopeful* – 1st class lugger, 53 foot long, 36 tons, built Porthleven 1898, bought by owner skipper Thomas Matthews in 1900, 26hp motor fitted 1915, broken up in 1927.

PZ635 *Our Maggie* – 1st class lugger, 51 foot long, 33 tons, built Porthleven 1898 by J. Bowden, bought by owner Benjamin Trewavas in 1899, skipper Richard Humphreys, sold to owner skipper Richard Humphreys in 1911, sold to Brighton 1914.

PZ658 *Dreadnought* – 2nd class lugger, 23.5 foot long, 4 tons, built Porthleven 1877, bought by owner skipper Nicholas Praed in 1907, broken up in 1924.

PZ688 *Sepoy* – 3rd class rowing boat, 14.6 foot long, 5.3 beam, 1 ton, bought by owner skipper John Gruzalier in 1917, registration cancelled 1923.

PZ697 *Our Katie* – 1st class ketch, 56 foot long, 16.4 beam, 35½ tons, built Porthleven in 1917, owner Richard Pentreath bought her in 1931, skipper Richard Wallis Johns, sold to owners Richard and Vivian Johns in 1932, sold to owner Edward Pentreath in 1938, skipper Richard Wallis Johns, WW2 service for Ministry of Air, went back fishing until the 1970's.

PZ699 *Betty* – 2nd class motor boat, 18 foot long, 5.1 beam, 1½ tons, built Bosham in 1913, owner skipper Charles Murrish bought her in 1917, registration cancelled in 1926.

PZ704 *Monica* – 2nd class lugger, 20.6 foot long, 6.7 beam, 1½ tons, built Falmouth in 1913, motor fitted, owner skipper Bertram Jenkins bought her in 1942, sold to William Richards in 1944, worked WW2, in Mousehole until the 1960's.

This is most of the fishing vessels working from Mousehole or gave Mousehole as their home port from 1869 until 1944 taken from the Customs and Excise registration forms that are held at County Records Office, Truro.

All seine boats were 3rd class vessels and some around Newquay were up to 60 foot, larger than most 1st class luggers.

Porthleven was by far the biggest boatbuilders during this period but the records fail to mention who they all were, this applied to all ports where boats were built. In the majority of cases there was no mention of where or when they were built. In Mousehole the registration forms show that 43 boats were built in the village, but it could well have been more.

The largest vessels built in Mousehole was carried out on what is now the Wharf Car Park by the old quay. This was a large open area much bigger than it is now. Medium sized vessels were built by the village clock, there were no shops, village clock or houses near the harbour office then. Small punts, horse carts and hand carts were built where the Bank Car Park now is, that area was the dumping ground for 100's of years and was regularly washed away, the dumping was stopped in the 1980's when granite armour was placed around that area to stop the sea eroding it away.

Appendix III
Glossary of Cornish Words Not Now in Use

THESE WORDS ARE taken from an old Cornish book lent to me by Clifton Pender in the 1960's. They are by no means all the words used today in isolated villages, mining areas and fishing ports, they are getting less frequently used except in those places mentioned above. Some of the words are now used nationally and will not be lost. Depending on exactly what area you come from then certain words are spelt differently but mean and sound the same, JAFFLE and YAFFLE for example. You can have several little fishing coves only a few miles apart that use a word with just one letter altered but meaning the same, WHIFFING is the commonest used but some coves say WIFFLING – to list them all would probably take a book in itself. The ones listed below are those you are most likely to hear around villages, harbours and mining country.

ABROAD	wide open
ADDLE POOL	a cesspit
ADVENTURER	a shareholder
AFERED	afraid
AGAR	ugly
AGIN	against
AGLETS	hawthorn berries
AIRY MOUSE	a bat
ATWEEN	between
AX	ask
AXED OUT	asked out
BACKLET, BACKSIDE	backyard
BAGLE	troublesome person
BAL	a mine
BALK, BAULK	large square timber beam
BAL-MAIDEN	girl who works at mine's surface
BARWELL	fisherman's apron
BASTING	a beating
BEAUTY	used as a term of contempt
BEETY	to mend fishing nets
BELLY TEMBER	good solid food
BERRIN	a funeral
BLACKJACK	the coalfish
BLAWED	out of breath

BLINK	small light or flame
BLOWING HOUSE	place for melting tin
BOLT	a stone built drain
BOTHIC	the pouting
BOTTOMS	valley or old tin stream works
BOWGIE	shed for sheep or cattle
BOWJOULER	roller for hauling ropes through
BREEDY	to make a fishing net
BRIMING	phosphorescence at sea
BRIT	very small shoal fish, (whitebait)
BROWSS	pulped fish used to attract others
BUFFLEHEAD	a fool
BULL-WRA	the wrasse
BUNT	belly in a sail or fishing net
BUZZA	large earthenware jar
CANTOR	wood frame for winding fishing line on
CARKER	the scorpion fish, Father Lasher
CARN, CAIRN	large pile of rock or stone
CAWNSE	pavements stones
CHACKS	cheeks
CHAD	small bream

CHEEL	a child
CLABBY	wet and sticky
CLACKER	a woman's tongue
CLICK PAW	left handed
CLODGY	sticky, muddy
CLUNK	to swallow
COB	mixture of clay & straw for building
COLLOPING	a good thrashing, beating
COOSE	cold or chilly
COWAL, KOWAL	fish basket carried on back
COWL	fish's air bladder
CRAN	800 herring
CREASE OIL	creosote
CREEPER	a small grapnel
CRIB	a small meal or lunch
CROWST	a meal or feed
DAG	pick used by miners
DAGGIN	longing or ready for it
DAHN	a marker buoy
DOLLYMOP	a vulgar flirt
DOUSE	throw water over, put out
DRECKLY	presently
DRETHEN	underwater sand bank
DRUGS	oily fish waste
EFT, EVET	the newt
EMMET	a foreigner, not from Cornwall
EVAL	three pronged fork
FAIRMAID, FUMADE	a cured pilchard
FER	far
FISH FAG	a fish wife
FISH JOUSTER	selling fish from a van
FITTY	suitable, proper
FOGOU	a cave, hole or cavern
FOUSTER	to work hard
FRAP	not proper, a mess, bind tightly
FULSOME	rich or sweet food
GAD	a wedge for splitting rock
GALLAVANTER	an incurable flirt
GALLAVANTING	running around, flirting
GARRA, GERRA	tall rocky hill

GARRICK	the garfish
GARM	to shout
GEAGLED	dirtied, dirty, filthy
GEKE	to look or stare
GOONHILLIES	small breed of extinct horse from Goonhilly Downs
GRAFTED	covered or coated in dirt or dust
GRAMMER SOW	the woodlice
GRIGGAN	the grasshopper
GRIZZLE	to grin or laugh
GRUNG	to grind your teeth
GULGE	to drink quickly
GURNICK	the gurnard fish
GURRY	a hand barrow
GURT	big or large
GUT	a narrow gap or passage
HALE	to haul, pull or drag
HARDAH	blue elvin rock
HEAVING	damp and sweaty
HEVAH	here, in this place
HOBBLE	well paid odd job
HOLIDAYS	areas missed in painting or dusting
HOLM	the holly tree
HOOTIN	crying
HORNFISH	the lobster or crawfish
HORNY WINK	a slug
HUER	a lookout, mainly for fish shoals
ISS	yes
JACOB'S LADDER	the Milky Way
JADES	salted herring
JAFFLE	plenty, a handful
JIGGER	a small mizzen sail
JOUSTER	travelling fish seller
KEDGE, KILLECK	stone used as an anchor
KEEL ALLEY	place for playing skittles
KEIVE	a large tub or vat
KELTER	in good condition
KICKER	small mizzen sail used in fishing

KIDDLIWINK   an ale or beer house, an inn
KISKEY   dry & brittle, especially wood
KITEY   hairbrained, eccentric, impulsive

LASH UP   a bad mistake
LASHING   to pour with rain
LAST   strip of bait from mackerel tail
LAUNCE   the sandeel
LAUNDER   guttering on a building
LEARY   tired, hungry or faint
LEECH   bottom edge of a fishing net
LERRUPIN   a beating, also something large
LIDDEN   telling the same old story
LINHAY   a lean-to shed or outhouse
LOUGGY   tired, sleepy
LOUSTER   very large or big, also hard working
LUD   a large heap or pile
LUMBERS   the gaps between ribs and keel

MACKEREL BIRD   the manx shearwater
MADDRICK GULL   the black headed gull
MARINADE   fish cured in vinegar
MAUNGE   to eat or chew noisily
MAZED   bewildered
MERLE, MURL   single link in a chain
MIDJANS   small bits or pieces
MOR, MUR   the guillemot
MUN   rotten or decaying fish
MUNDIC   rotten granite
MURGY, MORGYE   the lesser spotted dogfish
MURRIAN   the ant

NEFLIN   Newfoundland cod

OOZLE   throat or windpipe
OUTLANDER   a foreigner, not Cornish
OVER NIGH   close or nearby
OVICE   eaves of a house
OWL   the small eyed ray

PALLACE   cellar for baulking pilchards
PEART   brisk or lively
PEAS   the hard roe of fish

PEECHER   very good, fishing bait
PEEL, PEAL   the sea trout
PEZZACK   a broken backed pilchard, rotten
PILCHARD HOG   the pilot whale
PILL   a pool or creek
PINNICKIN   very small & weak
PLAT   a small flat area
PLUM   stupid, soft
PLUS FOUR   the greater fork beard fish
PROPER   exactly, perfect
PUT GOING   killed or murdered

QUEENS   a small scallop
QUIDDLE   the spider crab

RAB   heavy clay or granite rubble
RADGELL   an excavated tunnel, the fox
RAG   a large irregular roofing slate
RANY   half tide reef
RASH, RASHING   fish shoal breaking surface
RAW MILK   milk straight from the cow
RAW FRY   suet fry up
ROKER   the thornback ray
ROUSER   resounding, as with singing
ROW   underwater reef of rocks

SCALPIONS   dry salted fish
SCAT   hit, break or smash
SCAT ABROAD   burst open
SCRAN   food
SCREECH LIKE A WHIT-NECK   scream or cry, see WHIT-NECK
SCROLLED   split boiled pilchards
SCUD   low clouds and rain
SCULLIONS   onions
SHALES   fish scales
SHEEVO   a fuss, argument or row
SHONG, SHRONG   broken single mesh of fish net
SHOOT   cast nets into the sea
SHOT   fish that has spawned
SHRIMMED   chilled
SKEET   to squirt, also a strong wind
SKEG   boats keel
SKEW   thinly drizzly rain, off-centre

SKILLET	cooking pot with 3 short legs
SKUDDY	patchy sand & rock seabed
SLAG	misty rain or sleet
SLEEPY	stupid, also dry rot in wood
SLEWED	drunk, intoxicated
SMEECH	thick black pungent smoke
SODGER	a red herring, also soldier
SPANKER, SPANKING	very large or big
SPILGARN	the shag or cormorant
SPILLER	a ground line with many hooks
SPLATTY	patchy seabed, scattered fish
SPONNEL, SPUNNEL	calm water downtide of rock
SQUINCH	thin twine for stitching nets together
STANK	to walk, tread on or squash
STARVING, STEEVING	very cold, to be cold
STINT	to take your turn
STRAMMER	very large
STROME	a streak or line
STROVE	try, force or compel
STUGGY	short and fat, thickset
SUMP	bottom of a mine shaft
SUW, SEW	boat aground with ebbing tide
SWELLACK, SWOLLICK	the bird redwing
TAFFLE	tangle
TAILINGS	the last or refuse ore
TALLY	total
TEASER, TAYZER	first net to be shot
TEEL	to plant or sow crops
TEELED	buried or planted
THONGS	bootlace seaweed
THURT-EYED	cross-eyed
TIDDLY	smart or clean
TIER	row of moored boats, nets or crab pots

TIFFIN	a small meal, sandwiches
TIFFLINS	small fragments of material
TOD	a tangle
TOKENED TO	betrothed to
TOR	mountain, huge rock on hill top
TOTELIN	imbecile or senile
TOUSER	a large apron
TOWAN	sand dunes covered in grass
TOWRAG	sun-dried cod, ling, etc, derogatory term for a person
TRAAPSE	to go for a walk
TRAMMEL	type of fishing net
TRIG	to prop up or wedge
TRUCK	trash, rubbish, not getting involved
TUB	the red gurnard
TUBBANS	clods of earth
UGLY	bad tempered
VORE	a furrow or small ditch
VUGG	
cavity in mines encrusted with crystals	
WEATHER DOG, SUN DOG, or MOON DOG	the halo around sun or moon heralding bad weather
WEET	to pull or drag
WHEAL	a mine
WHIFFING	trailing lures behind a boat
WHISHT	feeling tired or sad
WHISTLER	3 or 5 bearded rockling fish
WHIT-NECK	the weasel
YAFFEL	plenty, a handfull
ZARK	the sea urchin
ZAWN	a sea cave or rocky inlet

366